T0305718

COVID-19 AND THE GLOBAL POLITICAL ECONOMY

Covid-19 and the Global Political Economy investigates and explores how far and in what ways the Covid-19 pandemic is challenging, restructuring, and perhaps remaking aspects of the global political economy.

Since the 1970s, neoliberal capitalism has been the guiding principle of global development: fiscal discipline, privatisations, deregulation, the liberalisation of trade and investment regimes, and lower corporate and wealth taxation. But, after Covid-19, will these trends continue, particularly when states are continuing to struggle with overcoming the pandemic and violating one of neoliberalism's key principles: balanced budgets? The pandemic has exposed the fragility of the global political economy, and it can be argued that the intensification of global trade, tourism, and finance over the past 30 years has facilitated the spread of infectious diseases such as Covid-19. Therefore, economies in lockdown, jittery markets, and massive government spending have sparked interest in potentially re-evaluating certain features of the global political economy. This volume brings together leading and upcoming critical scholars in international relations and international political economy to provide novel, timely, and innovative research on how the Covid-19 pandemic is impacting (and will continue to impact) the global economy in important dimensions, including state fiscal policy, monetary policy, the accumulation of debt, health and social reproduction, and the future of austerity and the fate of neoliberalism.

This book will be of great interest to students, scholars, and experts in international relations and international political economy, as well as history, anthropology, political science, sociology, cultural studies, economics, development studies, and human geography.

Tim Di Muzio is Associate Professor in International Relations and Political Economy at the University of Wollongong, Australia and Associate at the Centre for Advanced International Relations Theory at the University of Sussex, UK. His research examines economic inequality, energy policy, and global debt and money.

Matt Dow received his PhD in Political Science in 2019 from York University, Canada. His research examines fossil fuels, the global monetary and debt system, settler colonialism, and climate change.

RIPE SERIES IN GLOBAL POLITICAL ECONOMY

Series Editors: Susanne Soederberg *(Queen's University, Canada)*, Adrienne Roberts *(The University of Manchester, UK)*, Samuel Knafo *(University of Sussex, UK)* and Naná de Graaff *(Vrije Universiteit Amsterdam, the Netherlands)*.

For almost two decades now, the *RIPE Series in Global Political Economy* published by Routledge has been an essential forum for cutting-edge scholarship in International Political Economy, which we understand to be a broadly defined area of research that may cut across other disciplines. The series brings together new and established scholars working in critical, cultural and constructivist political economy. Books in the *RIPE Series* typically combine an innovative contribution to theoretical debates with rigorous empirical analysis.

The *RIPE Series* seeks to cultivate:

- Field-defining theoretical advances in International Political Economy.
- Novel treatments of key issue areas, such as global finance, trade, and production, both historical and contemporary.
- Analyses that explore the political economic dimensions of relatively neglected topics, such as the environment, gender, race, and colonialism from both Western and non-Western perspectives.
- Accessible work that will inspire advanced undergraduates and graduate students in International Political Economy.

Capital Claims: Power and Global Finance
Edited by Benjamin Braun and Kai Koddenbrock

For more information about this series, please visit: www.routledge.com/RIPE-Series-in-Global-Political-Economy/book-series/RIPE

COVID-19 AND THE GLOBAL POLITICAL ECONOMY

Crises in the 21st Century

Edited by Tim Di Muzio and Matt Dow

Routledge
Taylor & Francis Group

LONDON AND NEW YORK

Cover image: Ann Solecki variation on iStock Image 1218467204 (alashi)

First published 2023
by Routledge
4 Park Square, Milton Park, Abingdon, Oxon OX14 4RN

and by Routledge
605 Third Avenue, New York, NY 10158

Routledge is an imprint of the Taylor & Francis Group, an informa business

British Library Cataloguing-in-Publication Data
A catalogue record for this book is available from the British Library

Library of Congress Cataloging-in-Publication Data
Names: Di Muzio, Tim, editor. | Dow, Matt, editor.
Title: COVID-19 and the global political economy : crises in the 21st century / edited by Tim Di Muzio and Matt Dow.
Description: Abingdon, Oxon ; New York, NY : Routledge, 2023. |
Series: RIPE series in global political economy |
Includes bibliographical references and index.
Identifiers: LCCN 2022014098 (print) | LCCN 2022014099 (ebook) |
ISBN 9781032168210 (hardback) | ISBN 9781032168197 (paperback) |
ISBN 9781003250432 (ebook)
Subjects: LCSH: International economic relations. |
International trade. | International finance. |
COVID-19 Pandemic, 2020–Economic aspects.
Classification: LCC HF1359 .C726 2023 (print) |
LCC HF1359 (ebook) | DDC 337–dc23/eng/20220603
LC record available at https://lccn.loc.gov/2022014098
LC ebook record available at https://lccn.loc.gov/2022014099

ISBN: 978-1-032-16821-0 (hbk)
ISBN: 978-1-032-16819-7 (pbk)
ISBN: 978-1-003-25043-2 (ebk)

DOI: 10.4324/9781003250432

Typeset in Bembo
by Newgen Publishing UK

The OA version of chapter 8 was funded by Australian National University

For Ophelia, Max, and Remi
and
For Rosalie

CONTENTS

NOTES ON CONTRIBUTORS

Tatiana Andersen is a PhD Candidate and academic teacher at the University of Wollongong, Australia. Her transdisciplinary research explores the political economy of the biosciences, focusing on the complex intersections between finance, ownership, and technoscientific research.

Tom Barnes is an economic sociologist and precarious work researcher at the Australian Catholic University (ACU). He is currently researching global warehouse logistics and automotive manufacturing.

Solomon Benatar is Emeritus Professor of Medicine at the University of Cape Town (UCT), South Africa, and Adjunct Professor at the University of Toronto's Dalla Lana School of Public Health, Canada. He was Chief of Medicine at UCT and Groote Schuur Hospital for 19 years and Founding Director of the UCT Bioethics Centre for 20 years. His academic interests have included respiratory medicine, health services, human rights, academic boycott, medical ethics, cross-cultural dialogue, and global health.

Dan Bousfield is an assistant professor at the University of Western Ontario, Canada. He researches social movements, protests, and critical political economy, with an emphasis on psychoanalysis, technology, pedagogy, and resistance. His methodological frameworks draw on critical pedagogy to examine the everyday exclusions built into technology and politics through race, gender, and settler colonial sensibilities.

Sophie Cotton is a PhD Candidate in Political Economy at the University of Sydney, Australia, researching Australian migration. They work on automation, displacement, and warehousing work at the Australian Catholic University Institute for Humanities and Social Sciences.

Laura Davy is a research fellow at the Australia New Zealand School of Government and Crawford School of Public Policy at the Australian National University.

Helen Dickinson is Professor of Public Service Research and Director of the Public Service Research Group at the School of Business at the University of New South Wales, Australia. Her expertise is in public services, particularly in relation to topics such as governance, policy implementation, and stewardship of 4th industrial revolution technologies. In 2015 she was made a Victorian Fellow of the Institute of Public Administration Australia, and in 2019 awarded a Fellow of the Academy of Social Sciences.

Tim Di Muzio is an associate professor in International Relations and Political Economy at the University of Wollongong, Australia, and Associate at the Centre for Advanced International Relations Theory at the University of Sussex, UK. His research examines economic inequality, energy policy, and global debt and money.

Matt Dow received his PhD in Political Science in 2019 from York University, Canada. His research examines fossil fuels, the global monetary and debt system, settler colonialism, and climate change.

Rakesh Kumar is a doctoral scholar at Western Sydney University, Australia. He researches platforms, labour, and migration in Australia and is interested in the impact of technology and automation on labour and organisations. Trained in International Relations and Economics, he brings two decades of work experience in the education technology sector to academia.

Adam Lucas is a senior lecturer in Science and Technology Studies at the University of Wollongong (UoW), Australia. His research focuses on the history and sociology of early modern and premodern machine technology, and contemporary climate change and energy policy. He is particularly interested in processes of innovation and the democratisation of technological decision-making. Previously, he worked as a researcher and policy analyst for the New South Wales Government.

Philip McMichael is a professor of Global Development at Cornell University, USA. He works with the Civil Society Mechanism in the UN Committee on World Food Security (CFS).

Sara C. Motta is a mother, poet, political theorist, popular educator, and associate professor who convenes the Politics Discipline at the University of Newcastle, Australia. She has worked for over two decades with communities in struggle forging emancipatory and decolonising pedagogical and epistemological practices and resistances/re-existencias in, against, and beyond patriarchal capitalist-coloniality in Europe, Latin America, and Australia. She was winner of the 2019 best Gender Theory and Feminist Book (International Studies Association).

Natasha Popcevski is a doctoral candidate in International Political Economy and an Academic Tutor and Research Assistant at the University of Wollongong, Australia.

Richard H. Robbins is a distinguished teaching professor of Anthropology at the State University of New York at Plattsburgh, USA.

Sandy Smith-Nonini is a research assistant professor of Anthropology at the University of North Carolina at Chapel Hill, USA. Her work has often focused on the intersection of medical anthropology and political economy, with a strong systems orientation—including projects on politics of health systems, resurgent infectious disease epidemics, working conditions/political ecology of meat processing, and the relationship of oil/gas dependence to energy poverty.

Dillon Wamsley is a PhD candidate in the Department of Politics at York University, Canada. His research focuses on global and comparative political economy, social policy, and state restructuring in the post-2008 era.

ABBREVIATIONS

AGRA	Alliance for a Green Revolution in Africa
AMG	Annual General Meeting
AUSMIN	The Australia-U.S. Ministerial Consultations
BAU	Business-as-Usual
BRI	Belt and Road Initiative
CDC	Centers for Disease Control and Prevention
CHSP	Commonwealth Home Support Program
COP	Conference of the Parties
CRISPR	Clustered Regularly Interspaced Short Palindromic Repeats
CRPD	Convention on the Rights of Persons with Disabilities
CSM	Civil Society and Indigenous Peoples' Mechanism
CEO	Chief Executive Officer
CSOs	Civil Society Organizations
DAI	Dangerous Anthropogenic Interference
DHHS	Department of Health and Human Services
DNA	Deoxyribonucleic Acid
DOD	Department of Defense
DPH	Department of Public Health
EBC	Earth Bank of Codes
ESOPs	Employee Share-ownership Plans
EU	European Union
FAO	Food and Agriculture Organization
FERN	Food and Environment Reporting Network
FPE	Feminist Political Economy
GDP	Gross Domestic Product
GFC	Great Financial Crisis
GHG	Greenhouse gas

GM	Genetically Modified
GOARN	Global Outbreak Alerts and Response Network
H1N1	Swine Flu
H5N1	Avian Flu
HHS	Health and Human Services
HNWIs	High-Net-Worth-Individuals
IFC	International Finance Corporation
IMF	International Monetary Fund
IoT	Internet of Things
IPC	International Planning Committee for Food Sovereignty
IPE	International Political Economy
IPES-Food	International Panel of Experts on Sustainable Food Systems
IPRs	Intellectual Property Rights
JPEO-CBRND	Joint Program Executive Office for Chemical, Biological, Radiological and Nuclear Defense
LMICs	Low and Middle Income Countries
M&As	Mergers and Acquisitions
MIC	Military Industrial Complex
MMR	Maternal Mortality Rates
MMT	Modern Monetary Theory
MSH	Multi-stakeholder Co-operatives
NAFTA	North American Free Trade Agreement
NDCs	Nationally Determined Contributions
NDIA	National Disability Insurance Agency
NDIS	National Disability Insurance Scheme
NSA	National Security Agency
NCF	National Care Forum
OECD	Organisation for Economic Co-operation and Development
OSHA	Occupational Safety and Health Agency
OWS	Operation Warp Speed
PAYE	Pay as You Earn
PDFOs	Participatory Democratic Forms of Organization
PHEP	Public Health Emergency Preparedness Cooperative
PhRMA	Pharmaceutical Research and Manufacturers of America
PPE	Personal Protective Equipment
PPPs	Public-Private Partnerships
RDT&E	Research, Development, Testing, and Evaluation
RET	Renewable Energy Technology
RCSA	Recruitment, Consulting and Staffing Association
RLW	"Real" Living Wage
RUP	Real Utopias Project
SVM	Shareholder Value Maximization
TRIPS	Trade-Related Aspects of Intellectual Property Rights
UN	United Nations

UNFSS	United Nations Food Systems Summit
USDA	United States Department of Agriculture
WB	World Bank
WEF	World Economic Forum
WFH	Working from Home
WFS	World Food Security
WHO	World Health Organization

INTRODUCTION

The Covid-19 Pandemic, International Political Economy, and Social Reproduction

Matt Dow and Tim Di Muzio

> There have been as many plagues as wars in history; yet always plagues and wars take people equally by surprise
>
> —*Albert Camus, The Plague, 1947*

> The plague only exaggerates the relationship between the classes: it strikes at the poor and spares the rich
>
> —*Jean-Paul Sartre, Les Temps Modernes, 1957*

> If it is true that the leper gave rise to rituals of exclusion, which to a certain extent provided the model for and general form of the great Confinement, then the plague gave rise to disciplinary projects... in order to see perfect disciplines functioning, rulers dreamt of the state of plague
>
> —*Michel Foucault, Discipline and Punish, 1995*

There can be little doubt that 2020 was a watershed year for the global political economy. By mid-March 2020, a highly contagious virus proliferated worldwide, causing international travel, trade, and commerce to slow and entire societies to lockdown. There is still little known about the precise geographic and transmission origins of coronavirus SARS-CoV-2 or Covid-19. However, the virus was first identified in Wuhan, a province of China, at some point during December of 2019 (Gebrekidan 2020; Mallapty 2020). What is known is how the virus transfers from one host to another and that it is a global pandemic of respiratory illness that has infected an estimated three hundred million people worldwide and claimed more than five million lives (and counting) (WHO 2021).[1] What is novel about the Covid-19 pandemic, though, compared to previous global pandemics, was the abundance of warnings and information accumulated by global medical experts, journalists, and security studies specialists predicting there was a looming

DOI: 10.4324/9781003250432-1

pandemic threat (Brannen and Hicks 2020; Davis 2020; Hammond 2020; Henig 2020; ; Schoch-Spana et al. 2017; Snowden 2020; Sun et al. 2020). In 2003–2004, governing a pandemic already witnessed a glimpse of what was to come from the original SARS-CoV virus outbreak that spread across 29 different countries and territories, roughly infecting 8,000 people and causing 774 deaths (CDC 2020a). In addition, recurring global influenza (flu) outbreaks like the global swine flu (H1N1) in 2009 and the recurring variants of the global avian flu (H5N1,) and of course, the common flus, continue to claim an estimated 250,000 to 650,000 lives each year (CDC 2020b). Although there are a variety of vaccines for the novel coronavirus, new variants such as Delta and Omicron have also appeared, challenging the scientific and broader international community (CDC 2021a). Yet, despite our knowledge of past historical plagues, present warning signs, and data about the looming viral pandemic, Covid-19 largely took the international community by surprise. But we must ask, why?

The primary explanation is identified as global governance is currently struggling between the potential end of the *International Liberal Economic Order* and the rise of an *Authoritarian Liberal Order* (Anievas and Saull 2019; Babic 2020; Gill 2019; Sthal 2019). The international liberal economic order has had a *longue durée* of racist, sexist, and fascist tendencies and prioritises and protects capital accumulation over human well-being and the biosphere (Anievas et al. 2015; Anievas and Saull 2020; Barkawi and Laffey 1999; Bakker and Gill 2003; Berneria 1999; Bhambra et al. 2020; Di Muzio 2015a; Moore 2015; Persaud 2016; Vitalis 2017).[2] The creators of this post-WWII world order did attempt to build and foster international relations and institutions on the principles of liberalism: cooperation (e.g., United Nations), science (e.g., World Health Organization), and human rights (e.g., Declaration of Human Rights). However, these principles have been applied selectively and unevenly, with wars, human rights abuses and poverty persisting in many parts of the globe (Ikenberry 2018). In short, it was never a complete world order and never fully lived up to liberal ideals—particularly when these ideals obstructed capitalist accumulation and the geopolitical power of the West (Gowan 1999; Jahn 2013; Losurdo 2011).

The authoritarian liberal order, under the guidance of former United States President Donald Trump, Brazilian President Jair Bolsonaro, United Kingdom Prime Minister Boris Johnson, Russian President Vladimir Putin, Indian Prime Minister Narendra Modi and other far-right-wing elected leaders and parties throughout Europe, is an attempt to restore white Christian supremacy and nationalism as the guiding principles of global governance (Anievas and Saull 2020; Stewart 2020). This looming world order, even with Donald Trump's loss in the 2020 election, is still very active, incredibly organised, funded, and is committed to a potentially violent insurrection against the Biden Administration, with the endgame being some form of white supremacist-based authoritarianism (Rowley 2022). Moreover, these far right-wing social movements are still ideologically entrenched with conspiracy theories, anti-science, anti-vaccination and anti-masking and have become a global movement that strongly believes and disseminates that Covid-19 is a hoax

TABLE I.1 Top ten countries by Covid-19 cases

Global Rank	Country	Covid-19 Cases	Deaths
1	United States	61,263,030	859,356
2	India	35,708,442	483,936
3	Brazil	22,523,907	620,031
4	United Kingdom	14,475,192	150,154
5	France	12,111,218	125,438
6	Russia	10,650,849	316,163
7	Turkey	9,978,452	83,702
8	Germany	7,531,630	114,712
9	Italy	7,436,939	139,038
10	Spain	7,164,906	89,934

Source: Data retrieved from: https://www.worldometers.info/coronavirus/countries-where-coronavirus-has-spread/ (10th January 2022).

(Chotiner 2020; McGreal 2020; Parks 2021; Bond 2021). This has led many social forces to articulate that any Covid-19 preventive measures will sacrifice the world capitalist economy and the freedoms of individuals.[3] Thus, it is of little surprise that the top ten countries with the highest infection and death rates of Covid-19 belong to the movements above in some capacity (See Table I.1).

Although the relationship between the form of government and the spread of the virus is important to study further, we argue that analysing Covid-19 through the lens of global governance just scratches the surface of understanding the current crisis presented by Covid-19.

The pandemic has intensified the scholarly belief that the world order is in a crisis of global leadership and governance, it could be argued that this issue has continued to escalate since the Global Financial Crisis (GFC) of 2007–2008 (Babic 2020; Sthal 2019). The pandemic has uncovered the fragility of the global political economy's urban-centrism, trade, tourism, and financial architecture and it could indeed be argued that the intensification of global urbanism, business, tourism and finance over at least the last 30 years, facilitated the spread of infectious diseases like Covid-19 (Davis 2020). Yet, this is not necessarily an argument for re-localisation or autarkic states but recognition that local diseases can have global impacts on the health of all humanity. The primary reason for writing this edited collection is to investigate and explore how far and in what ways the Covid-19 pandemic is challenging, restructuring and perhaps remaking aspects of the global political economy.

Since the 1970s, neoliberal capitalism has been the guiding principle of global development: fiscal discipline, privatisation of public assets, deregulation of markets, the liberalisation of trade and investment regimes, lower corporate wealth taxation, environmental and labour standards downgraded in many places, and the extension and protection of both intellectual and physical property rights (Cahill and Konings 2017; Eagleton-Pierce 2019; Harvey 2005; Gill 2008; Plehwe et al. 2020). This latest phase of capitalism originated from the Washington Consensus (International Monetary Fund, World Bank, and the United States Treasury) as policy prescriptions (loans with strict conditions and guidelines) to allegedly help the "Third World" with their debt crisis of the late 1970s and 1980s as well as the former Union of Soviet Socialist Republics, with their government debt crises, and collapsed centrally planned economies in the 1990s (Di Muzio and Robbins 2016; George 1990; Sachs 2012; Williamson 1990). The Western capitalist core adopted these developmental policies to allegedly deal with stagflation and rising government debt of the 1980s and 1990s, ostensibly caused by government intervention and social spending (Nitzan and Bichler 2009: Ch 16; Di Muzio and Robbins 2016). This model of development quickly grew to incorporate an even larger membership and consensus with the opening of China, and much of Asia, to tourism, transport, trade and finance. As a result, the policies and practices of neoliberal governments and multinational corporations which have created an interconnected and interdependent neoliberal world order through what Stephen Gill has called "the new constitutionalism" and policies of "disciplinary neoliberalism" (Arrighi 2008; Gill 1995; Gill 2008; Gill and Cutler 2014). The concept of disciplinary neoliberalism highlights how nation-states are disciplined and embedded in the process of "intensifying and deepening the scope of market disciplines associated with the increasing power of capital in organizing social and world orders, and in so doing shaping the limits of the possible in people's everyday lives." (Gill and Cutler 2014: 6). For example, new constitutionalism represents the political-judicial counterpart to disciplinary neoliberalism as a mode of law or legal regulation that "secure[s] uncontested and extended protection for private property rights and investor freedoms on a world scale, locked in by basic laws, constitutions and treaties such that these rights are likely to stretch well into the future" (Gill 2014: 37). Yet even though the logic of neoliberalism has globalised, it has done so in differential, uneven and variegated pathways across the planet, largely due to the social forces and relations of power and resistance within and outside state structures (Bakker and Gill 2019; Brenner et al. 2010).

But after Covid-19, will these trends continue, particularly when states struggle with overcoming the pandemic and are in violation of one of neoliberalism's key principles: fiscal discipline? This is not the neoliberal world order's first encounter with a global crisis. What makes the current neoliberal capitalist world order potentially distinct from previous epochs is its resilience. For example, critical and mainstream scholars have pointed out for some time that neoliberal governance and financial capitalism have been a primary factor in various financial recessions and crises, predominately from the lack of governmental regulations that have plagued the global economy since the 1990s (e.g. the global north's 1990s recessions, Mexico's 1994 debt crisis, the Asian financial crisis 1997, the Russian financial crisis of 1998, the Argentine financial crisis 1999–2002, Dot-com bubble 2000–2002, the Great Financial Crisis of 2007–2009, European Sovereign debt crisis 2009–2019, etc.) (Albo et al. 2010; Gill 1999;; McNally 2011; Roos 2019; Stiglitz 2019; Tooze 2018). The solution to these crises has followed, more or less, the same neoliberal playbook: massive governmental bailouts (stimulus packages), further deregulation, tax cuts and subsidies for global businesses all the while the social burden and financial costs of these crises have been largely externalised onto ordinary citizens through increased government debt and intensified austerity measures (Blyth 2013; Di Muzio and Robbins 2016; Tooze 2018). Both critical and mainstream scholarship have tended to argue that the end of each global financial or legitimacy crisis would lead to the inevitable collapse of the era of neoliberal capitalism and neoliberal global governance (Plehwe et al. 2020). Perhaps strangely, the opposite has consistently taken place; neoliberal capitalism and governance have not only survived but have reinforced and expanded the supremacy of capital accumulation and market governmentality over the world economy and arguably seeped deeper into daily life as the sole development model and form of social reproduction (Brown 2015). The concept of social reproduction has many interpretations, the concept typically brings the readers' attention to the differential practices that reproduce the human, biological and ecological substance of everyday life—differential because communities and classes reproduce their lifestyles in different ways across space and time (Bakker 2007; Beneria 1979; Bhattacharya 2017; Luxton and Bezanson 2006; Elias and Rai 2019; Bakker and Gill 2003). For example, Isabella Bakker and Stephen Gill have conceptualised social reproduction as comprising three dimensions: "biological reproduction, the reproduction of labor power and social practices connected to caring, socialization and the fulfillment of human needs" (Bakker and Gill 2003: 4; see also: Bakker 2007). As important as these dimensions are, social reproduction can also be conceived in more general terms as to how any specific form of "society produces, consumes and reproduces its lifestyles, how it conceives of these lifestyles and how they defend them juridically or through the application of violence" (Di Muzio and Dow 2017: 9). Therefore, this collected volume makes the case that although the Covid-19 pandemic may not end neoliberal capitalism or its attendant governance regime, there are many important questions about how the pandemic has altered and challenged the political economy of global capitalism in various dimensions. Thus, a fundamental aim of this book is to explore and investigate how the pandemic has shaped and will shape and reshape the terrain of social reproduction and global capitalism.

This volume argues that it is important to understand how global pandemics are constituted in historical structures and have been one of the fundamental factors that have transformed and altered both the terrains of the world economy and social reproduction.[4] Most of the human social reproduction has historically taken place in what Fernand Braudel (1981) called "material life" or civilisation, which describes the "rich zone" or a "layer covering the earth" where most human beings reproduce their livelihoods through self-sufficiency, infra-economy, or informal economic activity. In other words, people re-produce through the exchange of goods and services within a small radius. This form of local material life or economy did place strict structural restrictions on movement as these populations were very susceptible to scarcity or inadequate food supplies and diseases found in the "biological *ancien regime*" (1981: 90ff). The biological *ancien regime* is an organic historical structure that shapes and reshapes the conditions of all demography, social life and economic interactions. This is not to be confused with the work of Thomas Malthus (1798[1998]) and what later would be known as the "Malthusian Trap", where overpopulation and consumption are seen as a natural law that produces scarcity (Clark 2010). Instead, the biological *ancien regime* highlights how human, plant, and animal disease, soil infertility, weather, and other naturally occurring phenomena impact human behaviour and social reproduction (Braudel 1981: 90ff). For Braudel, this historical structure established at times the very conditions of the existence of humanity and some "limits of the possible" over much of European civilisation until the 1800s (1981: 92). The primary reasons why Spain and Portugal, and later on, Britain and France, were able to overcome the structural constraints of the biological *ancien regime* and establish a Euro-centric world economy was through massive waves of internal state-led and violent enclosures, global warfare, colonisation and slavery, and with Britain transforming its economy from one premised on organic-based power to mechanical, industrial and coal-based power (Di Muzio 2015a; Federici 2004; Horne 2018, 2020; Malm 2016; Mann 1993[2012]; Marx 1867[1976] Mies 2001; Moore 2015; Wallerstein 1974). Finally, Marxist political economists Robert Brenner (1977) and David McNally (1988) have argued that the bubonic plague (1331–1354) in Europe that killed an estimated 75 to 200 million people (10 to 60 per cent of Europe's entire population) was one of the central reasons for the transition from European feudalism to capitalism. This is because all pandemics appear to expose differences of inequality within a hierarchical human population. In the case of the bubonic plague, most deaths were European serfs, forcing the European ruling elite to fundamentally alter the hierarchy, social property relations, and class configuration, from serfs to wage workers in England (McNally 1988).

The invention of quarantine in Europe, used during the Covid-19 pandemic, started in 1377, with foreign ships and sailors placed in quarantine by domestic rulers. Michel Foucault argues that it was the plague of leprosy at the end of the seventeenth century that gave birth to new surveillance and disciplinary society in Europe (1995: 195ff). For instance, Foucault noted that town gates "were fitted with observation posts, people were compelled to speak the truth under threat of death", and people were forced into fixed places under fear of becoming contaminated or punished (1995: 196). These surveillance and disciplinary projects may have emerged to separate the population into two factions: the sick and non-sick, to stop the spread of the plague. But Foucault argues that these projects of exercising power and discipline over the population did not end when the sickness disappeared but rapidly expanded. Rulers quickly realised that the greatest way to exercise power over their subjects was through surveillance and other disciplinary methods, which could be deployed and justified through the creation of binary divisions and the branding of the population (sick/healthy, mad/sane, dangerous/harmless) (Focault1995: 199). This European governmentality shifted during the nineteenth century with the emergence of liberal governmentality and the extension of biopolitics when the White horsemen of the Apocalypse were no longer the primary security threat to European society (Foucault 2008: 66). Instead, the primary security threats against the population became everyday dangers such as crime, disease and hygiene, the degeneration of the individual, family, race and the human species (2008: 67). For Foucault, as the so-called threats multiplied, so did surveillance and discipline over the population. Foucault uses Jeremy Bentham's idea of the panopticon to highlight growing surveillance practices "for institutions like schools, factories, and prisons which would enable one to supervise the conduct of individuals while increasing the profitability and productivity of their activity" and became potentially the very credo or formula of liberal governmentality (2008: 66–68).

To critically study the past, present, and potential future transformations of the global political economy, we should also consider what William H. MacNeil argues in his *Plagues and People* (1989). MacNeil argues that the driving force of human history could be summed up as the struggle with micro-parasitism (germs, viruses, and bacteria). No matter how socially and technologically advanced and complex human civilisations become, we are organically chained, not only to each other but to all living species and the biosphere, and this relationship will always foster future outbreaks, particularly if we continue to pursue economic growth and thereby disturb and destroy nature's ecosystems on which all species depend (Kolbert 2015).

The question then becomes, how far and in what ways will the Covid-19 pandemic change or intensify current patterns of neoliberal governance, the capitalist global economy, and social reproduction? We argue that the Covid-19 pandemic, unlike previous financial crises, or previous and current challenges to neoliberal hegemony, is vastly different and exposes some "morbid symptoms" or potentially fatal structural tendencies embedded in the current trajectory of global development and social reproduction. The first tendency is that the neoliberal world order and economy rest on a foundation of gross inequality in terms of global income, living standards, unpaid and paid labour, global consumption of resources, and environmental protection, which is embedded in historical classism, sexism, and racist philosophies and practices (Bhattacharya and Vogel 2017; Bodley 2015; Di Muzio 2015b; Chakrabarty 2017; Kenner 2020; Berkhout et al. 2020; UN 2020). For example, there are an estimated 7.8 billion people and roughly US$399.1 trillion dollars of personal wealth. The Credit Suisse *Global Wealth Report* (2020) argues that at the top of the global wealth pyramid, there are 175,000 individuals on this planet who have at least a net worth of over US$50 million dollars, and together, this class of people have roughly US$99.6 trillion in global wealth (25%) (2020: 29 and see Figure I.1).

The next class is considered the top 1%, which are 51.9 million households who hold 1 million dollars in financial wealth (after debt) and control 43% of all global wealth at US$173.3 trillion. If we look further down on the wealth pyramid, where most people are, they have a net worth of under US$10,000 dollars and hold 5.4 trillion or roughly 1.4% of all global wealth (p. 29). Although almost half the world lives on less than US$5.50 a day or the equivalent of US$2,007.5 a year (World Bank 2018).

The Covid-19 pandemic has unevenly exposed, inflicted, and killed those who are not only racial minorities, gendered, or in elderly vulnerable groups, but also

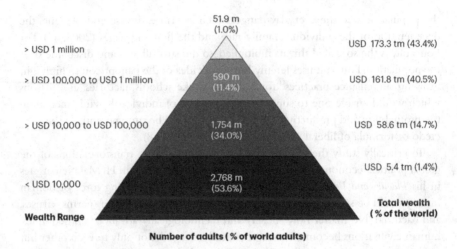

FIGURE I.1 The global wealth pyramid

Source: Credit Susses *Global Wealth Report* (2020: 29).

those predominately in low-income areas (Bambra et al. 2020; Botton et al. 2020; Long et al. 2020; StatsCan 2020). As noted by Sartre (1957) in the introductory quote, previous pandemics have greatly impacted the working poor and spared the rich, the Covid-19 pandemic under neoliberal governance, is no different. This is the result of not everyone being able to quarantine because their individual or family livelihood is dependent on their ability to work and the fact that most of the world's workplaces for essential services (e.g., food, transport, health care) cannot be transferred to their place of residency. Adding to the problem is that most jobs are precarious and unprotected (Jay et al. 2020; Gore and LaBaron 2019; Graeber 2019; Standing 2014). So even though the neoliberal world order has witnessed some progress in lifting people out of abject poverty in the late-20th and 21st centuries, could Covid-19 endanger this progress or engender new forms of wealth inequality?

The second tendency is global debt (Kose et al. 2020). One could conceive the neoliberal world order as a debt-growth-socio-economic restructuring nexus, highlighting how economic growth and debt have become fundamental ways in which a globalised society is organised and reorganised to meet the needs of creditors (Di Muzio and Robbins 2016). This is so because current patterns of financial accumulation, the social reproduction of livelihoods and economic growth are dependent on the ability to service the accumulation of mounting debts (Di Muzio 2015a; Di Muzio and Robbins 2017). In other words, the world economy may be better understood as "a single debt-based economy" (Rowbotham 1998: 159). For example, all major social forces are *deeply indebted* (see Table I.2).

Global debt (government, financial, and corporate bonds and household debt) stood at US$45 trillion in 1991 and now stands at over US$272.7 trillion in 2020

TABLE I.2 Total debt by category measured in trillion dollars

Type of debt	2000 (4Q)	2007 (4Q)	2014 (4Q)	2018 (4Q)	2019 (3Q)	2020 (3Q)	Per cent Increase Since 2000
Government Bonds	22	33	58	64	69.1	77.6	252.7
Financial Bonds	20	37	45	59	62.8	66.3	231.5
Corporate Bonds	26	38	56	70	73.7	79.6	306.1
Household	20	33	40	45	47.1	49.2	146
Total Debt as a % of GDP	246	269	286	318	320 (4Q)	365 (4Q)	48.4

Source: Data collected 2000 to 2014 is from (Di Muzio and Robbins 2016). For 2018, it is from Tanzi 2018. For 2019 and 2020, it is from Tiftik et al. 2020).

(Tifik et al. 2020). Just as important, over 90 per cent of the world's money supply is controlled, produced, and distributed by commercial banks as interest-bearing debt and based on the anticipated potential creditworthiness of their borrowers (Di Muzio and Robbins 2016, 2017). The neoliberal world order and economy have allowed both banks and credit rating agencies the power to deem individuals, corporations, and governments creditworthy or non-creditworthy; therefore, subjecting these social forces to potential market discipline (Gill 1995; Roos 2019; Sinclair 2008). With the continued spread of Covid-19, economies in and out of lockdown, jittery markets and massive government spending, we question will service and repayment of global debt continue to be a fundamental way the current world order and the economy is organised?

The third tendency is that neoliberal governance and the world economy are built on the assumption that infinite economic growth is possible on a finite planet (Hamilton 2004; Heinberg 2011). For example, to overcome global financial inequality and mounting debt, political classes the world over pursue evermore economic growth (see the conclusion to this volume). This has led the world order to be organised around economic growth (measured as gross domestic product) as a fundamental yardstick—measuring the success of both "economies" and "politicians" as it influences macroeconomic policies and priorities so that government spending and debt is influenced by the rate of growth (Fioramonti 2013: 14). For example, world gross domestic product has increased by 143.2 per cent since 2000 (see Table I.3). Most of this economic growth has come from non-Organisation for Economic Co-operation and Development countries.

All public goods (education, health care, national parks, etc...) are tied to gross domestic product growth, and if growth declines, societies are threatened with cuts in social spending unless the nation-state becomes more indebted or raises its sources of revenues (e.g., taxation, fines, fees) (Roos 2019). As a result, the gross domestic product has become *the* "global definition of power" to the extent that countries are globally ranked by their gross domestic product and allowed into global governance institutions based on their gross domestic performance (i.e.,

TABLE 1.3 World gross domestic product

Gross Domestic Product	2000	2007	2014	2018	2019	2020	Per cent Increase Yearly Average	Per cent Increase Since 2000
OCED	27.5	43.3	50.1	53.2	53.7	52	4.5	89.1
Non-OCED	6.1	14.7	29.4	33.2	34.1	29.7	19.4	387
Global	33.6	58	79.5	86.4	87.8	81.7	7.2	143.2

Source: Data collected from World Bank 2020 and OECD 2020.

Group of Seven or Twenty) (Fioramonti 2013: 10). These countries have incredible power as planetary leaders in shaping the terrains of globalised social reproduction. At the same time, countries with sluggish gross domestic performance are forced "into a vicious circle of structural adjustments and macroeconomic reforms, mostly dictated by the World Bank and the International Monetary Fund, in partnership with international investors and financial markets" (Fioramonti 2013: 32ff). What is important to note is that economic growth can only expand through the destruction, despoliation and commodification of the natural world comprised of limited and finite resources (Hickel and Kallis 2020). To put this in context, consider that global GDP stood at US$84 trillion in 2020.[5] If we apply a modest growth rate of three per cent, this means that by 2100, global GDP will have to be US$904 trillion. Yet, the planet's health is currently at a historical tipping point with the looming climate emergency, the sixth mass extinction, the destruction of important planetary carbon sinks (wetlands, forests, oceans, etc.), and the inevitable "peaking" and exhaustion of fundamental non-renewable resources for social reproduction (IPCC 2021, Rockström et al. 2016; Ripple et al. 2017). Moreover, there is mounting social and scientific research that has linked the increasing spread of certain global bacterial, virial, and other disease outbreaks to declining overall planetary health (Bernstein and Salas 2020). The key question is whether continued economic growth is possible and what the natural world would look like at that rate of monetising and commodifying nature? The unlikelihood of continued exponential growth is a key reason for mounting debates on the need for alternative patterns of social reproduction and new indicators for human well-being (Fioramonti 2017). For these reasons, we ask the question of whether the Covid-19 pandemic may force world leaders, market forces, and economic policymakers to rethink the current developmental trajectory of the world. As we point out in the conclusion of this volume, we find little evidence to suggest that a new political operating system is emerging to challenge the dominance of GDP. Still, scholars and practitioners have begun to re-evaluate the future prospects of the global political economy and the primary ideas that have initiated it.

This volume brings together established and upcoming critical scholars in international relations and international political economy to provide novel, timely and innovative research on how the Covid-19 pandemic is impacting and *is likely to* impact the global economy in several important dimensions including, but not limited to, state fiscal policy, monetary policy and the accumulation of debt, health and social reproduction, the future of austerity and the fate of neoliberalism. Finally, this volume provides some insights for those who would like to transform global society to focus on greater biospheric sustainability, greater economic equality, and human well-being rather than the accumulation of power and profit. To do so, we have structured this volume into three main sections. Below, we detail the book's organisation by theme and chapter.

Part I: Global Power, Inequality, and Climate Change

The first theme of this volume explores dimensions of the pre-existing global crises that have arguably been accelerated by Covid-19: increased financial inequality, the tyranny of the rate of return for global investors, and the perils of climate change. Questions that animate this section include (1) how much longer can institutional investors and other capitalist social forces continue to expect a rate of return on their money no matter the consequences; (2) how has Covid-19 transformed or accelerated the need for a rate of return; (3) how will mounting corporate and government debt impact the global economy; (4) what are the connections between Covid-19 and climate change and how might climate change reinforce the spread of more deadly diseases and (5) with both the growing need to get a rate of return and to finance tremendous debt loads, how will these pursuits impact the climate change movement?

The opening chapter by Richard H. Robbins provides an empirical and vigorous account of the contradiction that the Covid-19 pandemic is providing an "opportunity of a lifetime" for global investors during the largest global health crisis in over one hundred years. This "opportunity of a lifetime" is rooted in predatory behaviour by global investors to capitalise on the chaotic disruption and lockdowns, services and goods shortages, suffering, and death. So far, the global billionaires' class have increased their wealth by over 60 per cent in eight months (March 2020 to November 2021). This is the result of two important features of the global neoliberal capitalist economy, the first being that "financialization" has become embedded in the very process of how societies reproduce themselves. To put this into context, Robbins asks the reader to visualise a world whereby everyone belongs to a nation-state and a "state of finance"—where people pay their taxes and pay their debt, interest, and rents. From 2010 to 2020, Americans paid US$30 trillion in interest, US$4.5 trillion in rents, and only US$20 trillion in federal taxes. The second feature is the logic of "rates of return-on-investment capital", which means that global investors want specific returns on their investments. As a result, global investors are very selective in what they do and do not invest in, which has tremendous impacts on global society, as every facet of human life has become increasingly tethered to accessible finance. Furthermore, Robbins demonstrates how macroeconomic policies in the United States have been created to eliminate or minimise potential threats to "rates of return". These "threats" include inflation, taxes, labour/wages, responsibility for negative externalities, lack of investment opportunities, competition and default. He concludes by stating that while the future remains unknown and contested, a fundamental fact is that in a post-Covid-19 economy, global investors will continue to pursue the logic of the rate of return at the expense of the rest of global society if they continue to remain unimpeded.

Natasha Popcevski's contribution reveals that the Covid-19 pandemic is not "the great leveller" of rich and poor nor a "socially neutral disease". Instead, one major outcome of the pandemic has been the rise of billionaire wealth. There has been extensive literature on explaining wealth inequality, and yet most of the dialogue remains grounded in two dominant explanations. The first is from neoclassical economics, where wealth is distributed by the "production function". The "production function" claims that wealth is distributed by how much labour or capital contributes to production or economic output. But if we follow this logic, then Elon Musk is "2,020,408 times more productive than the average worker at Tesla", which is absurd. The other explanation for wealth inequality is rooted in Marx's work. Marxists argue that wealth inequality can be easily explained by focusing on labour exploitation. Popcevski demonstrates the shortcomings of this explanation as well. As Marxists have never been able to solve "the transformation problem" (converting labour time into prices). She then draws on the capital as power theory to demonstrate why global inequality continues to grow. The capital as power perspective argues that the reason global inequality continues to grow, even during the pandemic, is largely the result of organised power that is embedded in capital accumulation and the capitalist system. As people do not become billionaires, nor are corporations profitable or highly valued through just productivity and the exploitation of others alone. Popcevski demonstrates that most of the wealth of billionaires stems from their ownership of income-generating assets—typically large equity stakes in corporations they either founded or takeover. Popcevski concludes that a way to stop the escalating global inequality and power of the global 1% would be to introduce a more progressive tax system where the rich finally pay their fair share.

The next chapter by Dan Bousfield reveals that the Covid-19 pandemic has deepened the crisis of liberal governance in the Global north, especially the United States. This crisis is anchored in global liberal governments and institutions inability to address "the role of social media in rising authoritarianism, racism and vaccine hesitancy during the Covid-19 pandemic." This is seen in how liberal societies treat both rational and irrational argumentations as credible because processing them is primarily up to the individual's discretion. This is one reason why Adorno saw the persistence of irrationalism in a liberal society. This irrationalism is coupled with the fact that as societies become more complex, the need for "experts" arises. This is a fundamental contradiction in liberal societies because individuals are imagined as having unlimited freedom to make their own decisions in a society that needs ever-more "organizational obedience for it to function". Global public trust has rapidly deteriorated in liberal institutions on both the right and left of the political spectrum. The fundamental difference between the camps is that the authoritarian and far-right have always created a narrative (conspiracy theory) that there is something happening "behind-the scenes" whereby racialised and sexualised minority groups are replacing the "white race" and their "culture" in insidious ways. On the left, the Black Lives Matter and indigenous protests often challenge the hypocrisy, inequalities and injustices created by liberal institutionalism and society. Bousfield illustrates how the Covid-19 vaccine hesitancy, authoritarianism and racism have been connected to online radicalisation and the role of social media and yet this is protected under liberal free speech law. In other words, everyone has the right to their own opinion even if they can be proven incorrect. Hence, the real power behind social media is not necessarily to spread verifiable information but to influence people to act in one way or another. Bousfield concludes by noting that the cruel optimistic underpinnings of liberalism "now appears in the distinction between the vaccinated and unvaccinated, as the manifest racialized inequalities under capitalism are reflected in the global pandemic response."

The following chapter is by Adam Lucas. He argues that the commitments contained in the Paris Agreement require national governments to make emission reductions consistent with maintaining global average surface temperatures at no more than 2 °C by 2100. Those commitments include a "preferred ambition" of 1.5 °C. The logic of the global carbon budget implies that to have a 50% chance of maintaining the 2 °C goal, developed countries would have had to begin emission reductions in the order of 8% to 10% per year as of 2013, which they did not do. In 2011, James Hansen and colleagues warned that if global emission reductions were delayed until 2020, the required rate would be 15% per year. In 2013, William Nordhaus argued that between 1% and 2% of world income would be required to achieve the 2 °C target, constituting between 5% and 9% of global GDP. One of the few positive outcomes of the Covid-19 pandemic has been the radical reduction in global transport emissions due to regional, national, and international travel restrictions. The pandemic will result in 7% global emission reductions during 2020 if those restrictions remain until the end of the year. In September 2020, it was estimated the global economic downturn resulting from COVID would reduce global GDP by 4.4%. Ironically, COVID offers the world's governments an opportunity to hit a "reset" on deep decarbonisation and achieve the emission reductions required. This chapter explores the extent to which they have taken up that challenge.

The final chapter in this section is by Sandy Smith-Nonini. Her study shows a significant connection between industrial meat production, climate change, and the Covid-19 pandemic. The connection rests on the fact that the leading scientific thesis on the origins of the Covid-19 pandemic is that it is a "spillover" effect from the growing destruction of ecosystems, humanity's increased interaction with wildlife, and humanity's growing obsession with meat-based diets. Combined, the three largest meat processing firms—JBS, Tyson, and Cargill—emit more greenhouse gasses than the country of France. Moreover, the Big Meat industries are one of the primary actors responsible for the mass destruction of forests, wetlands, and other ecological sites as they convert them to pasture and crop fields for livestock. Smith-Nonini then investigated a wide variety of meat-processing plant outbreaks in the United States' Midwest, where she found that there is ample evidence to suggest that the meat industry was responsible for "the largest industrial source of viral spread". For example, in June 2020, "77% of people sick with the virus were of working age and, in meatpacking counties". The Big Meat executives tried to cover this up with the help of Republican governors and the Trump administration. Smith-Nonini argues that meat-processing plants are a major site of Covid-19 infection due to the union busting and deregulation of the industry Big Meat championed. Yet, this industry is still heavily dependent on "state-facilitated subsidies", corporate tax breaks, low-wage and racialised labour (often immigrant) workforces, and lax governmental and environmental regulation. In conclusion, we learned that the Big Meat corporate-food regime is not only unsustainable because it contributes to climate change and mass environmental destruction but also that it is one of the fundamental factors that led to the pandemic.

Part II: Global Health, Social Care, and Reproduction during the Covid-19 Pandemic

The second theme explores the dimensions of global neoliberalism and the impacts of previous austerity measures on health and social reproduction about the pandemic and its aftermath. It interrogates how neoliberal governance and development have impacted global health before and after Covid-19. Questions that animate this section include (1) how has the neoliberal world order impacted global health; (2) how far and in what ways has the Covid-19 pandemic potentially highlighted some shortcomings of global health under neoliberal governance and how is this connected to social reproduction; (3) how far and in what ways has neoliberalism dismantled (through austerity) key government institutions, policies, and structures surrounding global health that could have prevented or helped combat Covid-19; (4) how do we understand the relationship between inequality and health in the Covid-19 pandemic and what has the pandemic taught us about the merits of private versus public health care systems and (5) finally, how far and in what ways can we imagine better health care provisioning in the future up to and including preventative measures?

In the opening chapter of Part II, Wamsley and Benatar argue that there has been a fundamental reversal in how global health has been carried out in capitalist societies. These transformations have made the global population much more at risk and vulnerable to the Covid-19 pandemic. From 1945 to 1980, global populations witnessed significant improvements in global health outcomes, reflecting how both citizens and social movements exerted pressure on nation-states to develop national health and social policies. As a result, after WWII, public officials rapidly expanded public health, raised per capita incomes, made vast improvements in technology and medical care, and were able to make significant improvements in global health outcomes. In the following era, from 1980 to 2008, under neoliberal capitalism, there was a shift from public health finance and healthcare provision towards private market finance and private healthcare provision. This has undermined public health in two ways (1) directly "through cuts in health care services and privatization of insurance" and (2) indirectly "through unemployment and privatizing social risk". They illustrate that the consequences of the Global Financial Crisis of 2008 meant intensifying both austerity and the marketisation of global health. This has made the preparation for viral pandemics more difficult for global and national health institutions. Indeed, Covid-19 emerged when national health care systems across the globe have never been so defunded and fragile, and yet "the world has become more susceptible to globalized disease outbreaks." As the Covid-19 crisis and pandemic continue, we have learned that neoliberal capitalism contradicts and undermines public health. What is truly needed is rebuilding domestic and global public-led health and environmental capacities combined with poverty reduction.

In the next chapter, Tatiana Andersen's vital contribution explores the persistent logic of vaccine inequities, rooted in a "complex and yet strategic enmeshment" among "war-biomedical logics, asset accumulation logics and intellectual property logics". The unequal access to the Covid-19 vaccine and other therapeutics is not a natural market outcome but part of a long history of how proprietors of the biomedicine industry have consistently and strategically controlled knowledge and produced medication as a privately owned asset. Andersen explores how the United States has dramatically increased government spending within the private defence sector. This has led to biomedical innovation being directly connected to militarised defence. She shows the power behind the biopharmaceutical sector or techno-scientific knowledge and how they aim to have their knowledge and innovation turned into income-generating assets. The fundamental difference between commodities and assets is commodities are simply bought and sold where profit is made at the point of sale, whereas assets generally generate income for a given period, through the power of ownership and thereby, the exclusion of others. She highlights that intellectual property rights are a form of Veblenian sabotage, which is "understood as the strategic and deliberate restriction of productivity and creative innovation". Thus, biopharmaceutical firms "claim ownership over techno-scientific knowledge as assetized property, but they also make claims on how societies engage with health and illness". The market value of biopharmaceuticals pivots on their ability to capitalise on uncertainty (global or national health crises) and their ability to provide, yet at the same time, restrict access to essential bio-scientific knowledge and medication. Finally, Andersen argues for key structural reforms in the global biopharmaceutical industry. We learn that public officials and concerned citizens must challenge the industry's *modus operandi* lest inequities in global vaccines and other therapeutics continue.

The final chapter in this theme is by Laura Davy and Helen Dickinson who offer a case study on Australia's care sector that reveals how most care "largely happens behind closed doors". The fundamental reason is that Australia's political economy, like other capitalist economies, have historically structured "the management of care and support" to be placed involuntarily into the private sphere, which is generally a "feminine responsibility". The Covid-19 pandemic has exposed that biological, social reproduction is fundamental to the economy and, thus, has dragged the care sector into public consciousness. Davy and Dickinson reveal that many elderly and disabled people who were greatly impacted and the most at risk for Covid-19 were not the primary recipients of Australia's additional governmental services and vaccines. For example, 1,841 people died from Covid-19 in Australia, with 1,483 of these deaths being those aged 70 or over, and 45% of these people were living in "government subsidized aged care facilities". The authors further point out that, in previous decades, governmental social care was driven by austerity and market reforms for Australia's disability and aged care services. These changes have helped escalate the crisis of care. An Australian Royal Commission has made public that there are major challenges for the future of care in Australia. One difficulty is staffing, as workers in the care sector are highly underpaid, have poor employment conditions, and have limited opportunities because most of the workers are largely women. As feminist scholarship has demonstrated, care work is systematically undervalued in society despite its crucial importance. In this sense, the Covid-19 pandemic highlighted the contradiction between their essential work and their ill-treatment. In conclusion, the authors argue the need for reinvestment in social care through a human-rights approach not motivated by market logic or profit. We learn that without social reform, future emergencies will continue to disproportionately affect the elderly and disabled.

Part III: The Future of Production, Money, Energy, and Food Regimes

The final theme examines and investigates how the pandemic may change the future of the global political economy in four key areas: work, money, energy, and food. Chapters in this section are animated by the following questions (1) what will the future of work and the monetary system look like? Will cheap credit continue to be the lifeblood of neoliberal capitalism, and what are the consequences of the current fiscal and monetary order across nations? Are there alternatives worth consideration; (2) what will the future of the global energy system be? Oil prices have collapsed and rebounded but will this ebb and flow continue, and how does the price of oil impact upon the future of energy systems and global social reproduction? Will renewable energies finally take over from fossil fuels? Are there limitations to a renewable energy transition in the post-pandemic world order and (3) what lessons does the pandemic have for the future of work and food regimes and food security/sovereignty?

The opening chapter of this theme is by Tom Barnes, Sophie Cotton, and Rakesh Kumar. The authors highlight how the Covid-19 pandemic may or may not worsen the growing problem of precarisation in Australia, the United Kingdom, and the United States. They investigate how the pandemic may impact the future of work. Although the concept of precarisation is still very much debated, the authors argue that precarisation can be broken down into three elements: (1) access to sufficient paid work; (2) income security; (3) and collective voice. There are two explanations for the rise of precarisation. The first is that there has been long-term stagnation in global manufacturing productivity which has led to a surplus of labour, and thereby, a "world of poorly paid workers". The second is that precarity is connected to the cyclical nature of booms and busts cycles in neoliberal capitalism, as seen in the last four recessions. The authors assess both accounts using rigorous empirical data on unemployment, income insecurity, collective voice, and associational power to demonstrate "that precarization is a process in which the social and economic risks of life in capitalist society are passed onto workers". Yet, this process does not happen purely by the cyclical nature of boom and bust cycles nor by linear manufacturing trends. Rather, it results from neoliberal capitalist path-dependency in the long and short runs. In other words, "precarization is best conceived as *a path-dependent and cumulative process punctuated by periodic crises of job loss and unemployment*". This labour trend has emerged over several decades, and when an economic crisis unfolds, like the Covid-19 pandemic, it worsens the already fragile conditions of vulnerable and unprotected workers. And most of these workers are usually from racialised and gendered groups who are already disenfranchised. The Covid-19 impact on the future of work remains unclear, but the pandemic has revealed the tremendous differences in how work and workers are valued. For instance, the minority of privileged and professional white-collar workers can work from home whereas most workers who do manual or person to person labour (manufacturing, construction, hospitality, travel, food, health and social care, etc.) still must be present in their physical formal workplaces and are "exposed physically to the coronavirus". Although the Covid-19 pandemic crisis may intensify the prevailing trends of precarisation in Australia, the United States and the United Kingdom, we learn that it may also open new sites of resistance and contestation to overcome worsening labour and living conditions within global capitalism.

The following chapter is by Tim Di Muzio. Di Muzio aims to re-politicise the nature of how monetary policies operate and, in doing so, critiques both neoclassical and Keynesian assumptions on debt, monetary policies, and inflation. The Covid-19 pandemic has become the "the biggest borrowing spree in history" by the OECD countries seeking to stave off another great depression. For decades, the OECD countries have attempted to follow the first commandment of neoliberalism—fiscal discipline. With the pandemic, budget constraints disappeared virtually overnight. This return to quasi-Keynesian economics of "priming the pump" has garnered greater attention in Modern Monetary Theory (MMT). The fundamental difference between MMT and the fiscal-monetary paradigm of balanced budgets is that MMT argues that "running deficits can be beneficial for human well-being and the economy if the government is monetarily sovereign". Di Muzio highlights that both theoretical monetary paradigms have largely no historical framing and have depoliticised and naturalised governmental monetary policies and capitalism. He provides a brief historical analysis of the history of money, banking, and fiscal spending, focusing on the financial revolution in England. This is important because it exposes that "the Bank of England (and later commercial banks) had control over the issuance of credit". This has become a global blueprint for a "fiscal lock in" that forces governments into debt if they wish to spend more than their revenues. The other important feature of Di Muzio's historical analysis is how poverty was turned into a "moral choice" and not "a structural feature" under British capitalism. The second part of the analysis is to challenge the "economic assumption" that massive government deficit spending creates massive inflation, as suggested by MMT critics and some followers. Di Muzio dismantles this assumption by providing empirical evidence that shows no correlation between federal budget deficit spending and inflation. Instead, the evidence seems to suggest the opposite. He argues that there is a fundamental contradiction embedded into the capitalist system, which is capitalist cost-plus accounting, which MMT scholars do not engage with. Simply put, due to capitalist cost-plus accounting, "there is a dearth of purchasing power or aggregate demand in the economy". This means that there is always a shortage of purchasing power for outstanding goods and services, and thus, commercial banks provide the essential credit to keep the system functioning. Moreover, MMT largely overlooks how most new money that enters the economy comes from commercial banks issuing loans to willing borrowers, which account for roughly 92% of new money in the United States. In conclusion, Di Muzio argues there is no natural reason why commercial banks should have this power to be the primary issuers of credit, and humanity does not have to be under the rule of fiscal-monetary policies, which has historically reinforced debt fright, austerity policies, and inequality. We thus learn that the pandemic has unintentionally opened a potential site of contestation and re-politicisation over monetary policies which is deeply needed.

The next chapter is by Matt Dow. Dow critiques the literature that presumes, even before the Covid-19 pandemic, that the global political economy was transitioning from fossil fuels toward renewable energy. This literature ignores the fundamental facts that "the global political economy is completely dependent on fossil fuels and that global financial accumulation is betting on a fossil fueled future, not renewable energy". The reason for this is that the world's total energy needs are still supplied by fossil fuels at 80.9 per cent. Moreover, although initially there was a significant decrease in overall market capitalisation in the fossil fuel industry because of the Covid-19 pandemic and an oil price war, this has quickly rebounded. As global investors still do not believe that "renewable energy has the capacity to replace fossil fuels as the prime mover for global society for a variety of technical, political and social reasons". Dow suggests we need to shift our theoretical lens away from Realism and Liberalism when it comes to theorising the future of energy and focus on two structural components of the global political economy. The first is the reciprocal relationship between increasing debt and the pursuit of economic growth, which has been predominately fulfilled by fossil fuels for the last 300 years. The second structural component is that the current petro-market civilisation is not just the outcome of the ability of the Carbon Majors to reinforce the centrality of fossil fuels in everyday life. Instead, this global civilisational order would be impossible without the help of governments and other industries, the global power elite, and a significant amount of humanity who enjoy their fossil fuel livelihoods and lifestyles. This reflects a fundamental contradiction of how global energy consumption, carbon emissions, financial power, human agency, and inequality are intertwined. Finally, Dow suggests that the growing climate denialist movement can be conceptualised as social forces of annihilation because of their ability to prevent and stall the transition to low carbon patterns of social reproduction through the ballot box. The future of energy has become possibly the largest paradox in human history in that humanity may choose "its annihilation" by maintaining a global political economy based on fossil fuels, power, and profit instead of attempting to build a global political economy based on well-being and the logic of livelihood.

The last chapter on this theme is by Philip McMichael. McMichael argues that the Covid-19 pandemic could be a turning point in the direction of the world food system. The current world food system is one where transnational food corporations promote false claims of "feeding the world" meanwhile their global supply chains often source cheap labour and appropriated land from the global south. Since the 1990s, global small-scale farmers, in the global south, have been subjected to intense liberalising trade and foreign investment policies whereas farmers in the global north have been able to retain protections and subsidies by their governments. The global south now has become subjected to "Public-Private Partnerships", which have used "public monies subsidized land enclosures and commercial land corridors for producing foods for export", which has left small-scale farmers increasingly controlled by corporate value chains and monocultural-industrial farming practices. This world food system is responsible for "50 percent of zoonotic diseases" because of the mass deforestation and habitat destruction that increases the interaction between humanity and wild/domesticated animal species. Whether or not Covid-19 originated in Wuhan is important, but what might be more important is how China's aggressive agro-industrial expansion dispossesses small farmers. These small farmers are then forced to either hunt or raise exotic wild animals for human consumption that exposes them to "exotic pathogens" coupled with the fact that factory farming already has direct linkages with previous viral outbreaks. The Covid-19 pandemic, then, not only shows the unsustainable nature of the current "corporate food regime" but also how unequal global food distribution has become. Corporate food supply chains have raised food prices during the pandemic, which caused roughly an additional 821 million people into food insecurity in low-income countries. Devastatingly, the solution to this growing world food crisis by the partnership between the United Nations and World Economic Forum is greater market-driven solutions. This is seen in how the global food system is now changing from food chain ownership, like Monsanto and Walmart, to agribusiness mergers with asset managers like BlackRock and the Carlyle Group taking control. This change in ownership is leading the global food system towards digitalisation and financialisation, enabling new frontiers of market power and further monocultural-industrial logic over the global food system. Indeed, the future of food has been labelled as "Food-as-Software" whereby food production will be "agriculture without farmers and humans". In conclusion, McMichael argues the future of food rests on peasants' demands over a quarter century ago for "food sovereignty". We learn that the current global corporate food regime is not only unsustainable, unequal and unjust but deadly as it will continue to contribute to future viral pandemics.

The concluding chapter is by Tim Di Muzio and Matt Dow. They close the volume by surveying the critical arguments made throughout the edited collection. They also consider the future prospects for neoliberalism as many of its defects as rationality of rule have been exposed during the present crisis. Di Muzio and Dow finish the chapter by introducing three hypotheses that can help us explain why political leadership is doing precious little to overcome the multiple crises we face in the twenty-first century.

Notes

1 https://covid19.who.int/ (January 10, 2022).
2 Critical scholars have often pointed out that neoliberalism, as a political ideology and neoliberal capitalism, has deep origins and connections to far right extremism (Slobodian 2018; Stewart 2020).
3 An extreme example of this was by Texas Lieutenant Governor Dan Patrick who argued that vulnerable people and communities may have to volunteer to die to save the United States economy (Beckett 2020).
4 For historical structures, we draw from Fernand Braudel (1980), which are political, cultural, values, economic, hierarchical and other social relations and arrangements derived from human history not a historicism or immaterial idealism. This should not be confused with structural determinism whereby human activity is always determined by structures. Historical structures are constituted by hierarchies, persistent social practices, rhythms in everyday life and are made by collective human activities and transformed through collective human activities that are always embedded in a history where things could have been otherwise.
5 https://data.worldbank.org/indicator/NY.GDP.MKTP.CD (January 10, 2022).

PART I

Global Power, Inequality, and Climate Change

1

"A ONCE IN A LIFETIME OPPORTUNITY"

Covid-19 in the Age of Finance

Richard H. Robbins

I know you're not supposed to say this, but it's a once-in-a-lifetime opportunity. You're not going to see this again: Where you've actually got an economy that's fine, and you've got a Fed pumping trillions of dollars in.
— *Marc Lasry, CEO Avenue Capital Group, 2020*

Introduction

Covid-19 marks the first pandemic of the age of Finance. Previous widespread disease outbreaks, such as the flu epidemic of 1918, or the plagues that struck Early Modern Europe or the Roman Empire, occurred in industrial or pre-industrial economies. Their consequences included dramatic population declines, increased wages, decline in investment opportunities and lower inflation trends (Barro et al. 2020; Rapley 2021; Jordà et al. 2020; Bonam and Smădu 2021). Early returns as of 22 months into the Covid-19 pandemic prove the prescience of Marc Lasry in June 2020 (see epigraph) of an "opportunity of a lifetime" for investors. The Dow Jones Industrial Average opened at 25,590 on March 1, 2020, and closed at 35,619 on November 22, 2021, and the wealth of global billionaires increased by over 60 per cent (Institute for Policy Studies 2021, see also Popcevski this volume). Overall, the top 20 per cent collected more than 70 per cent of the increase in household wealth and almost a third went to the top 1 per cent (McCaffrey and Shifflett 2021).

However, the full economic outcome of the Sars-CoV-2 pandemic is still uncertain as of the preparation of this volume and will depend on such factors as continued efficacy and availability of vaccines, the possible emergence of new variants, the long-term impact on poor countries and, most of all, the economic growth necessary to repay what countries borrowed to avoid a recession or worse. But it will also occur during a period of increasing financialisation of the global economy. By financialisation I mean:

DOI: 10.4324/9781003250432-3

the process by which the reproduction of societies as a whole becomes ever more dependent on finance, credit, debt, and on the logic of speculative money capital; a historical predicament in which the imperatives of finance increasingly capture and dictate the social and political forms that feed it.

Kalb 2020: 2; see also Robbins 2020, 2022

We see the growing power of Finance in the growth of global investment capital. Total estimates vary, but wealth managers in 2020 controlled over $100 tn, greater than the total GDP of all the countries worldwide (Watson 2020; McKinsey 2020); add to this more than $100 tn controlled by pension funds and insurance companies (OECD 2020) and the amount controlled by banks and other private investors, and the approximate total in 2020 exceeded $350 tn, and by 2024 is projected to reach over $450 tn (Shorrocks 2019: 37). In comparison, in 1990 global financial assets amounted to only $51 tn (Sanyal 2014), a 250 per cent increase over the period adjusted for inflation.

We see financialisation also in the share of national incomes that go to labour in the form of wages and salaries and the share that goes to investors in the form of dividends on stocks, interest on loans, profits from the sale of properties and securities, and rents on property. In 1960, in the United States, 50 per cent of the national income went to labour and 17 per cent to investors. By 2007, investors' shares climbed to 47 per cent before falling to 30 per cent in the global economic collapse of 2007, climbing back to near 40 per cent, while labour's share hovered just above 40 per cent.[1]

Finally, the share of the U.S. GDP captured by the financial service industry doubled between 1960 and 2010, a pattern repeated in most of the Eurozone (Greenwood and Scharfstein 2013: 4).

Of course, citizens do not share equally in investment income. Between 2010 and 2016, the share of income-generating financial assets owned by the top 1 per cent of income earners in the United States grew from 50.4 per cent to 55.6 per cent, whereas the bottom 90 per cent decreased from 12.0 to 9.2 per cent (see Table 1.1). Further, the bottom 90 per cent held over 70 per cent of the debt, compared to under 7 per cent for the top 1 per cent (Wolff 2012, 2013, 2017a, 2017b; see also Hagar 2014).

Pavlina R. Tcherneva's (2014) research on the distribution of income during the economic expansions that followed downturns in the United States provides further evidence of the resilience of Finance to thrive in a crisis. She discovered that going back to 1949 and in every case over the past 60 years, the top 10 per cent appropriated a continually larger share of the economic recovery, and "in the 2009–2012 expansion," captured over 115 per cent of the income growth (2014: 55; see Figure 1.1).

This chapter concerns how and why the top 10 per cent managed to capture an increasing share of the national income following a downturn and how such an analysis might that help us understand the post-COVID economic situation. The

TABLE 1.1 Income generating assets and total debt by percentile of wealth, 2010 and 2016

Asset Type	Top 1 per cent		Next 9 per cent		Bottom 90 per cent	
	2010	2016	2010	2016	2010	2016
Stocks and mutual funds	48.8	53.2	42.5	40.0	8.6	6.8
Financial securities	64.4	64.6	29.5	29.2	6.1	6.2
Trusts	38.0	51.4	43.0	33.2	19.0	15.4
Business equity	61.4	65.7	30.5	28.5	8.1	5.7
Non-home real estate	40.0	40.0	43.6	42.1	20.9	17.9
Total assets for group	**50.4**	**55.6**	**37.5**	**35.2**	**12.0**	**9.2**
Total debt	**5.9**	**6.7**	**21.6**	**20.9**	**72.5**	**72.4**

Source: Wolff 2012, 2013, 2017a, 2017b; see also Hagar 2014.

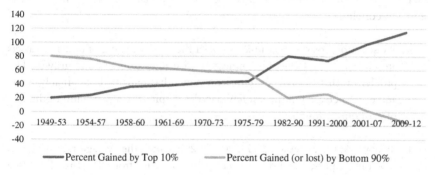

FIGURE 1.1 Distribution of average income in the United States following economic expansions, 1949–2012

Source: Data from Tcherneva (2014).

chapter proceeds with a heuristic that imagines Finance as a sovereign state whose aim is to increase their returns over a period against the democratic opposition. The chapter then considers seven major threats to the rate of return and some of the tactics used to safeguard and enhance capitalist returns. The chapter ends with the call for future studies on the power of Finance and its potential opposition post-pandemic.

Finance as a Sovereign State

In this chapter, I want to assume that virtually everyone in the world holds dual citizenships, one to the nation-state to which they pay taxes and the other to the abstruse state of finance to which they owe interest and rents. The latter, divided into net creditors and net debtors, is more autocratic and demanding and continually captures a greater portion of the economic pie than the former. Americans, for example, pay more interest on debt than they pay in Federal taxes. Over the past decade (2010–2020) they have paid to Finance more than $30 tn in interest (Bureau of Economic Analysis 2022a) in addition to $4.5 tn in rents (Clark 2019; Brant 2020). Over that period, Federal revenue totalled $20 tn (U.S. Bureau of Economic Analysis 2022).

Although most of the attention from economists and economic policymakers focuses on increasing economic growth rates as a measure of economic health, for the state of finance, the ultimate goal is maintaining, if not increasing, benchmark rates of return on investment capital. Generally speaking, investors expect a 10 per cent annual return from equities and a 3–5 per cent return on the less risky bond market (see e.g. Speights 2021). This does not necessarily diminish the importance of growth since there is a strong relationship between the rates of return on capital and economic growth. In a seminal paper, Dean Baker, Brad DeLong and Paul Krugman (2005) worked out the mathematics of the relationship and concluded:

> We see strong reasons to think that, over the long run, rates of return on assets are correlated and causally connected with rates of economic growth. The problem is that the rate of return on capital has remained remarkably stable and even increased in the last few decades despite a steady erosion of the rate of economic growth.

In their work, Òscar (et al. 2017a; 2017b; 2019) map the average rate of return on bonds, bills, equity, and housing across 16 countries from 1870 to 2015 (see

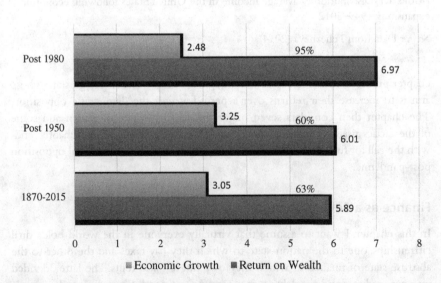

FIGURE 1.2 Rate of return on investments and economic growth, 1870–2015

Source: Data from Òscar et al. (2017a; 2017b; 2019).

Figure 1.2). They found that the rate of return averaged 5.89 per cent and the rate of economic growth 3.05 per cent over the entire period. After 1950, the average rate of return was 6.01 per cent with an economic growth rate rising, as expected to 3.25 per cent. However, between 1980 and 2015, although the rate of return rose to 6.97 per cent, the rate of economic growth fell to 2.48 per cent.

This relationship between the rate of return and economic growth is consistent with Piketty's conclusion in *Capital in the Twenty-First Century* (2014) that the rate of return over the past 150 years, with the exception of the decades associated with the two world wars and the Great Depression, consistently exceeds economic growth—or as he draws it, r > g. As the rate of increase in investment capital exceeds overall growth (and essentially the rate of increase in wages), Piketty (2014: 377) concludes that this contributes to growing economic inequality.

Although some economists assume that economic growth can perpetually increase, some predict future growth up to 20 per cent a year (e.g. Basu 2017), economic growth rates are clearly slowing (see Figure 1.2) and most economists, as well as wealth managers, predict continual slowing Piketty (2014: 93–94) sets future annual growth at 1.5 per cent at best.

Part of the decline in growth rates is attributable to what economists call the "convergence factor" (Barro and Xavier Sala-i-Martin. 2004:14), a tendency of emerging economies to approach the lower rate of growth of wealthy economies. But "convergence" is simply a descriptive term. It does not explain why the rate of growth declines as wealth increases.

There are good reasons, the most significant being that the growth rate is exponential, not arithmetic. For example, in the 18 years between 1999 and 2017, the automobile industry increased automobile production by 41 million, a 2.8 per cent

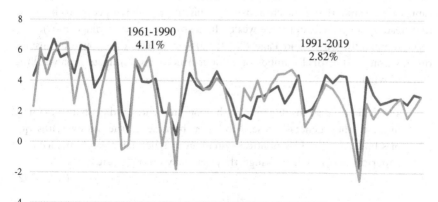

FIGURE 1.3 United States and global rates of economic growth, 1961–2019

Source: https://data.worldbank.org/indicator/NY.GDP.MKTP.KD.ZG (CC BY 4.0).

annual growth rate. If the same 2.8 per cent growth rate was maintained for the following 18 years, it would need to produce 58 million more cars (OICA 2017).

Consequently, Finance has a problem. The rate of return on capital should vary with the rate of economic growth, but economic growth is slowing and somehow the rate of return remains steady and even growing. But how?

Who Determines National and Global Economic Policy?

The elite of Finance and their institutions—wealth managers, banks, insurance companies, pension funds, etc.—have enormous power conferred by their wealth (see e.g. Ferguson et al. 2017; Page et al. 2018). They use it to help select government leaders. For example, the top 1 per cent in the United States provides 95.8 per cent of all political donations (Opensecrets n.d.) Sovereign states depend on investors to fund a government and consequently have a vested interest in maintaining high rates of return to repay their debts and maintain access to investment capital at low interest rates (Ferguson 2001: 197; see also Roos 2019). Investment banks such as Goldman Sachs, J.P. Morgan Chase and Barclays maintain access to the highest levels of government, often supplying the finance ministers who dictate economic policy. Of the past thirteen U.S. Secretaries of Treasury, seven were investment bankers (three from Goldman Sachs), two were corporate CEOs, two came from the Federal Reserve, another from the financial services sector, and one from the practice of law (U.S. Department of the Treasury, N.D.). Once scattered around individual banks, wealth managers and advisors are now concentrated in behemoth asset management funds, such as Blackrock, with almost $10 tn under control (Hamlin 2021). Finally, the largest allocators of capital share common interests with propaganda-pushing media moguls who often exaggerate the societal contributions of investment banks. "We help companies to grow," said Lloyd F. Blankfein of Goldman Sachs, "by helping them to raise capital. Companies that grow create wealth. This, in turn, allows people to have jobs that create more growth and more wealth. It's a virtuous cycle" (Arlidge 2009).

Consequently, Gilens and Page (2014, 2018) conclude that powerful business organisations and a small number of affluent Americans dominate policymaking, and that when:

> a majority of citizens disagrees with economic elites and/or with organized interests, they generally lose. Moreover, because of the strong status quo bias built into the U.S. political system, even when fairly large majorities of Americans favor policy change, they generally do not get it.
>
> *2014: 22–23*

These policies generally correspond to those part of the so-called neoliberal agenda, which gained momentum in the 1980s after the so-called "stagflation" of the 1970s. These policies and their enabling legislation address the most significant threats to the rate of return, which include

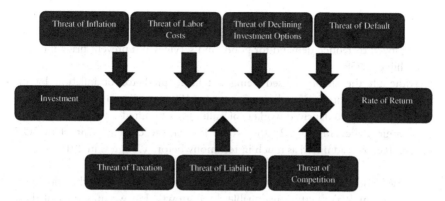

FIGURE 1.4 Threats to the rate of return on capital

Source: Author.

- Inflation
- Taxes
- Labour/wages
- Responsibility for negative externalities
- Lack of investment opportunities
- Competition
- Default

The following analysis suggests that if these threats to the rate of return, absent steady economic growth, were not addressed by governments, there would likely be no return on capital.

Figure 1.4 summarises some government policy decisions that address these threats, and we will examine briefly how they may affect the economy post-Covid-19.

Reducing the Threat of Inflation

Economists treat controlling inflation as one of the three or four major areas of macroeconomic policy research, whereas central banks treat it as their major, if not only, job. Ostensibly, their goal is to maintain price stability, although increases in the rate of inflation may be the greatest threat to the rate of return. A 6 per cent rate of return with 6 per cent inflation is nominally zero, or as one wealth advisor succinctly put it, "inflation rots bonds" (Collins 2018). Generally, central banks set a target rate for inflation and by raising or lowering the interest rates that banks charge each other (the prime interest rate), seek to prevent it from rising above that target rate of 2 per cent a year—it has averaged 2.2 per cent since 2000 (World Bank. 2022).

In the past, central banks used employment figures to predict inflation rates relying on the theory that at least at 5 per cent of the workforce should be unemployed to reduce demand for goods and services and prevent price increases (see Phillips 1958).

Although the theory ceased being a reliable predictor of inflation by the mid-1980s, its continued application into the 1990s unnecessarily cut an untold number of jobs and deprived workers of millions, or hundreds of millions, in wages (Economic Policy Institute 2020). Jerome Powell, the current chair of the U.S. Federal Reserve, admitted as much in testimony before Congress in 2019:

> We're missing 10 years of [wage] growth… I think that's really the underlying problem. We're getting reasonable wage growth, but we missed all of those years beginning at the beginning of the century. It's a very serious problem, and we should do a better job of calling it out.
>
> *cited in Irwin 2019*

Raising or lowering short-term interest rates constituted the main tool for central banks to control employment and, ostensibly the money supply. The banks could also adjust the money supply through open market operations either by buying assets, generally long-term government bonds and mortgage-backed securities, thus injecting money into the economy (i.e. quantitative easing), or by selling them, thus reducing the money supply.

To offset the decline in economic activity attributed to Covid-19, central banks have reacted by injecting $24 tn into the global economy. In a jobs-oriented economy, the goal would be to create jobs and support wages. However, when the goal is to alleviate threats to the rate of return, it should be to support Finance. During the economic crisis of 2007–2008, most of $700 bn of the so-called economic stimulus went to bail out banks and insurance companies. The result was the paradoxical rise in the amount of money in the economy but a decline in its velocity—the rate at which it is spent (see Yi Wen and Arias 2014). Between 2000 and 2010, each dollar circulated 1.9 times, and between 2011 and 2021, only 1.5 times (U.S. Bureau of Economic Analysis 2022c).

The pattern is the same in the euro area, where "Money velocity … is currently less than 1 which means that money being printed (even notionally) isn't even circulating once" (This Time is Different 2019). Consequently, we can expect that with central bank policy designed to alleviate threats to the rate of return, investors will capture the larger portion. At the beginning of the pandemic, the U.S. Congress allocated funds through banks intending to target the so-called small companies (below 500 employees), but banks funnelled the money to big companies or favoured clients less likely to spend it (Guida 2020).

At the time this chapter is being prepared, inflation globally has spiked, reaching 6 per cent in previous months in the United States. Causes include the additional spending of consumers freed from the constraints of the pandemic, higher wages for workers prompted by labour shortages, and bottlenecks in the global supply chain creating a scarcity of goods (see e.g. Krugman 2021). Absent in the present doomsday chatter over inflation is the fact that inflation mostly harms investors, but benefits the majority of the population, whose income will rise along with prices, as will the value of their homes (the major asset of the middle classes) and their ability to repay their debts (see e.g. Schwarz 2021). However, if the past is any guide, and given the power of Finance, governments and central banks may act quickly to quell inflationary pressures (Plender 2021, see also Fix (2021) on differential inflation).

Reducing the Threat of Taxation

Taxes are a second threat to the rate of return on capital. The lower the rate of taxes on investors and corporations, the higher their rate of return and dividends. According to the International Monetary Fund (IMF 2019), between 1990 and 2018, the tax rate on corporate income in high-income countries went from 38 per cent to a bit over 22 per cent. A corollary of this is that corporate taxes decline relative to taxes on individuals. In the United States in 1990, total corporate tax payments were about 20 per cent of total individual tax payments, but only about 12 per cent in 2018 (Tax Policy Center 2020). Changes in the tax system would mean that corporations keep more of what they make and so have more to dis-tribute to investors, either in stock dividends or in buybacks that reduce the number of shares but raise their value.

In the United States, the tax system also means that investors get to keep more of their investment income than ordinary people keep from their wages. In 2019, personal income tax rates for heads of households ran from 10 to 37 per cent, and taxes for capital gains on assets held for more than 1 year ranged from 0 to 20 per cent. In all, tax rates and changes have benefited corporations and those who have the capital to invest.

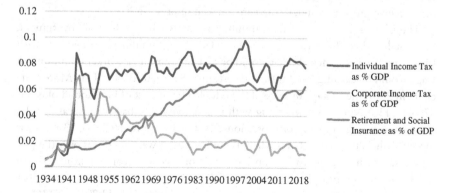

FIGURE 1.5 U.S. Government tax receipts by source as a share of GDP: 1934–2020

Source: Data from www.whitehouse.gov/omb/historical-tables/ (Table 2.1).

To compound this, the weak enforcement of tax laws globally provides opportunities to avoid taxes for those whose income arises from their invested capital rather than their wages, which usually have tax deducted from wages before the worker receives them (see e.g. Harrington 2016; Henry 2012). Gabriel Zucman (2015: 3–4) estimates that 8 per cent of global household wealth is held in tax havens, whereas U.S. multinationals book almost 60 per cent of their profits in low-tax countries (Saez and Zucman 2019b: 77). As Saez and Zucman (2019b) point out, it seems relatively easy to get international cooperation in multilateral institutions such as the IMF and WTO when promoting investment. However, because of the political influence of investors, it seems impossible to get such cooperation to recapture that tax money.

There are limits to what governments can do, particularly in the United States, to resist Finance. When the Biden administration first proposed tax rate increases on the wealthy in 2020, partially in reaction to the pandemic, they consisted almost exclusively of taxes on wages and salaries and virtually nothing on investment income (see Cassady 2021). Republican Representative Kevin Brady characterised a proposed increase in capital gains taxes as "dangerous," and added that Republicans had launched an "all-out effort" to prevent the proposal from becoming the law (Jagoda 2021).

Reducing the Threat of Rising Wages

Finance also depends on low labour costs, which boost business profits and the dividends paid to shareholders. In fact, keeping wages low does double duty for investors. It improves return on equities, since more corporate income can be directed to dividends and stock buybacks. It also helps keep inflation low by preventing a rise in labour purchasing power. Furthermore, minimising wage increases stimulates borrowing, and accounts for the rapid rise in household debt in the United States from 24 per cent of GDP in 1952 to 75 per cent of GDP in 2Q of 2021 (FRBNY 2021). In effect, households borrowed money that should have been received in wages and, in the bargain, paid interest on it.

The United States does have a minimum wage set by the federal government, but that has done little to help workers. Had the minimum wage kept up with labour productivity since 1968, it would be $24 an hour, and a worker on minimum wage would be earning $48,000 a year instead of $15,080 (BLS 2019a). More generally, in 2007, the average income of the middle 60 per cent of U.S. households was $76,443. Had income grown along with productivity as it had for several decades before, the average income of those householders would be $94,310, 23 per cent more (Mishel et al. 2015). Even where there have been wage increases over the past 40 years, they have gone to the top 5 per cent of U.S. wage earners: from 1979 to 2018, the increase in real hourly wages of the top 5 per cent of workers was 56.1 per cent. For the bottom 70 per cent, it was 17.1 per cent (Gould 2019: 35–36).

The result in the United States is that even in the period of high employment before the Covid-19 pandemic, wages of workers in the bottom 50 per cent remained well below that needed for an adequate living. The median wage of the lowest 44 per cent of U.S. workers aged 18–64 was $10.22 an hour or $18,000 a year (Ross and Bateman 2020). Their position could be improved by collective action, but government policies have favoured investors by reducing the collective bargaining power of workers: the rate of unionisation in the United States fell by more than half over the past 30 years, to just about 10 per cent of the workforce (BLS 2019b).

Regarding the effects of Covid-19 on labour, the greatest changes have been on the acceleration of trends in remote work and virtual interactions, e-commerce and digital transactions, and deployment of automation and AI. McKinsey estimates that 17 million U.S. workers will need to change jobs by 2030 (Lund 2021). Regardless, it is likely that employers under pressure to protect and increase the rate of return will use the pandemic to reduce labour expenses and increase worker productivity. Remote work, for example, apparently increased worker productivity in those jobs where education level was essential (see Maurer 2020). Employers may also favour remote work because it lessens the effectiveness of labour organising efforts.

Reducing the Threat of the Cost of Negative Externalities

Another way of maintaining the rate of return on investments is to allow corporations to pass on some of the costs of doing business to the public or future generations (see Robbins and Beech 2018), generally in the form of negative externalities. Externalities are costs that affect a third party who did not choose to incur that cost. For example, car manufacturers do not charge medical expenses associated with air pollution. It is understandable then that the private sector spends heavily on lobbying, campaign donations; and public relations to minimise the cost of government regulation that would reduce those externalities and to weaken the enforcement of existing regulations.

Attempts have been made to estimate the total externalised costs of doing business. The United Nations, in 2010, came up with an annual figure of $2.2 tn in environmental costs alone, or one-third of the annual profits of the 3,000 largest corporations in the world (Jowit 2010). Since that excludes health costs, it is reasonable to assume that the total return on equities for a few is roughly equal to the indirect costs paid by the rest. The Intergovernmental Panel on Climate Change (IPCC) estimates that, depending on the extent of temperature increases, Climate Change alone, by 2080, would cost over $1 tn a year.

Reducing the Threat of a Lack of Investment Opportunities

With some $350 tn seeking a place to grow, finding investment options that produce a competitive rate of return becomes more complex and riskier. Consequently, privatisation of state services or resources is one of the favourite options of Finance. Proponents of privatisation argue that it will make those assets more efficient, but, as Harvey (2010: 28, 216) notes, the real attraction of privatisation is that it creates new places to invest money and keep it growing.

Moreover, it is not clear if the private sector is more efficient. Contrary to the thinking of mainstream economists, Mariana Mazzucato argues that public enterprises are at least as efficient as private enterprises, if not more so, and that important parts of private enterprise are based on public money. As she puts it,

> without strategic public investments we would not have any of the technologies in our smart products from the Internet to GPS and SII. We would also not have the renewable energy solutions that might create a green revolution or most of the radical new drugs to treat diseases.
>
> *Mazzucato 2015: xxi*

The question is, how will the Covid-19 pandemic affect the drive of Finance toward the privatisation of services or resources? There is already evidence that the successful privatisation of nursing homes increased infection and death rates in those facilities (see e.g. Armstrong and Bourgaeult 2020) but, despite that, does the pandemic further increase opportunities for investors to profit from public services?

For example, when Cardinal Timothy Dolan, the Catholic archbishop of New York, in an interview with Betsy DeVos, Secretary of Education under Donald Trump, asked her whether she was using the pandemic to boost private schools, DeVos replied "absolutely" (Barnum 2020; Flannery 2020). Various educational services are promoting online education as a way for school districts, strapped for money given the costs of the pandemic, to economise on education costs. In 2021, federal, state and local governments budgeted almost three-quarters of a tn dollars on K-12 education, an attractive target for Finance (Hanson 2021), and there is a question of whether the pandemic will further the privatisation of public health as another way for local and federal governments to reduce pressure on taxpayers (see e.g. Parramore 2021).

Reducing the Threat of Anti-Trust Legislation

Competition is another enemy of Finance and the rate of return because it puts downward pressure on prices as businesses seek to attract more consumers. The effects on the public of reducing competition are described by a French economist, Thomas Philippon.

When he arrived in the United States in 2000, he noted that prices of essential goods (e.g. laptops, cellular telephone service, air travel, telephone calls) were cheaper than in Europe. However, since that time, as he documents (Philippon 2019), these essential items have become less expensive in Europe and elsewhere around the world than they are in the United States. Why are U.S. monthly broadband prices $66.17, whereas in South Korea they are $29.90 and $35.71 in Germany? Why have airlines in the United States posted a profit of $22.40 per passenger mile, whereas, in Europe, it was $7.84? The major reason, Philippon suggests, is the surge in corporate mergers and acquisitions over the past three decades. In 1985, there were 2,309 mergers and acquisitions, and in the next year there were 3,477. The figure roughly doubled by 1994 (8,076), almost doubled again by 1998 (14,780). In 2019, there were 18,882 mergers and acquisitions. Globally, there were almost 50,000 M&As. (IMAA 2021). Philippon argues that market sectors increasingly are likely to be dominated by a shrinking number of corporations (see also Nitzan 2004). This, he (2019: 97) suggests, leads to "increasing concentration, increasing entrenchment of industry leaders, increasing profits and payouts to shareholders, decreasing investment, and decreasing productivity growth." He also says that corporate mergers and market concentration are costing the average American $300 a week. Philippon finds that the increasing concentration of firms has little to do with economic or corporate efficiency. Rather, it is driven by the lobbying power of corporations in the United States, a power largely absent in Europe.

The pandemic promises to provide an opportunity to further increase market concentration because of the increase in business failures and permanent closures, as opposed to temporary ones. Estimates of small business and firm closures vary from the permanent closure of 400,000 firms above what would be expected (Hamilton 2020), to some 200,000 (Crane et al. 2020), particularly during 2020, the first year of the pandemic. It is also possible that sectors with an already high degree of concentration, such as airlines or cruise ship companies, supermarkets and drug store chains, agricultural producers, and wireless providers, will face weaknesses as a result of the pandemic and argue for quick merger appeals that will further cement their control over prices and wages to the detriment of everyone else (Baer 2020).

Patent protection and laws regarding intellectual property, both dear to Finance, also confer monopoly rights on producers, and may have profound effects on the pandemic, as patent protection and intellectual property rights for Covid-19 vaccines have contributed to preventing the acceleration of vaccine production and limited their availability in poor countries (but see Boland 2021). The failure to vaccinate poor populations increases the likelihood of more contagious and more lethal variants appearing and will further devastate the economies of poor countries reeling under austerity restrictions. The monopoly rights over the vaccines have been upheld despite the $18 bn provided to pharmaceutical companies by the United States through Operation Warp Speed (see Kim et al. 2021; Burleigh 2021), and the failure to recognise the provision in the World Trade Organization (WTO) rules regarding the cancellation of copyright stipulations in an emergency.

Reducing the Threat of Default

Of all of the above threats to the rate of return, including inflation, none strikes greater fear into net creditors than net debtors failing to pay what they owe. If the Covid-19 pandemic influences the trajectory of the economy with significant effects on the larger society, it will likely be because of the measures taken to reduce the threat of default.

As Dow and Di Muzio note in this volume (see Introduction), governments and central banks, in a direct response to the pandemic, have injected some $24 tn into the global economy, virtually all in some form of debt (Jones 2021), bringing the total of global indebtedness to almost $300 tn or more (Ranasinghe 2021).

Preventing default will require authoritarian methods and intensifying surveillance greater than anything we have yet experienced, creating, as Shoshana Zuboff (2019) labels "The Fight for a Human Future at the Frontier of Power." In effect, the pandemic may be responsible for a decisive shift to the authoritarian liberal order discussed in the introduction to this volume.

The shift will be apparent in at least three ways: the first will be in the austerity measures imposed on sovereign governments to ensure the repayment of sovereign debt. The second will be in the surveillance methods used on debtors to assess their willingness and ability to repay their debts and force them to do so, regardless of the personal costs. Finally, courts will make the declaration of bankruptcy more difficult.

The mechanisms available to creditors to force sovereign debt payment are relatively recent. Consequently, in the past, as Roos (2019) notes, sovereign debt default was not uncommon (see also Reinhart and Rogoff 2009). Before the Second World War, those who bought government debt tended to be small investors who were disorganised and were unable to present a unified front to debtors. Roos argues that things are different now. The increased integration of global financial institutions (see Eccles 2019; World Bank 2020) has given Finance greater power over governments. If a country threatens to default on its foreign debt today, delays

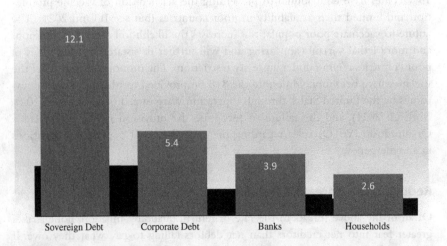

FIGURE 1.6 Amount of added global debt in trillions

Source: Data from Jones (2021).

payments or refuses to recognise it, lenders have ways to retaliate. They can refuse to extend further credit or renew existing loans, leaving a country to face devastating damage to its domestic economy. In addition, the integration and concentration of global financial institutions enable lending institutions, as well as large private investors, to influence the elite groups in indebted countries so that they are aligned ideologically with foreign creditors. The result, says Roos (2019: 15), is to reconfigure domestic power relations so that the views of the elite in indebted countries accord with those of international Finance.

Investors can now even influence the selection of finance ministers who treat debt repayment as more important than domestic spending (e.g. Do Rosario and Gillespie 2019). The effect of this concern seems to be to eliminate democratic deliberation of whether the country ought to pay its sovereign debt and, if so, how. When a country has trouble repaying loans, creditors can force the country to shift revenue from domestic needs to debt repayment. Generally, this is done by raising taxes, devaluing currency, cutting services such as education, public health, policing, poverty reduction, and shifting the savings to pay the debt. The power of Finance was illustrated when, in 2012, Greeks voted overwhelmingly for parties favouring default over austerity (Smith 2012), after which the German finance minister, Wolfgang Schauble, famously said that the Greeks "can vote however they want, but whatever the election result we have will change nothing about the actual situation in the country" (in Roos 2019: 17). The austerity imposed on Greece, and which is likely to be imposed on other debtor countries whose economies are battered by the pandemic and forced to borrow to meet the basic needs of their citizens, will again place the burden of repayment on the poorer and weaker groups in the countries and on emerging economies already struggling with a "debt boom" (Sugawara 2021, see also Di Muzio this volume). The lesson seems to be, to sacrifice the weakest to save the strongest, but be sure that investors realise their expected rate of return (see especially Boyce and Ndikumana 2011).

The situation faced by sovereign states may not be much better for businesses, families, and individuals who, while taking advantage of increased credit availability during the pandemic, find themselves unable to service, let alone repay their debts in full. In the United States, consumer debt alone is almost $15 trillion, 75 per cent of the current GDP (see Figure 1.7).

Historically, Finance reduced exposure to default by lobbying governments to impose stricter bankruptcy laws or permit more information gathering on prospective borrowers. Responding to a surge in bankruptcy filings between 1980 and 2004 (see Garrett 2006), for example, in 2005 the U.S. Congress based legislation, The Bankruptcy Abuse Prevention and Consumer Protection Act, restricting the ability of debtors to default by increasing the costs of filing for bankruptcy, using income means testing regarding liquidation and repayment and requiring credit counselling. A more debtor-friendly modification of the act introduced in 2020 by Senators Elizabeth Warren and Jerrold Nadler, The Consumer Bankruptcy Reform Act, was given virtually no chance of being enacted (Atkisson 2021).

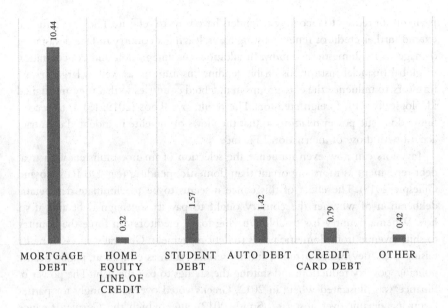

FIGURE 1.7 U.S. Consumer debt in trillions as of 2021 Q2

Source: Data from www.newyorkfed.org/newsevents/news/research/2021/20211109.

The credit score evolved over some 200 years, begun by merchants to sys-tematise rumours regarding debtors' character and assets (Trainor 2015). Critics alarmed at the possible abuses of this data-gathering emerged almost immediately. A contributor to Hunt's Merchant Magazine in 1853 lamented that "[g]o where you may to purchase goods, a character has preceded you, either for your benefit or your destruction." In 1936, TIME Magazine wrote of the astonishing surveillance powers of credit bureaus (Trainor 2015). These efforts of Finance to rate borrowers on their reliability resulted in the now widely used FICO score developed by Fair, Isaac and Company and implemented in 1959.

Of course, these surveillance efforts pale in comparison to the data-gathering and dissemination possibilities of the computer age and the data mining abilities of Google, Facebook, TikTok, Instagram, Twitter, and other platforms or apps such as Fitbit that record what you purchase online, what online sites you visit, where you are at any given time, who your friends are, how many hours you spend playing video games, and what bills and taxes you pay (or don't pay). Then imagine, asks Botsman (2017), the state using this information to create a Citizen Score to deter-mine how trustworthy you are and publicly displaying the score to allow viewers to determine whether you can get a mortgage, a job, or even your chance of getting a date. In 2020, China implemented just such a program. Its Social Credit System can restrict people from buying plane tickets, acquiring property, or getting a loan. Different localities can set their own criteria for the system, and they include not paying fines when you're deemed fully able to, misbehaving on a train, standing up a taxi, or driving through a red light (see Kobie 2019).

One can imagine, also the power that such systems can confer on the state of Finance and its data priesthood in charge of oversight and control as it struggles to realise its desired rate of return. It goes beyond the market capitalism's ambitions that seeks to turn people into consumers, and instead seeks to convert them into reliable debtors. Zuboff (2019: 21) uses the term "surveillance capitalism" to articulate this shift, describing it as a:

> coup from above, not an overthrow of the state but rather an overthrow of the people's sovereignty and a prominent force in the perilous drift toward democratic deconsolidation that now threatens Western liberal democracies. Only "we the people" can reverse this course, first by naming the unprecedented, then by mobilizing new forms of collaborative action: the crucial friction that reasserts the primacy of a flourishing human future as the foundation of our information civilization. If the digital future is to be our home, then it is we who must make it so.

Conclusion

This chapter has considered the fundamental relationship between creditors and investors seeking a rate of return (the state of Finance) and the general public's well-being both before and during the pandemic. The chapter argued that neoliberal governments have helped support capitalists in their quest for a healthy rate of return by stifling seven major threats to increasing returns to capital. We remain unsure how the mounting debts—state, personal and corporate—accumulated during the pandemic will play out in future policies and the trajectory of capitalist economies but one thing remains clear: focusing on the rate of return and the strategies employed by capitalists to safeguard and enhance it are increasingly important aspects for understanding the state of Finance in the global political economy. Undoubtedly, the social forces of the rate of return have and will confront opposition to their aims. Perhaps, the ultimate question for the 21st century might be: how far and in what ways can labour and debtors overcome the power of Finance and the pathological quest for an ever-greater monetary return at societal expense?

Note

1 Federal Reserve Bank of St. Louis: Wages and Salaries Received https://fred.stlouisfed.org/tags/series?t=wages, Federal Reserve Bank of St. Louis: Monetary Interest Paid https://fred.stlouisfed.org/series/A2061C1A027NBEA, Bureau of Economic Analysis: Dividends https://apps.bea.gov/iTable/iTable.cfm?reqid=19&step=2#reqid=19&step=2&isuri=1&1921=survey, Department of the Treasury, and Office of Tax Analysis: Capital Gains www.treasury.gov/resource-center/tax-policy/tax-analysis/Documents/Taxes-Paid-on-Capital-Gains-for-Returns-with-Positive-Net-Capital-Gains.pdf www.treasury.gov/resource-center/tax-policy/tax-analysis/Documents/Taxes-Paid-on-Long-Term-Capital-Gains.pdf

2

THE BILLIONAIRE BOOM

Capital as Power and the Distribution of Wealth

Natasha Popcevski

Introduction

Undoubtedly, the pandemic will prove to be a landmark moment in the history and politics of the distribution of wealth. Indeed, during the pandemic, the world's billionaires increased their net worth to unprecedented historical heights. This was an impressive feat for the world's richest, who took to celebrations by launching themselves into outer space, hosted factory mega-raves, and perhaps more prudently sailed away from the virus on their mega-yachts during the mass suffering caused by the global health crisis.[1] Whether billionaires have profited *during* the pandemic, or whether billionaires have profited *from* the pandemic may be difficult to detect with any certainty. However, we know that the accumulation of billionaire wealth has transcended previous orders of magnitude set before the crisis. As Sharma notes, the "total wealth of billionaires worldwide rose by US$5 tn to US$13 tn in 12 months, the most dramatic surge ever registered on the annual billionaire list compiled by *Forbes* magazine" (2021: np). Even before the pandemic, one observer wrote that billionaire net worth represents "the greatest concentration in wealth since the Gilded Age of U.S. plutocrats at the end of the 19th century" (Wagstyl 2019). The latest pandemic has once again demonstrated that the trend toward increasing wealth inequalities is itself endemic to pandemics. Contrary to how pandemics most often increase economic inequalities, the Black Death was the only pandemic in history to reduce economic disparity among people. For example, where large-scale pandemics appear to have reduced inequality, Alfani suggests that the mechanism responsible for this reduction lies in the extermination of the poor. The Cholera outbreaks disproportionately affected society's poor, "thus it tended to curtail the lower part of the distribution—which would have led to a reduction in inequality among the survivors even in the absence of any other distributive effect" (Alfani 2020). But beyond the pandemic, critical enquiries into the cause and effects

DOI: 10.4324/9781003250432-4

of inequality—both within and between nations—have recaptivated the field of International political economy (IPE) and the general public (Di Muzio 2015b; Dorling 2015; George 2010; Milanovic 2018; Piketty 2017, 2019; Wilkinson & Pickett 2011; Shaxson 2011; Standing 2014a; Stiglitz 2012, 2016). At least since the Occupy movement of 2011, there has been significant interest in the rise of the so-called 1 per cent and popular concern that the levels of socioeconomic inequality experienced in the 21st century are set to increase over time, creating an even greater divide between billionaires and the rest of global society (Piketty 2017). Given the fact that their levels of wealth are on public display (for instance, on *Forbes* and *Bloomberg*), even the billionaire class fears a societal backlash (Neghaiwi and Jessop 2021). But why care about economic inequality, and furthermore, do the billionaires really deserve their wealth, and if so, on what basis? According to the United Nations:

> Inequality threatens long-term social and economic development, harms poverty reduction and destroys people's sense of fulfilment and self-worth. This, in turn, can breed crime, disease and environmental degradation. We cannot achieve sustainable development and make the planet better for all if people are excluded from the chance for a better life.[2]

There is also evidence to suggest that highly unequal societies are more prone to social problems, are less happy, and contribute to poor public health outcomes (Wilkinson & Pickett 2011). And as we shall discuss below, it is doubtful that the billionaires deserve their wealth based on their individual productivity (Alperovitz and Daly 2008). Thus, what is at stake in this chapter is no less than the question of differential power and wealth, and unequal life chances.

Specifically, this chapter contributes to IPE debates on inequality by shedding light on the rise of the billionaire class before and during the pandemic. In the financial literature, the 1 per cent are labelled "High-Net-Worth-Individuals (HNWIs)". These are individuals who hold at least US$1 mn in investible assets. This being the case, billionaires represent a very exceptional class within HNWIs. By "class", I do not mean to imply that billionaires all share the same interests, worldview, and act unanimously to shape and reshape the world for their own benefit as a class. Although billionaires have not necessarily acted as a class *for itself*, I contend, based on empirical data, that we can consider billionaires as a class *in itself*, defined by their inordinate wealth and power by extension. As of 2021, according to *Forbes* (see figure 2.1 below), there are 2755 worldly billionaires, up from just 13 in 1985, or an increase of just over 21,000 per cent.

Although the number of billionaires increasing over the neoliberal period is plain to see, with a few exceptions, the critical political economy has been slow to account for the rise of this class (Di Muzio 2015b; Petras 2008).[3] In this chapter, I use the capital as power framework to argue that ownership and exclusion (institutional power) rather than individual productivity or the exploitation of workers can help us account for the rise of the billionaire class and its increase in wealth

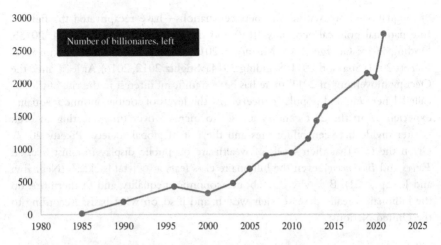

FIGURE 2.1 Rise of the billionaire class in the neoliberal era

Source: *Forbes* World's Billionaire List (compiled by various reports).

throughout the pandemic. However, although ownership and exclusion are key factors in the rapid accumulation of wealth, so too have the unprecedented fiscal stimulus and loose monetary policy of governments and central banks during the pandemic. At least in the United States, there is some survey evidence to suggest that a considerable amount of stimulus checks given by the Biden administration ended up in financial markets, boosting share prices, and thus the wealth of billionaire shareholders like Elon Musk of Tesla (Friedman 2021).[4] This chapter considers two additional main factors: The turn to neoliberalism and rapid technological change. To demonstrate my argument, I have divided this chapter in the following manner. First, I consider the rise of the billionaire class before and during the pandemic. Second, I consider the neoclassical and Marxist understandings of the distribution of wealth and contrast this with the capital as a power perspective before discussing some of the reasons for the rise in billionaire wealth. In the third section, I briefly consider whether billionaires should exist and canvass some recent proposals to address the divide between billionaires and the vast majority of citizens. The chapter then ends with a short conclusion.

The Rise of the Billionaire Class

Far from the virus being *the* "great leveller" of rich and poor alike, as many social and political commentators earnestly professed, the globalisation of Covid-19 has only served to exacerbate and intensify long-standing economic, geographic, gender and racial inequalities across the world (Goldin 2021; Oxfam 2021; Sokol & Pataccini 2020; see also Bousfield this volume). Indeed, the virus has shown that it is by no means a "socially neutral disease", evident in the significant disparities in morbidity and mortality rates experienced across populations (Bambra et al. 2020).

The sweeping yet necessary mobility restrictions enacted by governments worldwide to curb the spread of the virus created the immediate conditions for an economic recession at a level not experienced in almost a century (OECD 2020d). A year on, global growth levels appear to be returning with global GDP projected to grow 5.6 per cent in 2021, thanks largely to the economies of the United States and China. Tellingly, global economic recovery will be experienced disproportionately across the world (IMF 2020; OECD 2020d). It took several years for the world economy to recover from the global financial crisis of 2007–2009 (Tooze 2018). Here too, the super-rich were not exempt from slower recovery rates, requiring just 4 years for wealthy shareholders to bounce back to wealth levels resembling pre-global financial crisis figures (Collins 2020). In comparison, the rate of wealth accumulated since the start of the Covid-19 pandemic has been nothing short of arresting. The world's billionaires experienced a US$700 mn dip in aggregate wealth from US$8.7 tn in 2019 down to US$8 tn at the peak of the outbreak in March 2020 (Forbes 2021a). By April 2020, the total wealth of all billionaires had already recalibrated to near pre-COVID figures. In 2021, the combined net worth of the world's billionaires totalled an unprecedented US$13.1 tn dollars or a growth of 64 per cent since the beginning of worldwide lockdowns (Forbes 2021b), which means since the start of the Covid-19 pandemic, the global billionaires have become US$5.1 tn richer as a class. The resilience of the 1 per cent and their billionaire counterparts may be expressed in part by the burgeoning fortunes of "pandemic profiteers" who are capturing gains in the arenas of technology, global healthcare, and online retail (Collins et al. 2020, Oxfam 2020). These developments point to an inconvenient truth—HNWIs are riding out a markedly different tide of pandemic – and on a comparably bigger superyacht.

The global billionaires are a microscopic and exclusive but growing population of transnationally dispersed elites with both diverse and collective ownership interests who comprise the top of the global wealth pyramid. Though they only account for 0.00002 per cent of the global population, billionaires are disproportionately represented by their vast ownership claims over globalised income generating assets, and the numbers have been rising historically. According to the Forbes annual billionaire list in 2021, there were 2,755 billionaires, which is the first publication to keep a running record of the world's billionaires since 1987.[5] Their numbers climbed up by 660 entries from the previous year for a 24 per cent increase in billionaires. Notably, of those entries, 493 became first-time billionaires during the pandemic, with nine new entrants making their fortunes from vaccinations largely funded by the public purse. Backed by their governments in Germany and the UK, these billionaires are sabotaging cheaper vaccinations for the Global South by jealously guarding their exclusionary patents (Oxfam 2021; see also Andersen this volume).

Billionaire fortunes had been an uncommon but not unprecedented phenomenon, up until the end of the 20th century. American oil tycoon-cum-philanthropist[6] John D. Rockefeller is considered the first official dollar billionaire, a status he achieved through calculated industrial sabotage and consequent monopolisation of the nation's oil industry through the institutional power of Standard Oil (Bichler and Nitzan 2007). Today, there are a growing number of publications that produce datasets that track and rank the world's billionaires by wealth. Although it should be noted that each publication may differ slightly in their methodologies to identify a billionaire, one fundamental feature shared by this exclusive group is that an individual must possess a personal net worth of at least 1 bn units of a major reserve currency, predominantly the U.S. dollar. Financial institutions commonly refer to individuals with investable assets of at least 1 mn dollars as High-Net-Worth-Individuals (HNWIs). In 2020, the total number of HNWIs equalled 1.1 per cent of the global adult population and owned US$191.6 tn or 45.8 per cent of the total pool of global wealth (Credit Suisse 2021: 22). Yet, there exists a steep gradient of wealth even in the top 1.1 per cent of global owners. Billionaires account for only 0.0049 per cent of all HNWIs across the world, yet they own 6.8 per cent of global HNWI wealth. Clearly, billionaires and their wealth claims are significantly vast and far removed from the wealth of other non-billionaire HNWIs. For instance, there is a substantial difference between an individual who owns US$1 mn in investable assets and a billionaire who owns US$1 bn in investable assets. Both are considered HNWIs in the extant financial literature; however, at a ratio of 1:1000, it is unmistakable that the billionaire has greater financial leverage than their millionaire counterparts, so we should be careful not to treat billionaires as possessing similar qualities and abilities to other HNWIs. This leverage lends the billionaire, both as an individual and member of the billionaire class, greater differential control over capitalised assets and greater access to finance. Furthermore, a hierarchy of capitalised power exists within the billionaire class itself. Billionaires with the largest global fortunes have greater claims over the social process than other billionaires that rank further down the list by wealth. For example, the differential accumulation exercised by island owner and Oracle founder Larry Ellison, currently the 7th richest person in the world (US$93 bn), will have a comparatively greater impact than Alibaba receptionist-turned-Chief People Officer Judy Tong Wenhong (US$1 bn) who is tied with 150 other billionaires as the 2,674th entrant on the billionaire list in 2021. Highlighting the hierarchical nature of the global 1 per cent and the hierarchy within the billionaire class itself demonstrates the need for distinct critical inquiries into a largely overlooked group that holds decisive power to reshape broader patterns of social reproduction through their ever-increasing ownership claims of capitalised corporations and their unique access to credit. Specific focus on the apex of the global wealth pyramid is significant in the context of the pandemic for three reasons. First, 2020 witnessed the largest total growth in billionaires since financial publications began recording their annual numbers (Forbes 2018). Second, only in the last few years, the global economy has seen the creation of a handful of centibillionaires.[7] Of the four centibillionaires in this world, three were minted during the global pandemic. Furthermore, the remaining top 10 owners are also teetering on the edge of centibillionaire status (Forbes 2018). Finally, the global billionaire club has increased in membership year-on-year since the 1980s, and yet there have been few critical academic studies to explain the rise of billionaires. To help account for the rise of the billionaire class and the distribution of wealth, I now turn to the capital as power framework in critical political economy.

Capital as Power and the Billionaire Class

Political economy and its mainstream economics counterpart have long sought answers for the distribution of wealth (Nitzan and Bichler 2009: 70ff). As Polanyi (1985: 83) suggests, the question of why poverty goes with capitalist plenty stretches back to the origins of political economy as a field of knowledge, and in his study of capitalism in the 15th to 18th centuries, the great French historian Fernand Braudel also questioned this riddle of disparity:

> Conspicuous at the top of the pyramid is a handful of privileged people. Everything invariably falls into the lap of this tiny elite: power, wealth, a large share of surplus production. Is there not in short, whatever the society and whatever the period, an insidious law giving power to the few, an irritating law it must be said, since *the reasons for it are not obvious*. And yet this stubborn fact, taunting us at every turn. We cannot argue with it: all evidence agrees.
>
> *1982: 466 my emphasis*

Outside the capital as power perspective to be discussed momentarily, there are two major traditions that have tried to address Braudel's "stubborn fact". First is the neoclassical tradition whose definition of capital is tangible and intangible capital goods that underpin the production process. Along with labour, these goods are considered productive of economic output; thus, the capitalist who owns these goods should be rewarded in proportion to their contribution to the output production. This is encapsulated in the infamous "production function", which argues that if we can discern how much labour and capital contribute to production, we can divide the wealth produced accordingly (Nitzan and Bichler 2009: 69). For example, if labour contributes 50 units of work and capital contributes 50 units of productivity, then we know that the monetary value of the economic output should be divided equally. In sum, each "factor of production" is financially rewarded according to their involvement in production. If we examine this claim with a real-world example, we can start to see the absurdity of the argument. Founder and owner of Tesla and Space Exploration Technologies, Elon Musk, is the world's richest human worth US$279 bn in November 2021.[8] Making up the bulk of his wealth are his ownership claims over Tesla standing at US$198 bn. According to the compensation software and data company, PayScale, the average salary for a worker at Tesla is US$98,000.[9] From the perspective of individual productivity, this comparison would suggest that Musk is 2,020,408 times more productive than an average worker at Tesla. For anyone who has ever worked alongside another person, this strains credulity. There is little doubt that people differ in education, experience, drive, skillsets, ability and intelligence, but to claim that one human is over two mn times more productive than someone else is bizarre and difficult to justify by differential physical acumen or philosophically.[10] Although there is no doubt that Elon Musk contributes to the production processes at Tesla in various ways, there must be another reason for his accumulated wealth than the individual productivity proposed by the neoclassicals (see Fix 2021). A further critique of the production function is that the present value of any capital good used in production is calculated by discounting the expected future profit by the rate of interest and some factor of risk (Nitzan and Bichler 2009: 77). Since present value is calculated based on an expectation, which can vary widely in reality, we can never truly know the precise value of capital goods. Although the production function says that we can know the precise value, it is virtually useless in accounting for the division of wealth.

A second attempt at explaining the division of wealth is the Marxist argument that workers are exploited during the labour process. By exploitation, Marx and Marxists mean that workers are not compensated for the full value of their labour time during the production process. This "unpaid surplus labour" is the source of capitalist profit for Marxists. It follows that increasing profit means increasing the rate of exploitation. This can happen in two ways: The capitalist forces factory workers to become more productive during the working day (create more output for a similar wage), or the capitalist forces the workers to toil for longer hours. Due to this exploitation, it is reasoned that we can understand how workers earn far less than their capitalist counterparts. However, the major problem is that labour time and wages in money are incommensurate units—one is measured in seconds, minutes and hours, and the other in cents and dollars. So there is no way to empirically demonstrate Marx's interpretation of exploitation since labour time would have to be converted into prices.

Furthermore, Marx and Marxists make a distinction between those productive workers who add value to the production process and unproductive workers who merely consume value. However, there is no *objective* way of discerning productive from unproductive labour in capitalism (Nitzan and Bichler 2009: 84ff). Although the Marxist tradition has some appeal in that it tries to theorise the relationship between capital and labour and understand unequal power relations, it fails to provide us with an empirically valid theory of the distribution of wealth. For this reason, I now turn to the capital as power perspective to see how it can contribute to our understanding of the rise of the billionaire class and how they profited during the pandemic.

The capital as power framework is a novel critical contribution to the study of IPE that aims to remediate existing theoretical gaps concerning the contested concept of *capital*. As we have discussed, both the neoclassical and Marxist camps frame capital as a narrow economic or material entity. As suggested above, while these conceptions offer something, it becomes increasingly difficult to rationalise or critique the magnitude of accumulation experienced by dominant owners by the existing theories of capital.[11] The prevailing neoclassical and Marxist conceptions of capital rest on the premise that capitalism is a mode of production. By doing so, these traditions obfuscate the centrality of capitalism as a *mode of power*. The distinction here is important. A mode of production limits itself to the weight of mechanised and organic labour forms in reconstituting social reproduction, whereas conceptualising capitalism as a *mode of power* emphasises the necessity of organised power and its exertion over the entire socio-political field (Nitzan and Bichler 2009: 263ff). To understand accumulation, we must move away from solely focusing on labour relations and toward the wider exertion of power over a social field. This entails that profit and wealth are not narrowly determined by the production of goods and services but by a wide array of circumstances and factors. Though capitalists do not always get it right, the factors that affect earnings over time are supposed to be priced into the asset's value (i.e. share price). Therefore, the capital as power perspective focuses on capitalisation as the dominant ritual of capitalism. It is true that capitalists/investors are chasing expected future corporate earnings and that this expectation is discounted into a present share price for the firm. Yet, as Nitzan and Bichler (2009: 208) remind us, earnings are a matter of exercising power over the terrain of social reproduction. To keep with Tesla, the profitability of the company and, therefore, its capitalisation (also known as market value) does not only just depend on producing electric vehicles but on a range of issues such as hype, patent protection, litigation, laws that encourage more electric vehicles, the oil price, and price of electricity, availability of consumer credit and charging stations, free trade deals, the quality of battery life, the rise of competitors such as Lucid Motors and many other factors. Yet, investors are capitalising on the power of Tesla to influence the market and broader society and should this power wane, so too will Tesla's capitalisation and Musk's fortunes, as the majority of his wealth is derived from his ownership of shares in the company. For this reason, the capital as power approach understands capital as *commodified differential social power* symbolically measured in monetary units. In this way, capitalist accumulation does not rest on the accumulation of productive capital goods, nor does it solely rely on labour exploitation during the production process. Instead, capitalist accumulation rests on the capacity of dominant capital to shape, against opposition, social reproduction in their favour (Nitzan and Bichler 2009: 17–18). *Dominant capital* refers to the leading corporations and key government organs at the epicentre of differential accumulation (Nitzan and Bichler 2009: 10). Notably, the very foundation of capitalist accumulation rests on ownership and exclusion (2009: 228). If capital is to be conceived as symbolic of accumulated social power, then accumulation must be understood as a differential process of capitalist development—some accumulate more than others in the hierarchy due to their differential ownership of income-generating assets (2009: 150–151).[12] Thus, the objective for the capitalist is to accumulate more and faster than their rivals trying to do the same (2009: 17–18). And yet the differential accumulation of quantified power commanded by increasing rates of return requires the exponential extraction, reconfiguration, and destruction of our finite Earth for private gain and consumption. Herein lies a giant contradiction of capitalist order and the billionaire's place in it: The dollar rate of billionaire private fortunes is a symbolic quantification of this power process that transforms and commodifies nature (Smessaert et al. 2020). Moreover, dominant owners apply the same logic to their consumptive practices, meaning billionaires leave a larger ecological footprint than those with lesser wealth and income. As money is no object, consumption becomes a differential process to out-consume peers at rates that are unsustainable and quantitatively disproportionate to the rest of humanity (Di Muzio 2015a; Kempf 2008; Kenner 2020). Understanding capital *as a mode of power*, where power is measured in money (since money is a claim on society and nature), allows for greater leverage in studying transformative billionaire accumulation and consumption in the 21st century. As suggested above, this power is primarily rooted in private ownership and the right to exclude. As argued by Nitzan and Bichler:

> The most important feature of private ownership is not that it enables those who own, but that it disables those who do not. Technically, anyone can get into someone else's car and drive away, or give an order to sell all of Warren Buffet's shares in Berkshire Hathaway. The sole purpose of private ownership is to prevent us from doing so. In this sense, private ownership is wholly and only an institution of exclusion, and institutional exclusion is a matter of organized power.
>
> *2009: 228*

This passage suggests that billionaires are not billionaires because of their individual productivity and contribution to production; the billionaire class exists and has expanded because of their disproportionate ownership claims over powerful income-generating institutions or corporations that act to shape and reshape the socioeconomic fabric in the quest for earnings. If this concentrated ownership and the power to exclude others were ever challenged, then the wealth of the billionaire class would significantly dwindle to zero. To provide one example of how exclusion works to accumulate vast fortunes, consider the case of the pandemic profiteers that became billionaires due to the pandemic (Brenner 2020). According to Fierce Pharma, the industry's daily monitor, Moderna received US$2.48 bn in public money for research and development into a vaccine.[13] Yet, despite the public subsidy, it appears that the CEO and two of its founding (now) billionaire investors want to accumulate even more by sabotaging the availability of the vaccine for the world's poor unless they get their ransom of profit. As Oxfam reports:

> Vaccine billionaires are being created as stocks in pharmaceutical firms rise rapidly in expectation of huge profits from the COVID-19 vaccines over which these firms have monopoly control. The alliance warned that these monopolies allow pharmaceutical corporations total control over the supply and price of vaccines, pushing up their profits while making it harder for poor countries, in particular, to secure the stocks they need.[14]

This passage demonstrates that vaccine billionaires are not just minted by the fact that they have overseen or have invested in pharmaceutical companies that create vaccines, but perhaps more importantly, by their ability to exclude others from accessing a vaccine without going through a steep paywall protected by their patents. A more prominent example of putting profit before people during a global health crisis where the poor are the hardest hit is difficult to find.

Although the institutional power rooted in ownership and exclusion is paramount to explaining the rise of the billionaire class and wealth inequality more generally, other factors are incredibly important to consider.

More than likely, what also contributed to billionaire wealth leading up to and during the pandemic were the record low interest rates which made credit seriously cheap.[15] This has been exceedingly advantageous for the ultra-wealthy who can afford to borrow more and follow the logic of buy-borrow-die, using continuous lines of credits against paper wealth assets to fund their activities and thereby avoid paying taxes on realised gains (Ensign & Rubin 2021).

It is difficult to know how much cheap credit ended up investing in the stock markets of the world. If total stock market capitalisation can be considered a potential indicator of the wealth added to the global economy by access to cheaper credit, then from 2019 to 2020, global stock markets increased by US$15 tn to US$94 tn (up from US$79 tn in 2019).[16] And as we know, with very low interest rates, capitalists are seeking returns in the stock market (see Robbins, this volume).

Other than cheaper credit, another factor to consider is how the transition to neoliberal rule facilitated greater capital mobility and transnationalisation of business accumulation (Gill 1995). At least since the transition to neoliberal world order, the processes of globalisation have helped to further mobilise transnational capital and the dominant owners who control the global circuits of accumulation, value chains and societal reproduction. This is largely manifest in the global spread of neoliberal socioeconomic order since the late 1970s and its dominion over state restructuring in response to the "failures" of Keynesianism in the global North and the debt crisis in the South, instituting market-friendly policies as the new "common sense" (Harvey 2007). Part of this "common sense" has been the rollback of wealth taxes experienced during the Keynesian era, which contributed to capital increasing its share of the wealth generated by society as a whole (Piketty 2017). It also gave capital access to a greater pool of cheap labour as China and other Asian countries went through a period of economic opening.

Another prominent reason for the rise of the billionaire class is how their institutions have piggybacked on decades of government defence spending on research and development. Through defence contracts, the tech corporations of Silicon Valley continue to have a close relationship with the Pentagon.[17] The internet, rapid technological change, disruption to traditional business models, and the overall productivity growth of the economy are largely encapsulated in what economists call the network effect, all can be traced to massive defence spending throughout the Cold War (Wagstyl 2019). The network effect refers to a phenomenon where greater value is created for both companies and consumers as more people join the network or use compatible products. Many technology billionaires like Mark Zuckerberg and Larry Page have profited immensely from the digitalisation of society, the network effect and their monopoly over a platform (Ouellet 2019: 81–94). Like Standard Oil and other trusts, these new monopolies are now being questioned by both citizens and politicians (Kang and McCabe 2020). Not surprisingly, the tech giants are loath to break up their empires, with their monopolies or near-monopolies the chief source of their wealth, influence and power.

Should Billionaires Exist?

It should be clear by now that we have entered a Second Gilded Age where the wealth held by billionaires continues to escalate well above the rest of humanity. Without serious government intervention, this trend is likely to continue in the post-pandemic era, further exacerbating the divide between the ultra-wealthy and the working class. In some quarters, this has prompted the public, politicians and organisations to ask whether billionaires should exist at all. The most famous was Presidential candidate Bernie Sanders who publicly proclaimed that "billionaires should not exist". In one of the Presidential debates, the moderator Erin Burnett asked Sanders if his goal was to tax billionaires out of existence. This is what he said:

> [T]he truth is, we cannot afford to continue this level of income and wealth inequality, and we cannot afford a billionaire class whose greed and corruption has been at war with the working families of this country for 45 years.
>
> *Sanders as cited by Astor 2019*

Although Sanders did not win the nomination, his idea of taxing billionaires to fund social and infrastructural programs in the United States did not die a slow death. Leading the charge now is Senator Ron Wydon, a Democrat from Oregon, who proposed a federal wealth tax for the United States. At the time of this writing, the tax is still being debated, but the crux of the proposed billionaire tax is interesting to consider. The tax would levy a 23.8 per cent charge on the appreciated value of all tradeable assets owned by the billionaire class even if they are not liquidated. Traditionally, billionaires, like other investors, only pay capital gains tax when they sell shares. If the tax passes Congress, what this means is that if a billionaire's wealth appreciates by US$5 bn over a year, then they will be taxed at 23.8 per cent on this amount even if they refuse to sell their shares to realise monetary gains. Moreover, those who make US$100 mn in income over three consecutive years would also be subject to the tax. Senator Wydon suggests that his Billionaires Income Tax would force billionaires to pay taxes every year just like ordinary working Americans (Ponciano 2021). At the time of this writing, it appears doubtful that the proposed bill will pass Congress, given the political opposition and intense lobbying. Even if it does pass Congress, many anticipate that the tax will encounter significant legal obstacles in the courts and invite innovative legal gymnastics to evade taxation. However, if the tax does manage to pass Congress, not only would it be a historic win for the majority of working Americans who have suffered during the pandemic but also act as a beacon to other democracies questioning the existence of the billionaire class and what this small group tells us about capitalist hierarchy and privilege. Taxation is not the only way to eliminate the billionaire class, but, at present, it appears to be the only major proposal.

Conclusion

This chapter focused on the rise of the billionaire class that has grown in numbers and wealth during the worst scourges of Covid-19. It then considered two major schools of thought that have tried to account for the massive disparity in wealth and power: The neoclassical and Marxist perspectives. It then argued that the capital as power perspective offers a more convincing answer as it focuses on the institutional power rooted in ownership and exclusion. Indeed, private ownership is central to capitalism as the vast majority of the wealth held by billionaires is not in cash, but in the capitalisation of owned income-generating assets. This chapter also considered some additional factors that can help us account for the proliferation of billionaires such as generous fiscal and monetary policies throughout the pandemic, the turn to neoliberalism that favoured capital over labour and the technological revolution rooted in decades of American defence spending that lead to the growth of tech billionaires.[18] I also briefly examined how the wealth of the billionaire class may be challenged by public authorities seeking a fairer and more equitable economy in an age of vast disparity in power, life chances and privilege.

Notes

1 As of July 2021, Amazon founder Jeff Bezos was the world's richest human 4 years running and the first billionaire to launch himself into space with Blue Origin, a private space company he founded in 2000 (Rincon 2021). By late September 2021, Elon Musk officially topped Bezos and sustained the position of the richest individual in the world. In October 2021, the Tesla founder held a 9000-person rave on a whim at his Gigafactory in Berlin (Eede 2020). American business magnate and billionaire David Geffen failed to read the room on March 29, 2020, tweeting from the refuge of his US\$590 million mega-yacht, "Isolated in the Grenadines avoiding the virus. I'm hoping everybody is staying safe." accompanied by sunset-backed pictures of the grand private vessel. Geffen deleted the tweet soon after (Luscome 2020).

2 www.un.org/sustainabledevelopment/inequality/ (accessed November 16, 2021).

3 I do not engage the literature on the Transnational Capitalist Class due to space limitations but see (Van Der Pijl 1998,2012; Gill & Law 1989; Robinson & Harris 2000; Sklair 2001, 2002; Gill 2008; Carroll 2010).

4 I do not discount privatisation of state assets, corruption, and family-ties as a key source of billionaire wealth but note that these ill-gotten resources or gains still end up as ownership claims over an enterprise and thus involve the practice of institutional power and exclusion (Petras 2008).

5 Prior to this, Forbes documented American billionaires in *The Forbes 400* list, which debuted in 1982. Thirteen billionaires were recorded that year.

6 Rockefeller donated US$35 million to develop the University of Chicago, the cradle of neoclassical economics.

7 A centibillionaire has a personal net-worth of at least 100 bn dollars.

8 www.bloomberg.com/billionaires/ (November 16, 2021). It should be noted that his wealth obviously fluctuates with the value of Tesla shares.

9 www.payscale.com/research/US/Employer=Tesla_Motors/Salary (accessed November 9, 2021).

10 One could argue that since Musk is paid in company stock, he is taking on an incredible risk in ensuring the company remains profitable and grows over time to return shareholder value. But here too, we would have to measure risk, and there is no objective way to do so.

11 The term "dominant owners" was introduced by Di Muzio (2015b) to account for those owners with the largest capitalised assets.

12 Anything that can be subjected to the price system can and will be quantified into ownership claims, "everything that can be owned, from natural objects, through produced commodities, to social organizations, ideas and human beings—can also be quantified" (2009: 151).

13 www.fiercepharma.com/pharma/after-nearly-1b-research-funding-moderna-takes-1-5b-coronavirus-vaccine-order-from-u-s (accessed November 9, 2021).

14 www.oxfam.org/en/press-releases/covid-vaccines-create-9-new-billionaires-combi ned-wealth-greater-cost-vaccinating (accessed November 9, 2021) The alliance refers to The People's Vaccine Alliance, a collaboration of organisations fighting for universal access at affordable prices for the world.

15 https://fred.stlouisfed.org/series/FEDFUNDS

16 https://data.worldbank.org/indicator/CM.MKT.LCAP.CD (accessed November 9, 2021).

17 https://techinquiry.org/SiliconValley-Military/ (accessed November 9, 2021).

18 This chapter has not considered how being White, male, and born in a rich country can also contribute to billionaire status due to space limitations and the fact that this would require a larger study.

3

NEOLIBERALISM, RACE, AND IGNORANCE IN AN ERA OF COVID-19

Dan Bousfield

Introduction

This chapter examines how Covid-19 has accelerated the crisis of contemporary liberalism exemplified by turning toward authoritarianism and ignorance in political decision-making. Beginning with Adorno's provocation about the persistence of irrationalism in modern society, this chapter frames the propagation of ignorance under liberalism, neoliberalism and contemporary capitalism as a failure of regulation exemplified by responses to the global pandemic. The main argument in this chapter is that the ingroup logic of global liberalism has been unable to address the role of social media in rising authoritarianism, racism and vaccine hesitancy during the Covid-19 pandemic. Without efforts to address ignorance as a political problem, liberalism will continue to propagate the inequalities magnified by the pandemic and fail to develop viable political solutions to increasing global polarisation. To explore this argument, this chapter focuses on ignorance as a political failure of regulation rather than a lack of access to information. This failure stems from the valorisation of liberal principles of free speech, individualism and non-intervention manifesting in rising authoritarianism, racism, and the inability to respond to the global pandemic equitably. Consequently, the hierarchical inequalities of racism are exacerbated in the context of the global pandemic. The chapter first considers Adorno's take on irrationalism and modernity before linking this discussion with neoliberalism and the contradictions of social media in the context of the pandemic. The final two sections of the chapter explore the challenges of ignorance and racism in the constitution and reconstitution of liberal order and then offers a brief conclusion.

DOI: 10.4324/9781003250432-5

Adorno on Irrationalism

The chapter explores Adorno's reflection on the powerful tendencies toward authoritarianism and anti-rationalism embedded in enlightenment and modernity. Adorno connects authoritarian irrationalism and liberal society to explain how racism and anti-Semitism are integral to the production of authoritarian propaganda. In a series of essays dealing with astrology, occultism and anti-Semitism, Adorno criticises the way in which "irrationality" is an oversimplification of the depersonalisation and deference to authority that makes the scientific process "legible". As he argues:

> astrology, just as other irrational creeds like racism, provides a short-cut by bringing the complex to a handy formula and offering at the same time the pleasant gratification that he who feels to be excluded from the educational privileges nevertheless belongs to the minority of those who are 'in the know'.
>
> *Adorno 2007: 61*

Complex modern societies necessitate our subjective interpretation of information beyond an individual's capabilities to comprehend, necessitating deference to expertise. This means that the "publicness" of rational argumentation and irrational claims are identical, as they require shared conceptions of public interest, individual choice and democratic authority to authorise thought. In the postwar era, Ratna Kapur has characterised this as "fishbowl liberalism" or the key role of hegemony in bounding human freedom and human rights through a specific historical Western experience (2020: 3). Those inside of liberalism champion the benefits of progress, whereas those outside endure the "cruel optimism" of illiberal social conditions framed as unrealised liberal ends. The central contradiction of liberalism is the idea that individuals are supposed to have unlimited activity, freedom and ruggedness in a society that requires ever-increasing organisational obedience for it to function. As Adorno argues, "the same person can hardly be expected to be thoroughly adjusted and strongly individualistic at the same time" (Adorno 2007: 105). Consequently, he explains the need for a supplement to overcome the inherent tension of information and expertise in liberal ideology, which is the key position for the authoritative expert. The shared liberal understanding is that expertise and "those in the know" are somehow beyond the power structures and politico-economic relationships that establish their hegemony. In the broadest sense, the postwar liberal order has been accused of reinforcing this in the idea that global institutions suffer from a democratic deficit and a lack of public input, yet expertise demands the public defer to these organisations for decision-making (Moravcsik 2004; Nye 2001; Porter 2001). Adorno argues it is quite easy for challengers to this framework to replace the dominant ingroup with others, by providing alternative experts (as in astrology) and the idea that "behind-the-scenes activities" are projected onto the other groups (as in anti-Semitism) (Adorno 2007: 119). From Trump's assertions against "globalists",

Snowden's National Security Agency revelations, to QAnon and conspiracy theories, globally networked societies have seen increased access to information and declining centralised editorial over information. The liberal ingroup consensus has recently been challenged by the death of George Floyd and the subsequent Black Lives Matter global protests, as well as postcolonial and settler-colonial critiques of racial capitalism. Finally, as Berberoglu has argued, growing income and economic inequality alongside successive economic crises have eroded global public trust in liberal institutions, reinforcing authoritarian alternatives as legible policy options (Berberoglu 2020). Thus, although postwar liberalism attempted to establish a political agreement around shared public policy ideals, contemporary capitalism and global neoliberal policies have eroded those claims by increasing authority privatisation from previously public mechanisms.

The Neoliberal Premise

As a subset of liberalism, neoliberalism represents an intensification of the contradictions between individualism and authoritarian impulses of market actors. As Mirowski has argued, the origins of neoliberalism as an ingroup "thought collective" have not resulted in a coherent framework to assess neoliberal ideals. He argues that it is dangerous to think of neoliberalism as an exclusively economic theory; instead, it should be seen as an inherently political project to make "economics apolitical" in everyday common sense (Mirowski et al. 2009: 427). In other words, like liberalism's rational fishbowl (liberal actors are rational, not political). In this sense, neoliberalism reinforces the idea that key economic principles (for instance, market forces such as supply, demand and equilibrium) should be understood as off-limits for political intervention. By characterising neoliberalism as thought-collective, Mirowski argues that championing individualism, free markets and restraint on government intervention creates an ingroup of "persons mutually exchanging ideas and maintaining intellectual interaction", promoting epistemological discipline through a common theoretical orientation (Mirowski et al. 2009: 429). This argues that we should view neoliberalism as an academic epistemic bubble or the basis for like-minded political ideals, more aptly characterised as an echo chamber (Mirowski et al. 2009: 430). As Nguyen argues, epistemic bubbles are a social structure where voices have been excluded through omission, whereas an echo chamber is a consequence of other relevant voices being actively discredited (Nguyen 2020: 142). A key aspect of the distinction between epistemic bubbles and echo chambers is the framing of ignorance. An epistemic bubble has poor connectivity to alternative sources and perspectives, whereas the echo chamber actively prevents contrarian voices and relies on ingroup trust to discredit information (Nguyen 2020: 142). Ignorance emerges from a poor breadth of scholarship and the refusal to engage with ideas that challenge key theoretical assumptions. This understanding of neoliberalism frames knowledge as inherently political, or as Stephen Gill argues, neoliberalism is a combination of hierarchical and social structures, in the idea of a Gramscian hegemonic struggle between competing social forces (Gill 1995: 400). Neoliberalism can be framed as a fishbowl, epistemic bubble or echo chamber, meaning Kapur, Mirowski and Gill see neoliberalism as the dominant liberal discursive formation in global policymaking (Gill 1995: 406). In this way, neoliberalism has undergone narrowly constrained debates from monetarism and Thatcherism to the Washington Consensus and to the contemporary framing of neoliberalism as integral to multinational corporations and global value chains (Gereffi 2014). Both sympathetic and critical examinations of neoliberalism identify the authoritative coordination and discipline of thought supporting Adorno's claim that ignorance and authority are necessary supplements to order. Explanations that help frame the "disciplinary" character of contemporary neoliberalism as both structural and behavioural (imposed on the individual by society or imposed on states by the international order) reinforce the idea of efficacy of control by the proponents of neoliberal policy (ingroups) (Gill 1995: 411). In other words, critical framings of the ideology of contemporary neoliberalism overemphasise the coherence and rationality of these political processes in their effort to explain them. In the context of Covid-19, this is easily exemplified in the framing of "essential" workers, necessary to the economic functioning of the system regardless of public health threats. On the one hand, this framing applied to healthcare workers responding directly to Covid-19, yet it easily was co-opted to mean minimum wage service workers for multinational companies under the guise that these minimally renumerated and often racialised communities are "essential" to the global economy. In both cases, it is ignorance and authority that authorise the conflation of essential workers through the ideological merging of health and markets as material justification for otherwise contradictory understandings. If health workers are deemed essential, whereas minimum wage workers are also deemed essential, the idea of essential reflects power and authority, not a sense of reasonable claims.

The Role of Social Media

Ignorance is inherently hierarchical and tangible, as it reflects social power and also embeds institutions, norms, and neoliberal framing of regulation. In the context of Covid-19 and discussions of vaccine hesitancy, authoritarianism and racism have been integrally connected to online radicalisation and the role of social media. It is no secret that the pandemic arose in an era of social media whereby Silicon Valley represents a highly visible aspect of global inequality. The convergence of liberal notions of free speech, neoliberal framing of non-intervention in the sector, combined with the concentration of wealth and power in large technology firms have become an important vector of vaccine hesitancy. The primary mechanism of the privatisation of public speech stems from the regulatory framework of Section 230 of the American Communications Decency Act, which protects online companies from the content they host, under the abstract liberal principle of free speech (Adria 2010: 373). Unlike other forms of media, which have liability for the content produced on their platforms, Section 230 treats social media firms as infrastructure intermediaries rather than legally liable media platforms. In practice, the network effects of the monopolisation of technology and social media platforms (such as Facebook, Twitter and Google) privatise decision-making about public speech, concentrates power in technology billionaires' ability to monetise and control what Zuboff has framed as capitalism driven by private surveillance and authority (Zuboff 2019). The dystopian foreshadowing of Mark Zuckerberg's mantra "move fast and break things" can be seen in the sector's tax avoidance, aggressive lobbying to avoid regulation and the amplification of extreme and polarising content to maximise shareholder values. As Zuboff argues:

> Section 230's hands-off stance toward companies perfectly converged with the reigning ideology and practice of "self-regulation," leaving the internet companies, and eventually the surveillance capitalists among them, free to do what they pleased.
>
> *2019: 139*

The neoliberal convergence around free speech, regulatory avoidance (and eventually regulatory capture) and concentration of decision-making authority undermine public reason and contribute to the proliferation of irrationality. Google and Facebook's duopoly of the advertising market amplified echo chambers, and targeted advertising from keyword searches such as "Jew Hater", "How to burn Jews", "evil Jews" and "Jewish control of banks" to monetise and control the attention of social media users (Zuboff 2019: 624). To the extent that the online world mirrors and reflects the offline world, the neoliberal premise of markets as self-regulating has amplified racism, oppression and exclusion through fragmentation and polarisation of existing social norms (Noble 2018). The twinning of neoliberalism and the liberal ideal of free speech allows the propagation of injurious, defamatory, and confidential information and is implicated in a series of direct social harms, including the propagation of hate speech, advertising and platforming disinformation and misinformation, as a key vector of vaccine hesitancy (Adria 2010: 373). As Puri et al. (2020: 2587) have found, anti-vaccine content engenders more user engagement, higher likes and amplifies hesitancy debates taking place in society. Even brief exposure to anti-vaccination content increases the likelihood of vaccine hesitancy, in part because social media can propagate misinformation through vivid narratives and powerful imagery. With character limits on Twitter, and the promotion of visual content and memes on social media, these platforms have been designed to maximise emotional appeal, especially to demographics with lower digital literacy rates (Puri et al. 2020: 2588). The failure to regulate social media reflects the tension of neoliberalism's apolitical markets premise taken to logical extremes as private interests drive *de facto* social policy in the exchange of communication.

Moreover, the neoliberal belief in self-regulating markets and the initial failure to intervene in the proliferation of irrationalism also helps us explain the absence of preparation for Covid-19. The continual erosion of regulatory intervention as social media grew and the belief that the private sector was a source of innovation resulted in a lack of capacity to respond to the Covid-19 pandemic. The recurrent theme of ignorance here is its wilfulness, conscious efforts made to ignore data and evidence that directly contradicts political or ideological assertions (through forms of ingroup bias). Vaccine hesitancy is a long-standing and persistent public health issue but has often been framed in terms of risk assessment, free riding or other ways in which individual choice is valorised as significant for choice-making (Dubé et al. 2013; Jin et al. 2020; Capurro et al. 2018). Indeed, the effort to frame "vaccine hesitancy" versus the language of "anti-vaxxers" itself reflects the notion that ignorance is simply the lack of persuasive information. The rational underpinnings of free speech adopt the liberal language of persuasion to frame vaccine hesitancy as a "knowledge deficit" rather than addressing the absence of global regulation over forms of social media that platform and encourage high-value engagement through controversial positions (Meyer et al. 2019). For instance, the notorious Wakefield et al. *Lancet* study that prompted many forms of current anti-vaccine sentiment, can be seen as an explicit tension between the role of reason in medical science-as-practice into the role of the expert proposing science-as-truth (Goldenberg 2021). The liberal premise of "pro-vaccine campaigns" to create the conditions for mass public compliance—by shutting down dissenting views in amplifying the "pro-vaccine message" has been undermined by the perceptions of market-driven capitalist relationships between academic medicine and pharmaceutical companies (Goldenberg 2021: 30). In the Canadian case, where a single-payer public insurance should have mitigated some of the concerns about pharmaceutical conspiracies, social media efforts directly conflicted with public health mandates. Efforts by the Ontario government to insist that non-medical exemptions for school entry vaccine requirements resulted in a 0 per cent conversion rate for the thousands of parents forced to attend (Goldenberg 2021: 34). A key distinction is that the advertising-driven model of social media transforms information into persuasion, reinforcing the role of markets as superior to government and unregulated business as beneficial to society.

The design of social media systems was influenced by the persuasive technologies lab at Stanford University in the early 2000s. Utilising a combination of psychology, technology and computer design, the development of social media was a framing of the information on the internet with intent. As the director of the institute, BJ Fogg, explained, "The Web is not about information ... It's about influence" (Bourzac 2010). Fogg's legacy over social media design principles represents the inherent tension between deregulated information framed as "free" and market-driven information designed to "influence". Neoliberalism provides the rationale to reinforce the dual character of individualism and authoritarianism in the framing of information being free, but the influence is controlled. Section 230 allows social media companies to privately and arbitrarily decide when the public is negatively affected rather than providing a foundation for ideas like collective health. One example of the priming of vaccine hesitancy on social media platforms and the arbitrary capacity to regulate was demonstrated in the 2018 "Tide Pod Challenge". This viral campaign encouraged participants to place brightly-coloured laundry detergent pods in their mouths and chew, despite the highly toxic chemicals in the pods. Memes, internet debates and public discussion about the increasing number of deaths related to Tide Pod consumption resulted in Facebook and Instagram removing content that showed misuse of the laundry pods (Nelson et al. 2019). YouTube arbitrarily enforced the idea that it prohibited content with an inherent risk of physical harm (Nelson et al. 2019). The advertising and attention-driven social media models rarely employ non-copyright restrictions and have produced a form of regulation reinforcing the arbitrary and authoritative powers of social media platforms. It is arbitrary in that censorship is only adopted when direct correlative harm can be demonstrated, yet privatised, as the criteria and decision-making for content restriction are considered proprietary. Consequently, although public health was used as a justification to restrict the amplification of eating Tide Pods, the problem itself was created through the influence and advertising designed and monetised by the social media platforms. As one commentator argued, eating Tide Pods was economically rational on these platforms, as they were designed to amplify social reach and extreme content (Murphy 2019). Key is the arbitrary demarcation of public health in the context of Tide Pods, and Covid-19 is how one was framed as direct harm and the other enjoyed long-standing monetisation of vaccine hesitancy under individual speech. These platforms reject social norms through the valorisation of shareholder value, proprietary knowledge and individualism but arbitrarily decide when to restrict content that causes harm. In this way, social media platforms reflect Adorno's assertion about the propagation of irrationality, as social media is designed to propagate fads, memes and viral content alongside the idea that individuals should be free from influence or control over their actions.

The coherence of global liberal policy has been eroded by material and social conditions of inequality and by denying the authoritarian and irrational elements used to maintain these systems. Adorno framed irrationalism, expressed through occultism and anti-Semitism, as twinned characteristics of contemporary liberal societies. Adorno warns against marginalising irrational claims, as they are both calculated and logical and develop coherence within their asserted constraints (Adorno 2007: 223). In Anderson's work on epistemic bubbles, the danger of self-segregated social networks of like-minded people is a failure to update beliefs in response to new information (Anderson 2021: 11). Anderson focuses on group polarisation and cultural cognition as key dynamics in explaining recent support for authoritarian, racist beliefs, and conspiracy theories. Group polarisation and the willingness to accept extreme beliefs stem from the idea that cognitive biases impact risk perception, and individuals seek ingroup or outgroup coherence (Anderson 2021: 13). High degrees of individualism are expressed as resistance to social conformity, which perversely corresponds to acceptance of authoritarian leadership (Anderson 2021: 13). This follows Adorno's affective framing of authoritarianism, or that fascist leadership provides a form of gratification for its audience that is both ritualistic and celebratory (Adorno 2007: 226). From Trump's desires to have military parades, to literally hugging and kissing the American flag, authoritarianism provides an emotional supplement framed by irrational understandings of politics and policy. In the context of Covid-19, vaccine hesitancy has largely become intertwined with authoritarian justification about freedom, control and individual choice, encouraged by ingroup associations who reject social obligation. The idolatry of billionaires and "strongmen" has been seen throughout Covid-19, from Elon Musk's violation of public health orders to ensure a massive personal compensation package (US$55 bn), to leaders around the world advocating herd immunity, including Boris Johnson's desire to be intentionally infected on live TV to reinforce this point (Bienkov and Colson 2021; Heilweil 2020; Kiersz, 2021). Consequently, a central contradiction of what Adorno saw in the support for fascism and authoritarianism is also an expression of the loss of self-control, challenging the self-contained individual, with affective irrationality (Adorno 2007: 225–226). A common theme of fascist agitation is the focus on the status quo as both challenged and lost, drawing on the power of nostalgia and ingroup success, exemplified by the "Make America Great Again" slogan (Arendt [1951]1973: 177). Fascist rituals of innuendo allow leaders to return to the idea of a hidden outgroup versus the authentic ingroup, drawing on the revelatory notions of downfall, collapse, and catastrophe (Adorno 2007: 228). The rise in Asian racism, hate speech and emboldening of racist attacks are reinforced by ingroup politics supported by abstract liberal ideals like free speech. Trump's racist characterising of Covid-19 as the "Chinese Virus" or "Kung-Flu" was directly linked to increased anti-Asian sentiments online (Hswen et al. 2021). Giroux argues that under neoliberalism "political culture has been increasingly emptied of democratic values as collective life is organized around the modalities of privatization, risks, deregulation and commercialization" (Giroux 2008: 3). Subsequently, authoritative action is valued over reasoned debate, and consumerism is foregrounded as the most effective way to achieve a better future as a form of social Darwinism (Giroux 2008: 3). Ingroup thinking selectively reinforces liberal ideals to justify anti-Black racism, Sinophobia or Islamophobia on the justification of patriotic jingoism (Giroux 2008: 61). The freedom of market forces in the realm of public ideas magnifies racism as a matter of taste, lifestyle or heritage rather than framing racism as "politics, legal rights, educational access or economic opportunity" (Giroux 2018: 69). The murder of George Floyd and the ongoing efforts to address Black Lives Matter protests in the context of Covid-19 exemplified this intersection through what has been characterised as "woke" capitalism, the superficial rearranging of values and attitudes to avoid addressing institutional and structural problems of racial capitalism. Authoritarianism expressed through racial entreaties in defence of liberalism is simultaneously met by cultural shifts in affect to prevent regulatory ones.

Studying Ignorance

Adorno's arguments mirror the insights drawn from the emerging field of ignorance studies, which takes ignorance as a key aspect of enlightenment thought. As Gross and McGoey argue, ignorance as "the unknown" has long been the primary mechanism by which education is framed. Productive framing of ignorance sees it as something to be overcome or how new information and new ideas produce notions of progress (Gross et al. 2018: 1). As they note, however, "Hans-Georg Gadamer once suggested that the fundamental prejudice of the Enlightenment is the prejudice against prejudice itself", which is to say that enlightenment thinking has a blind spot when it comes to the notion of progress, coming directly from the belief that greater knowledge equals better outcomes (Gross et al. 2018: 3). Liberal scientific study has had difficulty conducting social scientific analysis if rationality itself is not a structuring principle of social order. The problem identified by Adorno is that ingroup and outgroup prejudice can form the basis of rationality through ignorance. In other words, knowledge and its absence are inherently political. In the context of Covid-19, this has been driven to the fore, where a lack of scientific consensus, evidentiary data, and policy outcomes percolates to a proliferation of conspiracy theories, alternative justifications for vaccine hesitancy and irrational claims of racism in the absence of coherent public authority. This was exemplified in the early days of the pandemic in the efforts to a blunt inquiry into the possible origins of Covid-19 from the Wuhan Virology Laboratory in China, as Sinophobic and racist. In an early effort to deal with health implications on the platform, Twitter banned the account of the conspiracy theory website Zero Hedge on January 29, 2020, under the guise of improper disclosure of personal details (so-called personal doxing) that were publicly available on the virology laboratory website (Gross et al. 2018: 3). In 2020 the *Washington Post* framed Republican Senator Tom Cotton's questions about the Wuhan origin thesis as a debunked "conspiracy theory", which it later modified (Firozi 2020). Both Facebook and Twitter maintained restrictions on discussing the Wuhan speculation and the origins of the Covid-19 through May 2021. By this time, the Bulletin of The Atomic Scientists openly inquired about the possibility of Covid-19's emergence from the laboratory and efforts to squash the inquiry as unscientific. As the *Lancet* had published a letter publicly denouncing the lab-grown origins of Covid-19 as conspiracies on February 19, 2020, the Bulletin of The Atomic Scientists responded that:

> A defining mark of good scientists is that they go to great pains to distinguish between what they know and what they don't know. By this criterion, the signatories of the *Lancet* letter were behaving as poor scientists: They were assuring the public of facts they could not know for sure were true.
>
> *Wade 2021*

The epistemology of science has been an integral aspect of the Covid-19 pandemic, as ingroup decision-making, authority and irrational actions highlight how the practice, slow collection of data and application of tacit liberal assumptions are ingrained in contemporary notions of public health and expertise. By May 2021, the Biden administration began official inquiries into the origins of Covid-19 and the "lab leak theory", re-establishing the need for a scientific foundation of previously dismissed claims. Liberal responses to racism as irrational and ignorant risk the public authority of decision-makers as they attempt to develop science-as-liberal, liberal-as-science responses. This kind of blind assertion of public authority replicates the enlightenment assumptions about the relationship between scientists and the public as rational. As Sloterdijk has argued:

> Enlightenment, which strives for the reification and objectification (Versachlichung) of knowledge, reduces the world of the physiognomic to silence. The price of objectivity is the loss of closeness. Scientists lose the capacity to behave as neighbors of the world; they think in concepts of distance, not of friendship; they seek overviews, not involvement. Over the centuries, modern science excluded everything that was incompatible with the *a priori* of objectifying distance and intellectual domination over the object: intuition, empathy, *esprit de finesse*, aesthetics, erotics.
>
> *Sloterdijk 1987: 140*

The ability to develop enlightenment critique necessarily assumes proximity, which it engages and reinforces attitudes about ignorance (Sloterdijk 1987: xxxii). In the context of the liberal fishbowl, the support for a reason as the basis of ingroup thinking is tautological; either reasoned liberal society is rational, or alternatives are claimed to be irrational. As Seth has argued, the influential liberal theorist John Rawls abandoned rationality as providing a moral basis for decision-making, arguing that "effective formal or procedural defense of modern morality and liberal politics" is beyond the capability of liberal theory (Seth 2020: 66). Jürgen Habermas was more explicit about the inability to establish a universal basis for privileging reason over other ways of understanding, connecting it directly with "our Occidental understanding of the world" (Seth 2020: 69). As Seth argues:

> In all versions of this narrative—Weberian, Hegelian, Marxist, Habermasian and others—the core presumptions of modern knowledge are not yet another set of parochial assumptions claiming universal validity like a proselytizing religion, but rather embedded in an account that purports to explain both why we humans were once bound to get things wrong and how it is become possible to get them right.
>
> *Seth 2020: 79*

Ignorance and reason are productively intertwined in the liberal narrative of universal rational thought but remain wedded to ingroup presumptions of authority and hierarchy that are contingent and not universal. The threat of a generational global pandemic was not only well-known but also it had been anticipated by successive governments around the world, and through the creation of the Global Outbreak Alerts and Response Network (GOARN) in 2000. However, in the context of the rising influence of anti-vaccination movements, particularly on social media, there was very little attention focused on the role of rising ignorance as a vector of the next global pandemic (Lakoff 2017). The manipulation of statistics for national pride and national interest in the context of pandemics was one of the primary motivations for reframing the WHO framework after the SARS outbreak, but very little work had been done to develop a scientific understanding of the role of ignorance in pandemic response (Ortega and Orsini 2020). This is a blind spot of enlightenment thought and liberal practice stemming from liberal assumptions about ignorance. The idea of a proper academic distance from the object of study assumes a narrative of divorced rational logic and assessment. This discourse presents information as pure fact, as if fallible subjects were not involved in its production (Dean 2012: 14). The problem that underpins these claims is threefold; first, the structures of knowledge are sustained by political practices and forms of hegemony and supremacy; second, every individual expert is a terse relationship between their expertise and subjective fallibility; and third, the researchers themselves are sustained by the authority conferred through their disavowal of subjectivity. Coming to terms with the role of ignorance in any assessment of knowledge means recognising that the individual academic's relationship to knowledge is in a way, itself inherently irrational. Scientific objectivity is sustained by its perverse and excessive reminder—this is typified by Charles W. Mills' racial critique of liberalism, whereby morally sensible and ethical theorists can justify slavery, racism, and apartheid with reference to necessity, tradition, or really existing conditions (Mills 2017). Thus, ignorance in the enlightenment liberal framing is a consequence of a lack of "education", yet when intersecting with issues of race or vaccine hesitancy, ignorance is a mechanism of power, an explicit way in which hierarchy manifests normalcy and its challenges.

Race and Ignorance

This chapter points toward the insights of Mills "epistemology of ignorance" to frame ignorance not simply as the absence of information, a reflection of hierarchal structures, and ingroup thinking based on race. Mills outlines this through a historicisation of racialised ignorance as a social construct, specifically in the mechanism of Whiteness in the translation from universalised enlightenment principles into 19th- and 20th-century thinking. Following Du Bois' *The Souls of White Folk*, the emergence of the race was a strategy to overcome the failure of religion to distinguish between the civilised and uncivilised (Du Bois 1910: 932). In other words, as outgroups increasingly adopted Western (and American) Christianity, it became increasingly impossible to exclude them from the public, necessitating race as construction of new outgroup segregation. Mills outlines ten different ways that ignorance and race intersect, but in terms of Covid-19, "not knowing" can be seen as the active *erasure* of information through dominant societal norms structured by historical White supremacy (Mills 2007: 21). The Canadian residential school system exemplifies how liberal education explicitly was strategised to "kill the Indian in the child" to supplant indigenous knowledge with authorised thought (Starblanket 2018). As Garner argues, one of the themes that emerge from fieldwork with white people is "their general unease at thinking of themselves as white *per se*" or how addressing Whiteness makes people "defensive about their social location" (Garner 2007: 36). The political corollary is the persistent debates about whether or not political statements are "racist", deflecting onto whether or not explicit references to race are necessary for opinions to be racist. As Haney-Lopez has argued, the long history of coded racial appeals has been a way to utilise normativity about permissive speech to continue to propagate racist ideas (Haney-López 2015). The persistent naming conventions about the origins of Covid-19 and its variants reflect how liberal scientific authority is deployed by experts to resist efforts by media members and politicians to frame the source of the pandemic as irrelevant. The danger of these strategies is that they can inadvertently replicate George Wallace's use of "non-racial" language as an explicit strategy to perpetuate White supremacist ideals by making sure to "never mention race" (Haney-López 2015: 22). The study of dog-whistle politics has focused on the "multivocal" communicative aspects of such speech, the coded nature of words, and the persuasiveness of the appeals (Albertson 2015). This approach replicates the normalcy of language and frames prejudice in terms of majoritarian ingroup sensibilities (the need to educate the public) rather than the deployment of irrationality and authoritarianism as political ignorance as active erasure (Kraus et al. 2019). Moreover, Mills frames the issue of White ignorance as an "inverted epistemology", a cognitive science issue framed in terms of wilful blindness or intentional lack of knowledge (Bailey 2007). Liberal education is inherently political and needs to be framed regarding the ingroup biases against outgroup resistance to liberal education. In the American case, politicised ignorance is integral to white supremacy, as liberal tolerance (the cruel optimism of progress) is eroded by the failures to address resurgent or new forms of racial prejudice and organisation. A contemporary expression of "not-knowing" in the context of the death of George Floyd and the subsequent Covid-19 protests is the *New York Times* 1619 project detailing the ongoing legacies of American slavery and White supremacy in contemporary American society. The effort was hastily responded to by the Trump administration's 1776 Report (since redacted by the Biden administration), as an effort to defend the abstract idealism of liberalism through defence of individualism against the critiques of American systemic racism. The role of education in replacing information with dominant values is central to Trump's claims, presenting a framing of American liberalism as universal and "authentic" (Arnn et al. 2021). The 1776 report's framing of education as "liberation from ignorance and confusion, from prejudice and delusion, and from untamed passion and fanciful hopes that degrade and destroy us as civilized persons", is in this sense, a very specific defence of both liberal universalism and enlightenment principles (Arnn et al. 2021: 37). Trump's report framed ignorance explicitly in terms of political strategies of "not knowing" or "the ignorance of not realizing what they lack" and the support for abstract universal liberal ideals against "skills-based, job oriented training" (Arnn et al. 2021: 35). Despite the report being widely reviled (for its lack of sources, citations and academic historical authors), Trump's report reinforces the ingroup redemptive ideals of liberalism, albeit in a dystopian framework of "patriotic education" (Flaherty 2021). In a much more nuanced and detailed way, Mills argues for the defence of liberalism by arguing that the egalitarian underpinnings of liberalism are redeemable alongside its dominant and globally hegemonic project (as a kind of fishbowl optimism) (Mills 2017: 14). So as he argues, "liberalism in general (both nationally and internationally) has been shaped by race, but that does not preclude reclaiming it" (Mills 2017: 26). The whitewashing of history, political thought and liberal ideals is addressed by foregrounding the role of white ignorance as a material condition of the contemporary world as inherently normative (Mills 2017: 59).

Racism, capitalism, and policies of neoliberalism provide the framework to understand how political ignorance frames responses to Covid-19. This is to follow DuBois' famous framing of whiteness as a "public and psychological wage" given to poor labourers to distinguish themselves from other workers through "public deference and titles of courtesy" while directing the opposite at racialised (Black) bodies (Du Bois 1998: 700–701). Authoritarian leaders' capacity to encourage refusal of Covid-19 vaccinations by privileged group draws on the irrationalism of ingroup identity and the rejection of outgroup values (in the myriad and continually changing anti-vaccine narratives). Moreover, this racialised logic of privilege reinforces the inherent legacies of racism, the Tuskegee experiments and the lower Social Determinants of Heath of marginalised and racialised communities. This cycle perpetuates the pandemic, which disproportionately impacts minority communities and the unequal and discriminatory policies of opportunity, housing and access to health care that are also highly gendered along racial lines (Hooijer et al. 2021). The racialised ignorance of the pandemic exemplifies Cedric J. Robinson's framing of racial capitalism, or how the whitewashing of the origins of enlightenment thought continues in the ignorance deployed as a strategy of capitalist accumulation at the expense of marginalised lives (Robinson 2021: 14. As Shilliam has argued, "there is no politics of class that is not already racialized" which is to challenge the idea that we can think about political ignorance outside of identity issues (Shilliam 2018). Race thinking allows us to recognise the contingent and specific dynamics that allow claims about Whiteness, Blackness and anti-Black racism to emerge (Reed 2013). The deployment of race is a hierarchical framing of contingent arbitrary claims, and needs to be understood politically; therefore, foregrounding ignorance as political helps dispossess the idea of education as an inherent good. As discussed above, principles of science have a key role to play in the construction of ignorance. As a form of racism, Nazi anti-Semitic arguments tried to establish an objective foundation for their beliefs through the mechanisms of science and modernity to establish a reality that did not exist. As Mills and Garner, and others have outlined, Whiteness is axiomatic in the difference between the Black, Indigenous and Jewish, Italian, Irish, and European immigrant experiences, namely that some groups had the option of attaining Whiteness (ingroup identification) that was restricted to other groups (Garner 2007: 100; Mills 2009: 276). The informal or meta-agreements that construct shifting racial hierarchies specify "phenotypical/genealogical/cultural" and other criteria as "white" with "non-whites" as inferior moral in status (Mills 1999: 11). This option of "passing" was therefore part of the postwar economic prosperity, combined with the grouping of Jews with the categories of Whites in the GI Bill of Rights and the Federal Housing Authority, whereas effectively continuing to exclude Black veterans from housing (Garner 2007: 100–101). How non-Whites (and indigenous groups in particular) are excluded from the categories of society, modernity and enlightenment stem directly from the material hierarchies of contemporary capitalism, which are framed through wilful or clandestine ignorance. As Sloterdijk has argued, modernity altered the social economy of intelligence, whereby stupidity can no longer be innocent, as it is linked to the problems of deception and complexity (Sloterdijk 1987: 493). This is why Kapur characterises progressive liberalism as "cruel optimism", because it denies the role of outgroup marginalisation by valorising ingroup successes exemplifying the new tensions between the vaccinated and the unvaccinated (Kapur 2020: 3). Progress, enlightenment and growth were supposed to overcome the idea of ignorance, a belief that continues to pervade liberal responses to racism today. As the first 25 weeks of the Covid-19 pandemic overturned 25 years of Western aid and progress, this cruel optimism will continue to refrain from the liberal response to ongoing political ignorance (Gates and Gates 2020).

Conclusion

This chapter has explored the role of ignorance in the Covid-19 pandemic and how contemporary liberalism has largely denied the deep complexities of its reign in the face of authoritarian, irrational and racist tendencies. The depoliticisation of government regulation in neoliberal advocacy by Silicon Valley contributed to the priming of vaccine hesitancy and was a largely unanticipated vector of pandemic response. The liberal conflation of information, expertise, and authority as scientific were unable to address the way that social media design maximised market influence, fads and viral content through the ideal of freedom of speech. Despite evidence that the platforms were capable and had previously addressed public health concerns directly and with intent, the confluence of abstract liberal values and privatised decision-making by technology firms using proprietary justifications played a key role in the unfolding of the pandemic and anti-vaccination campaigns. What Adorno long ago identified as ingroup opposition to liberal reason emerged in response to the pandemic as the deployment of political ignorance as a hierarchal strategy of racism, authoritarianism, and White supremacy. Beginning with Adorno's provocation about the persistence of irrationalism and racism in contemporary society, this chapter frames ignorance under ingroup or "fishbowl" liberalism as unable to address the inequalities of racialised capitalism. Ignorance studies help us frame the erasure of knowledge as a specific racialised strategy of supremacy and explain how the liberal logic of education as transmitted information is inherently linked to ingroup and outgroup political dynamics. The cruel optimism of liberalism now appears in the distinction between the vaccinated and unvaccinated, as the manifest racialised inequalities under capitalism are reflected in the global pandemic response.

4

COVID-19

Decarbonisation Under Duress

Adam Lucas

Introduction

There is growing international awareness that the window of opportunity is rapidly closing to stabilise greenhouse gas (GHG) emissions and avoid catastrophic changes to the global climate before the end of this century (Lucas 2020). The lack of progress in reducing anthropogenic emissions over the last three decades by most developed and developing countries has been a major focus of attention before, during and after the COP 26 negotiations in Glasgow in November 2021. A common refrain throughout this period has been the lack of ambition of most nation states' commitments to decarbonisation. One of the overriding messages from multiple sources has been that humanity's continued reliance on fossil fuels as its primary energy source is driving the global climate toward disaster (e.g. Hansen et al. 2011; DiMuzio 2012; Anderson & Bows-Larkin 2013; Delina 2016; Lucas 2020a; Climate Council 2021; cf. IPCC 2018; IPCC 2021). The terrible irony for humanity and the billions of other living beings with which we share this planet is that it is that very reliance that has empowered the ruling elites and corporations that have benefited most from this situation to delay taking action and systematically undermine efforts to do so.

According to Climate Action Tracker (2021), "current policies presently in place around the world are projected to result in about 2.7 °C warming above pre-industrial levels." If Nationally Determined Contributions (NDCs) are implemented, average global atmospheric surface temperatures will likely rise by 2.4 °C above preindustrial levels by the end of this century. If binding long-term net-zero targets are actually met there is a 66 per cent or greater chance of limiting warming below 2.3 °C (Climate Action Tracker 2021). Whether or not we agree with the goal of net-zero emissions, these commitments remain inadequate to return the climate to a "safe operating space for humanity" (Rockström et al. 2009),

DOI: 10.4324/9781003250432-6

with an ambition gap for 2030 of 19 to 23 Gigatons of CO_2 (Climate Action Tracker 2021). The fact that major fossil fuel-producing and financing nations and corporations continue to approve the expansion of oil, coal and gas production demonstrates their commitments to achieve net-zero emissions are a sham (Daley et al. 2021; Diski 2021; Disterhoft 2021; Morton & Pridham 2021).

Although Article 2 of the United Nations Framework Convention on Climate Change sets binding obligations on nation states to reduce their GHG emissions to achieve "the stabilization of GHG concentrations in the atmosphere at a level that would prevent dangerous anthropogenic interference with the climate system" (UNFCCC 1992), there is abundant evidence from multiple research fields that some forms of dangerous anthropogenic interference have already been happening for at least a decade (Anderson et al. 2008; Barnosky et al. 2012; Betts et al. 2011; Lenton 2011; Pittock 2006; Schneider 2009: Summarised in Lucas 2020). These changes have already created enormous social and economic hardship for millions of people in the worst-affected regions due to extreme weather events. In 2020 alone, more than 30 mn people were displaced due to more than 1,770 weather-related events (Aguilar Garcia et al. 2021). Those numbers will rise to the hundreds of millions over the next several decades unless urgent and radical action is taken to reduce anthropogenic emissions and draw carbon from the atmosphere (Kulp and Strauss 2019; Xu and Ramanathan 2017; cf. New et al. 2011; Rigaud et al. 2018).

Given that the fossil fuel industry remains primarily responsible for driving climate disruption, the Covid-19 pandemic arguably provides a useful lens through which to observe how fossil-fuelled interests have subsequently responded to the more ambitious demands recently made of them (Kenner and Heede 2021). It has been widely reported that one of the few positive consequences of the pandemic was a significant (but short-lived) downturn in fossil fuel use due to national and regional governments imposing comprehensive travel restrictions in 2020 to limit the spread of the virus. The pandemic resulted in a 6.4 per cent to 7 per cent reduction in CO_2 emissions during 2020 of 2.3 to 2.4 bn tons (Garthwaite 2021). Compared with 2019 figures, France saw the largest drop by country, at 15 per cent, while the United States and the United Kingdom were both down 13 per cent (Harvey 2020; Tollefsen 2021). By industry sector, the largest reduction was in global aviation emissions, which reduced by 48 per cent (Tollefsen 2021). However, global emissions of CO_2 surged again in 2021, with industrial emissions returning close to their pre-pandemic levels, with a 4.9 per cent increase over 2020. CO2 emissions from burning fossil fuels in 2021 are set to rise in every country and region in the world compared to 2020 (Garthwaite 2021).

In September 2020, it was estimated that the global economic downturn resulting from COVID would reduce global GDP by 4.4 per cent (UN News 2020). Comparing the extent of this downturn to the estimated cost of taking significant global action to prevent climate disruption by one prominent contemporary economist provides an informative comparative yardstick. The U.S. economist, William Nordhaus has argued that between 1 per cent and 2 per cent of world income would be required to be dedicated to climate mitigation measures to achieve the 2 °C target, constituting between 5 per cent and 9 per cent of global GDP (Nordhaus 2013). Assuming Nordhaus' arguably optimistic assessment is correct (cf. Bichler and Nitzan 2018; Stern 2006: xv), the world would have to sustain *for several decades* a similar level of expenditure on zero-carbon infrastructure and adaptation measures to the socioeconomic downturn we saw in 2020 to have any hope of achieving the 2 °C target, let alone the 1.5 °C target. However, unlike the major downturn that has resulted from COVID, which has generated historic levels of unemployment and the further concentration of wealth in the hands of a tiny global elite (see Popcevski this volume), the kinds of expenditure required to avert catastrophic climate change will at the very least necessitate harnessing all the wealth that has been pillaged from nation-states since the early 1970s by this same global elite. In 2016, economist and lawyer James S. Henry estimated that between US$24 tn and US$36 tn was sitting idly in tax havens around the world (Henry 2016). The intervening 5 years of corporate plunder clearly indicate the total sum is now considerably higher. Although this growing stock of unproductive capital could and should be used to decarbonise our societies, such an approach is fundamentally antithetical to the economic thinking espoused by Nordhaus, who assumes that the world can harness some form of "green growth" to mitigate and adapt to any of the adverse consequences of anthropogenic forcing of the climate based on what might generously be described as a "heroic" discount rate (cf. Bichler and Nitzan 2021).

In this chapter, I will outline the dominant role of fossil fuels in forcing climate disruption, and how the financial and regulatory elites of those countries and corporations that have benefited the most from the production and consumption of fossil fuels continue to act as major obstacles to decarbonisation.[1] Given that most of our countries continue to be ruled by the very same fossil-fuelled regulatory, financial and military elites that have brought us to this impasse, I will then demonstrate through a brief overview of current commitments to expanded fossil fuel production and dependent infrastructure in the United States, the United Kingdom, and Australia, that while these elites may now be publicly acknowledging the need to phase out fossil fuel use by 2050, they continue to support policies and forms of investment and development that will hasten climate catastrophe. The flurry of commitments from both developed and developing countries to net-zero emissions by 2050 both before and during COP26 will remain hollow until those same countries introduce, implement and enforce policies and actions that radically reduce their own emissions and those of other countries that lack the wealth and resources to do so on their own. It will also require the provision of adequate levels of finance to research and develop safe techniques for drawing CO_2 from the atmosphere and oceans. As I will attempt to demonstrate, an important contribution to providing the finances required to make a sustainable energy transition and mitigate the worst consequences of climate disruption will involve the repatriation of the vast sums of wealth that have been pillaged from our countries since the early 1970s by a tiny cadre of multi-millionaires and billionaires. This will, in turn, require the repeated exposure of the financial, legal and accountancy firms that continue to enable such activities and the political parties that have empowered these firms to embed themselves in multiple forms of contemporary governance.

Fossil Fuels, Finance and Decarbonisation

It is a historical fact that fossil-fuelled production systems have colonised virtually every corner of the earth over the last two hundred years and continue to dominate the decision-making processes of political, military, business, and industrial elites throughout the world (Mitchell 2009, 2013; DiMuzio 2015; Malm et al. 2021). The continued dominance of fossil fuels throughout the world's energy systems was not only instrumental in creating the current civilisational order, but it also poses an existential threat to the very civilisation it helped to create as the result of its primary role in contributing to anthropogenic forcing of the climate (DiMuzio 2012; Malm 2015). Fossil energy sources have generated around 60 per cent of historic GHG emissions (Pittock 2005; IPCC 2007; Heede 2014), and more than 65 per cent of current anthropogenic emissions (UNEP 2020). Averaged over the decade from 2007 to 2016, 91 per cent of global CO_2 emissions were from extracting, transporting, and burning fossil fuels and the industrial activities they facilitate (Pidcock 2016).

Since the international community began to focus on the issue of dangerous anthropogenic interference (DAI) with the world climate in the early 1990s, it has become increasingly clear that powerful interests in the fossil fuel and resource extraction industries have been expending considerable time, effort and resources undermining the science of climate change. They have also actively opposed national and international efforts to reduce fossil fuel use and any attempt to promote more ecologically sustainable forms of production and consumption (Beder 2000; Frumhoff et al. 2015; Hamilton 2007; Jacques et al. 2008; Pearse 2007, 2009; Oreskes & Conway 2010; Supran & Oreskes 2017; 2017a). Dubbed the "climate change counter-movement" in the United States, there is clear evidence from the United States, Canada, and Australia that fossil-fuelled corporations and their allies in politics, business and associated industries have ramped up their efforts to sow the seeds of doubt and confusion concerning DAI as the body of evidence of their culpability for climate forcing grows (Dunlap et al. 2022).

Because the wealth and political power of global elites is largely dependent on the continuation of fossil-fuelled production, along with the exploitation of labour and the environment, which has enabled 30 years of activism to reduce that dependence and decarbonise our societies has met with every possible form of resistance and sabotage that it is possible to imagine (Lucas 2020a, 2021, 2022). However, as more of these strategies and tactics have been exposed by academics, investigative journalists and environmental and social justice advocates, growing public recognition of a direct causal link between fossil fuel use and global climate destabilisation is manifesting itself in more interventionist popular movements among schoolchildren (School Strikes4Climate), investors (fossil fuel divestment) and civil society activists (e.g. Extinction Rebellion, Insulate Britain, Stop Adani), causing some discomfort for the fossil fuel industry and its supporters (Ayling 2017; Ayling and Gunningham 2017; BBC News 2021; Bergman 2018; Boulianne et al. 2020; Catanzaro and Collin 2021; Cojoianu et al. 2021; Colvin 2020; Gunningham 2019; Hannon and Clarke 2021; McKnight 2020; Slaven and Heydon 2020; Thackeray et al. 2020; Westwell and Bunting 2020).

Although there has been a noticeable change over the last year or so in the public rhetoric concerning decarbonisation and net-zero emissions espoused by the international finance industry and major fossil fuel producing nations, they remain committed to the continued exploitation of fossil fuel resources (Kenner and Heede 2021). This is clearly revealed through the financial, policy and program commitments they have made over the last several years and continued to make before, during and after COP26.

Regarding the international finance and banking industries, it was recently revealed that 39 banks that signed up for inclusion in the Net-Zero Banking Alliance at COP26 provided a total of US$575 bn in loans and underwriting to the fossil fuel industry in 2020. The world's 60 largest banks provided US$ 3.1 tn in fossil fuel financing between 2016 and 2020, amounting to 82 per cent of total financing (Disterhoft 2021). Exxon-Mobil, one of the largest recipients of finance industry largesse, is continuing its exploration efforts for new reserves and has made no commitment to decrease its emissions by 2030 or cut back production in line with a 1.5 °C target. Exxon has also paid zero income tax on its hugely profitable gas projects in Australia. Both of Australia's major political parties have been complicit in enabling this situation to come about, and both have refused to make fossil fuel companies pay income taxes commensurate with their profit-taking (Lucas 2021).

As the world witnessed, to the dismay of millions during the COP26 negotiations, the largest producers and consumers of fossil fuels remain steadfastly committed to maintaining their central role in the energy mixes of our societies and continue to support their further expansion. The Australian delegation joined Saudi Arabia, India, China, Brazil, Russia and Mexico in blocking multilateral agreements regarding fossil fuel phase-out and further delayed what most reasonable people agree is an inevitable transition to renewable energy sources. In the month before COP26, the BBC revealed that Saudi Arabia, Japan, India and Australia were also among several countries that sought to water down the text of the next Intergovernmental Panel on Climate Change (IPCC) assessment report that urges the need to move rapidly away from fossil fuels (Rowlatt & Gerken 2021; IPCC 2021).

During COP 26, the same countries' climate negotiators made it abundantly clear that they are determined to protect the fossil-fuelled forms of development, which they continue to endorse openly. Their behaviour during COP 26 demonstrates that they are prepared to do whatever it takes to maintain the economic dominance of the fossil energy sector and the political power that its dominance ensures. The fossil fuel industry had the largest delegation at the climate summit, with 503 people with links to fossil fuel accredited to attend the summit, and 27 country delegations including fossil fuel lobbyists (McGrath 2021).

Even among those countries that supported net-zero targets by 2050, their governments and the political parties that have historically benefited from supporting the global hegemony of the fossil fuel industry continue to endorse its further expansion by approving gas and oil exploration and new infrastructure reliant on that expansion. A recent report by a consortium of NGOs led by the University of Sussex has revealed that although the United States has pledged to halve its emissions by 2030, it has committed US$20 bn in annual support to the fossil fuel industry (Daley et al. 2021). The United Kingdom hosted the COP26 talks but refused to support the Beyond Oil and Gas Alliance formed by Denmark and Costa Rica (Nasralla & Abnett 2021), while U.K. Export Finance has provided US$1 bn in support for a major gas project in Mozambique (Seabrook 2021). The U.K. government is also expected to approve the exploitation of the Cambo oil field in the North Sea which contains around 255 mn barrels of oil, while Canada has provided US$17 bn in public finance to three fossil fuel pipelines between 2018 and 2020, and Norway has granted in this year alone more than 60 new permits for fossil fuel production and access to 84 new exploration zones (Daley et al. 2021). Australia is currently considering the approval of more than 100 fossil fuel projects that will contribute 5 per cent of global industrial emissions should they go ahead (Morton & Pridham 2021).

Had all these entities been prepared to act in a more socially and environmentally responsible manner from the outset of international negotiations, most countries would arguably have made far more progress in their mitigation and adaptation efforts, and we would collectively be in a much less precarious situation today.

Table 4.1 records the top 20 GHG emitters in 2020 and the proportions of their electricity production by source, along with their contributions to global GHG emissions in 2017.

These countries collectively contribute more than 83 per cent of total global GHG emissions. China and the United States remain responsible for the largest proportion of these emissions, at 28 per cent and 14 per cent, respectively, with India responsible for around 7 per cent and Russia around 5 per cent. Most of the remaining 16 countries are responsible for around 1.5 per cent to 3 per cent of total emissions. Only five countries (Germany, Canada, Brazil, the United Kingdom and France) source less than half of their electricity from fossil fuels, although this obviously does not include their transport fuels or reflect their total energy consumption and consequent dependence on fossil fuels. Although half of these high-emitting countries have more than doubled the proportion of the electricity they derive from renewables over the last two decades, many of them did so from a very low base. Only two countries (Canada and Brazil) derive more than half their electricity from renewables, and only Germany, Brazil, Turkey, the United Kingdom and Italy saw any significant growth in the proportions of electricity derived from renewables over the same period. Iran, Indonesia, Saudi Arabia and South Africa remain laggards, with Saudi Arabia sourcing almost none of its electricity from renewables, despite having the abundant potential to do so and enormous reserves of capital to make a sustainable energy transition.

TABLE 4.1 Top 20 GHG emitters and their electricity production by source, 2020 (per cent of total)

	Country	Fossil Fuels	Nuclear	Renewables	2017 contribution to GHG emissions (Mt)
1.	China	66.17	4.80	29.02	9,300
2.	United States	60.05	19.50	20.44	4,800
3.	India	74.46	3.32	22.22	2,200
4.	Russian	59.16	19.74	21.10	1,500
5.	Japan	69.14	4.57	26.29	1,100
6.	Iran	91.52	1.75	6.73	567.1
7.	Germany	43.77	11.33	44.90	718.8
8.	Indonesia	83.05	0.00	16.95	496.4
9.	South Korea	65.78	28.56	5.66	600
10.	Saudi Arabia	99.96	0.00	0.04	532.2
11.	Canada	16.64	14.84	68.52	547.8
12.	South Africa	88.58	5.17	6.25	421.7
13.	Brazil	13.60	2.17	84.23	427.6
14.	Mexico	75.22	3.74	21.03	446
15.	Australia	75.13	0.00	24.87	384.6
16.	Turkey	56.89	0.00	43.11	378.6
17.	United Kingdom	40.74	16.96	42.30	358.7
18.	Italy	56.83	0.00	43.17	321.5
19.	France	9.47	67.21	23.32	306.1
20.	Poland	83.09	0.00	16.91	305.8

Source: Data from www.sbs.com.au/news/interactive-fossil-fuels-vs-renewables-where-the-world-s-top-20-emitters-stand/7f050390-ddbf-414b-bd29-299757d42d6d; https://worldpopulationreview.com/country-rankings/greenhouse-gas-emissions-by-country.

Many observers from a wide range of backgrounds have noted that although ruling elites have generally been reluctant to pay anything but lip service to the science of climate change, they have been far more willing to act on scientific advice concerning COVID. Although COVID has certainly provided important lessons about the most appropriate and effective responses to one of the biggest socioeconomic shocks in a century or more, the lesson yet to be widely acknowledged is the extent to which fossil-fuelled economies are vulnerable to disruption from naturally-occurring pathogens that have been displaced and dispersed by fossil-fuelled forms of unsustainable development (Malm 2020).

Although it may be a truism that planetary physics, chemistry and biology are immune to the conservative fiscal preferences and climate war rhetoric of those who oppose radical climate action, denial of the reality of the earth's climatic past will not prevent those outcomes for which we are, yet, unprepared. The hard lessons of COVID offer the world leaders an opportunity to hit a "reset" on deep decarbonisation. Although the majority of climate scientists agree that we no longer have the luxury of making modest, incremental changes to our energy and governance systems over many decades, they also argue that we almost certainly do have sufficient time to avert the worst possible consequences if we increase the intensity and geographical extent of our current efforts (IPCC 2018, 2021; Xu and Ramanathan 2017).

The Scientific Rationale for Deep Decarbonisation

It is now widely accepted within and outside the climate science community that if we want to return the climate to a "safe operating space for humanity" (Rockström et al. 2009), anthropogenic contributions to GHGs in the atmosphere and oceans will have to be completely removed by the middle of the century ("decarbonisation"), and CO_2 levels in the atmosphere and oceans returned to preindustrial levels through a variety of biological and artificial techniques by the end of the century ("sequestration") (Hansen et al. 2011; Xu & Ramanathan 2017). The fundamental questions, which arise from this widespread consensus are, how do we achieve these twin goals after 30 years of denial, indecision and obstruction by powerful nation states and those dominant corporations within those nations that remain committed to fossil-fuelled development? And how do we ensure that the new processes we put in place will be socially and environmentally just, transparent and democratically accountable? Although these questions assume a commitment to values that may not be shared by all national governments, abandoning these Enlightenment values means also abandoning any commitment to scientific methodologies and reasoned argument.

Given the Paris Agreement endorses the principle that 60–90 per cent of remaining fossil fuel reserves constitute "unburnable carbon", the rationale for complete decarbonisation of the global energy sector remains incontrovertible (Campanale et al. 2011; Leaton, 2012; Meinshausen et al., 2009; IPCC 2021; Steffen & Rice 2015). The commitments contained in the Paris Agreement require national governments to make emission reductions consistent with maintaining global average surface temperatures at no more than 2 °C above preindustrial levels by 2100. Those commitments include a "preferred ambition" of 1.5 °C, an ambition that became the central focus of the COP 26 negotiations in Glasgow. However, several recent studies indicate that there is now a high probability of mean global surface temperatures rising by 1.5 °C above preindustrial levels between the late 2020s (Henley & King 2017; cf. Johnston 2017) and the early 2050s (Gabbatiss 2018; Mauritsen & Pincus 2017). There is also a growing probability that mean global temperatures will rise between 2 °C and 3 °C above preindustrial levels by 2060 (cf. Stern, 2006: vi). The former finding was recently confirmed by the IPCC in its 2018 report with a high rate of confidence (IPCC 2018: 6) and again in 2020 by the World Meteorological Organization (WMO 2020).

The logic of the global carbon budget implies that to have a 50 per cent chance of maintaining the 2 °C goal, developed countries would have had to begin emission reductions in the order of 8 per cent to 10 per cent per year as of 2013, which they did not do. In 2011, James Hansen and colleagues warned that if global emission reductions were delayed until 2020, the required rate would be 15 per cent per year. Clearly, the levels of emission reduction required to maintain a 1.5 °C target are much higher. More disturbing is the growing body of evidence indicating that even if global atmospheric surface temperatures can be sustained at 1.5 °C above preindustrial levels by the end of the century, this will not stabilise the global climate over the medium to longer term. A recent paper by climate scientists Xu and Ramanathan (2017) concludes that a continuation of business-as-usual (BAU) has a higher than 50 per cent chance of generating more dangerous climatic changes within three decades, i.e. more than 1.5 °C above preindustrial levels, and that there is a 5 per cent probability that warming along this pathway will become catastrophic by 2050. They cite evidence from the Eemian period of 130,000 years ago, which suggests that sustained warming of 1.5 °C or more over centuries can cause catastrophic sea level rise of between 6 and 9 metres (Xu & Ramanathan 2017: 10318; cf. Hansen et al. 2007; Lucas 2020).

During a recent public presentation in the lead-up to COP26, climate scientist Will Steffen pointed out that with regard to about global emissions, "when you look at the so-called paleo record … there is only one other time in the 4.5-billion-year history of earth that you can see a rise this fast". He went on to explain that "Since 1970, the global average temperature has risen at a rate about 200 times the background rate over the past 7,000 years" (Climate Council 2021). Indeed, the last time in earth's history that atmospheric burdens of GHG emissions were at their current levels was during the Middle Miocene 14–16 mn years ago when average global surface temperatures were 3 to 6 °C higher and sea levels were 25 to 40 metres higher than at present (Tripati et al. 2009; cf. Lucas 2020).

The shrill claims of climate confusionists about the coming economic Armageddon if we were to switch our energy sources to renewables sound increasingly hollow in this context. Nevertheless, the lack of progress to date in confronting industrial civilisation's dependence on fossil fuels has ensured that radical social change will confront humanity over the coming decades, whether that change be driven by the goal of radical emission reduction, or by the unintended outcomes of radical climate destabilisation (Anderson & Bows 2013; Delina 2016; Harvey 2016; Matthews & Caldeira 2008). In Australia, average surface temperatures have already increased by about 1.4 °C since 1910 (IPCC 2021; cf. Morton & Readfearn 2021), yet, the Australian Government under the Coalition of the Liberal and National parties remains committed to expanding its fossil export trade. My recent research into the Federal Coalition's intransigence on this issue demonstrates that it has been captured by the fossil fuel industry in much the same way as conservative political parties in Canada and the United States (Lucas 2021, 2022; cf. Ali 2022; Carroll et al. 2022; Doreian and Mrvar 2022).

According to Climate Action Tracker, the only countries worldwide that have introduced policies that are almost sufficient to achieve the 1.5 °C ambition are Costa Rica, Ethiopia, Gambia, Kenya, Morocco, Nepal, Nigeria and the United Kingdom, all of which could achieve it by making moderate improvements to current policies and commitments (Climate Action Tracker 2021a). In other words, most countries have failed to introduce or enforce policies to enable them to achieve the level of reductions required to avoid climate catastrophe. Fifteen countries were rated "highly insufficient" and six others "critically insufficient", the latter including Iran, Russia, Singapore, Thailand, Turkey and Vietnam.

Although the political leaders of many countries voiced their commitment to net-zero emissions by 2050, during the recent international climate negotiations in Glasgow, most of them have not put in place any firm plans to achieve that goal. As explained in the previous section, many key players continue to either approve or tacitly support projects and financing that further expands fossil fuel production and infrastructure developments contributing to higher burdens of GHGs in the atmosphere and further global temperature increases.

Mainstream Political Discourse: The Second Major Obstacle to Decarbonisation

In the wake of the rolling international financial crisis, which began in late 2008, mainstream political discourse concerning action to avert DAI with the Earth's climate has tended to polarise around two seemingly antithetical positions. The first is focused on implementing policies and programs aimed at securing nation-states and their populations from the medium- to long-term threats posed by DAI. The second involves efforts to demonise any policies or programs that threaten short-term economic growth and the continuation of a slightly modified BAU. The former position tends to be endorsed by socialist, social democratic and other leftist and broadly progressive governments, whereas the latter tends to be espoused by neoliberal, neoconservative, and right populist governments (cf. Christoff 2013; McDonald 2015). Although there clearly are differences in the political rhetoric associated with these two positions, they are not antithetical. We have only to look at the behaviour of many of the so-called "centre-left" political parties, such as the Australian Labour Party under Anthony Albanese and British Labour under Keir Starmer, to see how the two positions can be deployed strategically for different occasions and audiences.

The strategic deployment of these two positions is particularly evident in the policy responses of centre-left and centre-right parties to radical improvements in the cost and reliability of renewable energy and storage. Numerous studies over the last 15 years have demonstrated that, for both GHG emissions and the total life cycles of the technologies concerned, solar and wind technologies are con-siderably less environmentally harmful than fossil fuel alternatives or the nuclear option (Fthenakis et al. 2007; Hertwich et al. 2015; Pehl et al. 2017; Weisser 2007).[2] Although the assumptions and system boundaries informing these studies clearly affect their findings (Jones et al. 2017), the relative superiority of solar and wind as the most economically and environmentally sustainable forms of renewable energy technology (RET) has nevertheless been demonstrated in many jurisdictions for at least 5 years (Belot 2017; Christoff 2016; Johnstone et al. 2017; Parkinson 2018). In both developed and developing countries, new-build RET systems are now considerably cheaper than new-build coal, gas, or nuclear alternatives, and will soon also be true in more countries even when storage is considered. Indeed, it is now the case in the United States, China and elsewhere that established coal and gas plants are being outbid on competitive energy markets in which the merit order effect frequently favours wind and solar on price, even when the capital expenditure costs of established fossil fuel plants have been amortised (Barnard 2021; Goldenberg and Dyson 2018; Leitch and Willacy 2020; Morris 2017).

In the case of developing countries, RETs offer the real possibility of "leapfrogging" over fossil-fuel-based economic development, an insight which has been recognised by governments in India, Africa and several Pacific Island nations. Nevertheless, although many cities, municipal councils, regions and medium-sized developed and developing countries have committed to completely decarbonise their energy systems by 2050 or earlier, recent commitments by major developed and developing countries to net-zero emissions do not constitute commitments to complete decarbonisation.

A distinct reluctance to accept the relevant "market signals" concerning the increasing costs of fossil-fuelled energy provision and decreasing costs of renewables has been most evident in those developed countries where neoliberal rhetoric concerning the supposed superiority of "free markets" to deliver improved social and economic outcomes has been the most politically successful and influential. It is no coincidence that they are all Anglophone countries with abundant fossil fuel resources where so-called "climate skepticism" has flourished among their political, business and industrial elites, i.e. the United States, Canada and Australia (Ali 2022; Carroll et al. 2022; Doreian and Mrvar 2022; Lucas 2021, 2022).

Directly contrary to the claims of neoliberalism, which asserts that unfettered markets enable competition between firms to determine which enterprises will set the lowest prices based on their market performance and efficiency, the reality is that monopolistic control of major international markets has become the norm (Birch 2015; Hertel-Fernandez 2019; Lindsey & Teles 2017). Therefore, it would seem that neoliberal rhetoric is only deployed when it supports those political and economic goals which the relevant parties deem to be politically useful in supporting a continuation of the status quo and the systematic undermining of democratic norms.

Here, it is useful to consult the work of Jonathan Nitzan and Shimshon Bichler who have argued that the main goal of capitalist enterprises is not simply profit-making, but differential accumulation. In other words, corporations attempt to accumulate capital at a higher rate of return than their competitors to ultimately eliminate them or absorb them through corporate takeovers (2009: 334ff). The ultimate aim of corporations is to create vertically and horizontally integrated companies which span geographical and physical levels of scale, i.e. regions, nations and continents (Nitzan and Bichler 2009). It should, therefore, be clear that those public and private corporations which dominate the energy sector—being amongst the most highly capitalised, and therefore, some of the most politically and economically powerful companies in the world—have an extremely strong incentive to ensure that their market dominance remains intact for as long as possible (DiMuzio 2015; Lucas 2021). Neoliberal rhetoric is simply a mask for the continued dominance of these monopolistic (more precisely oligopolistic) interests.

As the warnings from climate scientists concerning the dangers of human forcing on the global climate system become more urgent, more certain, and more pointedly fixated on decarbonising the world's energy systems, the rhetoric of political, business and industry leaders in most countries now acknowledges the urgency to act but continues to endorse the very activities that have led us to the current impasse. We regularly hear them and their spokespeople mouthing platitudes about their commitment to reducing emissions. Yet, their actions and behaviour indicate to the contrary, an ongoing commitment to extracting and burning fossil fuels at a growing rate, supposedly to generate more "economic growth". Nor does it seem to matter how precipitously the costs of renewable energy decrease and its reliability increases year after year. Our leaders remain committed to continuing to invest heavily in fossil fuel infrastructure and the future that it entails. This includes the allocation of explicit price subsidies and the implicit environmental, health and tax subsidies (a.k.a. "externalities" in neoclassical economics) that arise from fossil fuel use, which were estimated by the International Monetary fund at US\$5.9 tn in 2020. Considering that the International Energy Agency's net-zero roadmap estimates that US\$5 tn will need to be spent annually by 2030 to put the world on the pathway to a safe climate, the fact that the annual costs of fossil fuel use to society and the environment already exceed this amount should be receiving far more public attention (Carrington 2021). Unwilling and perhaps unable to confront the fact that the kinds of futures they continue to endorse, involves the further immiseration of billions of people over the coming decades and the destruction of vast swathes of infrastructure and biodiversity, so long as fossil-fuelled political, business, industrial and military elites can maintain the continuation of a slightly modified business- and politics-as-usual and stay on top of the growing chaos their actions are generating, they are more than happy to keep on keeping on.

Of course, openly admitting that this is what they are doing is not permissible, even though the evidence is clear. Investing in fossil fuels is more profitable than investing in renewables, at least in the short term (Di Muzio 2011; Hager 2021). For as long as financial markets continue to over-value fossil fuel revenue-generating assets without having to factor in any of their "negative externalities" or the financial risks they pose to investors, they will continue to attract significant investment from those institutions and individuals who are not just privileging profit over principles, but profit over pragmatism. They understand that if these trends continue, their ability to make profits will decline even more quickly than the billions of livelihoods they are undermining as the social, economic, and environmental effects of climate disruption and global heating become more and more severe. Differential accumulation can only be maintained in this situation by restricting new market entrants, strangling innovation, preventing competition and colonising all forms of goods and service provision, including health, education and welfare (cf. De Loecker et al. 2020; MacLean 2017; Mayer 2017).

We thus face several seemingly intractable, interconnected obstacles to change (see the conclusion, this volume). First, is the ongoing duplicity of the fossil fuel and other major polluting industries and their billionaire enablers who publicly express their commitment to reducing emissions but privately undermine policy and legislation that could hasten that process through overt and covert means at their disposal (Ali 2022; Brulle 2014; Brulle et al. 2012; Carroll et al. 2018; Carroll et al. 2022; Doreian and Mrvar 2022; Farrell 2015, 2016, 2019). Second, is the ongoing failure of the finance sector to factor into ratings and valuations of companies the climate risks they face. Third, is that the major political parties in most countries remain beholden to the corporate donors who finance their increasingly expensive election campaigns and the post-political careers of their elected functionaries (Brulle 2018; Lucas 2021, 2022; Taft 2018).

The Looting of National Economies by Global Elites and Why Tax Havens Should be Raided to Finance Global Decarbonisation

The toxic influence of global corporations in contemporary political discourse and practice is, in fact, symptomatic of much wider and deeper problems with current forms of governance across the political spectrum. Although the COVID pandemic has been the most significant historical driver of GHG reductions following decades of policy failure by most world governments, it has also witnessed one of the most significant transfers of wealth to global elites in world history (see Popcevski this volume). During the first year of the pandemic, the world's 10 richest men acquired an additional US$540 bn in personal wealth. At the end of 2020, global billionaires' wealth sat at US$12 tn, eight times Australia's annual GDP (Oxfam International 2021). The world's super-rich now hold the greatest concentration of wealth since the Gilded Age at the turn of the 20th century. Yet, none of this accumulation of wealth would have been possible without the continued existence of a global financial system rooted in the exploitation of the vast majority of people and the environment a financial system that is utterly dependent on the continued domination of fossil fuels in the global energy mix.

These institutionalised forms of global exploitation, that the late German sociologist Ulrich Beck called "organized irresponsibility", have undoubtedly contributed to the rise of populist movements throughout the world (Beck 2010). Although many people in putatively liberal democracies are conscious of being given a raw deal by the mainstream political parties that govern them, they are poorly served by a corporatised mainstream media that generally fails to expose the extent to which transnational corporations and national and regional oligopolies; routinely ensure that any legislation which threatens their incumbency is diluted, opposed and defeated (Bichler and Nitzan 2017; Gilens and Page 2014; Hertel-Fernandez 2019;

Lindsey & Teles 2017; MacLean 2017; Mayer 2017; Murray and Frijters 2017).The political power of the fossil fuel industry in Australia, Canada and the United States is emblematic of the ability of dominant capital to shape whole polities and their legislative apparatuses but is rarely subjected to any sustained scrutiny by the so-called "fourth estate" (Ali 2022; Brulle 2014, 2018; Carroll et al. 2022; Farrell 2015, 2016; Lucas 2021, 2022; Taft 2018). Organised irresponsibility is further enabled by important policy decisions being contracted out to global consultancy firms, such as Deloitte, KPMG, Ernst and Young, PriceWaterhouseCoopers and McKinsey and Company, enabling the governments that employ them to further hollow out their own bureaucracies' policy expertise and hide behind multiple veils of secrecy (Anonymous 2019; De Luce and Salam 2021; Sguazzin and Bowker 2021; Turnbull 2021; West 2016, 2018, 2018a).

Attempts to hold elected officials and government bureaucracies to account for incompetence, maladministration, nepotism, malfeasance and other forms of illicit, illegitimate and corrupt behaviour via freedom of information (FOI), conflict of interest and whistle-blower provisions are now routinely met by incumbent governments and senior officials with contempt. A general culture of impunity has emerged in which it is now routine in many countries for governments to redact or withhold documents, which they deem embarrassing or potentially incriminating. The weakening of FOI laws and whistle-blower protections and the reduction of funding and resources to government oversight bodies has been an almost constant complaint among social and environmental justice advocates for almost a decade. The ways in which Julian Assange, Edward Snowden and other whistle-blowers and investigative journalists have been relentlessly persecuted and victimised in recent years clearly indicate that authoritarian forms of governance are on the rise.

It is a cruel irony of the COVID pandemic that already existing inequalities within and between the countries of the North and the South have been exacerbated, further entrenched and institutionalised as a rapacious global oligarchic elite has tightened its grip on power throughout the world with the support of our countries' political leaders. Although there is some historical evidence from past pandemics that mass deaths have ultimately contributed to greater equality (Gingerich and Vogler 2021; Scheidel 2017; Snowden 2019), the current pandemic has so far compounded them. The "vaccine apartheid" enabled by the United States and European governments that provided the public funds for the development of the same COVID vaccines that Big Pharma is now refusing to provide at a low cost for developing countries, is but one symptom of this destructive behaviour.

According to a report published in 2020 by the Tax Justice Network, Public Services International and the Global Alliance for Tax Justice, US\$427 bn in tax each year is lost to nation-states by international corporate tax abuse. The press release for the report states that "Lower-income countries lose more than half what they spend on public health every year to tax havens … OECD countries are collectively responsible for nearly half of all global tax losses." The report reveals that

TABLE 4.2 Developed countries primarily responsible for global tax losses

Jurisdiction	Responsible percentage of global tax loss	Annual tax loss (USD)
British Territory Cayman	16.5	<70 billion
United Kingdom	10	<42 billion
Netherlands	8.5	<36 billion
Luxembourg	6.5	<27 billion
United States	5.53	<23 billion
TOTALS	**47.03**	**<198 billion**

Source: Data from www.globaltaxjustice.org/en/latest/427-billion-lost-tax-havens-every-year.

US$245 bn is directly lost to corporate tax abuse by multinational corporations and US$182 bn to private tax evasion. Multinationals have shifted US$1.38 tn worth of profits out of the countries where they were generated and into tax havens. Financial assets worth over US$10 tn have been shifted by private tax evaders into offshore tax havens. It states that the greatest enablers of global tax abuse are "the rich countries at the heart of the global economy and their dependencies—not the countries that appear on the EU's highly politicised tax haven blacklist or the small palm-fringed islands of popular belief." These countries account for 98 per cent of countries' tax losses, whereas lower income countries are responsible for only 2 per cent. Table 4.2 records the five jurisdictions responsible for almost half of all countries' tax losses. The results will no doubt surprise many readers (Global Alliance for Tax Justice 2020).

Based on extensive research into the vast sums of taxpayer funds and capital diverted annually to corporate interests in Australia through direct and indirect subsidies, tax concessions and other forms of corporate favouritism (Lucas 2021; Murray and Frijters 2017; West 2016, 2018, 2018a), it seems reasonable to conclude that the many forms of corporate largesse routinely conferred upon dominant corporations by successive governments throughout the world over the last several decades have deprived most of humanity of the capital that could have been used to not only make a global sustainable energy transition and decarbonise our societies over the next few decades, but to provide the majority of the world's population with minimum standards of healthcare, welfare and education. The vast bulk of this capital has been illegitimately and illicitly shifted into tax havens or spent on conspicuous and inconspicuous forms of consumption that serve no other purpose than to finance the profligate, carbon-intensive lifestyles of a tiny global elite. It must surely be the responsibility of every person of good conscience throughout the world to raise our fellow citizens' awareness of this situation and to direct their wrath and appetites for genuine social, economic and environmental reform towards these individuals and the overt and covert networks of influence they have systematically constructed since the end of the Second World War to further their own interests and undermine democratic norms (MacLean 2017; Mayer 2017; Dunlap et al. 2022). Rest assured that these individuals will do whatever it takes to prevent this from happening.

Conclusion

In the current political environment, any global commitment to the wholesale transformation of the world's energy systems within the timeframe, which climate scientists tell us is necessary to avert DAI appears highly improbable. It should be abundantly clear from the previous analysis, however, that the powerful business and industry interests discussed in this chapter see democracy and democratic reforms as a direct threat to their power and influence and have done and will continue to do their utmost to distort the public will in their favour, and to undermine and discredit any efforts which oppose them (Anonymous 2019; Levitsky & Ziblatt 2018; MacLean 2017; Mayer 2016; Runciman 2018; Wolin 2010). With enormous economic resources at their disposal, they will continue efforts to marginalise any political party, labour organisation, NGO or individual that tries to promote democratic reform or any efforts to create institutional, regulatory or legal checks on their power. Whether those efforts are open or covert is irrelevant. The fact is that they *are* involved in such activities and will not resile from them unless and until they are not only exposed, but regularly and publicly humiliated, hounded and prosecuted for engaging in them. If we as citizens are not prepared to do our utmost to turn the current situation around, we may as well simply give up any pretence that the democratic reforms fought for and won by our forebears were in any way sustainable or worthy of extension and renewal.

If we are prepared to think of this in purely demographic terms, there are compelling reasons for believing that it may be possible to refashion the current global regime over the next few decades. Given that there are approximately 10 mn of these individuals who are currently hiding their pilfered wealth offshore, with perhaps another 100 mn enablers who are willing to assist them and perhaps aspire to emulate their odious ways of life, and more than 7 bn others who do not share their interests, we at least have the physical numbers to effectively oppose them, if not defeat them effectively. The future of humanity and our fellow living beings are the stakes in play.

Notes

1 I use the terms financial and regulatory elites in the sense articulated by Sovacool and Brisbois (2019), informed by the work of Scott (2008) and Mann (2012). Financial elites include corporate directors, investors, property owners and businesspersons "who control access to capital or industrial assets that therefore influence the calculations of others", while regulatory elites include political representatives, members of political parties, lawyers and national planners "who can use the legal system as a form of political power". Business and industrial elites are part of the broader financial elite, and political elite part

of the broader regulatory elite. Military elites form part of the broader coercive or physical elite, along with the police and organised criminals, "who control access to the means of violence and are able to dominate others into obedience."

2 The latter study by Pehl, et al. (2017) has, however, noted that large-scale hydroelectric projects and biomass have considerably "higher specific indirect energy inputs and specific indirect GHG emissions than nuclear-, wind- and solar-based power supply."

5

ENGINEERING THE CORONAVERSE

The Wild, Wild Sovereignty of Big Meat in the Age of the Corporate State

Sandy Smith-Nonini

Introduction

The Coronavirus pandemic is a phenomenon that conflates personal, social, and planet-wide risks in an unprecedented way. These overlapping risks parallel the pathogen's emergence from a complex interplay of degraded ecosystems and unregulated industrialisation. This chapter explores the relationship of Covid-19 spread associated with the rapidly globalising meat industry in a period when corporate power increasingly overlaps or supersedes the control of states.

The complex aetiology of Covid-19 arises from the ways climate change, industrial meat production and emergent diseases feedback on each other. For example, a widely held thesis of coronavirus origin involves a "spillover" of contagion from an animal host in ecosystems degraded by climate chaos and unrelenting capitalist development of wild habitats (Wallace 2020). Disrupted rainforest ecosystems reproduce risks for emergent contagions like SARS-CoV-2 (Ellwanger et al. 2020), which many epidemiologists believe was brought to Wuhan, China, through the Asian wildlife trade. Covid-19 follows the Bird Flu, a 2016 emergent contagion linked to agribusiness that wiped out wild birds and poultry populations in over three dozen countries across four continents (Sharma 2018).

Climate change, in turn, is driven in part by greenhouse gas (GHG) emissions from meat and dairy operations. A recent study found that the three largest meat processing firms—JBS, Tyson and Cargill—emitted more GHGs than France, placing them on par with leading oil companies. Surprisingly, the five largest meat and dairy firms were slightly ahead of Exxon for GHGs (IATP et al. 2017), but corporate secrecy undermines their social accountability. Climate accords, negotiated between nations, assume governments are willing and able to regulate corporate emitters. Yet, the expansion of corporate power in recent decades makes that unlikely, an oversight that could doom the Paris Agreement.

DOI: 10.4324/9781003250432-7

The Food and Agriculture Organization found that livestock alone represented 15 per cent of all global GHG emissions, exceeding those from transportation. Beef production was the worst offender with 41 per cent of livestock emissions—four times higher than pork or poultry. Worse, over a third of livestock emissions are methane, a potent GHG that speeds short-term climate change. The vast bulk (84 per cent) of emissions is not from meat processing or transport but from producing feed and growth of livestock. Nearly half of livestock emissions are tied to feed production, including the conversion of forests to land for pasture and crops. For beef, regional emissions from pasture expansion are most intense for cattle grazed in Latin America (Gerber et al. 2013).

During the pandemic, industrialised meat processing also became a major site of Covid-19 infections in many countries, representing a worst-case scenario of the climate/Covid-19/inequality nexus. This has historical roots. Ranching's low labour costs have long made it a preferred fall-back strategy of rural elites in times of low prices or peasant uprisings. Big Meat's push for deregulation and embrace of union-busting and mergers exemplifies the neoliberal response to systemic risks that challenged capitalist accumulation after the 1970s energy and economic crises. Elite solutions to the fall in profits depended on harnessing states to policies that accelerated temporal and spatial dispossession of public assets (Harvey 2005).

After the mid-1990s the trend accelerated with the emergence of what Bruce Kapferer dubbed "corporate-state sovereignty" (2004: 11; 2018), as nation-states themselves became more privatised, serving capital more instrumentally, ceding sovereignty over oligopolies and devolving to them former state functions (including provisioning), even as corporations become more de-territorialised and difficult to monitor or regulate. The neoliberal shift after 1980 saw major meatpackers pioneering vertically-integrated production and linking "contract" farming of animals with processing and international sales under giant corporate entities. Yet, as this analysis shows, such conglomerates rely on a myriad of state-facilitated subsidies, tax breaks and access to low-wage (often immigrant) workforces, cheap natural resources and environmental sinks for air and water pollution (Crossa and Cypher 2020).

Seeing the Coronavirus crisis through the lens of industrial meat illuminates the nexus of risk and exposes the fragility of global systems built on neoliberal accumulation without regard to environmental and social degradation. Adam Tooze (2021) dubbed the pandemic "the first comprehensive crisis of the Age of the Anthropocene—an era defined by the blowback from our unbalanced relationship to nature."

The first half of this chapter draws on findings from epidemiological surveys by the author and two colleagues[1] about Covid-19 spread among the so-called "essential" workers at meatpacking plants in two states of the U.S. southeast between June and September 2020. A "Crisis Epidemiology" of Meatpacking and Covid in the US South presents the main findings of that study. Our follow-up research, discussed in Unregulated Workplaces; Expendable Workers, illustrates how large meat monopolies used political influence and a legacy of deregulated workplaces to deflect public scrutiny during the pandemic, while causing illness and death among their workers and in the wider community (Smith-Nonini 2021).

The second half focuses on a case study of JBS. In little more than a decade this Brazilian meatpacker morphed into the world's largest meat producer, exemplifying the multifaceted dilemma of the corporate state. *Corporate Rule: Cowboys in the White House* explores how JBS-USA emerged as a leading source of Covid-19's spread in the United States and the company's use of political influence and federal subsidies to mitigate impacts of the pandemic on its profits. *Global Meat—Outlaws on the Run* follows JBS back to Brazil to examine its outsized role there in viral spread and controversies over its role in the Amazon deforestation and bribery of officials to sidestep regulations and gain state-financing of its global expansion. The conclusion discusses the phenomenon of the food sector corporate-state monopolies that pose multiple systemic risks and evaluates implications for the (optimistically "post-pandemic") future and potential for reforms.

A "Crisis Epidemiology" of Meatpacking and COVID in the U.S. South

Beyond environmental harms, meatpackers face a social reproduction problem due to heavy dependence on immigrant workers, which the pandemic made visible. *The Jungle*, Upton Sinclair's 1906 expose of immigrant working conditions, brought the appalling working conditions of meatpackers to public attention, but initial reforms focused on food safety. In the late 1930s, the industry became unionised, but most of these gains were lost in the 1980s as the industry moved to rural areas, adopting weaker safety standards and lower wages. Multibillion-dollar corporate owners broke unions, deskilled jobs and globalised, creating fast-moving production lines increasingly dependent on Black and immigrant workers. The North American Free Trade Agreement (NAFTA), which pushed Mexico to cut farm credits, accelerated illegal migration north. Today, Hispanics, many undocumented, make up 35 per cent to 45 per cent of meatpacking workers and a half or more of the workers on processing lines (Crossa and Cypher 2020; Fremstad et al. 2020; Halpern 2005).

As the pandemic emerged in early 2020, a series of meat-processing plant outbreaks drew public attention in the Midwest. In late May, the Food and Environment Reporting Network (FERN) found that rural counties with meatpacking outbreaks had infection rates five times higher than the average for US rural counties (Douglas and Marema 2020). Although elder-care homes and prisons were legally required to report positive cases to health authorities, reporting was voluntary for other U.S. workplaces. This became a hugely consequential loophole as evidence mounted that the meat industry was the largest U.S. industrial source of viral spread (Marema 2020; Taylor et al. 2020).

Meatpacking's high risks arose from crowded workstations on fast-moving processing lines and frigid airflow systems, which likely boosted viral contagion. Workers in many places reported pressure from supervisors to resume work while sick or soon after exposure. Once infected, immigrant workers who often commute in packed vehicles and live in crowded households, face a high risk of spread. Unions and workers at many plants reported that managers were slow to adopt safety protocols (Parshina-Kottas et al. 2020; Taylor et al. 2020).

Nationwide, 22 large meat plants closed temporarily due to worker absenteeism and/or plant "cleaning" after the Covid-19 outbreaks in April. As citizens began navigating a new terrain of economic lockdowns and "stay-at-home" orders, the enigmatic toilet paper shortage gave way to rumours of meat shortages and price hikes in some regions—a scare fed in part by an industry media blitz warning of risks to the meat supply chain as part of a campaign for federal protection.

Although President Donald Trump had earlier declined to use federal power to resolve shortages of hospital medical supplies, on April 27 he invoked the Defense Production Act to prevent shutdowns of food manufacturers on the condition that they adhered to as yet unpublished guidelines for "critical infrastructure" workplaces being prepared by the Centers for Disease Control and Prevention (CDC) and the Occupational Safety and Health Agency (OSHA). Richard Trumka (2020), president of the AFL-CIO union federation, called Trump's order to reopen plants without proper safety protocols "dangerous and disgraceful." By mid-May, most large meatpackers began promoting masks and safety protocols. Many hung thin plastic sheets between processing line workers and ended demerits for sick days. However, worker advocates and union leaders reported that adherence to the voluntary measures varied.

Covid-19 outbreaks in meat plants received less publicity in the South. The two states we studied ranked among the top five nationally for their leading meat industries—pork in North Carolina and poultry in Georgia (Douglas 2020a). In both states the industry grew rapidly in recent decades, backed by Republican politicians with solid legislative majorities.

Case Study of North Carolina

North Carolina was already home to more hogs than people when I first studied the industry in 2001. Worker turnover in meat plants was near 100 per cent a year due to low pay, abysmal working conditions and ergonomic injuries. The plants increasingly relied on undocumented Mexican labour (Smith-Nonini 2003). Two decades later, as the pandemic bore down, FERN reported that by April, 65 per cent of Covid-19 outbreaks at US food processors and farms were in meatpacking, most at plants of industry leaders Tyson Foods, JBS, and Smithfield (Douglas 2020b). That June and July, I combined epidemiology with investigative journalism (my pre-graduate school occupation) to gather data on Covid-19 spread linked to North Carolina meat plants. In mid-June, worker advocacy groups reported major outbreaks in at least five major NC meat plants, but the state Department of Health and Human Services (DHHS) updates made little mention of workplaces. The scale of the problem became clear when DHHS responded to my email query, confirming that 2,772 meatpacking workers had tested positive for Covid-19 in outbreaks at 28 plants (Smith-Nonini 2020).

My survey of infection rates found surges in 14 rural counties with large meatpacking plants, including a hotspot in the state's southeast where pork production employs 19,000 workers.[2] 12 of the 14 counties were among the highest in the nation for Covid-19 cases (New York Times 2020).[3] Such high case rates were rare outside cities at that time. One such example was Duplin County, at the heart of the meatpacking region. Why did rural Duplin with the highest infection rate in the state have close to twice the rate of Covid-19 cases as Mecklenburg County, home to Charlotte, our largest city? The high ranking was not explained by outbreaks in nursing homes or prisons (Smith-Nonini 2020), but not less than four large Duplin-based meat processors had confirmed outbreaks at that time.

In July, we mapped rural telephone zip codes with high infection rates near meat processing plants.[4] The largest cluster, also in the Southeast, had at least nine plants with outbreaks, and we found that zip codes within commuting distance of two or more plants had the highest case rates (Smith-Nonini and Marema 2020). Most zip codes with high case rates had large minority populations.

By late June, 77 per cent of people sick with the virus were of working age and, in meatpacking counties, disproportionately Hispanic, consistent with their predominance in plant workforces. Despite the risk to communities, DHHS kept locations of plant outbreaks secret, citing a lack of regulatory authority (NC Watchdog Reporting Network 2020). This was not unusual. A national survey found only four U.S. states provided full data on food industry outbreaks. (Douglas 2020c).

Indeed, the pork industry wields enormous clout in the state. An industry leader served in the legislature for nearly a decade protecting industry interests, and one survey found half of NC legislators taking pork donations even as hurricanes caused hundreds of hog waste ponds to overflow, contaminating rivers (Democracy NC 1995). Smithfield, which runs the world's largest hog processing plant, pumped over US$4 million into political donations over 23 years, most of them going to the Republicans.[5]

Case Study of Georgia

In August 2020, we shifted focus to Georgia, the top US poultry producer. Despite a high case rate and reports of Covid-19 outbreaks at several meat plants, state politicians and health officials depicted viral risks as contained. At the behest of Gov. Brian Kemp, Georgia was the first state to reopen its economy in late April, and like many Republicans, Kemp opposed mask mandates.

The heart of Georgia meatpacking was Hall County in north Georgia, where a water tower declares it "Poultry Capital of the World." The astounding 13 meat processing plants in the county employed 6,780 workers, many Latinx. The county was also home to the state's highest Covid-19 rate (3,521 cases per 100,000)—40 per cent higher than metro-Atlanta.[6] This was remarkable, since high rates were mostly found in large cities at that time.

An Emory University team found one-quarter of 450 meatpacking workers tested in Hall County to be COVID-positive. Latinx people tested positive at over twice the rate of whites (Smith-Nonini and Paschal 2020). Georgia's Department of Public Health (DPH), despite partnering with the Emory study, echoed state officials' praise of the chicken industry for its response to the virus and blamed cultural issues like large families and parties for the spread in worker communities (Redmon and Bluestein 2020; Smith-Nonini and Paschal 2020).

But Georgia's data suggested otherwise. Using the DPH Covid-19 database, we found Georgia's average case rate for 11 rural counties with large meat plants was close to 3 times the average for rural counties without plants (Smith-Nonini and Paschal 2020), a problem also documented nationally (Douglas 2020d).

DPH downplayed meatpacking's role in the pandemic despite media reports that four workers died after a Covid-19 outbreak at a Tyson Foods plant in southeast Georgia, while a nearby plant had sent 619 workers home to quarantine (Saunders 2020). None of this hindered the Georgia Poultry Federation from issuing an upbeat statement, picked up by national papers, that the state's chicken production was unaffected by Covid-19, in contrast with the Midwest, where plant closures had slowed meat production (Richards 2020).

After touring a large poultry plant, Gov. Kemp praised the industry to reporters and blamed workers' cultural practices for high caseloads. A state health official on the tour echoed his comments. Georgia DPH responded to my open records request in August 2020 with old, already published data from a May report to the CDC. Text at the top read: "These cases do not represent plant 'outbreaks' …" and "THIS DOES NOT ASSUME INFECTIONS WERE ACQUIRED IN THE FACILITY" [*emphasis in original*] (Smith-Nonini and Paschal 2020).

Unregulated Workplaces; Expendable Workers

Debbie Berkowitz, a safety specialist at the National Employment Law Project, expressed little surprise at our findings, noting, "To protect the public from Covid-19, you have to protect workers. If you don't, it continues to spread." In the pandemic, she said, "worker health became public health." Her warning was verified by a December 2020 epidemiology study in the Proceedings of the National Academy of Sciences, which estimated the real toll from the viral spread in meat plants was far higher than official reports suggested. Based on data through July 2020, the researchers estimated that meat plants had been point sources for 236,000 to 310,000 infections (fully 6 to 8 per cent of the U.S. cases) and 4,300 to 5,200 deaths, with the "vast majority" of spread *in communities* due to plant workers carrying the contagion home (Taylor et al. 2020). The implications were stark since meatpacking outbreaks continued into 2021, albeit at a lower rate. As of August 3, 2021, 574 US meatpacking plants had seen confirmed cases of Covid-19., with at least 58,913 meatpacking workers becoming ill and 297 who died, according to FERN's ongoing tally (see: Douglas 2020b).

The tepid response of state authorities was manifest in the variable responses of meat plants. According to worker advocates, one unorganised plant in North Carolina waited six to eight weeks to implement safety protocols, and pressured infected workers to return to work,. Some Georgia plants were hobbled by high absenteeism due to illness, fear and quarantine (Smith-Nonini and Paschal 2020). Police dispersed a protest of 40 workers after a walkout at one plant. Unions helped provide workers leverage in some cases, but most plants are not unionised; both states rank very low nationally, with less than 5 per cent of workers organised, in part due to anti-union "right-to-work" legislation passed in the 1950s, which limits union bargaining power.[7]

According to Scott Mabry, an OSHA spokesperson, despite a surge of Covid-19 complaints, OSHA did not routinely inspect plants. Mabry blamed cuts in staffing.. Although OSHA had been underfunded for decades in the neoliberal era, Trump cut down even further, eliminating a fifth of inspector jobs. Workplace visits dropped further with the pandemic, whereas fatal workplace incidents rose to record levels (Yerardi and Campbell 2020).

A key problem was that new CDC guidelines for "critical infrastructure" workplaces were effectively voluntary.[8] Berkowitz, a former OSHA chief of staff under Obama, described the language as watered down with phrases like "if feasible" and "consider doing this," making the regulations unenforceable. The guidelines controversially allowed workers exposed to infected employees to continue working if they did not have symptoms. This incentivised companies to not offer Covid-19 testing onsite since a positive test would require quarantine.

In North Carolina, internal emails obtained by ProPublica showed how weak regulations hobbled health policy. One county health official argued that posting cases on the state website would be "very detrimental to any cooperative relationships that we have with the plants." A county health director responded to an email saying she could not force Tyson Foods to socially distance workers because health officials were only "educators" and "do not have regulatory authority." In two counties, health officials co-edited reassuring joint press releases with plant officials, featuring county seals alongside company logos. Press inquiries about outbreaks were referred by health officials to the companies, which declined to give details (Documenting Covid-19 2020).

The weak enforcement of worker safety reflected the *laisse faire* approach of Trump (and prior administrations), essentially allowing large agribusiness giants to dictate federal safety policy.[9] On April 26, the day before Trump's order protected meat plants from closure, John Tyson, Chairman of the Tyson Foods board, placed alarming ads in major newspapers claiming the "food supply chain is breaking."

The industry leader, Tyson, who spent US$5.89 million on lobbying since 2016, headed up a pressure campaign, asking state governors and Trump to declare food plants critical infrastructure, exempt from bans on public gatherings or curfews. His overture to Gov. Kemp's office asked Georgia officials to "encourage workers to continue to work while healthy"—effectively a request to circumvent the CDC's

10—14 day quarantine advice for people exposed to someone positive for Covid-19 (Documenting Covid-19 2020).[10]

The implicit threat of Trump's order was that "essential" workers who were not fired but chose to stay home due to Covid-19 risk, would lose access to unemployment benefits. Author Mike Davis described the policy as an impossible choice forced on tens of millions of Americans who need to work to put food on the table but doing so poses risks they will bring a deadly disease home to their loved ones (Democracy Now 2020).

Corporate Rule—Cowboys in the White House

A year earlier, on May 23, 2019, Trump stood at a White House podium in front of men in cowboy hats to announce a US$16 billion agriculture bailout aimed at "American" farmers impacted by new tariffs on food exports to China. Controversially, Brazilian-owned JBS-USA benefitted from US$78 million of this taxpayer largess (Kindy 2019), despite its foreign ownership and soaring profits. The US subsidiary had rapidly grown into a major player nationally in just over a decade as part of a company plan to enhance its access to capital and distance itself from a reputation for degrading the Amazon. It emerged as one of the top three U.S. meat industry political donors by 2020 (Center for Responsive Politics 2021).

In the Midwest, where Covid-19 first emerged in meat plants, six JBS-USA plants had outbreaks. The largest, in a plant located in Greeley, Colorado, took more than 6 months to get the outbreak under control. As of February 2021, 465 Greeley workers had contracted Covid-19 in the plant, and seven had died, out of 3,200 employees. The crisis began in late March when hundreds of workers began to call in sick at the plant, located in Weld County, even as the company offered incentives for attendance and reminded workers of the Trump order that food workers were exempt from stay-at-home orders. A Denver Post investigation found that at least two Covid-19 infected workers were fired for staying home and nine of 14 infected workers reported they had gone to work while sick. A few days later, after three workers died in a week, County Health Director Mark Wallace ordered the plant's closure (Bradbury 2020a; Bradbury 2020b).

JBS drew on its political connections to contest the order. According to emails obtained by the Post, a Greeley plant administrator replied that he understood the governor did not want the plant closed. Then, the head of the Colorado State health agency, Jill Hunsaker Ryan, emailed Wallace saying the director of the CDC had called her at the behest of Vice President Mike Pence, asking her to intervene. She wrote: "They want us to use the CDC's critical infrastructure guidance (sending asymptomatic people back to work even if we suspect exposure but they have no symptoms) even with the outbreak at present level. Are you okay with that? I am if you are." Wallace agreed, but he later moved ahead with closing the plant. Both Hunsaker Ryan and Wallace retired two months later (Bradbury 2020b).

In September 2020, JBS-USA earned the rare distinction of being fined by OSHA for Covid-19 violations at the Greeley plant and two others in Worthington,

MN, and Green Bay, WI. Greeley union leaders dismissed the "proposed" fine for their plant, US$15,615, as a pittance; indeed, JBS-USA earned nearly US$28 billion on its pork and beef divisions in 2020 (McCarthy 2021). JBS appealed the fines which allowed the company to postpone improving safety protocols and avoid admitting liability (Kirkham 2021).

The pandemic record fits with a longer pattern of worker injuries, a category for which the meat industry stands out compared to other sectors. Yet JBS-USA stands out more, with the highest rate of serious worker injuries among US meat companies, and the second-highest rate among all companies, according to recent Congressional testimony (Food Safety News 2020a). This chronic disregard of workers' safety brings to mind Wendy Brown's (2015: 38) observation that corporate pressure on the state has a depoliticising effect. "When everything is capital," she wrote, "labor disappears as a category."

The mystery of JBS-USA's rapid rise to power in the U.S. meat industry is explained in part by shady or explicitly illegal state subsidies. Congressional testimony in early 2020 revealed that despite its many fines for violations, JBS received tens of millions (US dollars) in routine subsidies from the US Department of Agriculture (USDA) (Food Safety News 2020a). The problems dated to 2008 when the company bought Smithfield Beef and Pilgrim's Pride poultry company with funds company officials later acknowledged were illegally obtained from the Brazilian National Development Bank (BNDES) (Freitas et al. 2017).

Since then, JBS has thrived through an aggressive growth policy of buying out its rivals, which led to revenues that more than justified paying the occasional fine. JBS-USA was also sued by a coalition of US ranchers for allegedly conspiring with other large meatpackers to drive down beef prices and using a loophole to claim that its foreign pasture-raised meat is a "Product of the USA" (Mitchell 2019), The company was also implicated in a 2019 Salmonella outbreak that impacted 30 states (CDC 2019).

This string of controversies attests to the dangers of oligopoly control over US meat production, and the persisting pattern of corporate political donations that result in policies that pay firms back with state subsidies and protection from regulation.

Global Meat—Outlaws on the Run

The confluence of the pandemic, JBS's Amazon connections and JBS-USA's rapid rise in the United States led me to follow the company back to Brazil, where a massive, ongoing surge of Covid-19 was also linked to meatpacking and abysmal health policies of another right-wing, populist president. It turned out that the seeds of the JBS corporate-state strategy were planted nearly three decades ago.

The company remained small and regional for decades after 1953 when José Batista Sobrinho, the company's namesake and founder, opened a small slaughterhouse in Anápolis, Brazil. In 1993, the Batista family began buying up competitors, not with their capital, but with generous loans from the BNDES bank, as part of Brazil's strategy to aid the growth of selected national firms. By 2005, JBS dominated Brazil's meat sector and began looking abroad for growth. The company went global rapidly under leadership of Batista's sons, Joseley (2007–2011) and Wesley Batista (2011–2017), each forced to resign, in turn, due to charges of illegal practices (Freitas et al. 2017). The two spent an astounding US$20 billion, again much of it borrowed from BNDES, on takeovers of rival companies, with a focus initially on holdings in the United States and Australia, the two largest beef-consuming countries (Freitas et al. 2017). In 2015, JBS spent nearly US$3 billion to acquire U.S.-based Cargill pork operations and the British poultry producer, Moy Park, and announced plans for further expansion in Europe (Oberst 2015).

Similar to the US experience under Trump, Brazilian President Jair Bolsonaro, led an anti-science campaign against viral safety protocols and denied that Covid-19 posed a public threat, even as the contagion convulsed the nation, causing the second deadliest outbreak in the world (after the United States) with over 581,000 coronavirus deaths as of early September 2021 (Tracking Coronavirus 2021). Legislative hearings on Bolsonaro's inaction in April 2021 revealed that he had turned down three offers of vaccines in previous months before finally signing a contract. In May, protesters filled the streets by the thousands to denounce the regime (Barbara 2021). Bolsonaro, who has close ties to Brazilian agribusiness, has also been blamed for a steep rise in seasonal fires to clear land since he took office in 2018.

By September 2020, over 4,000 Brazilian JBS employees had fallen ill from Covid-19 in outbreaks affecting 23 plants in seven states (Mano 2020). National health officials believe three regional virus clusters originated with nearby meatpacking plants, including JBS facilities (Phillips 2020). Compared with the nominal U.S. OSHA penalties, in Brazil, where a judicial reform movement has targeted corruption for two decades, JBS was fined a much heftier US$3.6 million for Covid-19 violations at one plant and more fines were expected (Mano 2021).

Covid-19 fines are only the latest legal fracas for JBS in Brazil. In 2009, a public exposé by Greenpeace linked the company to cattle acquired from newly deforested areas, leading JBS to sign accords with the non-profit organisation and the government promising to monitor its supply chains. Reports of violations persisted, and in 2017, Greenpeace suspended its accord with the company after Brazilian authorities raided two JBS plants and fined the company US$7 million for buying cattle from illegally deforested areas (Estrada 2017).

Despite a new JBS pledge to clean up its supply chain, evidence shows the company continued to slaughter cattle from recently cleared forest land (Amnesty International 2020; Greenpeace 2021; TBIR 2019). This "cattle laundering" involves cows fattened on illegally cleared land, then transferred via middlemen to a legal ranch before they are sold to JBS. The Stockholm Environmental Institute's JBS beef supply chain audit linked the firm to at least 290 square kilometres of destroyed rainforest per year (TBIR 2019). The company claimed it had no control over indirect suppliers (Harris 2020). The recurrent linkages of JBS with Amazon deforestation vividly portray the "wildness" of corporate sovereignty, which Kapferer (2004) views as "most evident at peripheries of powerful state orders."

In March 2017, JBS CEO Joseley Batista, turned himself in to authorities to avoid arrest for his role in a multi-company scandal in which tainted meat was allegedly shipped abroad after firms paid off sanitary inspectors for falsified permits. Investigators led raids on three JBS plants and shut down ten beef plants for 20 days. Several foreign importers suspended meat purchases (Alerigi and Freitas 2017). Later, he and his brother Wesley were both jailed on bribery charges from Brazil's sprawling Car Wash (Lava Jato) corruption scandal. Both men became witnesses for the state in May 2017, shocking the country with testimony revealing a long-running scheme of paying kickbacks for favouritism at the BNDES development bank, which lent the equivalent of US$3.2 billion to finance JBS's phenomenal global expansion. A current and former president of BNDES and a government finance minister were indicted for accepting bribes (Phillips 2019).

The brothers' testimony included an audiotape implicating the then President, Michel Temer, as complicit in the kickbacks and revealed bribes of over US$220 million to 1,829 officials and politicians, mostly as political contributions. In return for a leniency agreement, the Batistas agreed to pay a US$3.6 billion fine over 25 years (Freitas et al. 2017). The scandal opened an unusual window into both the rationale and *modus operandi* of the corporate state, in which power becomes subordinated to the economy as firms pursue intensifying capital flows (Kalb 2018), which become entangled with apparatuses of the state (Kapferer 2018). The widespread media revelations of CEO malfeasance, alongside charges of rainforest clearing, led to a backlash from JBS shareholders.

Despite months of negative press and legal jeopardy, in late 2017, the Batista family, which controls 42 per cent of JBS shares, moved to salvage the firm's international reputation by spinning off holdings outside Brazil through an Initial Public Offering (IPO) to create a separate company called JBS Foods International. The plan aimed in part to separate the firm's most profitable assets from those in Brazil to reassure shareholders concerned over legal and environmental liability. Financial analysts, to their credit, were critical, rating JBS poorly for high political and legal risk (Debtwire 2018, Chain Reaction 2020). The Batistas postponed the IPO. Despite their global aspirations, the JBS legacy of just paying fines and moving ahead with corporate crime seems to have left Batista family owners blindsided by recent movements (however tenuous) for ecologically and socially conscious investing.

Conclusion—"Gun Fight at the OK Corral"

If not for the high stakes involved, the absurdity of the JBS rap sheet might evoke Hollywood gunslingers in the Wild West, but JBS is an arguably "modern" global company that does immeasurable damage by degrading the land of indigenous peoples and disdain for the welfare of workers, consumers, small farmers, and the wider public in multiple countries. Less colourful or blatantly illegal, Tyson Foods and Smithfield are variations on the model. Like the rise of racist, anti-science populist leaders such as Trump and Bolsonaro, following JBS's rise to power feels like a throwback to an earlier age.

Gezici (2020) reported that 75 per cent of U.S. industries are now more concentrated, with average sizes three-fold those of the mid-1990s, a trend promoted by neoliberal readings of anti-trust law that focus on consumer welfare and efficiency rather than effects on small firms. The political influence of business grew as well. The number of agribusiness Political Action Committees (PACs), disbursing funds directly from industry to politicians, rose from zero in 1974 when they became legal to more than 4,700 in 1990 (Nestle 2007). In 2020, the U.S. meat processors spent US$4.19 million on lobbying, more than half from Tyson, Smithfield and JBS-USA. Funds benefitted Republicans at double the rate of Democrats (Center for Responsive Politics 2021).

In a sense, this is an old story. Historically, the power of imperial regimes hinged on control over food, according to Philip McMichael (2013, 41), who defines today's "corporate food regime" as combining access to food resources with market forces that enhance power relations—through strategic provisioning of social classes and manoeuvres to monopolise market power. In addition to classic modes of state capture like political donations, hiring state officials with industry backgrounds, lobbying and media influence, Donald Nonini (n.d.) emphasises the role of the "rump state"—e.g. the turn to (underfunded) public-private partnerships to run welfare state food programs, greased by lucrative outlays to commodity producers, such as JBS. Subsidies for basic grains also benefit Big Meat since they shore up markets for animal feed and commodities like high-fructose corn syrup in processed and fast food.

Kapferer (2018) observed that oligarchic forms often arise from firms (like JBS) run by families or kin, which draw on loyalty to maintain exclusive control. Oligarchic powerbases both contribute to and gain from the rise of nationalistic populism that boosts candidates like Trump and Bolsonaro. The 2018 election of Bolsonaro, in the wake of the Car Wash scandal and an economic downturn, represented the resurgence of agribusiness elites. Ironically, although Brazil's BNDES bank aided JBS's global expansion during Inácio (Lula) da Silva's Worker Party regime, the model of public-subsidised development through private firms dates to Brazil's period of military rule (1964–1985). By 2010, the value to Brazil of loans to firms from BNDES was more than three times that of Brazil's World Bank lending. After 2000 the BNDES kept private equity from the deals, increasing its state entanglement (Aldo and Lazzarini 2014, 241–248).[11] The exponential rise of global JBS depended on BNDES mega-loans. Without them, as Joseley Batista testified under oath, "it wouldn't have worked" (Freitas et al. 2017).

Notably, the Brazilian state's retained assets from loans gave it leverage over JBS. The BNDES gained close to a third of the firm's shares when it rescued an overindebted JBS in 2009 by buying back its unsecured debt, later converting it to shares of stock (Debtwire 2018; Freitas et al. 2017). It would behove the United States to similarly retain equity or another form of control over corporate handouts. Instead, the Trump Administration overtly favoured agribusiness over farmers, labour or citizens in its trade-related bailout of JBS-USA (Kindy 2019) and inclusion of Big Meat in federal pandemic stimulus funds for agriculture (Dembicki 2020).

The global expansion of firms inevitably limits state sovereignty. After the Batista brothers' 2017 testimony, Temer made concessions to agribusiness to survive in office (Phillips 2019). The JBS globalisation tool chest for slipping the reins of the state included (1) building JBS-USA, currently the source of 83 per cent of JBS sales, to benefit from the stable U.S. dollar and distance itself from its reputation for rain forest destruction, (2) taking advantage of low tax havens like Ireland (at 12.5 per cent)—the home base of its subsidiary Moy Park and intended headquarters for the post-IPO JBS Foods International, and (3) the option to pivot back to Brazil for cheaper exports than its American competitors when beef prices are high and the Brazilian real is low (Pan 2015).

A corporate presence in the United States and Europe enhances JBS's access to financial capital and markets for further growth. JBS's earnings relative to peers have depended heavily on mergers (Chain Reaction 2017). The combination of recent low interest rates and financialisation reinforced pressure from shareholders to continue the merger and acquisition strategy to keep stock values high (Gezici 2020). Another strength of globalisation for JBS has been the firm's growing trade with China, the destination for most of its Brazilian exports. This hedges against losses from European boycotts over the Amazon connection or supply chain disruptions, as occurred in the pandemic, when meat firms took a blow from lost restaurant sales in countries with lockdowns.

As we envision a future beyond the pandemic, prospects for pushback to globalisation loom large. The crisis exposed the fragility of long-distance supply chains and risks to financial markets, including formerly solid assets like U.S. Treasury Bonds. Rescue packages, although essential, increased inequity again and showcased the vital role of states in fiscal bailouts (Tooze 2021). Public support for state-led progressive policies, including social reforms and climate change mitigation, is evident from polling and elections in the United States and Germany.

In 2020, polls showed vegetarians doubling their numbers in Brazil, reaching 30 million (Londoño 2021) and a 45 per cent increase in (already strong) plant-based meat sales in the United States (GFI 2021), with the phenomena attributed to health, climate and unsafe meat plant concerns. JBS recently acquired three plant-based protein companies to hedge against the trend (Smith 2021). Given the cultural significance of meat-eating in many cultures and the growing taste for meat in China's middle class, however, global markets for meat remain healthy (Godfray 2018) and still bode ill for GHG emissions, but the pandemic and media reports on meatpacking outbreaks may be boosting a dietary shift.

Trade-dependent firms like JBS, along with OECD nations, are vulnerable to supply chain breakdowns in the "post"-pandemic economy Energy price volatility, regional shortages of key commodities, tight supply margins and shareholder and citizen activism directed at social/environmental pariahs have roiled markets. In the event of a GHG tax or other "green" tax on transit or trade, price increases on meat would likely impact affordability and profits (Godfray et al. 2018). The slow rise of regional food markets gained a boost in 2021 as meatpacking COVID outbreaks and decades of low prices for their animals prompted many U.S. ranchers to peel away from dependence on Big Meat and set up their own regional meatpacking operations, now backed by US$500 million in USDA funds as part of a Biden push for more competitive (and resilient) food markets (McCausland 2021).

Non-profit scrutiny and mounting pressure on JBS to clean up its supply chain have borne fruit. Notably, in mid-2020, more than two dozen financial firms managing over US$3.7 trillion pressured the Brazilian government to stop deforestation, singling out meatpackers' role. A month later, Nordea Asset Management, a large Nordic investment group, removed JBS shares from its funds for environmental reasons. The Covid-19 meatpacking outbreaks provoked investor wariness as well. After record prices in 2019, JBS shares dropped 30 per cent during the initial months of the pandemic (Harris 2020).

An underappreciated strategy for reform is that of the Brazilian judicial reform movement, which has targeted corrupt practices since the early 2000s and was boosted under the Rousseff presidency, ultimately resulting in the Car Wash investigation. Right-wing forces leveraged the anti-corruption probes (despite weak evidence) to bring down Rousseff's presidency (Pahnke 2017), but the prolonged activism spurred new transparency and anti-graft rules and led to the appointments of thousands of new regional judges, including those imposing fines on meat companies with Covid-19 outbreaks. This approach deserves study by activists in the Global North for both its potential and its pitfalls—e.g., revolving door hires with corporate firms co-opted gains in recent years (Engelmann 2020). As the JBS-USA story attests, the rise of corporatised states offers little basis for assumptions that corruption is a Global South problem; it interpenetrates public and private sectors in the North as well. Activism to counter it must be similarly strategic.

The crackdown on the Batista brothers forced them out of direct management, required them to divest large assets to pay a multi-billion dollar fine, and continues to plague family control of the company (Freitas et al. 2017). The family's planned IPO spinoff of the JBS global food division was delayed five years after a poor reception on Wall Street, but in August 2020 the Batistas announced plans to move ahead with the offering in 2021. However, a shareholder uprising may put their plans back on ice.

The challenge, ironically, comes from the Brazilian state and investors. In a rare move, BNDES, which controls 30 per cent of JBS shares, joined forces with dissident investors in a vote by 72 per cent of shareholders to sue former CEOs Joseley and Wesley Batista for losses connected with their massive bribery of Brazilian officials. State authorities charged the brothers with selling large quantities of JBS stock to pay more than 1800 bribes, then repurchasing the shares at lower prices. JBS stock values also plummeted after their 2017 testimony about the crimes. (Food Safety News 2020b.

This unexpected turn, reminiscent of recent shareholder activism at Exxon and Chevron, implies increased investor scrutiny of environmental and social abuses. It also is a message for JBS that perhaps this is not the best time to woo shareholders with a new IPO. Wild sovereignty has its contradictions.

Notes

1 Tim Marema, reporter for the Daily Yonder (DailyYonder.com) and Olivia Paschal, reporter for Facing South, online magazine of the Institute for Southern Studies (facingsouth.org).
2 See: www.ncpork.org/north-carolinas-pork-industry-remains-economic-powerhouse/
3 Hard copy record of July 22 version of "North Carolina Coronavirus Map and Case Count" 2020 *The New York Times*; site updated since: www.nytimes.com/interactive/2020/us/north-carolina-coronavirus-cases.html
4 High infection rates were defined as 100(+) cases/10,000 residents. Typical commuting distance was assumed to be 15 miles.
5 See: followthemoney.org
6 See: https://dph.georgia.gov/covid-19-daily-status-report for official Covid-19 data from Georgia DPH.
7 See: https://en.wikipedia.org/wiki/Union_affiliation_by_U.S._state for source of data on union affiliation by state.
8 See: www.cdc.gov/coronavirus/2019-ncov/community/organizations/businesses-employers.html
9 In January 2021 President Joseph Biden ordered OSHA to strengthen safety rules and enforcement for Covid-19 in workplaces. Since then he has pushed OSHA and large firms to mandate vaccinations. Tyson Foods required its workforce to be vaccinated beginning in August (Hirsch 2021).
10 This archive of documents was obtained by Columbia University's Brown Institute for Media Innovation.
11 Like much of the Global South, Brazil relies on major commodity exports to earn foreign currency reserves to stabilise local currency values and pay sovereign debt, also many popular workers party social programs relied on these funds (Pahnke 2017: 50).

Bibliography

Aldo, Musacchio and Sergio Lazzarini. (2014). *Reinventing State Capitalism*. Harvard University Press.
Amnesty International. (2020). Brazil: Cattle illegally grazed in the Amazon found in supply chain of leading meat-packer JBS. July 15. Available at: https://www.amnesty.org/en/latest/news/2020/07/brazil-cattle-illegally-grazed-in-the-amazon-found-in-supply-chain-of-leading-meat-packer-jbs/ (Accessed: 05/13/22).
Alerigi, Alberto and Thais Freitas. (2017). 'Operation Weak Flesh' takes bite out of Brazil's meat exports. *Reuters*. March 24. Available at: https://www.reuters.com/article/us-brazil-corruption-food-exports/operation-weak-flesh-takes-bite-out-of-brazils-meat-exports-idUSKBN16V281 (Accessed: 05/13/22).
Barbara, Vanessa. (2021). The Unveiling of Bolsonaro's Supervillain Plot Is Weirdly Gripping. May 27. *The New York Times*. Opinion. Available at: https://www.nytimes.com/2021/05/27/opinion/brazil-covid-inquiry-bolsonaro.html. (Accessed: 05/13/22).

Bradbury, Shelly. (2020a). Two JBS Greeley employees say they were fired after staying home sick during coronavirus pandemic. *The Denver Post.* May 7. Available at: https://www. denverpost.com/2020/05/07/coronavirus-jbs-greeley-plant-fired-sick/ (Accessed: 05/13/22).

Bradbury, Shelly. (2020b). How coronavirus spread through JBS's Greeley beef plant. *The Denver Post.* July 12. Available at: https://www.denverpost.com/2020/07/12/jbs-greeley-coronavirus-investigation/. (Accessed: 05/13/22).

Brown, Wendy. (2015). *Undoing the Demos: Neoliberalism's Stealth Revolution.* Zone Books.

CDC. (2019). Outbreak of *Salmonella* Infections Linked to Ground Beef. Centers for Disease Control and Prevention. *Food Safety Alert.* March 22. Available at: https://www.cdc.gov/salmonella/newport-10-18/index.html (Accessed: 05/13/22).

Center for Responsive Politics. (2021). Open Secrets: Money to Congress. Agribusiness: Meat processing and products. Available at: https://www.opensecrets.org/industries/summary. php?cycle=2020&ind=G2300 (Accessed: 05/23/22).

Chain Reaction. (2017). JBS: Financial Restructuring Could Be Delayed Due to Serious Allegations. Chain Reaction Research. Washington, DC. June 28.

Corkery, M. and Yaffe-Bellany, D. (2020). As meat plants stayed open to feed Americans, exports to China surged. *The New York Times.* June 16. Available at: https://www.nytimes. com/2020/06/16/business/meat-industry-china-pork.html (Accessed: 06/17/20).

Crossa, Mateo and James M. Cypher. (2020). Essential—and Expendable—Mexican Labor. *Dollars and Sense.* July-August. Available at: http://www.dollarsandsense.org/archives/ 2020/0720crossa-cypher.html (Accessed: 05/13/22).

Debtwire. (2018). Batista Family fights to stay atop as scandals deepen. *JBS Shareholder Profile.* March 28. Available at: https://www.debtwire.com/info/shareholder-profile-batista-fam ily-fights-stay-atop-jbs-scandals-deepen (Accessed: 05/13/22).

Dembicki, Geoff. (2020). Trump Is Bailing Out Big Meat—and Further Screwing the Planet. *The New Republic.* June 1. Available at: https://newrepublic.com/article/157913/trump-bailing-big-meatand-screwing-planet (Accessed: 05/23/22).

Democracy NC. (1995). Hog Money Pollutes NC General Assembly. Democracy North Carolina. July 13. Available at: https:// demo crac ync org/research/july-1995-hog-moneypollutes-nc-general-assembly/ (Accessed: 05/ 13/ 22).

2020 Democracy Now. Mike Davis: Workers Face "Sophie's Choice" Between Income & Health as 50 States Reopen Amid Pandemic. Part 1. May 22. Available at: https://www. democracynow.org/2020/5/22/historian_mike_davis_increased_inequality_coronavirus

Documenting Covid-19. (2020). Brown Institute for Media Innovation. Columbia University. Available at: https://documentingCovid-19.io/ (Accessed: 08/15/20).

Douglas, Leah. (2020a). Charting the spread of Covid-19 in the food system. Food and Environmental Reporting Network, May 19. Available at: https://thefern.org/2020/05/ charting-the-spread-of-Covid-19-in-the-food-system/ (Accessed: 07/02/20).

Douglas, Leah. (2020b). Mapping Covid-19 outbreaks in the food system April 22. Food and Environmental Reporting Network. Available at: https://thefern.org/2020/04/mapp ing-Covid-19-in-meat-and-food-processing-plants/ (Accessed: 02/02/21).

Douglas, Leah. (2020c). Few states release data about Covid-19 in the food system. Food and Environmental Reporting Network. August 17. Available at: https://thefern.org/ ag_insider/few-states-release-data-about-Covid-19-in-the-food-system/ (Accessed: 08/25/20).

Douglas, Leah. (2020d). Covid-19 shows no sign of slowing among food-system workers. Food and Environmental Reporting Network. June 22. Available at: https://thefern. org/2020/06/Covid-19-shows-no-sign-of-slowing-among-food-system-workers/ (Accessed: 07/05/20).

Douglas, Leah and Marema, Tim. (2020). When Covid-19 hits a rural meatpacking plant, county infection rates soar to five times the average. Food and Environmental Reporting Network. 28 May. Available at: https://thefern.org/2020/05/when-Covid-19-hits-a-rural-meatpacking-plant-county-infection-rates-soar-to-five-times-the-average/ (Accessed: 07/16/20).

Engelmann, Fabiano. (2020). The 'Fight Against Corruption.' In: Brazil from the 2000s: A Political Crusade Through Judicial Activism. *Journal Of Law and Society.* Volume 47, Issue S1, October. ISSN: 0263-323X, S74–S89.

Ellwanger, Joel H., Bruna Kulmann-Leal And Valéria Kaminski, et. al. (2020). Beyond diversity loss and climate change: Impacts of Amazon deforestation on infectious diseases and public health. *Annals of the Brazilian Academy of Sciences.* 92(1): 1-33.

Estrada, Rodrigo. (2017). Greenpeace Brazil Suspends Negotiations with Cattle Giant JBS. Greenpeace. March 23. Available at: https://www.greenpeace.org/usa/news/greenpeace-brazil-suspends-negotiations-cattle-giant-jbs/ (Accessed: 05/13/22).

Food Safety News. (2020a). DeLauro challenges USDA officials about JBS corruption in meat industry. February 13. Available at: https://www.foodsafetynews.com/2020/02/delauro-challenges-usda-officials-about-jbs-corruption-in-meat-industry/. (Accessed: 05/13/22).

Food Safety News. (2020b). JBS, S.A. shareholders agree to sue Joesley and Wesley Batista. November 9. Available at: https://www.foodsafetynews.com/2020/11/jbs-s-a-shareholders-agree-to-sue-joesley-and-wesley-batista/ (Accessed: 05/23/22).

Freitas, Jr., Gerson, Tatiana Freitas and Jeff Wilson. (2017). The Dirty family secret behind JBS' $20 billion buying spree. *The Grand Island Independent.* Bloomberg - Washington Post News Service, June 3. Available at: https://theindependent.com/news/dirty-family-secret-behind-jbs-20-billion-buying-spree/article_367033a2-48a7-11e7-b6bf-93bbde853c2d.html (Accessed: 05/13/22).

Fremstad, S., Rho, H.J., Brown, H. (2020). Meatpacking workers are a diverse group who need better protections. Center for Economic and Policy Research. April 29. Available at: https://cepr.net/meatpacking-workers-are-a-diverse-group-who-need-better-protections/#:~:text=almost%20one%2dhalf%20(44.4%20percent,and%2022.5%20percent%20are%20black) (Accessed: 05/13/22).

Gerber, P. J., Steinfeld, H., Henderson, B., et. al. (2013). *Tackling Climate Change through Livestock – A Global Assessment of Emissions and Mitigation Opportunities.* Food and Agriculture Organization. Rome. Available at: https://www.fao.org/3/i3437e/i3437e.pdf (Accessed: 05/23/22).

Gezici, Armağan. (2020). Monopoly Everywhere. *Dollars and Sense.* January/February. Available at: http://www.dollarsandsense.org/archives/2020/0120gezici.html (Accessed: 05/13/22).

Godfray, Charles, Paul Aveyard, and Tara Garnett et. al. (2018). Meat consumption, health, and the environment. *Science.* Vol. 361, Issue 6399, 1-8. Available at: https://science.sciencemag.org/content/361/6399/eaam5324. (Accessed: 05/13/22).

Greenpeace. (2021). Making Mincemeat of the Pantanal: The Markets for Beef. March 3. Greenpeace International. Amsterdam. Available at: https://www.greenpeace.org/static/planet4-international-stateless/2021/03/77f3941a-0988_gp_pan_mincemeat_v9.95_mixedres.pdf (Accessed: 05/13/22).

Halpern, Rick. (2005). Packinghouse unions. *The Electronic Encyclopedia of Chicago.* Chicago Historical Society. Available at: http://www.encyclopedia.chicagohistory.org/pages/943.html (Accessed: 09/12/20).

Harvey, David. (2005). *A Brief History of Neoliberalism.* Oxford: Oxford University Press.

Hirsch, Lauren. (2021). After mandate, 91% of Tyson workers are vaccinated. *New York Times*. September 30. Available at: https://www.nytimes.com/2021/09/30/business/tyson-foods-vaccination-mandate-rate.html (Accessed: 05/23/22).

Kalb, Don. (2018). Challenges to the European State: The deep play of finance, demos and ethnos in the new old Europe. In B. Kapferer (Ed.), *State, Resistance, Transformation: Anthropological Perspectives on the Dynamics of Power in Contemporary Global Realities*. Herefordshire, UK: Sean Kingston Publishing, 23-65.

Kapferer, Bruce. (2004). Old Permutations, New Formations? War, State, and Global Transgression. *Social Analysis*. 48(1): 64-72.

Kapferer, Bruce. (2018). Introduction: Crises of the power and the state in global realities. In B. Kapferer (Ed.), *State, Resistance, Transformation: Anthropological Perspectives on the Dynamics of Power in Contemporary Global Realities*. Herefordshire, UK: Sean Kingston Publishing, 1-12.

Kindy, Kimberly. (2019). This foreign meat company got U.S. tax money. Now it wants to conquer America. *Washington Post*. November 7. Available at: https://www.washingtonpost.com/politics/this-foreign-meat-company-got-us-tax-money-now-it-wants-to-conquer-america/2019/11/04/854836ae-eae5-11e9-9306-47cb0324fd44_story.html. (Accessed: 05/13/22).

Kirkham, Chris. (2021). Exclusive: Most U.S. firms hit with COVID-19 safety fines aren't paying up February 18. *Reuters*. Available at: https://www.reuters.com/article/us-health-coronavirus-workplace-fines-ex/exclusive-most-u-s-firms-hit-with-covid-19-safety-fines-arent-paying-up-idUSKBN2AI1JT (Accessed: 05/13/22).

Londoño, Ernesto. (2021). Brazil Is Famous for Its Meat. But Vegetarianism Is Soaring. *The New York Times*. December 26. Available at: https://www.nytimes.com/2020/12/26/world/americas/brazil-vegetarian.html (Accessed: 05/13/22).

Mano, Ana (2020). Special Report: How Covid-19 Swept the Brazilian Slaughterhouses of JBS, World's Top Meatpacker. *Reuters*. September 8. Available at: https://www.reuters.com/article/us-health-coronavirus-jbs-specialreport/special-report-how-covid-19-swept-the-brazilian-slaughterhouses-of-jbs-worlds-top-meatpacker-iduskbn25z1hz (Accessed: 08/17/21)

Mano, Ana (2021). JBS ordered to pay $3.6 million after Brazil beef plant's COVID outbreak. *Reuters*. March 19. Available at: https://www.reuters.com/article/us-jbs-covid-payment/jbs-ordered-to-pay-3-6-million-after-brazil-beef-plants-covid-outbreak-idUSKBN2BB1XB (Accessed: 05/13/22).

Marema, Tim. (2020). The rural counties with highest rate of new infections. *Daily Yonder*. June 15. Available at: https://dailyyonder.com/new-infections-hit-counties-with-meatpacking-plants-prisons-and-non-white-populations/2020/06/15/ (Accessed 07/15/20).

McCausland, Phil. (2021). The Price of Meat is going up. Ranchers and Corporations are split on why. *NBC News*, October 2. Available at: https://www.nbcnews.com/politics/politics-news/farmers-biden-admin-push-change-meatpackers-status-quo-rcna2511 (Accessed 05/23/22).

McMichael, Philip. (2013). *Food Regimes and Agrarian Questions*. Fernwood Publishing.

Mitchell, Charlie. (2019). In Nebraska, cattle ranchers rally against big agribusiness. *The Counter*. October 3. Available at: https://thecounter.org/nebraska-cattle-ranchers-rally-ocm-usda/ (Accessed: 05/13/22).

NC Watchdog Reporting Network. (2020). How NC chose cooperation over transparency on meatpacking plants with virus outbreaks. *Raleigh News and Observer*. August 11. Available at: https://www.newsobserver.com/news/coronavirus/article244672767.html?fbclid=IwAR3Hu6elRWHY6EQKgfO4N_G_jeKafCxbXOuWhpTYhc00pWGFNYjD-exgrpM (Accessed: 08/18/20).

Nestle, Marion. (2007). *Food Politics: How the Food Industry Influences Nutrition and Health*. University of California Press.

Nonini, Donald. n.d. Our Food, The Alliance, and the Corporate State. In Donald Nonini and Dorothy Holland, *Food Activism in the Current Crises*. (In prep) New York City: New York University Press.

Oberst, Christofer. (2015). JBS turns to Europe for Processed Foods Expansion. Available at: https://www.delimarketnews.com/jbs-turns-europe-processed-foods-expansion/chr istofer-oberst/mon-09212015-1218/2131. (Accessed: 05/13/22).

Pahnke, Anthony. (2017). The Brazilian Crisis: Corruption, Neoliberalism and the Primary Sector. *Monthly Review Press*. Vol. 68(9): 43-54.

Pan, Kwan Yuk. (2015). Boom time for Brazil's JBS as real slides. *Financial Times*. March 30.

Phillips, Dom. (2019). The swashbuckling meat tycoons who nearly brought down a government. *The Guardian*. July 2. Available at: https://www.theguardian.com/environment/2019/jul/02/swashbuckling-meat-tycoons-nearly-brought-down-a-government-brazil (Accessed: 05/13/22).

Phillips, Dom. (2020). 'There's a direct relationship': Brazil meat plants linked to spread of Covid-19. *The Guardian*. July 15. Available at: https://www.theguardian.com/environment/2020/jul/15/brazil-meat-plants-linked-to-spread-of-covid-19 (Accessed: 05/13/22).

Richards, Doug. (2020). Industry: Georgia chicken plant production unabated by Covid-19. *11Alive News*. April 27. Available at: https://www.11alive.com/article/news/health/coronavirus/poultry-industry-Covid-19/85-76a95ff2-4668-419e-ae48-e069de380f80 (Accessed: 08/18/20).

Saunders, Jessica. (2020). Poultry processor sends 415 South Georgia employees home with pay. *Atlanta Business Journal*. April 7. Available at: https://www.bizjournals.com/atlanta/news/2020/04/07/poultry-processor-sends-415-south-georgia.html. (Accessed: 05/13/22).

Sharma, Shefali. (2018). Mighty Giants: Leaders of the Global Meat Complex. Inst. for Agriculture and Trade Policy. April 10. Available at: https://www.iatp.org/blog/leaders-global-meat-complex. (Accessed: 05/13/22).

Sims, Bob and Erica Shaffer. (2020). JBS sets earnings record in 2019. JBS SA. March 27. Available at: https://www.meatpoultry.com/articles/22838-jbs-sets-earnings-record-in-2019#:~:text=JBS%20USA%20Beef%2C%20which%20includes,compared%20to%208%25%20in%202018. (Accessed: 05/13/22).

Smith, Morgan. (2021). JBS Buys European Plant-based Food Producer Vivera. *ProFood World*. April 20. Available at: https://www.profoodworld.com/industry-news/news/21391581/jbs-acquisition-raises-its-global-position-in-the-plant-protein-market. (Accessed: 05/13/22).

Smith-Nonini, Sandy. (2021). "When Workers' Health is Public Health:" Meat-Processing, COVID-19 Spread and the Structural Complicity of Local and State Health Departments. In M. Singer, P. Erickson, & C. Abadia (Eds.), *A Companion to Medical Anthropology*. 2nd edition. Hoboken, NJ: Wiley-Blackwell.

Smith-Nonini, Sandy. (2020). Covid Confidential. The coronavirus is surging in rural counties with meatpacking plants. North Carolina officials are hiding data on clusters from the public. *INDY Week*, 12-13, July 1. Available at: https://indyweek.com/news/northcarolina/covid-19-meatpacking-plants/.(Accessed: 05/13/22).

Smith-Nonini, Sandy and Tim Marema. (2020). We Tracked the rural epicenters of coronavirus spread in North Carolina. The data point to meat-processing plants. *INDY Week*, 9-11, July 29. Available at: https://indyweek.com/news/northcarolina/coronavirus-meat packing-plants-data/. (Accessed: 05/13/22).

Smith-Nonini, Sandy and Olivia Paschal. (2020). As COVID-19 hit Georgia meatpacking counties, officials and industry shifted blame. *Facing South*. Institute for Southern Studies. Sept. 8. Available at: https://www.facingsouth.org/2020/09/covid-19-hit-georgia-meat packing-counties-officials-and-industry-shifted-blameTop. (Accessed: 05/13/22).

TBIR. (2019). Revealed: How the Global Beef Trade is Destroying the Amazon. The Bureau of Investigative Reporting. February 7. Available at: https://www.thebureaui nvestigates.com/stories/2019-07-02/global-beef-trade-amazon-deforestation. (Accessed: 05/13/22).

Taylor, C., Boulos, C., and Almond, D. (2020). Livestock plants and COVID-19 transmission. *Proceedings of the National Academy of Sciences* 117: 31706 – 31715. Available at: https://www.pnas.org/content/117/50/31706/tab-article-info (Accessed: 01/31/21).

Tooze, Adam. (2021). Has Covid ended the Neoliberal Era? *The Guardian*, September 2. Available at: https://www.theguardian.com/news/2021/sep/02/covid-and-the-crisis-of-neoliberalism. (Accessed: 05/13/22).

Wallace, Rob. (2020). *Dead Epidemiologists: On the Origins of Covid-19*. Monthly Review Press.

Yerardi, J. and Fernández Campbell, A. (2020). Fewer inspectors, more deaths: The Trump administration rolls back workplace safety inspections. *Vox News*. August 18. Available at: https://www.vox.com/2020/8/18/21366388/osha-worker-safety-trump (Accessed: 08/29/20).

PART II

Global Health, Social Care, and Reproduction During the Covid-19 Pandemic

6

GLOBAL HEALTH, COVID-19 AND THE FUTURE OF NEOLIBERALISM

Dillon Wamsley and Solomon Benatar

Introduction

In this chapter, we seek to situate the economic and health crises associated with Covid-19 within historical contexts, examining trends in health status at different periods of capitalist development in various world regions. We first examine the post-World War II period from 1945 to 1980 to illustrate how the emergence of public health models and national development dramatically improved population health, despite persistent inequalities between the Global North and South. Second, we examine the transformations ushered in under neoliberalism from 1980 to 2020, surveying critical shifts in public health finance and provision, and their implications for population health. Although this period was marked by improvements in certain aggregate health metrics, we contend that the rise of austerity and risk privatisation has generated substantial inequalities within and between countries, degraded population health in some regions, and obstructed the capacities of state and global health institutions in managing disease outbreaks. Third, we survey the emergence of the Covid-19 global pandemic, the accompanying economic crisis, state responses, and the multifaceted implications for global health. We maintain that while inequalities within countries have intensified, the effects of the crisis have been most deeply felt in low- and middle-income countries (LMICs) across the Global South. We conclude by examining possible lessons from the Covid-19 pandemic and assessing potential transformations in global health, the global economy, and our relationships to nature that may lead to improved health and social well-being in a post-pandemic world.

DOI: 10.4324/9781003250432-9

Postwar Capitalist Development and Global Health, 1945–1980

The European origins of public health date back to the late 19th century, often emerging from welfarist state-building and the inequalities of industrial capitalism. Perhaps the first European public healthcare model, Germany's national health insurance system, was established in the *Health Insurance Bill of 1883* as part of Otto Von Bismarck's social insurance legislation. The 1883 bill created a statutory health insurance system based on earnings-related contributions that insured eligible populations against particular social risks and provided basic health services free at delivery (Busse et al. 2017). Before the mid-20th century, however, most public health expenditures were virtually non-existent. Within OECD countries, before the 1930s, no country allocated 1 per cent of GDP to public health care expenditures, while by 1980, average OECD expenditures rose to 4–6.5 per cent of GDP (Ortiz-Ospina and Roser 2016).[1] In the aftermath of the Great Depression and the Second World War, healthcare institutions and global health governance underwent a period of development and rapid change as states exerted greater control over national economies and sought to address the social dislocations and public health crises of the inter-war period. Predicated on quasi-Keynesian macroeconomic policies, the postwar order saw the emergence of nationally oriented, welfarist models of capitalist development (Cox 1987; Panitch and Gindin 2012). This global developmental trajectory laid the foundations for some of the world's first public health models and many industrialised capitalist countries extended the Bismarkian system throughout the mid-20th century. The National Health Service (NHS), established in post-World War II Britain under the influence of Aneurin Bevan's Labour Party, was perhaps the most comprehensive model, guaranteeing comprehensive and universal health service free at the point of delivery as a right of citizenship (Webster 2002).

Across the Global South, national healthcare initiatives emerged throughout the 1960s and 1970s to pursue national development and de-colonisation (Gish 1979; Sanders et al. 2019). These ranged from the rural health care initiatives in countries across Asia, to national healthcare systems in communist countries, most successfully in post-revolutionary Cuba. This period saw the emergence of a global "Health for All" initiative based on primary healthcare and public health principles, which prioritised publicly guaranteed healthcare and a commitment to address the social determinants of health (Benatar et al. 2018; Holst 2020). This initiative was based on basic care principles, participatory democracy, and human rights, as outlined in the 1978 Alma-Ata Declaration (Gish 1979). Despite numerous gaps and persistent inequalities within and between countries, the diverse initiatives of public health pursued on a global scale during this era saw rapid improvements in population health outcomes. Tables 6.1 and 6.2 show that from 1945 through 1980, within both LMICs and wealthy countries, life expectancy at birth, child mortality rates, and maternal mortality improved significantly (Ortiz-Ospina and Roser 2016).

TABLE 6.1 Health and ecological metrics for world regions, 1950–1980

Regions	Africa		Asia		North America		Europe	
Years	1950	1980	1950	1980	1950	1980	1950	1980
Life Expectancy (years)	36.5	49.9	41.1	60.4	68.2	74.0	62.0	71.3
*MMR /100.000 live births	N/A	640	N/A	420	N/A	12	N/A	27
Child Mortality Deaths under 5 per 1000 births	32.3	19	24.4	11.8	3.81	1.48	10.9	2.37
Ecological Footprint Annual CO_2 emissions	93.4m	529.8m	483.8m	4.4 b	2.7 b	5.5b	2.4b	7.7b

Note: M = Million Tonnes, B = Billion Tonnes.

Sources: Our World in Data, available at: https://ourworldindata.org/ (Ortiz-Ospina and Roser, 2016); WHO. (1991). Maternal Mortality Ratios and Rates, A Tabulation of Available Information, Third ed. WHO. Available at: https://apps.who.int/iris/handle/10665/272290. *There was no regional MMR available in these world regions in 1950 and the MMR data under the 1980 column is based on available 1983 data.

TABLE 6.2 Health, economic, and ecological metrics for select countries, 1950–1980

Countries	Cuba		Malaysia		South Africa		United States		United Kingdom	
Years	1950	1980	1950	1980	1950	1980	1950	1980	1950	1980
MMR/100.000 live births	N/A	*40	533.9	**77.2	N/A	N/A	83.0	10.5	91.4	11.7
Life Expectancy (yrs)	58.2	73.8	53.3	68.1	43.6	58.1	68.2	73.9	68.7	73.6
Per capita GDP in US$	2482	4106	2440	5829	3819	6998	14179	29611	11088	20612
Ecological Footprint Annual CO_2 emissions	5.6m	31m	3.7m	28m	61m	228m	2.5b	4.7b	500m	579m

Note: M = Million Tonnes, B = Billion Tonnes.

Sources: Our World in Data, available at: https://ourworldindata.org/ (Ortiz-Ospina and Roser, 2016); WHO. (1991). Maternal Mortality Ratios and Rates, A Tabulation of Available Information, Third ed. WHO. Available at: https://apps.who.int/iris/handle/10665/272290. * For Cuba, MMR data is for 1981. ** Note for Malaysia, MMR data is 1979 not 1980 data.

We argue that these significant improvements in population health outcomes reflected a historical conjuncture in which many states committed to national development under quasi-Keynesian macroeconomic policies, often in response to pressures exerted by citizens and social movements.

Contributions to improved public health included (1) publicly funded payment for the health care of individuals, free at the point of delivery as in the United Kingdom, Canada and many other countries, (2) universal social policies as a means of poverty alleviation (Mkandawire 2005) and (3) substantial resources to finance public health institutions that socialised risks and targeted the social underpinnings of health—for example, *public health measures* such as provision of clean water, clean air, safe handling of sewerage, hygienic food preparation, vaccinations and other pandemic control measures—that contributed to substantial gains in population health in many world regions.[2]

Steadily rising per capita incomes also enabled states to finance public investments in research and development, leading to improvements in technology and medical care. Specific advances included (1) the discovery of many new drugs, including cortisone, streptomycin for tuberculosis and chlorpromazine that contributed to the revolution in psychiatry, (2) the birth of intensive care, open-heart surgery, kidney transplantation and hip replacement, (3) chemotherapy for curing some childhood cancers and (4iv) Crick and Watson's identification of the structure of DNA—and more (Le Fanu 1999).

Although social movements sought to extend public health improvements to hitherto excluded groups and remedy persistent inequalities, a deep crisis of global capitalism throughout the late 1970s and a global shift toward market provision frustrated the realisation of such efforts.

Neoliberalism, Risk Privatisation and the Reconfiguration of Public Health Financing, 1980–2008

The emergence of neoliberalism profoundly reconfigured policymaking frameworks and development paradigms around the globe, with significant implications for public health and healthcare institutions (Benatar et al. 2018; Labonté and Schrecker 2007). In contrast to the postwar era, characterised by commitments to target the social underpinnings of health through progressive public health finance and the socialisation of risks, neoliberal globalisation has been characterised by austerity, risk privatisation, and the deeper commodification and marketisation of healthcare. Despite aggregate improvements in certain population health metrics, public health under neoliberalism has seen the resurgence of non-communicable diseases associated with poverty, stagnation or declines in population health outcomes in regions exposed to austerity, and a retrenchment of the capacities of national and global health institutions in managing disease outbreaks, particularly in the Global South (Benatar 2016; Stuckler and Basu 2013).

Central to the imposition of neoliberal policies throughout the 1980s and 1990s was the implementation of austerity, i.e. economic policies that seek to reduce or consolidate public spending, prices, and wages to restore economic competitiveness (Blyth 2013). Austerity as a mode of governance was often administered through structural adjustment programs, i.e., economic reforms imposed by international financial institutions (IFIs) on debtor countries throughout the Global South prioritising debt repayment (Rowden 2009), but also reflected longstanding political and ideological commitments to fiscal retrenchment by domestic political forces in many world regions. Debt-servicing mandates and fiscal consolidation policies not only eroded state fiscal capacities (Stiglitz 2012), but also contributed to the broader deterioration of public health and, as we will argue, significantly undermined population health where they were implemented most stringently (Stuckler and Basu 2013). In sum, implementing austerity measures, particularly throughout the 1980s and 1990s, significantly reduced state fiscal capacities and public health finance.

From 1995 to 2002, for example, average health expenditures as a percentage of GDP *declined* in sub-Saharan African countries from 6.1 per cent in 1995 to 5.4 per cent in 2002, and from 6.3 per cent in 1995 to 6.2 per cent in 2002 in Latin America and Caribbean countries (Ortiz-Ospina and Roser 2016). As states across the Global South were compelled to accept loan conditionalities, debt servicing often took precedence over social and health expenditures (Forester et al. 2020). In 2000, for example, average domestic public health spending in low-income countries stood at 7 per cent while external debt service accounted for 11.7 per cent of domestic public expenditures (World Health Organization (WHO 2020). Even in OECD countries, average public health expenditures as a percentage of total health spending declined from 63.3 per cent in 1995 to 58.6 per cent in 2002 (Ortiz-Ospina and Roser 2016). These changes in healthcare expenditures reflected a reconfiguration of public health finance during the late 20th century, in which debt-repayment prioritisation and dynamics of "fiscal squeeze" compressed government health expenditures and contributed to the rise of marketised healthcare provision (Rudin and Sanders 2011; Turshen 1999).

Amidst the retrenchment of public health spending, healthcare expenditures were increasingly offloaded onto individuals as part of a broader "privatization of risks" (Bakker and Gill 2003). This included introducing user fees for healthcare services and the contracting-out of services and infrastructure to profitable private providers (Hunter and Murray 2019). Out-of-pocket health expenses, for example, rose dramatically during this period. In 1997, "Heavily Indebted Poor Countries" (HIPC) paid an average of over 52 per cent of total healthcare expenditures on out-of-pocket expenses, whereas "lower middle-income countries" paid on average of 59.2 per cent compared to 15 per cent in high income countries (Ortiz-Ospina and Roser 2016). These distortions in public health finance and healthcare provision over the past several decades have undermined much of the ethos of public health and the prioritisation of targeting the social determinants of health characteristic of earlier decades, producing a myriad of effects on population health.

The Dialectical Effects of Neoliberalism on Population Health

Mainstream analyses of global population health from liberal commentators often highlight aggregate improvements in population health metrics and socioeconomic indicators to construct a celebratory narrative of progress throughout the neoliberal era (Pinker 2018). However, while the neoliberal period has seen certain aggregate improvements in global population health outcomes often associated with declining mortality from infectious diseases, we contend that it has been punctuated by periods of declining health outcomes in many world regions associated with the imposition of austerity and risk privatisation, persistent national and global inequalities in health outcomes, and a declining capacity of public health institutions to manage disease outbreaks.

Although the determinants of population health outcomes are complex (Coburn 2000), a substantial literature has documented the adverse health effects associated with austerity. Stuckler et al. (2017) have identified how austerity measures can *directly* (through cuts to healthcare services or the privatisation of insurance) or *indirectly* (through unemployment or exposure to social risks) undermine population health. Throughout the 1980s and 1990s, many world regions exposed to these policies saw declines in many population health metrics, from declining life expectancy and increased morbidity to the resurgence of infectious diseases.

In Russia, for example, following the demise of the Soviet Union and the imposition of market liberalisation policies, public health expenditures as a percentage of total health spending declined from 73.8 per cent in 1995 to 58.9 per cent in 2002—as part of a wave of privatisation policies associated with a health crisis of declining living standards and declining life expectancy (Ortiz-Ospina and Roser 2016). Between 1990 and 1994, average life expectancy declined dramatically for men and women in Russia from 63.8 years and 74.4 years in 1990 to 57.7 years and 71.2 years, respectively. This arose alongside an epidemic of suicide, alcohol-related deaths, and resurgent infectious diseases (Notzon et al. 1998), associated with the effects of market liberalisation policies and prolonged unemployment (Stuckler et al. 2009). Similar studies have observed adverse health effects, from rising infant mortality to resurgent infectious diseases, associated with cuts to health expenditures and privatisation policies imposed in East Asia in the aftermath of the 1990s financial crises (Stuckler and Basu 2013; Wade and Veneroso 1998), as well as in Mexico, Argentina, and elsewhere (Stiglitz 2002). From the 1980s to the present, many of these socioeconomic adjustments were imposed on debtor countries by the IMF in exchange for debt relief (Forester et al. 2020).

Throughout the neoliberal period, one of the most common health reform policies has been a reversion to cost financing schemes that offload health expenditure to individuals (e.g. user fees). In addition to deepening poverty by imposing additional costs to access services (Ponsar et al. 2011), the implementation of user fees has undermined public health and population health outcomes. In sub-Saharan Africa, for example, numerous studies have illustrated the adverse effects of user fees on population health (James et al. 2006; Nanda 2002). By imposing financial barriers to access care, user fees reduce the likelihood of accessing healthcare facilities, predominantly for low-income populations, leading to delayed treatment of disease or unreported illnesses with a range of downstream effects. Underutilised primary care and delayed treatment, closely linked with user fee schemes, are strongly associated with increased mortality (Ponsar et al. 2011). Recent studies have also illustrated how, all else equal, the reversal of user fees and the implementation of public health finance can reduce neonatal and population mortality and improve post-hospitalisation health status (Qin et al. 2018).

Throughout the early 2000s, the failures of austerity and market liberalisation coincided with an attenuation of some of these trends (Ostry et al. 2016). In LMICs, public health expenditures increased modestly during the early 2000s, and external health aid increased substantially (WHO 2020). Significant resources from state, civil society, and (often unaccountable) wealthy donors devoted to curbing HIV/AIDS-related deaths and controlling malaria and tuberculosis led to significant reductions in child mortality and deaths from communicable diseases across the Global South. As Table 6.3 indicates, the period from 1995 to 2008 saw cross-country reductions in child and maternal mortality rates and increased life expectancy at birth (Ortiz-Ospina and Roser 2016). These improvements reflect technological advancements in medical care, knowledge diffusion and increased resources devoted to reducing death from pneumonia, and developing/using anti-retroviral drugs for HIV/AIDS. Other advances included completing the first full human genome draft, approval of the first Herpes virus vaccine, reductions in coronary artery disease deaths and increased survival rates for many malignancies (lymphoma, myeloma, leukaemia and more) (Whitty 2017).

TABLE 6.3 Health and ecological metrics for world regions, 1980–2008

Regions	Africa		Asia		North America		Europe	
Years	1980	2008	1980	2008	1980	2008	1980	2008
Life Expectancy (years)	49.9	57.1	60.4	70.2	74.0	78.6	71.3	75.5
MMR/100.000 live births	640	590	420	190	12	23	27	16
Child Mortality Deaths under 5 per 1000 births	19	10.3	11.8	4.6	1.48	0.76	2.37	0.76
Ecological Footprint Annual CO2 emissions	529.8m	1.17b	4.4b	14.7b	5.5b	7.16b	7.7b	6.4b

Note: M = Million Tonnes, B = Billion Tonnes. *MMA data not available for most countries until 1990.

Sources: Our World in Data, available at: https://ourworldindata.org/ (Ortiz-Ospina and Roser 2016); WHO. 1991. Maternal Mortality Ratios and Rates, A Tabulation of Available Information, Third ed. WHO. Available at: https://apps.who.int/iris/handle/10665/272290; WHO (2010) Trends in Maternal Mortality: 1980 to 2008.

Notwithstanding these aggregate improvements since the 1990s, many of the most substantial gains in population health and declining poverty occurred in Asia, where China, the most populous country, averted market liberalisation policies (Weber 2021). In addition, critical scholars have noted how vast economic inequalities (including relative inequality) deepened within countries throughout the neoliberal period, with direct effects on population health (Wilkinson and Pickett 2011). Similarly, as Table 6.3 highlights, substantial disparities in health outcomes (average life expectancy, rates of child and maternal mortality) have persisted between world regions throughout the neoliberal era. Non-communicable diseases associated with poverty in LMICs, and stark inequalities in access to food, nutrition, water and shelter were at the foundation of these inequalities (Benatar 2016).

Data on the ecological footprints in various countries and regions is included as a reminder that while increasing affluence improves lives, it does so in tandem with increasing ecological damage. This implies that achieving similar health goals in lower-income countries will be at an ecological cost. In the face of limits to economic growth, the challenge for all, including wealthy countries, is to do better with less (Bednarz and Bevis 2012).

Despite reductions in inequality between countries over the past several decades, inequalities in life chances continue to be sharply divided across world regions (Benatar 2016). Average life expectancy is strongly associated with per capita income, with affluent Western countries far outpacing other countries. It should be noted that there is a wide range of life expectancies at birth for any level of income and that similar life expectancies can be achieved across a range of income levels.

The aftermath of the 2008 global financial crisis (GFC) saw a return to austerity in many world regions (Ortiz et al. 2015).[3] While aggregate global spending on health grew during the first decade of the 21st century, these trends have been significantly affected, and in some cases reversed, by the effects of the GFC (WHO 2020). Persistent imbalances in public health finance have remained in the post-2008 era. As of 2018, low-income countries, on average, continued to depend on donor funding for 30 per cent of total health spending, with external aid increasing as a share of total health spending from 18 per cent in 2000 to 30 per cent in 2018 (WHO 2020: 5–6). Out-of-pocket spending, moreover, accounted for 41 per cent of total health expenditures in low-income countries in 2018, which has remained virtually unchanged since the mid-1990s (WHO 2020). These imbalances continue to bear significant implications for population health, as the preponderance of external aid targets infectious diseases and funds basic services and primary care. Consequently, when crises hit, many low-income countries see retrenchments in health expenditures and funding for critical services in primary care, often leading to declining utilisation of health services and declining health outcomes (Kirigia et al. 2011).

Although the effects of the GFC were severe across the Global South, austerity was arguably most forcefully embraced in the Global North. Within the United States, tepid post-crisis stimulus policies and decentralised austerity contributed to deepening economic and health-based inequalities (Alston 2018). Similarly, within the United Kingdom, an unprecedented commitment to austerity in 2010 saw declining average life expectancy within de-industrialised regions in Northern and Northwestern England (Marmot 2020). Within periphery countries in the European Union, enforced austerity measures associated with post-crisis loan conditionalities contributed to sharp declines in population health outcomes. In Greece, for example, rising unemployment and significant cuts to social programs and healthcare expenditures have been linked to increasing rates of mortality, suicide-related deaths, and the resurgence of infectious diseases (Kentikelenis et al. 2014).

Accompanying a return to austerity in the post-2008 period has been an increasing turn toward healthcare marketisation (De Schutter 2020). Alongside the incursion of market forces in global health over the past several decades, characterised by a steady expansion of global market share for pharmaceutical and private health insurance companies (Mikulic 2020), the post-2008 period has seen increasing financialisation of healthcare. As part of a growing "financialization-development nexus", healthcare finance has been marked by the "transformation of healthcare into saleable and tradeable assets for global investors" (Hunter and Murray 2019: 1264). This has included an increasing reliance on private investors to finance healthcare initiatives, which has created asset classes out of population health, particularly in middle-income countries. This has been facilitated by the International Finance Corporation (IFC), the private equity arm of the World Bank, as well as development institutions and private actors such as the Bill and Melinda Gates Foundation (Hunter and Murray 2019). In addition to facilitating the privatisation of healthcare infrastructure and insurance markets, these initiatives often increase government costs due to exorbitant interest rate payments. Social inequalities in access to care have been widened through user fees, and population health has been subordinated to the needs of profit-seeking investors (Marriott and Hamer 2014).

The return to austerity and marketisation in the post-2008 period has also exacerbated longstanding retrenchments in the capacities of states and global health institutions in managing globalised disease outbreaks and coordinating responses to public health emergencies. The successive emergence of viral pandemics and disease outbreaks throughout the 2000s, from SARS (2002–2004) and H1N1 (2009–2010) to Ebola (2014–2016) and Zika (2014–2016), exposed the lack of preparedness in global, national, and local health institutions in containing disease outbreaks (Smith and Upshur 2015). The inadequacies of public health capacities included under-staffed and under-resourced national health systems lacking surge capacity, a dearth of disease surveillance capacities, and an inability to mobilise a global response to assist with information/resource sharing and contract tracing (Smith and Upshur 2015). As the world has become more susceptible to globalised disease outbreaks, the effects of austerity at national and global scales have increasingly undermined the capacity to mobilise collective responses. From fragile national health systems subjected to cuts and outsourcing to a system of global health governance dominated by private donors and multinational corporations, the consequences of neoliberal austerity on public health were felt on a global scale in 2020.

Covid-19 and State Responses to the Crisis

The outbreak of the Covid-19 pandemic throughout 2020, characterised by successive waves of infections and rising case counts, increased the need for intensive care facilities and protective measures for healthcare workers, stretching the capacities of hospitals and healthcare systems around the globe. Despite state officials in high-income countries and global health institutions being privy to the ongoing threat of global pandemics (and coronaviruses) before the Covid-19 pandemic, many of the same fragilities and limited capacities of national and global health systems characteristic of the neoliberal era have again been revealed throughout the pandemic.

In response to the crisis, many governments issued various lockdown orders, ceased economic activity in many sectors, imposed travel restrictions, and implemented a variety of public health measures. The economic fallout from Covid-19 public health measures has generated mass unemployment not seen since the 1930s, marking a steeper economic contraction than the GFC, albeit for distinct reasons (Tooze 2020). The interlinking crises associated with Covid-19 throughout 2020 and 2021, and the various government responses to the global pandemic, offer important lessons for assessing the state of global health, the global economy, and the future of neoliberalism.

Rates of disease-related morbidity and mortality, particularly amongst elderly populations, those with underlying health conditions, and disabled and vulnerable populations, have been the most consequential population health-related effects of the Covid-19 pandemic. There have also been many concomitant effects on healthcare systems. Lowering rates of routine care, from antenatal care to elective surgeries and foregone care for non-communicable diseases, such as cancer and hypertension, and attendant effects of prolonged lockdown on mental health will likely contribute to ongoing and less detectible population health crises (WHO 2020). Disparities in the size and scope of health-related budgetary responses between countries have already emerged. A recent report from the WHO illustrates that most LMICs have spent less than US$10 per capita on health-related budgetary responses to Covid-19. In contrast, high-income countries on average have allocated over US$50 per capita (WHO 2020).

"A Pandemic of Poverty"

While few countries have successfully contained the Covid-19 outbreak, common measures have been implemented throughout the Global North. In response to the unprecedented economic crisis induced by public health and lockdown measures, the scope of fiscal and monetary responses in Western capitalist countries has been unprecedented, far outpacing post-2008 stimulus measures. The Federal Reserve in the United States implemented a multi trillion-dollar monetary safety net to avert a credit crunch and increasing interest rates (Wigglesworth 2020). Many affluent countries have implemented job retention schemes, covering upwards of 80 per cent of lost wages to discourage companies from laying off workers, extending unemployment benefits, and allocating payments to populations compelled to shelter at home (OECD 2020b).

Despite the depth of resources mobilised in response to the crisis, these efforts have been plagued by gaps, delays, and exclusions of inter-alia gig, part-time, or self-employed workers from job retention schemes; the use of no-strings-attached bailouts to highly profitable, exploitative and ecologically destructive multinational corporations (Solty 2020); and limited supports for rent, mortgage, and utility payment relief. Many countries have also failed to expand paid sick leave or offer adequate resources for undocumented, unhoused, or incarcerated populations and the millions of working-class populations fulfilling "essential services" that service affluent populations sheltering at home (Brenner 2020). Indeed, many millions have already fallen further into poverty even in affluent countries (Parolin et al. 2020; Stroud 2020) and calls for post-COVID "fiscal consolidation" have surfaced as governments have accumulated the largest public debt build-up in peacetime (Blyth and Sommers 2020).

Across many world regions, these failures have likewise been exacerbated by a failure of leadership, where politicians and state officials have inflamed xeno-phobic sentiment, sown doubt on the efficacy of public health measures, and proposed scientifically dubious and quasi-eugenicist "herd immunity" measures as substitutes for public health responses (Jones and Helmreich 2020; Woolhandler et al. 2021).

While there have been numerous *internal* inequalities within Western capitalist countries in response to the pandemic, the effects of Covid-19 have deepened a "great divergence" in the socioeconomic trajectories between the Global North and South (Georgieva 2021). The economic fallout across many LMICs has been severe. Countries dependent on tourism, foreign direct investment, commodity exports, and remittances have experienced the most severe economic contractions (WHO 2020: 21). These trends have been exacerbated by enormous capital flight, particu-larly from "emerging markets" where an estimated US$100 bn of investments was removed in the early months of the pandemic, over five times the fallout from the 2008 crisis (De Schutter 2020: 21), significantly undercutting local currencies and foreign exchange reserves (Stubbs et al. 2021). Despite being tempered by central bank monetary policies, an estimated gap of US$2.5 tn remains in these countries to meet financing needs (Stubbs et al. 2021). If not met, these fiscal gaps will have significant effects on budgetary priorities and likely divert resources away from health and social spending. Notwithstanding calls for debt relief for countries across the Global South throughout the pandemic, global institutions have failed to follow through substantively on such measures, pushing several countries toward IFIs for loans, some of which has already been devoted to servicing external debts rather than meeting social and health needs (Stubbs et al. 2021).

The consequences of these macroeconomic trends have already influenced government social protection schemes implemented in response to the pandemic. Indeed, the lockdown and job retention schemes implemented in many countries across the global north have simply been unfeasible in countries without the fiscal capacity or access to debt markets to pay populations to stay at home. Recent estimates indicate that so-called "advanced economies" spent an average of 24 per cent of GDP on fiscal measures in response to the COVID crisis, compared to only 6 per cent in middle-income countries and 2 per cent in low-income countries (IMF 2020).

Furthermore, shelter-at-home orders have been untenable in many low-income countries where populations have no access to shelter to lock down and crowded living conditions have significantly worsened Covid-19 outbreaks (WHO 2020). A recent UN study of over 1407 social protection measures across 208 countries during the COVID outbreak has illustrated the gaps within state responses to the pandemic, where over 55 per cent of countries surveyed have not introduced health protections and over 62 per cent of countries have failed to extend food or nutritional measures (De Schutter 2020). With many populations working in informal sectors across the Global South, substantial percentages of populations have been outside the reach of cash transfers and social protection, particularly in countries such as India (De Schutter 2020).

While the economic and social consequences of the pandemic are still unfolding, in October of 2020, World Bank estimates indicate that 88–115 mn people would be further pushed into extreme poverty because of Covid-19 (WB 2020), while UN measurements projected that populations facing hunger crises would likely double throughout the pandemic (De Schutter 2020). Given the well-documented methodological flaws of the US$1.90 a day poverty benchmark used by the World Bank (Alston 2020), these numbers likely dramatically underestimate the true fallout from the crisis. Indeed, even increasing the metric to US$3.20 a day, recent estimates indicate that over 176 mn will be pushed into poverty, leading the UN special rapporteur on human rights and extreme poverty to aptly term the current crisis a "pandemic of poverty" (Alston 2020).

Lessons from the Covid-19 Crisis and Alternatives to Neoliberalism: Recovering and Prioritising the Social

The dynamics of the global pandemic continue to change, and the full impact of profoundly adverse health effects with differing socioeconomic and racial incidences and death rates have not yet been fully foreseen. Yet several lessons have emerged throughout the Covid-19 crisis that offer important insights for assessing possible reforms and transformations not only in the realm of global health governance but also throughout the global economy to address longstanding imbalances, inequalities, and forms of (un)sustainability associated with neoliberalism.

First, perhaps the most palpable lesson emerging from the Covid-19 crisis over the past year has been the need to transform global health governance. The fragility of national and global health infrastructure in responding to major disease outbreaks, matched by a persistent dearth of preparedness, has been a consistent failure in the realm of global health governance (Smith and Upshur 2015). Superimposed on longstanding issues related to a lack of coordination between states in response to global disease and public health crises, partly due to the oversized role of private and philanthropic organisations in global health, Covid-19 has exacerbated a crisis of global health governance (Casale 2020). Associated failures exhibited throughout the pandemic range from the inability to share national disease surveillance data, failures to mobilise collective funds to countries without adequate fiscal capacity and stark asymmetries in global vaccine distribution, which some commentators have likened to "vaccine apartheid" (Byanyima 2021).

Seeking to remedy such failures will require addressing longstanding democratic deficits in global health governance (Casale 2020), particularly between low-income and affluent countries, and moving beyond forms of "biomedical and technocratic reductionism" characteristic of dominant approaches in global health (Holst 2020). Addressing major public health crises that require sustained collective commitments to public health orders requires more deeply democratic forms of governance and expanded ethical frameworks that can address the multifaceted social and economic underpinnings of health (Benatar et al. 2003; Gill and Benatar 2016).

Second, the Covid-19 crisis has revealed the centrality of prioritising equality in access to effective and affordable healthcare as a guaranteed public good. Such access should be socially ranked as of greater importance than frivolous consumption of energy and resources that add minimally to life or well-being. However, this aspiration must be tempered by recognising the limits of medicine and life and setting reasonable expectations of what can be achieved. Although few countries have displayed exemplary responses to the pandemic, there appears to be increasing evidence that countries most committed to paradigms of market-led development and public sector austerity, particularly in public health, have been most inept at containing disease outbreaks, protecting populations, and mobilising collective responses to the crisis (Assa and Calderon 2020; Mellish et al. 2020). From persistent outsourcing of public services such as disease surveillance and PPE procurement to for-profit providers, to under-resourced public health sectors and the prioritisation of economic profitability over public health, the initial pandemic responses by the United States and the United Kingdom, for example, encapsulated the consummate failures of neoliberalism in responding to a public health and economic crisis (Saad-Filho 2020). Recovering and extending the ethos of the Health for All movement requires recognising that public health and institutions of healthcare are irreconcilable with logics of market-based efficiency, competition, and outsourcing. In the face of global pandemics, healthcare institutions must be rebuilt and fortified with substantial and progressively financed resources that can withstand economic or public health crises and transcend discredited doctrines of austerity and budget balancing.

Given that the most powerful health-promoting forces are social (Birn and Kumar 2021), these necessary changes in global and public health must be matched by attendant transformations in the shape and trajectory of the global economy. The paths of post-crisis austerity pursued by most world regions in the aftermath of the 2008 GFC illustrated neoliberalism's enormous political staying power. However, gaping fractures have emerged within neoliberalism's intellectual and ideological edifice as illustrated by the depth of the crises associated with Covid-19. These crises have required the suspension of forms of market activity to prioritise public health as well as mobilisation of vast state resources to guarantee the stability of life and the social reproduction of its essential ingredients. Faced with the profound collapse of fraudulent and corrupt economies, even exemplar neoliberal states in the Anglo-American capitalist world, for example, have mobilised unprecedented resources in response to the crisis, revealing the intellectual bankruptcy of economic dogmas promoting budget-balancing at all costs, and the capacity of capitalist welfare states to supersede the logic of austerity amidst crisis (Saad-Filho 2020). However, while these realities of the pandemic may open opportunities, intellectual and ideological shifts are not synonymous with socio-political or institutional transformations. The increments in debt associated with mobilising resources for immediate needs may erode potential for future generations. In other words, unless they are accompanied by lasting progressive and redistributive fiscal and taxation measures, current rescue programmes will likely be paid for by future generations or shouldered by poor and marginalised populations.

Moreover, the same fiscal and monetary capacities of Western capitalist states do not exist in most countries. LMICs face an even greater historic debt build-up in response to the crisis. Without sovereign currencies and with little fiscal capacity, a renewed wave of fiscal austerity, debt-repayment prioritisation, and structural adjustments may not be far off the horizon, with devastating implications for social and health-related spending. These impending fiscal crises will be superimposed on longstanding and deep structural imbalances in global health finance.

Responses to the Covid-19 crisis thus must prioritise a globally coordinated mechanism of debt alleviation (or outright debt abolition) and the suspension of conditionalities for countries across the Global South (Stubbs et al. 2021), such that domestic investments in public health and social spending can be re-prioritised. These efforts must also work toward more long-term mechanisms of targeting tax evasion and raising state fiscal capacities to open avenues for sustained public investments in public health. Furthermore, given the depth of the hunger and poverty crisis preceding the pandemic, which has been significantly exacerbated over the past several years (Alston 2020), critical resources must be devoted to targeting not only high-profile infectious diseases and global pandemics, but also multifaceted non-communicable diseases. These efforts are closely intertwined with the need to rebuild domestic public health capacities and fiscal and social safety nets more broadly, which have long accounted for the preponderance of funds targeting non-communicable diseases associated with poverty.

Finally, our species' long-term plight, as revealed by the Covid-19 pandemic's destructive path, is resulting in long-overdue acknowledgement that globally entrenched socioeconomic and political forces have led to changes in our biosphere that are reaching *tipping points* and an unprecedented *complex global and planetary crisis*. Such global destabilisation could and *should* stimulate existential introspection, critical reflection through social, moral and ecological imaginations, and the socio-political commitment needed to produce a new "common sense" (Bakker, Gill and Wamsley 2021) and paradigm shifts in thinking (Benatar, Upshur, and Gill 2021).

All global health initiatives must come to terms with these ongoing existential planetary crises posing numerous interrelated threats to public health and sustainability (Gill and Benatar 2020), particularly as threats of viral pandemics have become increasingly frequent alongside unsustainable industrial, agricultural practices and environmental degradation. Incorporating planetary governance into global health is a challenge that will persist with ever-more urgency. While these monumental shifts in global health governance and the global economy require momentous shifts in existing balances of political power within and between countries, as well as transformative shifts in existing values and ethical paradigms, the depth of the ongoing public health and economic crises associated with Covid-19 may offer a unique window of opportunity to advance them.

We suggest that we have the knowledge, ingenuity, and potential for the technological and social innovation necessary to invigorate a massive coordinated, collective, global shift that adds the necessary ecologically motivated planetary stewardship to ensure the sustainability of our biosphere. But to achieve this will require the breadth and depth of courage that has seldom been observed except under war conditions. Our planet is dying from the war waged on it by humanly imposed unsustainable economic ideas and practices, overwhelmingly due to the exploitative and extractive practices of several dozen multinational corporations and fossil fuel companies (Griffin et al. 2017). It is within our ability to revive the planet but only through willingness to make great sacrifices for the benefit of future generations.

Notes

1 Data for public health expenditures in most non-OECD countries is not available during this period.
2 The advances in population health associated with postwar national development, however, were accompanied by substantial increases in energy and resource consumption, disproportionately in Western capitalist regions, as expressed in the size of the ecological footprint.
3 In the words of a recent UN report, the legacy of post-2008 austerity measures resulted in "severely underfunded public healthcare systems, undervalued and precarious care work, sustained declines in global labour income shares, and high inequality rates coupled with average decreases in statutory corporate tax rates" (De Schutter 2020, 1)

7

FROM OPERATION WARP SPEED TO TRIPS

Vaccines as Assets

Tatiana Andersen

Introduction

This chapter examines the political economy of biopharmaceutical innovation, focusing primarily on vaccines in the Covid-19 pandemic. This analysis aims to make visible the deep entanglements that entrench an extractive and dysfunctional innovation ecosystem, calcifying inequities in global access to essential medicines. The chapter argues that the current inequities in vaccine access are not new or anomalous and that they are the result of a complex yet strategic enmeshment among the logics of war and biomedicine, asset accumulation, and intellectual property. Uneven access to Covid-19 therapeutics can be traced to these three elements, which have built inequity into the political economy of biomedicine long before the current pandemic. The first section in the chapter teases out the first entanglement by unpacking Operation Warp Speed (OWS) as the culmination of a historical war-biomedical nexus driven by the United States, which has important implications for the global political economy of biomedical innovation and North-South asymmetries. The second section places OWS in the broader context of an extractive innovation ecosystem guided by a logic of differential accumulation characterised by the assetisation of publicly funded research. The final section explores how asset accumulation logics and unequal access to therapeutics are embedded in the international architecture of the Intellectual Property Rights (IPRs) regime. Before moving forward, I want to present two cases that illustrate these three logics' historical entanglements and how they intersect with the Covid-19 pandemic.

Operation Warp Speed had its genesis on April 13, 2020, when it was pitched to the White House by the then Health and Human Services (HHS) secretary Alex Azar (Diamond 2021). Originally called Manhattan Project 2, OWS was conceived as a colossal public-private partnership that would invest billions of dollars in

DOI: 10.4324/9781003250432-10

accelerating the development and manufacturing of vaccines, therapeutics, and diagnostics for Covid-19 (Diamond 2021). By April 2020, the name "Manhattan Project 2" had been retired, but the foundational entanglements with the U.S. Department of Defense (DOD) remained calcified (Diamond 2021). General Gustave Perna, in charge of the U.S. Army Materiel Command, was appointed as the Chief Operating Officer, and the DOD was assigned to support OWS in substantive ways (HHS 2020). As the pandemic entered its second year in 2021, OWS had provided over US$18 bn in funding for the Research, Development, Testing, and Evaluation (RDT&E) of vaccines and therapeutics that were intended specifically for the U.S. population (Lancet Commission Task Force Members 2021).

Ten years earlier in July 2010, Tekmira Pharmaceuticals was granted a US$140 mn contract by the DOD to develop a therapeutic candidate for the Ebola virus (Arbutus Biopharma 2010). Despite this research being publicly funded, Tekmira filed several successful patents for its lipid nanoparticle vaccine technology and found its stock rising dramatically in 2014 as the West African Ebola epidemic unfolded (Reuters 2015; World Intellectual Property Organization 2020). A year later, Tekmira acquired OnCore BioPharma to absorb its asset portfolio of patented research for Hepatitis B, rebranded as Arbutus Biopharma, and terminated all development for an Ebola vaccine to focus on Hepatitis B instead (Arbutus Biopharma 2020; Koons et al. 2014; Schnirring 2015). By then, the DOD had invested a total of US$157 mn which allowed Arbutus to patent publicly funded research as an income-generating asset, increase its market capitalisation during the Ebola epidemic, and leverage the subsequent financial performance to acquire the science needed to rebrand itself.

In the Covid-19 pandemic, one of the most significant achievements of OWS has been the mRNA vaccine developed by Moderna, which received a total investment of US$5.97 bn from the U.S. government (U.S. Congressional Research Service 2021). The publicly funded research on Ebola vaccines a decade earlier became a crucial piece of the Covid-19 vaccine puzzle. Moderna's mRNA vaccine relies on lipid nanoparticle technology which had been developed, in part, during the search for an Ebola vaccine (Gaviria and Kilic 2021). Some of the patents for this technology are still held by Arbutus Biopharma, and, as of writing, Moderna is pre-emptively challenging them while Arbutus investors speculate on the potential future earnings of royalties if said patents were to be upheld (Cooper 2021; Gaviria and Kilic 2021). By October 2021, Moderna had a market capitalisation of US$129.76 bn, signalling an increase of 1,872 per cent from December 2019. Meanwhile, three of its executives reached the Forbes 400 list with fortunes worth over US$5 bn each (Lonas 2021; see also Popcevski this volume). Such vast increases in accumulation relied not only on OWS investment but also on the mRNA vaccine platform technologies which the U.S. government partly funded long before the pandemic (Kuter et al. 2021). While Moderna and Arbutus clash in courtrooms over their right to profit from the ownership of publicly funded research as an income-generating asset, millions of people are dying across the world due to inequitable access to Covid-19 vaccines. This inequity has been internationally codified in a dysfunctional and extractive innovation ecosystem which prioritises the capital accumulation strategies of biopharmaceutical companies headquartered in the Global North over the lives of human beings in the Global South.

Operation Warp Speed and War-Biomedical Logics

Structured as a public–private partnership, OWS was characterised by a vast network of departments, agencies and programmes anchored to a matrix of state investment that has been expanding for decades (HHS 2020). While not alone in its efforts, the DOD became a foundational pillar of OWS, leading support in diagnostics, therapeutics, vaccines, production, and distribution (HHS 2020). The key companies that received OWS support for vaccine RDT&E funding and/or advanced purchasing agreements were AstraZeneca, Johnson & Johnson, Merck, Pfizer-BioNTech, Moderna, Novavax, and Sanofi-GSK (U.S. Congressional Research Service, 2021). The groundwork for this relationship was laid long before the Covid-19 pandemic through public funding for research on other viruses like SARS, MERS, Ebola, Hepatitis B, Dengue, and HPV (Kuter et al. 2021). The deeply enmeshed attachments between war and the biopharmaceutical sector in the 21st century are highlighted by the fact that the DOD was among the largest investors in these vaccine technologies. In recognition of this role, the Joint Program Executive Office for Chemical, Biological, Radiological and Nuclear Defense (JPEO-CBRND) became an integral actor within OWS (Slaoui and Hepburn 2020). The JPEO-CBRND is tasked with facilitating the development and acquisition of countermeasures against chemical, biological, radiological, and nuclear threats to "fight and win unencumbered" (DOD 2020). Such institutional entanglements between the DOD and therapeutic innovation also serve to excuse, and often justify, the continued expansion of the U.S. war-making apparatus. This is achieved through discursive and affective tools that present the DOD as an integral actor in global health investment and disease management (Terry 2017).

War-biomedical logics have evolved considerably in the last three decades, particularly after the doctrine of mutual deterrence shifted to a focus on counterproliferation (Terry 2017). These "pedagogies of preparedness" rationalised new trajectories of techno-scientific research and justified a fixation on biosecurity that obscured the distinction between peacetime and wartime (Terry 2017: 161). A key result of these measures was a significant entrenchment of networks between the defence community and the life sciences, evidenced by federal agencies tripling funding for biochemical countermeasures between 9/11 and 2008 (Reppy 2008; Terry 2017). Congressional support for this expansion was driven by an attachment to the defensive protection offered through biosecurity, the promissory hope of biomedical salvation, and the perceived economic growth opportunities through techno-scientific innovation (Mazzucato 2018a; Terry 2017). This continued during the Obama presidency, for instance through the National Bioeconomy Blueprint, which emphasised the role of DOD vaccine research in strategies for future economic growth (Obama White House 2012).

Increased government spending on the private defence sector has altered the landscape of techno-scientific research. Defence strategies can neglect important biomedical research pathways, as funding decisions are guided by assessments of threats and risks to U.S. national security (Ficke et al. 2012; Reppy 2008). For example, stem cell RDT&E for musculoskeletal polytrauma resulting from improvised explosive devices has been prioritised, alongside vaccine technologies for certain viruses due to the expectation of ongoing military presence in "high-risk" tropical regions (Christopherson & Nesti 2011). These decisions can create funding and expertise vacuums, leading to the marginalisation of alternative enclaves of investigation that potentially delay or outright eclipse other therapeutic innovation pathways for civilian patient populations, including those in the Global South. Reppy summarises these concerns by positing that "if we accept the argument that new knowledge is influenced by the conditions under which it is produced, we would expect the MIC [Military Industrial Complex] to have shaped the scientific knowledge produced" (Reppy 2008: 803). War-biomedical logics are also reflected in the reshaping of traditional public health structures, which have been weakened in favour of those led by defence strategies. For instance, the Public Health Emergency Preparedness cooperative (PHEP) within the Centers for Disease Control (CDC) had its annual budget reduced by 50 per cent from 2006 to 2013 (Terry 2017). In this way, war-biomedical entanglements are deepened by expanding defence-funded biomedical research and a corresponding displacement of traditional public health bureaucracies. As Terry argues, such attachments between biomedical innovation and war discursively justify the continued expansion of the U.S. defence budgets and bureaucratic reach (Terry 2017).

I want to extend this further and argue that war-biomedical entanglements help preserve the ontological security of the DOD and of the U.S. more broadly. In International Relations, ontological security refers to how states seek the "security of a consistent self" by constructing and reproducing autobiographical identity narratives (Subotić 2015: 613). These narratives serve to justify the existence and continuity not only of the state itself but also of its membership in the international community (Subotić 2015). My claim is that the deepening of war-biomedical entanglements is used by the DOD to preserve its ontological security and justify the continuing ballooning of its budgets, bureaucratic reach, corporate partnerships, and international presence. Narratives of biomedical salvation, biosecurity, and biosurveillance are employed to enmesh the very health of populations with the strength and reach of the DOD. The pivot to bioterrorism countermeasures since 9/11 has meant that the state can never have too much health or too much security (Terry 2017). This translates to the United States' self-appointed mandate as an enforcer of global biosecurity, an ongoing project that demands permanent international threat surveillance, disease management, and active intervention.

For the United States more broadly, the framing of its military as an indispensable leader in global health helps it remain secure in its identity as a global military power. Any threat to the integrity and magnitude of the U.S. defence structure (such as budget reductions) is framed as a threat to global health security and therapeutic innovation. Given that biosecurity becomes a project with no temporal or territorial limits, such framing justifies the existence and expansion of the U.S. defence apparatus and by extension, requires its continued diffusion across political and bureaucratic borders into an indefinite future where emerging biological threats reside in-waiting (Terry 2017). The entanglement between war-biomedical logics and the ontological security of the United States has significant implications for the political economy of biopharmaceutical research because the sector has co-evolved with counterterrorism and biosecurity approaches to U.S. defence in the 21st century. This entanglement will likely deepen in the coming years as the Biden Administration seeks to repair and reconstruct the identity of the United States as a global "leader" in health and disease management, particularly after the perceived disruption and dislocation of this identity during the Trump Presidency.

The Australia-United States Ministerial Consultations (AUSMIN) held in September 2021 present an excellent example of the future entrenchment of war-biomedical logics due to the Covid-19 pandemic. The AUSMIN joint statement commits both countries to robust biosecurity, biosafety, and biosurveillance in the Indo-Pacific region to "prevent, detect, and respond to emerging COVID-19 variants, and the emergence or resurgence of other infectious diseases" (AUSMIN 2021). The aim is to support the U.S. Global Health Security Strategy and reinforce existing cooperation with the DOD (AUSMIN 2021). Global biosurveillance networks and the simultaneous strengthening of research and manufacturing of therapeutic products are supposed to bolster the architecture of health security in the region (AUSMIN 2021). This joint statement is significant for three reasons. Firstly, a clear war-biomedical nexus is made evident by the plethora of security references and DOD involvement that justify an ongoing defensive presence in the region. Secondly, the United States and the DOD preserve their ontological security by reinforcing identities of leadership in global health (in)security in the eyes of the international community. Thirdly, the anticipatory and limitless approach to biomedical threat surveillance justifies continuous DOD funding for biopharmaceutical RDT&E. The problem is not the public financing of biomedical research in itself but rather the extractive and dysfunctional innovation ecosystem in which it takes place. This anticipatory mind-set is further entangled in the very logic of capital accumulation in the biopharmaceutical sector, as the speculative value of expected future earnings is attached to the prospect of unending and permanent biomedical insecurity. The justifying narrative, similar to the one used to preserve the ontological security of the United States, is that any threat to capital accumulation in the sector will result in a corresponding decrease in global health and a decrease in therapeutic innovation.

Asset Accumulation Logics

While war-biomedical entanglements are not the only issue, they exacerbate the dysfunctional and extractive nature of our broader innovation ecosystem in two major ways. Firstly, they entangle therapeutic innovation with defence imperatives, shaping the context and trajectory of the innovation that emerges. Each government agency or department that finances biomedical research infuses its own bureaucratic and institutional settings in the innovation process itself. As a result, RDT&E beholden to defence strategies is often bound by restrictive secrecy, classified status, redactions, and opaque progress disclosure which benefit corporate interests and disincentivise the sharing of scientific innovation (Reppy 2008). Secondly, the biopharmaceutical sector relies on the coercive power of the state to encode and protect its capacity for capital accumulation. This takes place through legal modules, which graft assets with requisite attributes to facilitate and maximise accumulation (Pistor 2019). War-biomedical entanglements enable the sector to recruit perhaps the most coercive branch of the state—its defence and national security bureaucracies. In doing so, the capacity for accumulation protected in domestic law and international treaties becomes further entrenched by the deeper and more impenetrable protection of national security and defence bureaucracies.

The broader therapeutic innovation ecosystem is characterised by extractive and dysfunctional dynamics that de-prioritise equitable health care access, instead favouring capital accumulation (Mazzucato 2018a; Roy 2020; UCL IIPP 2018). Echoing recent literature on techno-scientific capitalism, I argue the biopharmaceutical sector is mediated by the asset form (Birch 2017; Birch and Muniesa 2020; Kang 2020; Pistor 2019; Roy 2020). Studies on the political economy of the biosciences have traditionally examined commodification, fixating on the production and market exchange of therapeutic commodities like vaccines (Helmreich 2008; Birch and Tyfield 2013; Birch and Muniesa 2020; Mittra and Zoukas 2020; Roy 2020). Commodities are intended to be bought and sold, with value realised at the point of sale. Assets are instead designed to generate income via rent for a given period, through mechanisms of ownership, monopolised exclusion, and even Veblenian sabotage—understood as the strategic and deliberate restriction of productivity and creative innovation (Nitzan and Bichler 2009; Veblen 1904). As explained by Pistor, commodification is necessary but insufficient for maximising capital accumulation (Pistor 2019). Assets are the ideal vehicle, but to fulfil their promise, they must be legally encoded with four attributes: priority over other financial instruments; durability over time; universality whereby attributes are protected and enforced across national and international jurisdictions; and convertibility so asset holders can lock-in past gains by transferring asset ownership in market exchanges (Pistor 2019). All four attributes require the state's coercive power, and they rely on the law as a "powerful social ordering technology" (Pistor 2019: 17). In the biopharmaceutical sector, techno-scientific knowledge itself has become assetised through a range of legal instruments that fall under the banner of IPRs, which are in turn protected by the state domestically and by treaties internationally.

I extend this claim further, arguing that assetisation is guided by a logic of differential accumulation in line with a power theory of capital (Nitzan and Bichler 2009). Through this lens, capital is not a material expression of industrial productivity but an institution of power. This architecture of power is organised through relations of ownership, and its centre of gravity is the capitalisation of expected future earnings. Dominant firms seek to accumulate capital *differentially*, beating the average rate of return relative to other firms. Firms can shape and (re)configure techno-scientific research and development in the pursuit of differential accumulation by owning claims on scientific knowledge as an income-generating asset. In doing so, they not only claim ownership over techno-scientific knowledge as assetised property, but they also make claims on how societies engage with health and illness. These claims take the form of corporate ownership of the pace, trajectory, and accessibility of therapeutic innovations like vaccines. If we understand capital to mean differential social power expressed in monetary units, we can examine an asset as a mechanism that, once capitalised, enables the owner to exercise power over the trajectory of industries and even the pace of innovation. The legally-encoded attributes of an asset become particularly salient here. By extension of their ownership, dominant asset holders also benefit from priority, durability, universality, and convertibility of their differential power.

Like war-biomedical entanglements, asset accumulation logics also carry a discursive element to reinforce an extractive innovation ecosystem. The biopharmaceutical sector creates and disperses its own autobiographical narratives, including those that frame innovation as contingent on venture capital, increasing financial returns, and high therapeutic prices (Mazzucato 2018a; Pistor 2019; Roy 2020; UCL IIPP 2018). While these arguments influence public opinion, they are most valuable in their ability to recruit the backing of the state, which protects and enforces the legal coding of firms' assets. These narratives have been on full display throughout the pandemic. For instance, the powerful lobby trade group Pharmaceutical Research and Manufacturers of America (PhRMA) has aggressively opposed patent waivers for Covid-19 therapeutics through lobbying and public campaigning, claiming a waiver would undermine future biomedical discovery (PhRMA, 2021). These narratives naturalise an extractive innovation ecosystem, obfuscating and displacing the state's role to delegitimise claims that publicly funded innovation should remain part of a global public commons. These justifications can often permeate government agencies, departments, and legislative committees when they rely on inflated RDT&E costs provided by the industry to determine "acceptable"—yet ever-rising—therapeutic prices (Deangelis 2016; DiMasi & Grabowski 2007; Gotzsche 2012; Roy 2020). During the pandemic, these narratives have also been echoed by global leaders. The U.K. Prime Minister Boris Johnson claimed, in a rather spectacular fashion, that the "reason we have the vaccine success is because of capitalism, because of greed" (BBC News 2021).

While OWS invested mostly in late-stage clinical development and early manufacturing, a significant amount of the basic and exploratory research on which vaccine and therapeutic technologies relied had been funded by the U.S. government decades earlier. The stated intention of OWS was to bridge the "dead space" in pharmaceutical drug development, what is usually referred to as the "valley of death", where companies fail to translate scientific discoveries into commercially-viable products for mass consumption (Mazzucato 2018a; Diamond 2021). To do so, OWS supported promising vaccine candidates by facilitating parallel RDT&E and manufacturing capability, given that the "dead space" in pharmaceutical production often occurs in between those two stages (Mazzucato 2018a; Roy 2020; Slaoui and Hepburn 2020). This narrative presented OWS as a late-phase investor and facilitator who entered the picture only once robust clinical data from the private sector was available to correct a market failure in an emergency. This not only perpetuated the market failure theory of state investment, but it also served to hide the crucial role of the state throughout the entire innovation process, rendering it invisible until it re-entered the frame as a facilitator of last resort in the final act. By this stage, however, the research that had been publicly-funded decades earlier had been repurposed, reconfigured, and diversified through a complex matrix of corporate and legal mechanisms that serve to camouflage the role of the state and maximise accumulation for asset holders. This matrix corresponds with the increased financialisation of the biopharmaceutical sector, calcifying a dysfunctional and extractive innovation ecosystem through corporate amalgamation and share repurchasing.

Mergers and acquisitions (M&As) can be understood as mechanisms of corporate control aimed at taming, limiting, and controlling overall market efficiency (Nitzan 2001). Since amalgamation facilitates dominant firms' organised power, mergers have become a most potent form of differential accumulation by breadth—increasing earnings whilst reducing competition as a form of sabotage (Nitzan and Bichler 2009). Dominant firms then capitalise on this sabotage by strategically managing the resulting stagnation (Nitzan 2001). Historically, the biopharmaceutical sector has struggled with differential accumulation, primarily because blockbuster drugs with sales exceeding US$1 bn are relatively rare (Amir-Aslani and Chanel 2016). The sector has relied heavily on M&As to bypass the short-term demands of financial markets, which tend to become too overwhelming for small firms (Roy 2020). While aggressive M&As have proven lucrative as financial strategies, there is little evidence that they deliver higher product outputs. In fact, research productivity is negatively correlated with M&As as companies grow in size (Amir-Aslani & Chanel 2016). Large pharmaceutical companies can bridge gaps in research output by acquiring biotechnology start-ups and, more importantly, their IPRs and product pipelines like Tekmira did in 2015. For instance, in 2020, OWS funded research for a Sanofi/GSK mRNA Covid-19 vaccine candidate with US$30 mn and paid an additional US$2.07 bn in advance purchasing agreements (U.S. Congressional Research Service 2021). By August 2021, Sanofi had acquired Tidal Therapeutics in a US$470 mn deal, and all outstanding shares of Translate Bio which were valued at US$3.2 bn (Sanofi 2021b; Sanofi 2021a). Despite having acquired the mRNA technology of two leading companies, in September 2021 Sanofi announced it would discontinue its vaccine candidate due to the market saturation generated by competitors Pfizer and Moderna (White and Burger, 2021). This example demonstrates four key dynamics—an extractive public-private relationship where publicly funded firms prioritise financial returns; the assetisation of techno-scientific knowledge through IPRs; convertibility enabling the transfer of asset ownership across firms; and the reliance on M&As as a strategy to maximise differential accumulation.

As the sector begins to resemble an oligopoly through high concentration, natural ceilings to amalgamation emerge because biopharmaceutical giants simply run out of suitably large competitors to merge with (Morrison and Lähteenmäki 2016). Faced with the threat of differential de-accumulation, firms undertake share repurchasing programs (commonly known as share buybacks) to compensate for the natural ceiling to accumulation by breadth. Share repurchasing is a differential accumulation strategy whereby companies re-purchase their shares to increase the price of the remaining stock, benefiting shareholders and increasing the market capitalisation of the firm (Mazzucato 2018a; Roy 2020; UCL IIPP 2018). From 2016 to 2020, the top fourteen biopharmaceutical companies spent over US$219 bn in share buybacks and over US$358 bn in dividends, with the combined total surpassing their RDT&E expenditure by US$56 bn (U.S. House of Representatives 2021). Moderna, which received almost US$6 bn in public funding from the U.S. government during the pandemic, was authorised by its board of directors to spend US$1 bn in stock repurchases in 2021 (Speights 2021). The justification behind this strategy of shareholder value maximisation (SVM) is that shareholders are the most efficient allocators of firms' resources because they are the only investors with no guaranteed return, arguably making them rightful claimants of any residual revenue through dividends (Mazzucato 2018a; Pistor 2019; Roy 2020). The primacy of SVM was driven by a shift toward capitalisation becoming the primary model for assessing firm valuation, and the push to replace industrial managers with stock-compensated executives who would allocate resources to maximise dividends rather than expand industrial and innovation capacity (Krier 2009). A fundamental corollary of this trend is that therapeutic innovation and health care access are eclipsed by a logic of accumulation anchored to the monopolisation of techno-scientific research as an income-generating asset. These accumulation logics are used to enact and justify high therapeutic prices, concentrated sector amalgamation, short-term shareholder gains over RDT&E output, the enclosure of publicly-funded research for private gain, and the strengthening of legal modules that protect asset owners.

TRIPS and Intellectual Property Logics

Maximising differential accumulation from asset ownership depends on protecting assets' legal attributes across jurisdictions, rendering their codification as universal as possible for the longest duration possible. In the biopharmaceutical sector, IPRs are used as income-generating assets through exclusive ownership, temporarily enclosing techno-scientific knowledge. Ownership bestows IPR holders with governance functions over prices, supply, and distribution not only over the patented invention but also over its downstream applications (Kang 2021; McMahon 2021; Thambisetty et al. 2021). These governance functions demand further interrogation with defence funded innovations, given that security stipulations cloak RDT&E in additional layers of secrecy and bureaucratic opacity that benefit corporate interests. Since the decline of the individual inventor in the 20th century, most patents in the United States have been filed by corporate entities (Coriat & Weinstein 2012; Pistor 2019). This translates to corporate governance over techno-scientific knowledge, a governance model guided by a logic of differential accumulation which demands the expansion of assets' durability and universality to continuously exceed average rates of return. As Haunss explains, if controlling knowledge is a technology of power and "because power is a relational concept, knowledge can only so long serve as its base as a differential distribution is maintained" (Haunss 2013: 77). Through this lens, IPR regimes create monopolies over innovations only to release them to the public once they have "lost their differentiating potential" (Haunss 2013: 77). Dominant firms—in concert with lawyers, lobbyists, sympathetic legislators, and industry representatives—exercise the power of corporate governance to expand the differentiating potential of their assets in time (through durability) and place (through universality).

Conventional methods for prolonging the durability of IPRs involve securing patent protections that go beyond the standard twenty years, securing new patents with only minor or trivial variations, and strategically benefiting from trade secrets which can remain protected and undisclosed (Bell 2015; Kang 2021; Thambisetty et al. 2021). The universality of standard IPR protections across jurisdictions is pursued through a complex architecture of international treaties and agreements, forum shifting across international organisations, direct licensing agreements with firms, and bi-and-plurilateral agreements between countries that add protections beyond minimum standards (Haunss 2013; Kang 2021; Pistor 2019). Expanding the boundaries of durability and universality becomes an incomplete yet interminable project because the imperative for differential accumulation is interminable. The logic does not abide a limit to maximising shareholder value, exceeding average rates of return, or increasing market capitalisation relative to other firms. This ongoing project is enacted through legitimation narratives built on neoclassical and utilitarian economic foundations that present a causal relationship between IPRs, innovation, trade, and economic growth (Mazzucato 2018b; Pistor 2019).

Narratives legitimising maximalist positions on IPRs present them as the most effective mechanism for fomenting innovation. They posit that monopolies provide just rewards for productive undertaking, that temporary monopolies are necessary incentives because traditional market mechanisms will neglect public goods, and that monopolies encourage inventors to disseminate and disclose their work (Haunss 2013; Gabriel 2014; Mazzucato 2018b; Pistor 2019). Complementary justifications suggest that international IPR harmonisation fosters trade and economic growth in the Global South by protecting manufacturers in foreign markets and encouraging technology transfers (Haunss 2013). While a comprehensive critique of these arguments is beyond the scope of this chapter, I want to draw attention to three key issues. The first is that these narratives latch on to the ghost of the individual inventor, while most IPRs are held by corporations which "are creatures of law that have neither intellectual power nor creativity of their own" (Pistor 2019: 115).

The IPR regime in its current form is not designed to benefit inventors but rather the investors who, supposedly through their risk-taking and efficient allocation of resources, have been granted the right to capitalise on the ownership and governance of techno-scientific knowledge. The second issue is that this argument fails to cohere with the public financing of RDT&E, particularly given the risks taken by states throughout the entire innovation chain and their ability to create markets and not merely correct market failures (Mazzucato 2018a; Roy 2020). If the IPR regime were truly designed to benefit risk-taking investors, then most Covid-19 vaccines and therapeutics would be publicly owned and governed. The current IPR regime's logic is instead to facilitate differential accumulation by asset owners and their *private* creditors and investors, cementing an extractive and dysfunctional system that privatises publicly funded techno-scientific innovation. The third issue is how these narratives justify dysfunctional and often catastrophic power asymmetries between IPR-exporting and IPR-importing countries. The current North-South divide in access to Covid-19 vaccines is not an anomaly but a foundational pillar of the international IPR regime. It was proactively and strategically built into the very architecture of the Trade-Related Aspects of Intellectual Property Rights (TRIPS) Agreement (Haunss 2013; Kang 2021; Pechlaner 2010; Yinliang 2014).

The TRIPS Agreement of 1995 set minimum international standards in IPR protection that all 164 World Trade Organization (WTO) member countries must now abide by. Within TRIPS, there has been a constant tension between the maximalist position advocated by the corporate sector and IPR-exporting countries on one side and a network of state and non-state actors in the Global South advocating for equitable access to medicines on the other (Haunss 2013; Guan 2016). Before Covid-19, this conflict reached its apex during the HIV/AIDS crisis in the 1990s, leading to the Doha Declaration adopted by the WTO in 2001 (Correa 2004; Haunss 2013). Due to opposition from the corporate sector and IPR-exporting countries, Doha failed to amend TRIPS substantially and instead clarified flexibilities on compulsory licensing. These have been critiqued for being too cumbersome and asymmetrical, making them inadequate and insufficient to secure access to therapeutics in the Global South (Correa 2004; Guan 2016; Kang 2021; Thambisetty et al. 2021). In addition, IPR-exporting countries have sought to bypass flexibilities by embedding TRIPS-Plus clauses into bilateral and plurilateral trade agreements, threatening sanctions, litigation, and export market barriers unless fortified IPR protections are agreed to (Haunss 2013; Ido 2021; Kang 2021; Pistor 2019). The IPR maximalist coalition has traditionally argued that access to therapeutics in the Global South should be pursued through private market mechanisms like voluntary licensing and corporate philanthropy, international aid, and donations from the Global North (Haunss 2013; Thambisetty et al. 2021). These developments have coalesced with Covid-19, as the current North-South polarisation in vaccine access can be traced to the inadequacies of existing TRIPS flexibilities, the insufficiency of philanthropy and pooled donation systems like COVAX, and the adverse distributive effects of voluntary licensing agreements that facilitate vaccine hoarding by the Global North in secretive bilateral negotiations (Ariyarathna and Kariyawasam 2020; Brown 2021; Hanrieder 2020; Iacobucci 2021; Kang 2021; Spina Alì 2016; Thambisetty et al. 2021). Against this backdrop, India and South Africa proposed a comprehensive TRIPS waiver in October 2020 to temporarily waive patents, copyrights, and trade secrets relating to Covid-19 vaccines, therapeutics, and diagnostics (Thambisetty et al. 2021). While the Biden Administration endorsed a TRIPS waiver in May 2021, no such waiver has materialised as of writing due to strong opposition from the biopharmaceutical sector, industry lobby groups, and other IPR-exporting countries (Brown 2021; Kang 2021).

A TRIPS waiver would be an effective tool for improving global vaccine access precisely because it would disrupt the attributes of IPRs as income-generating assets, namely their durability, universality, and convertibility. In the case of convertibility, assets could face devaluation because they will have been released to the public much earlier than markets anticipated and before they reached the loss of their differentiation potential under conventional IPR standards. While necessary, a waiver of patents and trade secrets as undisclosed technical know-how is not a panacea. Countries in the Global South will need to rapidly expand their manufacturing capabilities, in-country vaccine technologies, and supply chain infrastructures (Brown 2021; Kang 2021; Labonté et al. 2021; Thambisetty et al. 2021). Legal certainty regarding patents' temporal delimitations through waivers and licensing flexibilities alleviate concerns over expensive litigation, economic sanctions, and trade disputes, leading to faster generic market entry and scaled-up manufacturing capabilities (Correa 2004; Iacobucci 2021; Ido 2021; Spina Alì 2016;). In contrast, stasis and uncertainty surrounding TRIPS flexibilities create difficult market conditions for generic entry and for the scaling up of manufacturing, leading to funding stagnation and chronically low infrastructure capabilities in many countries (Iacobucci 2021; Ido 2021).

The biopharmaceutical sector capitalises on this uncertainty and stasis as a form of industrial sabotage in a Veblenian sense, where accumulation is facilitated by the strategic management of industrial inefficiency (Nitzan and Bichler 2009; Veblen 1904). This prevents countries from rapidly scaling up their manufacturing capabilities and supply chain infrastructures, which could enable them to repurpose said capacity for future production beyond Covid-19 therapeutics. The risk for the biopharmaceutical sector is that an effective TRIPS waiver will create a significant legal precedent that threatens their assets' universality and durability while simultaneously facilitating the expansion of manufacturing capabilities and generic market entry in the Global South. Such developments could threaten accumulation in the sector not only in the context of Covid-19 but also through future manufacturing and distribution of existing and upcoming biomedical innovations. The loss of sales revenue from the commodification of vaccines and therapeutics is certainly a factor in opposition to a TRIPS waiver. However, I argue that the primary consideration is the potential for widespread asset devaluation that would threaten differential accumulation in the sector. The most pressing risk is not necessarily the loss of sales revenue from expanded manufacturing capacity or generic entry competition in the Global South but rather how these developments would disrupt market expectations of future accumulation from biomedical assets' durability, universality, and convertibility value.

Conclusion

Drawing on emerging biological threats, Terry has argued that in "this anticipatory mind-set, the future invades the present and takes it hostage by predicting risks and speculating on novel drugs" (Terry 2017: 146). While this framing takes war-biomedical logics as a point of departure, I extend it further to highlight the broader entanglement with asset accumulation and intellectual property logics. In a way, the present is taken hostage by the imperatives of differential accumulation that prioritise the expected future earnings from income-generating assets over the lives and health of human beings in the present. This polarised asymmetry between the public's health needs today and the potential for private accumulation in the future is codified in the very legal architecture that governs global health care access. The entanglements and their resultant inequities are justified through legitimation narratives that take the present hostage. These narratives create two tacit threats: that a dismantling of the war-biomedical nexus will result in greater global biological insecurity, and that any disruption to the legal codification of techno-scientific knowledge as an income-generating asset will lead to a standstill of biomedical innovation.

These entanglements place key actors like the U.S. government on an unsteady footing as they walk a seemingly contradictory tightrope when responding to health crises like the Covid-19 pandemic. The state must highlight its identity as a global leader in health security while diffusing this project's imperial nature; and it must visibly protect the legal codification of assetised techno-scientific innovation while simultaneously hiding its role as a major public investor of it. The logic of war-biomedical entanglements means that the United States is incentivised to continue indefinite biosurveillance, biosecurity, and disease management through an ongoing defensive presence in the Global South. Meanwhile, the international IPR regime perpetuates this dynamic by preventing the Global South from expanding its biopharmaceutical infrastructure and manufacturing capabilities to protect the asset valuations of IPR-holding companies in the Global North and, by extension, their differential accumulation. From an IPR maximalist position, the answer is to entrench the asymmetry even further through voluntary licensing, stronger IPR protections, corporate philanthropy, and donations.

While the Covid-19 pandemic has certainly brought many of these issues to public focus, the purpose of this chapter has been to demonstrate that these entanglements are neither new nor anomalous. From Operation Warp Speed to TRIPS, the pandemic has illuminated ahistorical and deep enmeshment of logics that underpin the political economy of global health care. Merely calling for more public funding for biomedical innovation, enhanced pandemic preparedness through biosurveillance, and cosmetic improvements to TRIPS flexibilities will not suffice. A complete reconfiguration of the current innovation ecosystem and its supporting legal architecture is required to dismantle such extractive and dysfunctional entanglements. These are embedded not only in public-private dynamics currently beholden to asset accumulation logics; they are further entrenched in colonial and imperial power asymmetries between the Global North and the Global South. Close attention must be paid to the specific agencies and departments that provide public funds to interrogate the legitimation narratives they employ and the bureaucratic imperatives they infuse in the innovation process. Likewise, the legal and economic legitimation narratives that justify the assetisation of publicly funded research to maximise differential accumulation must be robustly challenged. Without comprehensive structural reforms in the political economy of biomedicine, and as long as these entanglements continue to calcify, the Global South will continue to disproportionately suffer through health crises like the Covid-19 pandemic.

8

COVID-19 AND THE ECONOMY OF CARE

Disability and Aged Care Services into the Future

Laura Davy and Helen Dickinson

Introduction

When Covid-19 first arrived on Australia's shores in early 2020, the aged care and disability support sectors were already under enormous pressure and in considerable flux. This was vividly demonstrated by the fact that Australia had launched two Royal Commissions (formal public inquiries) into these sectors. Details of the many failings of these service systems were emerging almost daily from the in-progress Royal Commission into Aged Care Quality and Safety and the recently commenced hearings for the Royal Commission into Violence, Abuse, Neglect and Exploitation of People with Disability. Dramatic reform has occurred over the past decade within the disability support sector with the introduction of the National Disability Insurance Scheme (NDIS). A series of well-documented inquiries and scandals centred on staffing shortages and abuse in residential aged care had set the scene for major reform of this system very soon. This policy turmoil was taking place amidst demographic trends predicting increasing pressure on formal care systems in the coming years.

The pandemic exposed the deep, pre-existing fault lines within Australia's disability and aged care sectors and, more importantly, the devastating consequences of these flaws. Failures to adequately include people with disability in the policy response and vaccine roll-out, the interaction of workforce shortages with quarantine rules and vaccine mandates, and fear about the speed and ease with which the virus can—and has—spread through nursing homes, disability group homes and other congregate care settings, were all fixtures in national news media during 2019 and 2020. In this chapter, we argue that the Covid-19 pandemic exacerbated existing issues within the aged care and disability support sectors and shone a spotlight on them. Given that these issues have been illuminated so vividly, there is a

DOI: 10.4324/9781003250432-11

responsibility on politicians and policymakers to invest in the future of the care economy through systemic reform.

In the first part of the chapter, we provide a brief survey of the pre-pandemic care sector. We then explore the experiences of people with disability, older people, and care workers during the first waves of the pandemic. We examine how various structural features of Australia's disability and aged care systems created heightened risk for care service workers and clients. Both care workers and their clients faced an increased risk of contagion due to close living conditions in congregate care settings and the mobile nature of the care workforce. Care workers faced income loss, and people with disability and older people faced significant social isolation as services were cancelled or could not be sufficiently staffed. Compounding factors include a bungled Covid-19 vaccine roll-out to people with disability and a slow roll-out of vaccines to aged care and disability support workers.

Care largely happens behind closed doors—whether those doors lead to private homes, residential aged care facilities or specialist disability accommodation settings. Australia's political economy, like that of other contemporary capitalist states, is structured by a gendered logic of labour where the sphere of visible work and public action is predominately masculine and maintenance work—the management of care and support needs and the sustaining of bodies and minds within the private sphere—is configured as a primarily feminine responsibility. But Covid-19 has dragged the care sector out from the shadows and under the spotlight, into public consciousness.

Aged care and disability support are usually treated as distinct and separate policy domains. But the common challenges in both areas, which we describe together as the Australian care sector, suggest mutual opportunities for investment that can transform the future life outcomes of millions of Australians if they can be translated into concrete policy actions. Investing in the care sector to promote empowerment and security for both care workers and care recipients is critical for securing the future quality, safety, and sustainability of these essential support services.

In the final part of the chapter, we examine opportunities for future reform in the care sector. The care economy will increase significantly in the next few decades in Australia, due primarily to population ageing but also other demographic drivers. However, the aged care and disability support workforces, which are already feminised and low-paid, appear to be facing increasingly insecure employment arrangements, and it can be difficult to attract new workers into these expanding fields. The pandemic has demonstrated that issues of low pay and insecure work conditions are not just equity issues but are in themselves a public health concern. It has highlighted the essential nature of care and support work for a vast network of workers, older people and people with disability, family members and informal carers. We identify four areas that the Australian care sectors need to undertake substantial reform within if we are to more effectively serve the care needs of the population.

The Pre-pandemic Care Sector Landscape

The care sector is a complex landscape characterised by a mix of accountability structures and funding responsibilities. Responsibility for funding, regulation and policy development concerning aged care (which includes residential care and community-based support services) sits with Australia's federal government. Specialised disability services are predominately provided through the National Disability Insurance Scheme (NDIS), which is administered by the National Disability Insurance Agency (NDIA), a separate statutory agency. The NDIS was first introduced in 2013 in trial sites but has since been rolled out across all states and territories of Australia. The federal and state and territory governments all contribute to NDIS funding and decision-making processes. What is different to the previous system is that states and territories no longer directly provide specialised disability services. These are provided via a new care market comprising profit and non-profit organisations.

Service provision in both disability and aged care is mainly undertaken by non-government providers. Under the NDIS, eligible people with disability receive individualised funding packages to purchase support services that meet their personal needs and goals from a mixed market of non-profit, profit and government providers. The NDIS Quality and Safeguards Commission is the independent agency that regulates NDIS providers and seeks to improve the quality and safety of services. The aged care sector is similarly publicly funded but predominately outsourced to private and not for profit providers. Other mainstream services that people with disability and older people rely on, including public health services, are variously funded by the state, territory, and federal governments, and provided by a range of organisations.

In this chapter, we focus primarily on the clients of specialised aged care and disability supports because of the high impact of Covid-19 on these services, particularly on residential and accommodation services.[1] However, it is important to note that many older people and people with disability were greatly impacted by Covid-19 who were not recipients of these services. Most older Australians do not live in residential aged care, for example. From 2019 to 2020, 245,000 people were living in residential care facilities, whereas 840,000 people used the Commonwealth Home Support Program (CHSP), which includes services such as domestic and gardening assistance and meals on wheels (AIHW 2021). As of June 30, 2021, there were 466,619 participants in the NDIS (National Disability Insurance Agency, 2021, 5), which was designed to cater only to the disability-related support needs of the approximately 10 per cent of total Australians with disability assessed as having a severe and permanent disability. We lack good quality data about those who are not in these specialised services. For example, unlike in other countries such as England, there is no disability identifier in health data, meaning we have no clear picture of the number of people with disability who have contracted Covid-19 in Australia or died from it.

Australian disability and aged care services have experienced significant reform over the past decade. In much of the policy literature, it is suggested this has been prompted in part by rising expectations of older people and people with disability about the quality and convenience of the care and support services they receive. But it is also important to note that there have been longstanding concerns over the quality of these services and the life chances of individuals accessing them. In both sectors, the dominant discourse is that systems should be more "consumer directed" and that this will drive better services as individuals demand better services from providers or move their business elsewhere. The assumption in both cases is that the market will help drive improvement as individuals tailor services to their needs.

These reforms should signal that there are different expectations of the care sector now than there were in the past and that clients, their families and the community will hold providers to higher standards of accountability now than ever before. But when we examine the reform experience, we find research showing that the benefits of these reforms for clients have been both imperfectly realised and unevenly distributed. Individuals who are well-placed in terms of socioeconomic status and ability to self-advocate—or who have a network of supporters to assist them in negotiating the aged care or disability support system—are significantly more likely to experience choice and empowerment within consumer-directed systems. Conversely, people with cognitive disabilities, complex support needs, and people who do not have access to a support network of formal or informal advocates experience significant barriers to good conditions and support (Malbon et al. 2019). In both systems, there are also significant market challenges, with gaps in markets arising due to a lack of provision. This is particularly pronounced in rural and regional areas but is also an issue faced in urban areas.

The recent Royal Commissions highlighted several major challenges impacting the future quality and sustainability of these sectors. The first of these is staffing, in terms of both securing an adequate supply of workers and proper training and capacity building of these workers. The second is around models of care, and specifically how the environment within which care services are provided influences outcomes for clients. The third key issue is effective governance. This includes interface and coordination issues with other policy areas and the need to involve older people and people with disability in planning and decision-making processes. And the final issue, which is related to each of the previous ones, hinges on the need for more robust human rights underpinning to be at the centre of both aged care and disability support. We return to these issues indirectly in the next section while exploring the experiences of older people, people with disability and workers, and directly in the final section regarding opportunities for future reform.

The Experiences of People with Disability, Older People and Care Workers During the Pandemic

It was within the context of a care sector landscape already subject to considerable change and pressure that Covid-19 arrived on the scene, a virus with much deadlier consequences for older people and people with disability than many others in the community.[2] Some of the increased vulnerabilities and adverse effects experienced by these groups during the pandemic were due to disability or impairment related reasons, such as the presence of underlying health conditions or an inability to enact social distancing because of the physical nature of the care and support they might require. However, many were the result of contingent economic, political, and social arrangements such as barriers and discrimination within the health system (Dickinson, Llewellyn & Kavanagh, 2022) and more still were a result of structural features of the care and support sector that were exacerbated in the context of the pandemic.

From almost the very beginning of the pandemic, older people were identified as a population at high risk of contracting the Covid-19 virus and of becoming seriously ill or dying if they did so. In particular, the high proportion of older people with acute health conditions living in residential aged care settings led to the well-founded fear that the virus would spread rapidly through these facilities with devastating consequences. At the time of writing, 1,841 people in total had died from Covid-19 in Australia. The vast majority of these people were over the age of 70 (1,483 in total), and close to half (45 per cent or 835 people) were residents of government-subsidised aged care facilities (Australian Department of Health 2021). As outlined above, we do not know what proportion of those who have contracted COVID or died from it are people with disability because Australia lacks a consistent disability identifier in health data.

The recognition that older people were an "at risk" population allowed health authorities, aged care services, and older people and their families to take steps to mitigate this risk through infection control strategies such as limiting visitors to aged care facilities and priority access to protective equipment and vaccines. However, early recognition of their heightened vulnerability to Covid-19 also meant that older Australians experienced profound disruption to their lives over a long period. One of the key strategies adopted to reduce the risk of infection in residential care facilities was to restrict visitations from family and friends. Older people living at home with the support of community care services such as domestic assistance, community nursing, and meals on wheels also experienced reduced services, with some service provisions ceasing altogether. Others cancelled services themselves due to fear of infection (Pachana et al. 2020). Families were advised to not visit their older family members.

Several academics, advocacy groups and people with disability had seen what was unfolding in terms of people with disability being an "at risk" group in other countries and stressed the need for a tailored response (e.g. Kavanagh et al. 2020). However, the Federal Government was slower to identify that people with disability, like older people and First Nations people, were a priority group for developing policy. Many people with disability have pre-existing, underlying health conditions, which impact the intensity and duration of illness upon contracting the virus and the incidence of death. People with disability are also more likely to live on or below the poverty line and to live in poor quality and insecure housing or institutional settings than other Australians (Green et al. 2020), factors that contribute to the likelihood of exposure to Covid-19 and increased morbidity and mortality if infected. Even before the pandemic, people with disability had trouble accessing health and health services information in accessible formats, experienced low levels of participation and access to preventative health programs and encountered discriminatory practices within healthcare settings (Kavanagh et al. 2021).

Despite recognising these heightened risks, the early policy response in Australia largely failed to address people with disability. Left out of initial communications and consultation strategies, they found it difficult to access reliable information about Covid-19, the effects of the virus, and who was most at risk (Yates & Dickinson 2021). As Kavanagh et al. (2021) note, when guidelines for the management of outbreaks in residential care facilities were issued by the federal government in March 2020, disability accommodation was not mentioned at all. A range of commentators including people with disability, disabled people's organisations, families and carers and their organisations and academics, had been vocal about the dangers of the virus spreading rapidly through disability accommodation settings such as group homes and respite services from the very early days of the pandemic. The lack of concrete action on the part of governments to mitigate risks was galling and frustrating for many in the broader disability community, particularly in the face of the mismanagement of the federal government's vaccination program. But for many, it was also unsurprising and simply a reflection that people with disability are all too often forgotten about and deprioritised.

Australia's Covid-19 vaccine program commenced in late February 2021. The program initially prioritised staff and residents of both aged care and disability care and accommodation settings (see Table 8.1), in recognition that they were

TABLE 8.1 Australian government vaccination program priority groups 1a, 1b

Order of priority	Priority group
Phase 1a	
1	Quarantine and border force staff; frontline health care workers
2	Other frontline health care workers
3	Staff at residential aged care and shared disability care settings
4	Residents at aged care and shared disability care settings
Phase 1b	
5	People aged 80 years and over
6	People aged 70–79 years
7	Other health care workers
8	Aboriginal and Torres Strait Islander people aged 55 and over
9	Adults with an underlying medical condition, including people with disability
10	Critical and high-risk workers, including defence and emergency services workers

Source: This information was widely published by the Commonwealth Department of Health and other outlets during the first part of 2021 but is no longer available on government websites.

in a similarly vulnerable category due to living arrangements, reliance on paid support staff, and the high likelihood of pre-existing health conditions. The draft Commissioner's report from Hearing 12 of the Disability Royal Commission, which focused on the experiences of people with disability during the Covid-19 vaccine rollout, documents the many significant delays, miscommunications and implementation issues that occurred with the rollout of the vaccine program.

Official government announcements indicated that Phase 1a of the program, which included the priority vaccination of aged care and shared disability accommodation residents, would be largely completed within 6 weeks. It soon became clear that all phases of the vaccine program were delayed due to the failure of the federal government to secure a consistent vaccine supply. However, representatives from the Australian Department of Health further admitted[3] that despite the initial policy prioritisation of people with disability, the on-the-ground vaccination strategy had "pivoted" to focus solely on residents of aged care facilities, effectively de-prioritising people with disability (and by extension disability support workers). This "pivot" occurred without public notification, meaning many clients of disability housing and care services were still waiting for on-site vaccines well after members of the wider community could get vaccinated by their local General Practitioner (GP). Many disability support workers missed out on priority vaccination altogether and many of these ended up being one of the last groups in the community to have access to vaccination as they were in the younger age groups that were eligible later in the roll-out. Victoria and New South Wales are the states that have had the largest proportions of infections and deaths from Covid-19. These both have had heavy public health restrictions with extended periods of lockdowns. These restrictions were progressively lifted as the proportion of the population that had been vaccinated reached particular benchmarks. However, in both states, the vaccination rate for the general population ran ahead of the priority groups. That is, despite having been prioritised for nearly a year, people in the priority groups were, on average, less vaccinated than the general population. Without proactive government outreach, particularly to people with intellectual disabilities, people living in supported accommodation settings, and people who are geographically isolated, these groups experienced major barriers to getting vaccinated, including difficulty accessing information about when and how they could get a vaccine and difficulty getting to vaccination sites (Kavenagh et al. 2021).

Throughout the pandemic, aged care and disability support workers also faced higher risks from Covid-19, and these risks were further exacerbated by failures in the Australian Government's vaccination program and other aspects of the Covid-19 policy response. Care and support work often involves close physical contact with clients, and workers may come into contact with multiple clients over one day. This amplified the risk of workers catching the virus, given that care work by its nature usually has to be performed on-site and in close contact with other bodies. It also amplified the risk of workers transmitting the virus to others—to their own families after returning home after shifts, and to the people with disability and older people they work with, who may have health conditions that place them at high risk of dying should they catch it. Disability support workers were not included in groups receiving priority access to Personal Protective Equipment (PPE) at the start of the pandemic, which increased the risk of exposure for them and their clients. Support workers reported significant anxiety in the early stages of the pandemic about the lack of PPE and PPE training, and the limited and sometimes confusing information and guidance they received from their employers and health authorities (Cortis & van Toorn 2020).

The pandemic also heightened the effects of the often-poor employment conditions of aged care and disability support workers (Kavenagh et al. 2020). Disability and aged care workers are overwhelmingly female, and most are insecurely employed under part-time or casual contracts (see Table 8.2 for more detail). In many cases, the reforms to the care sectors over the past decade have worsened these conditions. Employment has transferred from state and territories to private and non-profit organisations and there is greater variety in the employment arrangements these providers have their staff. In the disability sector, the demand for flexible, person-centred support, while very positive for clients, has resulted in the increased casualisation of the workforce, as support may only be needed for a couple of hours at a time. These factors meant that during the pandemic, workers faced major blows to their financial security. If they came into contact with the virus, workers were required to cancel shifts while self-isolating to follow the directives of health authorities. One recent survey of disability support workers showed that only 47 per cent of those who took time off due to illness were paid sick leave (Kavanagh et al. 2020). Although some states (e.g. Victoria) moved to institute paid pandemic leave if people were required to isolate themselves for fear of infection, this was not common practice. This situation incentivised risky behaviours such as working while ill during a pandemic (Dickinson et al. 2020). The same survey of disability support workers found that during Melbourne's 2020 lockdown last year, one in ten disability support workers did not get tested for coronavirus after possibly encountering someone infected with the virus (Kavanagh et al. 2020). The health advice at the time stipulated that if you were deemed to be a "casual contact" you should self-isolate until you receive a negative test result. For people employed on a casual basis who may not have a savings pool to draw on, the loss of shifts these public health policies induced would have had a significant impact on financial security.

The impacts on care workers had flow-on effects for clients. At the height of the second wave of the pandemic in Melbourne, Victoria, staff shortages in some aged care facilities led to neglect of residents. For example, in one senior care facility, only six staff members arrived one morning to care for the facility's 115 residents (Curnow et al. 2020). At this point in the pandemic, we saw significantly higher numbers of Covid-19 in Victoria's privately run facilities than we did in those run by the state (Handley 2020). In part, this might be a reflection that state-run facilities were more likely to be in rural areas that had lower infection rates but it is also likely a product of the fact that there are strict staff ratio requirements in state facilities that are not mandated in the private sector. People with disability also missed out on essential support services due to a lack of available staff (Yates & Dickinson 2021). Some government initiatives were introduced to address these issues: the Department of Health established the Temporary Surge Workforce Support initiative to assist with worker shortages in residential aged care, and in late 2020 the NDIA contracted the Recruitment, Consulting and Staffing Association (RCSA) to provide a linking service connecting NDIS service providers to temporary staffing agencies should they need to fill Covid-19 related staffing gaps. However, shortages continued throughout the sector and information on the uptake and success of these initiatives is not yet available.

The experiences of older people, people with disability and care workers during the pandemic highlight specific aspects of several well-known challenges for the care sector in Australia in the future. Firstly, the challenge of ensuring adequate *supply* in the care sector workforce, a pre-existing issue that was particularly exposed by the need for a surge workforce in aged care and disability support to fill staffing gaps during the pandemic. Secondly, the challenge of the care *setting*, or the physical environment within which supports are delivered, was brought into the spotlight during the pandemic due to the rapid spread of the virus in some specialised care facilities. Third, the challenge of creating effective governance structures: the existing coordination and interface issues within aged and disability services predictably worsened in a public health emergency scenario, and older people and people with disability were too often excluded from consultation and planning processes directly impacting their lives. Finally, the need for a common core commitment to human rights to underpin future planning and reform of the aged care and disability support sectors. When service systems are stretched to capacity and those who work within them face challenges they have never faced before, violations of individual human rights can occur more easily. But it is precisely in emergencies that a baseline awareness of and commitment to upholding the human rights of older persons and persons with disability is needed, especially amongst government decision-makers and service providers. In the following section, we deal with each of these challenges in turn, exploring opportunities for future reform.

Opportunities for Future Reform of the Care Sector

Invest in the Care Sector Workforce and Improve Pay and Employment Conditions

Australia, like many other high-income countries, is facing a crisis in the care sector within the next decades, with steadily increasing demand for formal care services but limited funding and workforce supply to meet this demand under current policy settings. The Australian Bureau of Statistics predicts that the proportion of people aged 65 years and over in the overall population will increase from 15 per cent in 2017 to between 21 per cent and 23 per cent in 2066, almost a quarter of the population (ABS 2018). Around one in eight (13 per cent) people aged under

65 have some level of disability, rising to one in two (51 per cent) for those aged 65 and over, which means the proportion of people with disability will be rising significantly as well (AIHW 2020). At the same time, the working-age population (people between 15 and 64 years) is projected to decrease from 66 per cent to between 61 per cent and 62 per cent in 2066, which works out to be well below two out of every three people (ABS 2018). The sector is likely to lose some workers because of the pandemic, with some reporting burnout and feeling unsupported and others who refuse to comply with vaccine mandates choosing to leave the profession.

There is significant reliance on unpaid family carers to bridge the gap between the care and support people with disability and older people need and what is currently provided through funded care services. This stopgap is unlikely to remain in place to the same degree into the future, however. Lifestyle and demographic trends such as increased rates of workforce participation amongst younger female cohorts, increased family dispersion, changing family structures and changing expectations about familial care (Cullen 2019) are likely to reduce both the availability and propensity of younger generations to provide unpaid care at the same rate and intensity that their parents and grandparents did. This means the demand for formal care services is likely to continue to rise.

Feminist philosophers and political economists have long critiqued what they view as a systematic undervaluing of the role and importance of care work in society (Davy 2019; Hughes et al. 2005). Because caregiving has traditionally been a feminine responsibility, workers in the care sector (whether male or female) experience the low status associated with "women's work" (Hughes et al. 2005), and indeed, disability and aged care workers are overwhelmingly female (see Table 8.2). In the contemporary capitalist neoliberal state where independence and self-sufficiently are celebrated, people with disability, older people, and those who provide care to them are all marginalised by their association with the body, the private sphere, and the feminine. Despite the high demand for trained and experienced staff highlighted during the pandemic, care workers experience low pay, poor employment conditions, and limited opportunities for training and career development. The introduction of individualised support packages through the NDIS has only

TABLE 8.2 Profile of workers in major industry sectors in Australia

Industry	Workforce median age	% Employed full-time	% Female
Retail and Trade	33	50.4	54.1
Education and Training	43	62	71.5
Construction	38	84.6	13.2
Disability support and aged care	**47**	**20**	**80**

Source: Australian Government Labour Market Information Portal (2021a; 2021b; 2021c; 2018).

intensified these trends, leading to the creation of somewhat of a gig economy within the sector (Dickinson et al. 2020).

These conditions directly impacted the risks these workers and their clients faced from Covid-19, particularly given the delays in the vaccination program rollout. As Peisah and colleagues note, while restricting visitors was one of the key infection control strategies mandated by governments and adopted by residential care facilities, it was mainly staff who brought Covid-19 into these settings: "Around the world, despite restrictions on visitors through front doors of facilities, the virus quickly came through the back, carried by health care workers forced by low wages to work at multiple facilities simultaneously with insufficient PPE" (2020: 1201).

As well as bringing employment conditions to light, the pandemic also offers us the opportunity to reflect on these and the training and incentives that could foster good care and support, which have been seriously neglected in the shift to consumer-directed care in the aged care and disability support systems. A growing body of research demonstrates that positive relationships with paid support workers can lead to substantive improvements in the quality of life of people with disability and older people, particularly for people who have limited informal social support networks, people with cognitive disabilities, and people with complex support needs (Robinson et al. 2021). Providing enabling and empowering care and support requires complex skills in augmenting and supporting a person's ability to communicate and make decisions, managing social and emotional dynamics and boundaries, as well as personal traits such as patience, flexibility, attentiveness and responsiveness (Fisher & Byrne 2011; Marquis & Jackson 2000). For the benefit of both employees and clients of the sector, the specialised forms of practical knowledge and expertise that are central to supporting and empowering care work need to be recognised—and invested in.

One of the supplementary solutions to the care crisis may be to invest in new technologies that could replace some human care activities. Robotics offers some potential here and are one of the areas that saw a significant investment over the pandemic when other areas of the industry dropped off (Dickinson and Smith Forthcoming 2022). In countries such as Japan, where significant workforce shortages are already an issue, there have been some significant advances made in these technologies. Robots can fulfil a number of roles, from manual handling, carrying and cleaning to social interaction. They are of particular benefit in the context of a pandemic, where humans can carry infections. Robots do not get sick or tired and do not need to isolate because they have contracted a virus. As we have outlined, the response for many aged care facilities was to prevent visitors from coming into the facility, which led to some residents feeling extremely socially isolated. Social robots can be one way to keep individuals engaged without risking infection. Some suggest that robotics might be part of a solution to the care crisis, although this does not come without challenges from the perspective of people working in the care sector and people accessing these services (Dickinson et al. 2021). There are concerns that without appropriate protections, the expansion of these technologies might exacerbate inequities rather than help counter them.

These technologies raise a series of ethical concerns about where they might be used, which groups might access robotic care and which groups can access human care (Smith et al. 2021).

As a result of the Covid-19 pandemic there has been increasing recognition that care and support service staff are frontline "essential workers", providing critical services to people whose wellbeing and lives to depend on the continuation of this support. However, we have yet to see whether recognising the necessity of essential workers will translate to an increase in the respect and status associated with these professions or to an increase in their employment conditions and pay. Certainly, the recent history shows rather than being improved, the conditions and may have been substantially eroded for many, and this shows no sign of changing in the short term. Care and support work will clearly be a growing area of employment demand in the future due to the ageing population and the expanding NDIS market, but whether individuals want to move into these roles is another issue. There is an urgent need for robust workforce investment strategies to address the labour shortage, quality and equity issues that plague the disability and aged care sectors. Better career pathways and professional development opportunities are needed to attract new workers, particularly younger workers, to this expanding sector.

Invest in Supported Independent Living and Community Living Options

The physical space in which care and support services are provided played a significant role in amplifying risk during the Covid-19 pandemic. Congregate care facilities, whether in the aged care or disability support system, involve many people with heightened vulnerabilities to the virus living nearby. It is more difficult to enact social distancing practices. Combined with a highly mobile workforce working between different facilities, this makes them ideal settings for rapid viral spread. As Peisah et al. (2020: 1200) remark: "The default option of segregating older persons has exposed the heightened vulnerability of congregated settings, where it is intrinsically difficult to secure an adequate standard of health and social distancing."

The link between smaller home-like settings and better therapeutic outcomes is well known (Bigby & Beadle-Brown 2018; Brownie et al. 2014). The built environment structures our behaviour and routines: people living in an institutional environment are more likely to be treated institutionally—as bodies to be managed rather than as individuals. The findings from the Royal Commissions demonstrate that some forms of abuse and neglect are more likely to occur in institutional facilities that are segregated from the rest of the community. For example, the interim report from the Royal Commission into Violence, Abuse, Neglect and Exploitation of People With Disability describes the high incidence of violence and neglect in supported accommodation services (2020: 24–25), and the final report from the Royal Commission into Aged Care Quality and Safety observes that physical and sexual abuse of older people in residential care is "far from uncommon" (2021: 68). Despite this, large residential care facilities continue to be planned and built. Disability and seniors advocates have been calling on governments to invest in smaller-scale community living options for a long time, arguing that increased options about where people receive care services will enhance client choice and control and reduce the risk of abuse and neglect. Now that there is greater awareness of the heightened risks of Covid-19 transmission within congregate care settings, we hope their voices will be amplified by public health experts and officials in calling for greater investment in independent and community living options.

Establish Permanent Advisory Bodies to Give Older People and People with Disability a Voice in Policy Decisions

In Australia, and many other countries impacted by the Covid-19 pandemic, people with disability were left out of emergency planning frameworks, and neither group had much opportunity to participate in or inform policy and decision-making processes about how the pandemic would be managed. It was evident in the vaccine roll-out that little thought had been given to the nature of lives of people with disability. In many places, people with disability were told to attend mass vaccination settings, but these are not accessible for several people with disability for a variety of reasons. Had people with disability been involved in planning processes this would have been apparent early in the process, rather than being discovered much later. Appointing permanent advisory bodies for both groups that include a significant proportion of service users with lived experience, older persons representative organisations and disabled people's organisations, would go a long way toward ensuring this lack of voice does not happen again.

Foreground Human Rights in Future Care Policy, Planning and Practice

Although, so far, Australia has avoided the devastating numbers of deaths that occurred in other countries, harrowing stories have emerged that demonstrate how easy it is for the human rights of older people and people with disability to be suspended in an emergency pandemic situation. Cousins (2020) reports how residents in a Melbourne nursing home were left without food and water for up to 18 hours, had open wounds left unattended, and were basically locked in their rooms for the duration of the state's stay at home orders. Policies and procedures with nursing homes and specialist disability accommodation sites for allowing and managing visitors were largely left to the discretion of individual providers, which meant some older people and people with disability were prevented from seeing their family and friends for months at end. Explicitly including reference to the human rights of older people and people with disability in emergency planning frameworks is a crucial first step to ensuring that they remain "front of mind" and that policy responses adequately balance human rights with other concerns such as infection control.

Human rights awareness-raising and training amongst service provider staff and management is also critical, particularly within the aged care system. The purpose of senior care and disability support is currently couched in very different terms. Since the ratification of the United Nations Convention on the Rights of Persons with Disabilities (CRPD) in 2008, international human rights law has explicitly addressed the rights of people with disability in a way it has not yet done so for older persons.[4] The aged care sector has yet to have its watershed moment towards meaningfully instituting similar rights-based reforms—unless it is the current moment, in the wake of devastating global loss of life and suspension of human rights due to Covid-19. And although there has been a major paradigm shift in the underlying philosophies of disability policy and support in recent years, many within the disability community were dismayed with the speed at which some of Australia's human rights obligations were abandoned, including the obligation to "consult with and actively involve persons with disabilities" in decision-making processes.[5]

We argue that unless Australia embeds human rights within care services in a meaningful way, future emergencies will see these issues arise again. There are no easy solutions to this, it requires significant and ongoing work to ensure that the rights of older people and people with disability are realised.

Conclusion

While the situations of older people and people with disability are different in many ways, there are some critical similarities in the problems with the service systems designed to meet their respective needs. Without substantial investment, demand for care will soon outstrip supply. Poor pay and conditions negatively affect both care workers and their clients. Segregated and institutional environments result in poorer outcomes for older people and people with disability. In both service areas, failure to consult appropriately with those affected by public policy and public health actions results in policy and practices that are less fit for purpose and more likely to harm. The suggestions for future reform outlined above are not new. In senior care alone, there have been 20 reviews and inquiries over the past couple of decades. We hope that the confluence of factors overviewed in this chapter—and particularly the opportunity to frame these issues as matters of public health—will create further impetus for change. It is because the Covid-19 shone a light on the deep issues plaguing the sector that we have a window of opportunity now to address these issues through broad social and economic reform and investment strategies.

Notes

1 Specialised age or senior care refers to care for specific conditions such as MS, Alzheimer's and dementia, stroke or Parkinson's for example. This care is typically offered in the home by a trained health care professional.
2 www.cdc.gov/aging/covid19/covid19-older-adults.html (accessed November 19, 2021).

3 These details were first aired during public hearing 12 of the disability Royal Commission on the experiences of people with disability during the Covid-19 vaccine rollout (Royal Commission into Violence, Abuse, Neglect and Exploitation of People with Disability, 2021).
4 There is however a growing impetus for a United Nations treaty on the rights of older people, documented in Byrnes (2020) and Quinn et al. (2018).
5 United Nations Convention on the Rights of Persons with Disabilities, Article 4—General Obligations

The Future of Production, Money, Energy, and Food Regimes

9

COVID-19 AND THE FUTURE OF WORK

Continuity and Change in Workplace Precarity

Tom Barnes, Sophie Cotton and Rakesh Kumar

Introduction

Covid-19 and state responses to the pandemic have led to the deepest global economic crisis of the last 90 years. This chapter focuses on the relationship between the crisis and pre-pandemic questions about the future of work and employment (Benanav 2020; Peetz 2020). The pandemic and "Covid-19 Recession" have the potential to deepen the effects of several trends in work and labour markets related to technological change, globalisation and economic restructuring, with implications for unemployment, under-employment, insecure work, inequality, and rising financial precarity (Coibion et al. 2020; Connell 2020; Hodder 2020).

This chapter hinges the relationship between work and the Covid-19 Recession on the problem of increasing *precarisation*. This concept describes how the risks of economic survival and social reproduction in capitalist societies are transferred from the institutions of capital and the state onto workers and households (Kalleberg 2018; Standing 2014). It is closely related to the concept of precarity, which can be understood as a general state of vulnerability, anxiety and anomie about the future (Millar 2017), and the sub-concepts of precarious/ insecure work, which refer to poor-quality jobs with common features like low pay, employment insecurity and poor social protection (Kalleberg 2018). It is also linked to the idea of the "precarious worker" as an individual whose social and economic background makes them more likely to depend upon these jobs (Campbell and Price 2016).

Unanswered questions that arise at the present juncture are the extent to which the pandemic crisis will accelerate or deepen the process of precarisation and the extent to which the crisis will make the problem of precarisation worse in the long run. In beginning to address these questions, this chapter explores the temporality

DOI: 10.4324/9781003250432-13

and rhythm of precarisation: whether precarisation is a process of evolutionary change that transfers the costs and risks of economic life onto workers in a gradual way or whether it is better conceptualised as a history punctuated by major ruptures in the regulation of work and labour markets. The chapter considers whether it is possible to synthesise these long-run versus short-run dynamics into a single historical conception of precarisation as an historical order interposed by moments of crisis which threaten to deepen its effects while also presenting moments of opportunity for social struggle and counter-regulation. It also addresses how the Covid-19 Recession has introduced or exposed *new* dimensions of precarisation.

We pursue these questions in the following three sections. First, in 'The Temporality and Rhythm of Precarisation', we explain the idea of precarisation as a process, situating this "processual rendering" (Alberti et al. 2018) in the context of the recent debate about the future of work. This section also foregrounds the empirical content of the chapter and explains its methodology. In the second section, 'Precarisation as Trend, Precarisation as Rupture', we outline a "trend-and-shock" approach to data on the transformation of work and labour markets in high-income economies during the last 20 years, including data on the impact of the Covid-19 Recession. The third section, 'New Features of Work During the Covid-19 Recession', explores the extent to which the Covid-19 crisis is associated with new dimensions of precarisation by focusing on sectors and occupations which have been radically disrupted, such as retail trade, warehouse logistics or white-collar professional and managerial work. Finally, the 'Discussion and Conclusion' revisits the implications of these trends for the future of work and employment..

The Temporality and Rhythm of Precarisation

Within studies of precarious work, there is now a broad understanding that precarity is not just a state of vulnerability or individual exposure to the adverse effects of capitalism but *a process* in which the risks of economic life, survival, and social reproduction are transferred from the institutions of capital and the state onto workers and households. Precarity, in other words, has become synonymous with *precarisation* (Alberti et al. 2018; Barnes and Weller 2020; Standing, 2014). This process is also widely understood as cumulative; it involves risk "dumping" in which costs and consequences are overlaid and become more concentrated over time. Risk shifting has intensified precarity for workers over years and decades (Barnes 2021; Lewchuk et al. 2008).

However, there is much still to learn about the *rhythm* of precarisation. A debate has emerged among radical theorists about the temporality of precarisation and its roots and causes. Benanav (2020) argues that rising precarity is epitomised by persistent under-employment and underpinned by falling productivity and dramatic over-capacity in rich-country manufacturing. Long-term stagnation reproduces a surplus of labour on a global scale, leading to a "world of poorly paid workers" (Benanav 2020: 20).

Moody (2020) has criticised this thesis on several grounds, including the implication that job loss has occurred "in a straight downward line due to industrial overcapacity ... Rather, it has unfolded violently, first and foremost in the four major recessions of the neoliberal era". Moody refers to the global economic crises of 1980–1982, 1990–1991, 2000–2001 and 2007–2009—to which 2020's Covid-19 Recession can be added as a fifth case. According to Moody (2018), the restructuring and flexibilisation of work is driven, above all, by capitalism's inherently cyclical nature of boom and busts.

It is possible to frame the processual character of precarisation through the lens of this debate. On the one hand, precarisation can be presented as an evolutionary social and economic process in which risk-dumping is gradual. This version of precarisation underscores its long-term path-dependent nature; that pro-neoliberal state institutions have set the regulation of work and labour markets onto a self-reinforcing path of precarisation.

A contrasting view, in the vein of Moody's critique, is that precarisation represents a series of breaks or disruptions. In this framing, major crises lead to political conflict and social upheaval, which reset the rules of work and labour markets, radically disrupting social reproduction and reconfiguring the balance of class power. Precarisation can be thus portrayed as a chronology of major disruptions rather than organic gradualism. This disruption-versus-evolution duality has echoes of the "punctuated equilibrium" versus gradualism debate which originated in evolutionary biology (Eldredge and Gould 1972) and which was transplanted into political science (Baumgartner and Jones 1993) and management/organisation studies in the United States (Romanelli and Tushman 1994).

This chapter considers the tension between long-term trends and short-term shocks through an empirical study of the relationship between work, labour markets and economic crises. It sketches a "trend-and-shock" model of precarisation, which emphasises path-dependency in economic time series in both the long run and short run (Fine 1998). This contrasts with a "trend-with-fluctuations" model by conceptualising short-run crises as possible turning points, alongside "hysteresis" in the long-run, where variables can persist once established.

For the concision of analysis, we focus on trends in key indicators over the past two decades (2000–2020). An advantage of this timescale is that it includes the last three major economic crises; namely, the early 2000s recession (especially 2000–2001), the Great Recession (2008–2009) and the Covid-19 Recession (2020–?). While cognisant of global trends, we focus on change in three "liberal market economies" (Hall and Soskice 2001)—Australia, the United Kingdom and the United States—because of similarities in each country's political and institutional traditions. Documented trends reflect core elements of precarisation, namely, unemployment, under-employment, job insecurity, low wage growth, and declining union membership. In addition, we consider trends in the "future of work", which have garnered attention during the Covid-19 crisis, such as working from home and platform-based work in the gig economy.

Precarisation as Trend, Precarisation as Rupture

This section outlines our "trend-and-shock" approach to core data on the transformation of work and labour markets in Australia, the United Kingdom and the United States for the period covering the last three major economic recessions (2000–2001, 2007–2009 and 2020–?). Key trends are premised upon the idea of precarisation as a process of risk-shifting. We proceed by presenting a series of indicative datasets for the three countries. A broad overview of statistical measures of precarity in these three countries in the past two decades reveals a period marked by a consistent decline in workers' economic position and political strength, punctuated by the impacts of economic crisis.

Precarisation can be broken down into constituent elements, which include impediments to accessing sufficient paid work; inadequacy, volatility and unpredictability of income; and weak collective voice and associational power.[1] The first element—access to sufficient paid work—can be approximated by standard measures such as unemployment. The second element—income security—can be addressed by documenting wage growth as well as related measures of economic prosperity such as economic inequality and housing stress. The final element—collective voice—can be addressed by documenting trade union representation density changes and working days lost to industrial action. Each of these elements is considered below.

Unemployment

Unemployment and under-employment sit at the heart of precarisation, both through the impact on those left without paid work and by disciplining currently employed workers. Periodic economic crises are most immediately recognisable through spikes in the unemployment rate followed by periods of declining unemployment (Figure 9.1). Despite the strong fluctuation, the last two decades have not produced a clear positive or negative trend in the United Kingdom, the United States or Australia. Unemployment has risen and fallen with cycles in the capitalist economy in all three countries, including some notable differences such as the much greater rate of unemployment in the United States during the Great Recession and the Covid-19 Recession compared to the United Kingdom and Australia.

Another indication of labour market insecurity is under-employment, which measures the proportion of employees with unmet demand for more working hours. In the United States, involuntary part-time employment rose from 3 per cent from 1995 to 2007 to 4.7 per cent from 2008 to 2020 (BLS 2020). In Australia and the United Kingdom, where under-employment measures *all* workers who want more hours, under-employment rose from 7.1 to 8.4 per cent and 6.7 to 9 per cent respectively in the same periods, where data is available (ABS 2021b; ONS 2021b). These step-like increases in underemployment can be described as interrelated "trend and shock" effects. Moody (2020), for example, observes that under-employment tends to "rise and fall with capitalism's periodic crises", whereas

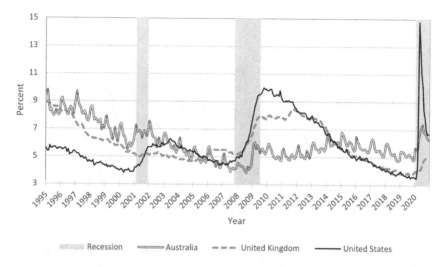

FIGURE 9.1 Unemployment rate

Source: ABS (2021a); BLS (2021); ONS (2021a).

Benanav's (2019: 129) argument that "unemployment will continue to spike during downturns and then give way to under-employment and rising inequality" helps to explain the cumulative process of risk-shifting.

Income Insecurity

Income security refers to all forms of social income, including money wages, enterprise or firm-based benefits, income from private savings or asset ownership, and state benefits such as welfare transfers, subsidised services, or unemployment insurance. A core dimension of precarisation is rising money wage dependency—a rising proportion of money wages in total social income (Barnes 2021). This shift has taken place over several decades. Therefore, individual worker and household exposure to capitalist volatility have become increasingly sensitive to trends in the basic hourly rate of wages.

Real wage growth has been consistently stagnant. Figure 9.2 shows these flat or downwards growth trends. In Australia and the United Kingdom, real wage growth has decreased over two decades. Australia's rate of real wage growth decreased from 2.9 per cent from 1998 to 2004, to 2.6 per cent from 2010 to 2014, to 1.5 per cent from 2015 to 2020. The U.K. real wage growth decreased from 2.4 per cent during 2000–2004 to 1.1 per cent during 2005–2009, −1.0 per cent during 2010–2014, before recovering slightly to 1 per cent during 2015–2019. The United States has seen flat real wage growth and periods of negative growth following the Great Recession. The rate declined from 2 per cent during 2000–2004 to 0.8 per cent during 2005–2009 and 0.3 per cent during 2010–2014, before recovering slightly to 1.5 per cent during 2015–2020.

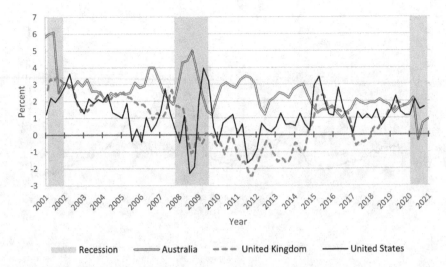

FIGURE 9.2 Real wage growth

Sources: ABS (2021c, 2021d); BLS (2021b, 2021c); ONS (2021c).

Another key measure of fiscal "health" in high-income countries is housing stress, defined as households which spend more than 30 per cent of total income on housing costs, including rental payments or mortgage debt (Yates 2007). Housing stress has increased markedly in recent decades, especially in major cities with high population density and high immigration. Across the United Kingdom, for example, housing stress increased dramatically following the Great Recession, from a low of 18.1 per cent in 2008–2009 to 24.4 per cent in 2014–2015 (DCLG 2013; DCLG 2016). In Australia, housing stress has increased steadily since the 1990s, spiking during the early 2000s Recession and the Great Recession. It rose from 19.6 per cent in 1995–1996 to 23.5 per cent in 2005/06 and then from 21.8 per cent in 2007–2008 to 25 per cent in 2011–2012 (ABS 2019).

A further sign of rising income insecurity is the rising proportion of renters, indicating the growing number of workers—especially younger workers—locked out of the mortgage market by declining housing affordability. Figure 9.3 shows that the proportion of renters increased markedly in all three countries following the Great Recession, although, in Australia, this reflected a longer-term trend which began in the 1990s. In the United Kingdom, the proportion of households renting increased from 30 per cent in 2006–2007 to 38 per cent in 2018–2019, accompanied by an increasing ratio of private-to-social renting. The proportion of renters increased in Australia from 25.7 per cent in 1999/2000 to 30.2 per cent in 2017–2018, and in the United States from 27.1 per cent in 2003–2004 to 31.9 per cent in 2015–2016.

A further dimension of the class inequality associated with precarisation is labour's falling share of national income in each country, as shown in Figure 9.4.

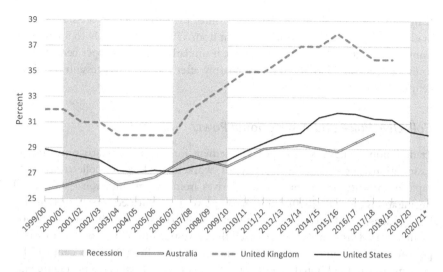

FIGURE 9.3 Households renting

Sources: ABS (2019); ONS (2001, 2002, 2005, 2006, 2007, 2019); US Census Bureau (2021, 2021a).

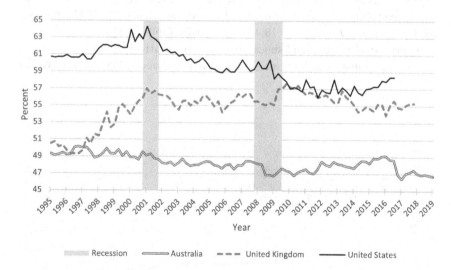

FIGURE 9.4 Labour share of income

Sources: ABS (2021e); BLS (2017); ONS (2018).

In Australia, the wages share of national income is much lower than in the United Kingdom or the United States, averaging 48 per cent since the 1990s, compared to 55 per cent in the United Kingdom and 60 per cent in the United States. However, the wages share has also fallen in these latter countries in recent years. In the United

Kingdom, the wage share has "flat-lined" since the early 2000s Recession and has gradually fallen since the Great Recession from 57 per cent in 2009 to 55 per cent from 2014 to 2018. In the United States, it similarly fell from 63 per cent in 2001 to 60 per cent in 2008 and dropped sharply after the Great Recession to 57 per cent in 2010.

Collective Voice and Associational Power

Trade union strength is an important element for resisting precarisation through "associational power"—the capacity of workers to bargain collectively with capitalist or state institutions, which derives from the mobilisational strength of organisations (Wright 2000). Trade union power has decreased over time, in membership density and willingness to undertake industrial action such as strikes. Union membership density has fallen consistently: in Australia from 32.7 per cent to 14.3 per cent over the time series; in the United Kingdom from 28.8 per cent to 21.0 per cent and, in the United States, from 14.9 per cent to 10.8 per cent (Figure 9.5). Strike density—the proportion of working days lost to industrial action—has also fallen dramatically since the 1990s, although data stabilised at a low rate during the 2010s. In Australia, this fell from a high in 1996 of 154.1 days lost to strikes per 1000 workers to an average of 15.8 from 2007 to 2020 (ABS 2008; ABS 2020c). The United Kingdom strike density has declined from an average of 22.7 days per 1000 workers in 1995–2006 to 18.4 in 2007–2019 (ONS 2019).

In terms of our "trend-and-shock" approach to precarisation, the data presented in this section mark out both long- and short-run changes. Collective voice, for

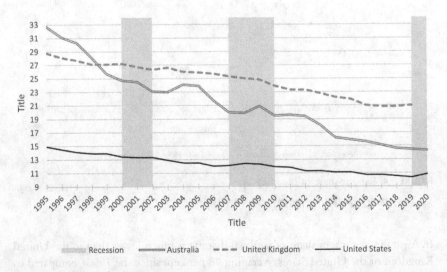

FIGURE 9.5 Union density

Sources: ABS (1996, 2013, 2020b); BLS (2019, 2021d); ONS (2020).

example, has been in secular decline over the last two decades and has not been radically affected in the short run by each successive economic crisis. In contrast, labour market insecurity has primarily reflected the shock of economic crises, declining during periods of capitalist growth and rising sharply during each recession.

Income insecurity, when measured in terms of rising wage dependency, stagnant real wages, rising housing stress and growing inequality, has increased steadily, punctuated by turning points in the crises marked by the economic recession. This was most obvious after the Great Recession, after which the proportion of renters rose, real wage growth fell, and the labour share of income fell. Macro-level evidence suggests that changes in income insecurity reflect both an ongoing trend and path-dependent sensitivity to economic shocks.

In short, different measures of precarisation may be more or less directly sensitive to ongoing trends or immediate shocks. When these measures are interpreted together, precarisation emerges as a process describable as *neither* pure trend nor pure shock, but rather as a path-dependent and cumulative process, as one in which economic crises, most evidently the Great Recession, can alter, deepen or induce processes of ongoing change.

We now discuss the Covid-19 Recession as the most recent example of such a qualitative "turning-point" in established trends. As we demonstrate, new features of precarisation have emerged during the Covid-19 Recession, which suggest a need to modify this concept further.

New Features of Work During the Covid-19 Recession

Covid-19 significantly impacted every sector of the Australian, British and American economies. Understandably, healthcare, including hospitals, aged care facilities and clinics, was the sector most *directly* impacted by Covid-19. Healthcare and social assistance is also the single largest-employing sector across the countries in this study, ranging between 12 and 14 per cent of the total workforce (ABS 2020a; BLS 2020a; ONS 2021). Although key sub-sectors of healthcare increased employment due to the priorities of the Covid-19 public health response, many workers lost jobs or working hours as routine, and non-elective care or surgeries and procedures unrelated to the pandemic were forcibly deferred or cancelled. In the United States alone, 1.6 million healthcare workers lost jobs during the first six months of the pandemic (BLS 2020). Job losses in the wider U.S. economy—around 20 million in the first three months of the pandemic—stripped most retrenched workers of medical insurance due to the employment-insurance-nexus which characterises the local healthcare system.

In other cases, entire industries were shut down, leading to mass job losses and drastic cuts to available working hours (see 'Precarisation as Trend, Precarisation as Rupture' above). Key examples include food and beverages, tourism, the creative arts, and higher education. The extent to which employment survived across many of these sectors depended upon the rollout of emergency "furlough" or wage subsidy schemes in which employers received funding to retain workers left idle on their payrolls. These schemes fell under the umbrella of unprecedented fiscal expansion by states (see the Chapter by Di Muzio in this volume). In the United States, for example, the Trump Administration's *COVID Aid, Relief, and Economic Security (CARES) Act 2020* allocated US$2.2 tn in spending, followed by the Biden Administration's *American Rescue Plan Act (ARPA) 2021,* which allocated US$1.9 tn.

However, in several cases, employers and workers were excluded from wage subsidy schemes. In Australia, the arts and higher education sectors were largely excluded from the wage subsidy scheme, known locally as "Job Keeper" (ATO 2021). On a broader scale, workers on temporary immigration visas were also excluded (Tham 2020). Covid-19 disproportionately affected racial or ethnic minorities' workers, although this was much greater in the United States and the United Kingdom than in Australia, where overall deaths were comparatively low (CDC 2021; ONS 2021).

The pandemic also entrenched gender disparities. Initial job losses were disproportionately borne by women due to high representation in sectors hit hardest by the recession (Dias et al. 2020; Wood et al. 2021). This was exacerbated in the United States by closing childcare centres (Collins et al. 2021; Lee and Parolin 2021). The long-term impacts are unknown, but even short-term disparities in unemployment can potentially exacerbate the pay gap.

Between job losses and pandemic lockdowns, the burden of unpaid domestic labour increased. Fathers in Australia and the United Kingdom performed paid work for fewer hours and unpaid work for more hours than before the pandemic. Very similar absolute changes in paid and unpaid work occurred for mothers, although from a starting point of much higher levels of unpaid domestic work and lower levels of paid work (Wood et al. 2021). In the United States, women lost substantially more hours of paid work than men (Collins et al. 2021). This pushed the absolute quantities of women's domestic labour to even higher levels (UN Women, 2020). Meanwhile, the family home failed to provide safety for many women, as shelter from the virus brought a greater risk of domestic abuse (Boxall, Morgan & Brown, 2020; Noman et al., 2020; Piquero et al.).

In the United Kingdom, the Coronavirus Job Retention Scheme provided a more generous wage subsidy than the Australian system but also contained loopholes. For example, workers with multiple jobs or those moving between jobs—including workers juggling precarious jobs to survive—were often excluded if part of their income was counted as self-employment (BBC 2021). In the United States, there was no equivalent furlough scheme; rather than unconditional cash subsidies, the *CARES Act 2020* and the *ARPA Act 2021* allocated loans to small-to-medium sized enterprises as well as tax credits, deferrals and deductions (US Treasury 2021). This less generous, credit-based approach partially explains why unemployment was significantly higher in the United States than in in the United Kingdom or Australia during the Covid-19 Recession. However, even in the United States, state fiscal expansion was generally effective in preventing widespread social collapse.

New technology has also shaped the experience of this pandemic-induced crisis. Radical advances in digital and smart technology had a transformative impact on working lives during the 2010s. Faster and more widely accessible broadband internet, the ubiquity of smart devices, social media, cloud computing and digital platforms have shaped the public and private experience of crisis adaptation, showing how crises and long-run trends can interweave to produce path-dependent precarisation. While technology does not principally determine or drive precarity, it should be conceptualised within the social process of precarisation as one important vector of influence.

Technological development during the 2010s made remote working and working from home (WFH) possible on a mass scale during the pandemic. Platform-enabled gig work and online consumption was similarly facilitated on a mass scale, parallel to an army of in-person "essential workers". The following sections explore changes in economic activity brought on by Covid-19 across three key sectors: office and remote work, food and accommodation, and retail trade and online shopping.

Office Work, Remote Work and Working from Home (WFH)

Remote work's role in society was elevated to new heights by the Covid-19 pandemic (Clancy, 2020). For example, in the United Kingdom, the proportion of workers who reported "usually" working from home increased steadily from 2.6 per cent in 1999 to 5.1 per cent in 2019, before spiking to an unprecedented 10.9 per cent by the fourth quarter of 2020 (ONS 2009; ONS 2021a). In April 2020, almost half of the workers reported "sometimes" working from home (ONS 2020a).

Employer surveys indicate WFH improved productivity by removing the compliance burden of direct or in-person workplace surveillance. In a survey of 15,000 businesses across 80 countries before the pandemic, 85 per cent of respondents said that remote work made employees more productive (IWG 2019). After the onset of the pandemic, a survey of 800 businesses found that 94 per cent reported productivity at the same level or higher than before (Mercer 2021). While WFH has, in some places, ebbed in line with the changing circumstances of the pandemic, many companies have chosen to regularise remote and flexible working arrangements (Dwoskin 2020; Sonnemaker 2021).

While this allowed many professional white-collar workers to avoid some of the occupational health risks associated with Covid-19, this was not true for most workers in manual labour occupations in manufacturing, construction, hospitality, travel, food and accommodation, and shopfront retail trade. For these jobs, the requirement of a physical presence in formal workplaces exposed workers physically to the coronavirus. Risks were exacerbated for workers without strong working conditions, including financially insecure workers in low-paying jobs, temporary jobs, or jobs that lack protection from arbitrary dismissals, such as "zero hours" contracts in the United Kingdom or "casual" jobs in Australia (ILO 2020).

Remote working arrangements have also brought occupational problems. Exposure to endless videoconference calls and the informal pressure of constant digital connection, including pressures outside standard or formally regulated working hours, have exacerbated prevailing trends in excessive working hours (Peetz 2020). The lines between working and personal lives, already blurred by cultures of work and technology, became fuzzier during the pandemic.

Finally, the temporary cessation of in-workplace surveillance has often been displaced or supplemented by technology-enabled monitoring and surveillance for remote work. Employers use software to monitor employees' website browsing, app use, time spent on various tasks, GPS tracking, or surveillance through real-time computer screenshots and keystroke logging (Hodder 2020).

Food and Accommodation

The hospitality sector was dramatically affected by the Covid-19 crisis as tourism shut down temporarily and dining out decreased drastically. After healthcare and retail trade, hospitality is one of the largest employers in affluent Western countries, ranging from 7.1 per cent in the United Kingdom to 11.9 per cent in the United States before the pandemic (BLS 2020; ONS 2021). The onset of Covid-19 saw dramatic falls in employment. In Australia, employment fell by 29 per cent from 2019 to mid-2020 (AISC 2020), with similar falls in the United Kingdom and the United States.

Lockdown conditions precipitated a rise in the United States of food delivery apps. In the United States, the top four food delivery apps (DoorDash, Grub, Uber, Postmates) doubled their revenue in April–September 2020 compared to the same period 12 months earlier (Sumagaysay 2020). The CEO of Deliveroo reported that the crisis brought forward forecasted food delivery demand by two to three years (Shead 2020).

The resulting spike in labour demand for gig workers, alongside mass unemployment, under-employment and exclusions from government support, accelerated a trend of financial stress-driven participation in gig economy jobs. Companies based in the gig economy are notorious for eschewing labour rights by insisting on workers' "independent contractor" or self-employed status. This has enabled platform capitalists to maximise risk-shifting onto workers in terms of reproduction costs, income insecurity and a lack of protection against hazardous working conditions. In Australia, rising labour demand for gig work was met with a rise in road accidents, including fatalities, in the opening months of the pandemic (SafeWork NSW 2020). Such cases highlight the physiological and economic consequences of risk-shifting in the gig economy.

Retail Trade, Online Shopping, and Logistics

Retail trade was profoundly reshaped during the Covid-19 crisis, both for front-end, consumer-facing workers such as store salespersons, cashiers, customer assistants, aisle stockers and supervisors, and for workers in the backend industry like those employed in transport and warehousing logistics. Both faces of retail trade have been disrupted by automation and eCommerce (Alimahomed-Wilson and Reese 2020; Gutelius and Theodore 2019; Hodder 2020).

In-store retail in "essential" services like groceries experienced sales growth during the pandemic, increasing demand for labour from major grocery supermarkets like Woolworths and Coles in Australia; Tesco and Sainsbury's in the United Kingdom, and Walmart in the United States. Most other new recruitment has been within casualised industries such as retail outlets and warehouses, distribution centres and fulfilment centres.

Online shopping also spiked under lockdown conditions. In the United States, the pandemic effectively squeezed five years of eCommerce growth forecasted before the pandemic into a six-month window. While sales for some product categories declined, such as clothing and consumer non-durables like groceries and alcohol, some durables like home improvement equipment and related services, grew by up to 16 per cent in the United States (IBM 2020). Many shops and food restaurants were forced to rapidly adapt to online sales to survive.

Rising eCommerce has increased demand for labour in online fulfilment centres where orders are received, sorted and dispatched. These jobs are mostly low paid, physically arduous jobs with limited employment security. In the United States, employment in these firms is also dominated by black and Hispanic workers (Alimahomed-Wilson and Reese 2020; Gutelius and Theodore 2019).

New technologies being implemented in retail trade and warehouse logistics include the deployment of mobile robots, automated conveyor systems, and autonomous vehicles enabled by the Internet of Things (IoT). Automation and the disruptive impacts of new technologies are ongoing features of capitalism (Benanav 2020; Wajcman 2017). The latest technologies continue to have a varied impact on labour; in some cases, displacing jobs and transforming labour market demand through the technological augmentation of jobs (Moore and Woodcock 2021).

One new feature in the labour process is "algorithmic management" of task allocation, performance, monitoring and discipline. Here, data is extracted from the labour process and fed into computerised algorithms, which through machine learning instruct or "nudge" workers to perform tasks within proscribed time limits. The extraction of data from the activity of workers in warehouses or retail outlets represents a form of "machinic dispossession" in which physical motions of the body are "datafied" or transformed into flows which record and analyse information about the sequence, speed and efficiency of tasks (Delfanti 2021).

Based on datafication, an algorithm can recalibrate work organisation on the shop floor by adjusting the tasks' order, operation methods, or the time allocated for completion. These are communicated to workers through various digital interfaces, especially screen-generated task lists as well as radiofrequency headsets or earpieces and, in some advanced workplaces, augmented eyewear or virtual "tethering" of bodies to "follow-me" automated mobile robots or guided vehicles, which obey algorithm-prescribed routes using floor markers or laser guidance systems (Gutelius and Theodore 2019). These forms of management, data extraction and algorithm-generated tasks occur in different ways in warehousing and logistics and the gig economy, whether through consumer-oriented platforms or more direct management control.

Algorithmic management has intersected with "despotic" workplace regimes, which rely on precarious jobs with low wages, limited employment security and little collective voice (Delfanti 2021; Wood 2020). It represents a new but rapidly spreading mode of articulation and exploitation that entangles precarisation, as an established process, with machines. Under algorithmic management, workplace relations are relatively impersonal and subservient to the calculative logic of machine-based processes. This is a novel dimension of precarisation that has been dramatically elevated in the context of the modern era's worst social and economic crisis. As in previous rounds of automation, however, these new technologies are not passively accepted by workers but are resisted and contested at the individual and collective levels (Kellogg et al. 2020).

Discussion and Conclusion: New Vectors in Precarisation?

Evidence presented in this paper demonstrates that precarisation is a process in which the social and economic risks of life in capitalist society are passed on to workers. The key economic data series measuring precarisation are neither purely cyclical nor linear trends with fluctuations. Instead, they exhibit genuine path-dependency in the long- and short-runs.

The punctuated element of precarisation is most evident in terms of insufficient access to paid work—what Standing (2014) characterised as "labor market insecurity". This has emerged as a periodic and cyclical feature which sharpens other trends in precarisation; problems of income insecurity and waning collective voice have been worsened by periodic and deepening crises of capitalism. Mass unemployment and under-employment during these crises have exposed workers' vulnerability to economic shocks—a vulnerability which has accumulated during prior periods of "headline" growth and stability.

Precarisation is a trend-based, cumulative and path-dependent process, described here through a processual "trend-and-shock" model. As well as ruptures and turning points, precarisation is epitomised by trends which have emerged over several decades. This is true for the key dimensions of income insecurity and declining worker protection via shrinking collective voice and representation.

Country-level differences remain important. For example, the unemployment rate spiked at much higher levels in the United States following the Great Recession and the Covid-19 Recession, compared to the United Kingdom and Australia. In Australia, under-employment was already trending upwards before the Covid-19 Recession, where the wages share of national income has also tended to be much lower than the United Kingdom or the United States. Despite these differences, all three countries have experienced rising income insecurity and shrinking collective voice, emblematic of a broader trend across the high-income economies of North America, northwest Europe, and parts of northeast Asia and many middle-to-high income economies across southern and eastern Europe. Market-based risks have been transferred onto workers' households, with women bearing the brunt of social reproduction in a cumulative fashion that has been sharply exposed during cyclical crises.

Based on this evidence, we can conclude that precarisation is best conceived as *a path-dependent and cumulative process punctuated by periodic crises of job loss and unemployment*. This process follows cycles of capitalist crisis and accumulation, which threaten to worsen workers' quality of life and drive a significant number into destitution. Capitalist crises represent moments in which fissures opened by the cumulative impact of precarisation threaten to make life and life prospects worse.

As the most recent crisis, the Covid-19 Recession also raises new questions. One is the unprecedented scale of state fiscal expansion in response to the pandemic (see 'New Features of Work During the Covid-19 Recession' above). The second feature emphasised in this chapter has been the role of new technologies, which were widely diffused during the 2010s. Key areas of working life influenced by the technological change have been remote work and WFH, eCommerce and online fulfilment, and platform-based gig work.

We have shown that the expansion of remote work has been enabled by major improvements in the quality of digital communication via faster internet speeds, smart devices, social media and consumer apps, which have become a ubiquitous feature of contemporary life, as well as cloud computing and, increasingly, the IoT. This has made WFH a feasible work option for millions of workers under conditions of community lockdown and physical distancing.

For many of these workers, WFH during the pandemic has had an ongoing impact on working arrangements and accepted notions of the "workplace", although the full scale and influence of these practices will take several years to be fully understood. By the late 2010s, eCommerce and online fulfilment were normalised to the extent that these consumption and distribution systems were able to expand to unprecedented levels during the pandemic, again with potentially ongoing impacts on consumer behaviour. The reorientation of the workplace through remote work also intersected with the ubiquity of platform-based apps, driving a spike in gig-based work.

Each of these technology-enabled aspects of life contains elements which intersect with or which sharpen precarisation. Remote working, for example, has exposed divisions between economic sectors and occupational groups, including a largely white-collar workforce which is able to work from home and those who cannot or who are prevented from doing so due to the nature of the labour process, the physicality of the producer-consumer relationship, the demands of managerial control, or a combination of these factors. For example, the benefits of WFH do not apply to most workers in sectors such as hospitals, aged care, retail supermarkets, or warehousing logistics and transport.

WFH has also generated new workplace issues. It has been associated with gendered inequality in the domestic sphere and an established tendency for workers in professional vocations to work excessive or unsociable hours, a problem exacerbated by technologies which enable employers to blur the boundaries between working time and leisure time or to monitor and discipline employees outside the confines of the traditional workplace.

Rising online fulfilment and gig work also highlights problems of poor job quality in high-demand occupations. Employment in warehouse logistics is notoriously precarious, with high numbers of casual, temporary and agency workers for whom labour market security is shaped by seasonal shifts in consumer demand, a tendency for employers to segment their workforces between permanent workers and workers without employment security or benefits, and a tendency toward physically demanding, low-wage work which leads to stress, injury, "burnout" and high labour turnover. The rising demand for warehouse work is intersecting with the prevalence of despotic labour practices in this sector.

Protections for gig-based workers are similarly poor, although this problem manifests differently in terms of workspace and formal employment arrangements— indeed, most gig workers are not even treated as formal "employees" by platforms, states or consumers, leading to a lack of employment security and protection from arbitrary, unjust or punitive treatment. Moreover, the spike in unemployment and under-employment during the pandemic has forced many workers to seek gig work under financial distress conditions.

Under social and economic crisis conditions, participation in work generated through online fulfilment and the gig economy is largely *precarity-induced*. A further feature common to both these forms of work, despite their differences in terms of workplace and workspace, is the tendency for task allocation and performance in the labour process to be monitored and disciplined via algorithmic management.

Whether the process of data extraction and machine learning is fed through consumer-based apps, as in the gig economy, or through wearable devices and scanners, as in warehouse logistics, the performance of workers is commonly now judged through an impersonal "datafied" process which humans, including managers, do not fully control. This dimension of machine-based precarity, in which the roots of workplace precarity appear to workers as impersonal, emotionless and impervious to "human" logic, is a product of the 2010s, which has been exposed on an unprecedented scale by the Covid-19 crisis.

The impacts of the Covid-19 crisis on the future of work are just beginning to unfold. This crisis has the potential to entrench prevailing trends of precarisation and to establish new path-dependencies through technology-enabled work practices. In contributing to the ongoing threat to make life worse with each successive crisis of capitalism, the biggest unanswered question is how "pandemic precarization" will open new sites of resistance and contestation.

Note

1 A more detailed outline of the constitutive elements of precarisation is provided by Standing (2014).

10

MMT, THE PANDEMIC, AND THE FISCAL DEFICIT FRIGHT[1]

Tim Di Muzio

As Covid-19 and its variants spread around the world, interrupting the "normal" operations of global capitalism, governments on the centre, left and right have been issuing large spending packages to fight recessionary conditions as businesses recalibrated their operations or shut down altogether and unemployment soared in a locked downed world (OECD 2020a, 2020b, 2020c). The crisis was made worse by the mountains of corporate and consumer debt that had accumulated to keep businesses turning over and households afloat well before the pandemic (Di Muzio and Robbins 2016; Soederberg 2014).

Surprising for some, against all prior devotion to "fiscal discipline" and so-called balanced budgets, public officials the world over shelved the first commandment of neoliberalism and collectively announced spending in the trillions. As *Bloomberg* noted, "in the battle against Covid-19, governments around the globe are on the cusp of becoming more indebted than at any point in modern history, surpassing even World War II" (Capo McCormick et al. 2021). This spending suggests that when it comes to preserving the class relations that structure our society—worker and employer, renter and landlord, debtor and creditor—it seems that money truly is no object during a crisis. At the time of this writing, no one knows the sum tally of the new spending, though it is certain to far exceed the bailouts witnessed during the Global Financial Crisis of 2007–2008. Indeed, echoing *Bloomberg*, the *Financial Times* dubbed this extravagance "the biggest borrowing spree in history"—and in early 2020, when the article was published, the pandemic was just getting started (Stubbington and Fletcher 2020).

As the pandemic deepened well into 2021, the economic turmoil unravelled while discretionary fiscal spending for relief programs mounted.[2] The ghost of Keynes seemed to be back in the fiscal saddle. To recall, Keynes argued that governments should spend by going into deficit in an economic downturn—particularly in a depression—and increase taxes and build surpluses to service debt

DOI: 10.4324/9781003250432-14

when the economy heated back up. Going into debt seemed the only solution to Keynes and his later acolytes (Keynes 2016). This thinking was based on the notion that businesses do not hire more workers nor increase or expand production during a depression due to less market demand for goods and services and greater uncertainty regarding future economic prospects (Skidelsky 2010). The only entity that can spend during a depression to get the economy going again and alleviate the misery of workers and businesses is the state itself. So, while the pandemic may be a once in a century bio-capitalist crisis with its peculiarities, it too has shined a bright light on the importance of government fiscal policy and borrowing to prop up the economy and support livelihoods and business.

Within this context and the scramble to find a new economic paradigm surpassing the orthodoxy of neoliberalism, a seemingly new set of ideas came to be debated beyond the ivory tower—Modern Monetary Theory (MMT) (Boxall et al. 2020; Mitchell 2020). As the *Economist* reasoned after surveying policy options during the pandemic: "What is clear is that the old economic paradigm is looking tired. One way or another, change is coming" (Anonymous 2020: 16). While proponents of MMT do not always agree on the way forward, at its very basic, MMT can be encapsulated in five main claims. First, national governments who are currency issuers always can service their debts, provided they are denominated in the national currency. This means that federal deficits, provided they do not contribute to runaway inflation, can be incredibly useful for achieving public policy goals. This suggests that MMT upholds a strong role for inflation monitoring. Second, the government does not have to wait around for tax receipts or bond sales to spend money on the economy. The treasury simply instructs the central or national bank to deposit payments in a recipient's account. In this sense, governments do not wait around for tax money to accumulate in a piggy bank before spending money on the economy, even in normal times. Third, deficit spending is an injection of money into the economy while taxes, fines and fees drain money out of the economy. In this sense, the government's deficit spending or debt issuance as securities is used by businesses when governments buy goods and services from them, by individuals who receive transfer payments or as a financial asset by citizens or foreigners who purchase government bonds. Fourth, the idea of chasing balanced budgets as an end goal in itself is an artificial constraint rooted in conceptualising the currency issuer as a currency user (for instance, comparing a government's finances to that of a household). Fifth, the government should strive for low inflation and full employment and towards this end, provide a job guarantee for those seeking paid work but unable to find it in the private sphere (Kelton 2020). In sum, MMT does not quarrel with the current way government finances are set up but rather seeks to show politicians and the public that running deficits can benefit human well-being and the economy if the government is monetarily sovereign (i.e. issues its currency). Of course, MMT is not without its detractors, mainstream and otherwise, but they too are largely caught within the legacy of the fiscal-monetary paradigm of which they appear to know little about the origins. The current fiscal-monetary paradigm that developed with the rise of capitalism has, over time, been depoliticised and naturalised as though things have to be the way they are and there is no accounting, financial or monetary alternative.

This chapter seeks to intervene in these debates and re-politicise the nature of the fiscal-monetary paradigm currently in operation. I argue that to understand contemporary debates on MMT and the COVID crisis, it is important to understand the historical context from which they are derived. It may seem strange to return to the origins of capitalism and the birth of the fiscal and monetary system in England, but if we fail to do so, our current debates will be intellectually impoverished and our policy options needlessly constrained. I contend that current discussions on what the pandemic has taught us about monetary and fiscal policy are myopic. It is the purpose of this chapter to broaden the political economy horizon so that we might think anew about pathways through the crisis and perhaps a new fiscal and monetary order. Part of doing so is understanding that capitalism was not born in a void but in unequal power relations and a massive social transformation that benefitted and, arguably continues to benefit, the few. Moreover, this chapter argues that while MMT has its virtues, it too misses two very important aspects of capitalism (1) *why* there is a constant aggregate demand problem in a capitalist economy and; (2) that the majority of new money creation is not issued by governments, but by commercial banks when they make loans to willing borrowers. To explore these arguments, this chapter is divided into three main sections and a brief conclusion. First, I return to the debates on the dearth of money in England and the vast pauperisation of the countryside as peasants were expropriated from their customary access to land and, thus, their self-provisioning. I show how these debates have long since been forgotten by economic orthodoxy but bear urgently and importantly on current fiscal and monetary debates, given that one of the main critiques of MMT is that it promises a "free lunch" (Epstein 2020; Scaliger 2021: 12). As we shall uncover, the early political economists argued that the able-bodied poor should in no way be relieved at public expense. In the second section, I discuss the virtues of MMT and empirically examine its main criticisms. In the third section, I outline MMT's oversights on aggregate demand and commercial banking and why this is not only important for our knowledge of the macro-economy but could also potentially broaden policy options. This is of particular importance given the centrality of money in capitalist society and the interconnected challenges our global community faces from climate change to an impending energy transition (Di Muzio 2015; Newell 2021). The chapter closes with a brief conclusion.

Power, Fiscal Lock-in and Pauperism

The literature on MMT and its critiques are largely ahistorical. They take the current fiscal-monetary system as a given as though things could not be otherwise. To paraphrase Marx, they assume as fact what has to be explained (in Morgan 1992: 1159–1160). For this reason, in this section, I provide some historical context of how we arrived at the present order of things and show how the transformation to a capitalist mode of power is intertwined with the monetisation of society and a fateful decision about how to expand the money supply to stimulate productivity and improvement.

For various reasons stretching back to King Croesus in Lydia in the 7th century BCE, where the first standardised coins were minted in electrum (an alloy of gold and silver), the so-called West came to believe that real money consisted of precious metals (Weatherford 1997: 30ff). The possession of gold and silver could raise and mobilise armies, pay for provisions and luxury goods and ultimately represent power and wealth in a geopolitically competitive Eurasia. The difficulty of tying an economy to the circulation of gold and silver as the only "real" currencies was that there was a limited supply of these metals. Thus, because of this monetary choice by those in power, a socially constructed and intersubjective limitation was put on the *potential* productivity of an economy and the wealth of rulers and subjects. The former is obvious, but the latter has to do with a ruler spending on the economy—generally for war. Once the expenditure is accomplished, a ruler only has limited options to restock treasury coffers: taxation (which is unpopular), finding a new mine through exploration or conquest, or capturing the gold and silver of others. Though some rulers were more successful than others, this dearth of money problem confronted all political communities who adopted gold and silver as their unit of account and official currency. This is one of the chief reasons the rulers of Western political communities tore themselves apart for precious metals, and merchants and conquistadors travelled to far-flung regions of the earth to find it (Vilar 2011; Kwarteng 2014). But by the early 1600s in England, the shortage of circulating money consumed social reformers and political authorities. At first, the problem of insufficient precious metals to stimulate improvement was met with the solution of alchemy. Was it possible to turn base metals into the precious metals of gold and silver to expand the money supply and promote the greater development of material resources? It was not, and so the problem persisted until, as Wennerlind's detailed study reveals, there was an epistemological revolution inspired by the work of the Hartlib circle, a European correspondence network sharing knowledge on scientific developments (Wennerlind 2011). Over time, the Hartlib circle realised that money was not a material substance but fundamentally an idea in the minds of men. Money, they reasoned, could theoretically be represented by any material substance. The belief that gold and silver had an intrinsic value and were thus the only "real" or "true" stores of value persisted, but that these precious metals could be represented *symbolically* by other instruments freed these early thinkers from the shackles of the precious metal fetish. It was now intellectually possible to expand the money supply, but one question loomed large; how to do so practically? Throughout the civil strife of the mid-1600s in England, social reformers introduced several proposals to tackle the dearth of money problem, while goldsmiths continued to expand the money supply through the extension of credit—albeit in a very restrictive way (Davies 2002: 250ff; Horsefield 1960). Ultimately, the solution came from capitalising the state's concentrated power to tax and extending credit notes on a relatively small amount of silver-backed by future taxes (Desan 2014; Dickinson 2016; Nitzan and Bichler 2009: 294–298). Toward this end, the Scottish trader and banker, William

Paterson proposed the creation of the Bank of England to extend loans to the Crown. This proposal was born in the crucible of King William of Orange's war with France, which was already six of nine years underway (1688–1697). In dire need of finance amidst the war, the proposal was accepted, and the Bank of England was established in 1694. As Wennerlind notes:

> A 1694 parliamentary act allowed the Bank to raise a capital stock of £1.2 million, the full value of which was to be lent to the government, paid out in notes or sealed bills, rather than coin, in exchange for tallies. In return, the government committed £140,000 per year to the Bank from a new tax on shipping and liquor, which was enough to pay subscribers an 8 percent dividend (£100,000 payable in cash and Exchequer Orders), provide a management fee to the Bank (£4,000), and allow the Bank to improve the returns on its reserves by acquiring annuities. The Bank's capital was subscribed in ten days by some thirteen hundred people and the Bank swiftly commenced its operations.
>
> *2011: 109*

While this financial revolution did not completely alleviate the shortage of money problem in England, it did lead to "Europe's and England's first widely circulating credit currency" (Wennerlind 2011: 109). It also leads to a unique capitalist fiscal and monetary arrangement that has largely spread worldwide through the power of finance and colonial violence. It should be recalled here that previous to the Glorious Rebellion of 1688, English sovereigns were *personally responsible* for their debts to moneylenders and could default at will because they could not be tried in a court of law. The Rebellion succeeded in subordinating the Crown to Parliament, with the Crown now only receiving a yearly stipend from the revenue raised by Parliamentary taxes. We should note that this was not a natural development but a political choice based on an asymmetry of financial power between English financiers and the monarchy in the age of the precious metal fetish. In sum, the issuance of credit for war came to be the primary way of expanding the money supply. As Brewer rightly argues, after 1688, England was fast becoming a fiscal-military state (Brewer 1989: 22). It was only much later that commercial banks would play a more important role in extending credit to businesses and households. But the lack of money was not the only problem plaguing England's early modern period. England was also beset by a plague of pauperism that was inextricably intertwined with the question of money.

Around the same time that social reformers and public authorities fretted about the dearth of money, they noticed another problem of the ruling class's making: the rampant pauperisation of the rural population. If the scarcity of money problem leads to how to expand the money supply to increase trade, productivity and improvement, then the problem of pauperisation leads to the question of what to do with the growing mass of unemployed paupers? As Polanyi suggested, there was no shortage of pamphlets proposing solutions to the problem, with Bentham's for-profit Panopticon proposal perhaps the most infamous (Polanyi 1957: 90). These early debates on what to do with the poor continue to inform current discussions on welfare and welfare reform and link up directly, as we shall see below, with MMT's proposal for a jobs guarantee funded by the central government—a program greeted with suspicion by MMT's critics.

The rise in pauperisation was due to the centuries long enclosure movement where peasant proprietors were denied customary access to their patch of arable land and the commons by violence and, over time, Parliamentary decree (Wood 2002: 109). As the countryside gradually monetised, the desire for profit and power grew fiercer among the lords of estates, and evermore peasants were evicted from the land so that pasture could be grown for sheep (Marx 1990: 879). The dissolution of the Catholic monasteries during the Tudor Protestant Reformation in the sixteenth century added more sub-tenants to the class of growing paupers, vagabonds and beggars, as did the dissolution of feudal retainers aimed at centralising the monopoly of violence in London. Those who could not find work had two unenviable choices: break the law or starve. As Marx argued in section eight of *Capital*, the scourges of pauperism and the dearth of employment opportunities were met with two major strategies employed by the ruling class, the increasing criminalisation and corporeal punishment of the poor and outdoor or indoor poor relief. Corporeal punishment came in the form of whipping, branding, torturing and even hanging the perceived beggars, vagabonds and criminals. Indeed, such was the threat to property by a growing mass of paupers that by the early eighteenth century, no less than 225 offences against the propertied could warrant the public hanging of an offender.[3] Poor relief evolved in fits and starts over the Tudor period and was orchestrated at the parish level. The poor could be given indoor relief, which meant entering an institution like a workhouse or poorhouse to be guaranteed sustenance. In contrast, outdoor relief did not require the relieved to enter an institution. The quality, level and coordination of relief varied as it was administered locally, and parishes did not have equal resources. However diverse and perhaps insufficient in many cases, the poor law statutes and acts at least gave the poor the "right to live" (Polanyi 1957: 81). Nevertheless, by the early eighteenth century, the "right to live" was incompatible with the emerging capitalist system and the pressing need for a labour market for capitalists.

The first salvo in the war on the poor and unemployed was launched by the writer of *Robinson Crusoe* fame, Daniel Defoe, in a pamphlet entitled *Giving Alms no Charity* in 1704. In it, Defoe "insisted that if the poor were relieved, they would not work for wages; and that if they were put to manufacturing goods in public institutions, they would merely create more unemployment in private manufactures" (Polanyi 1957: 108).[4] The next shot against relief was fired by the medical doctor and cleric Joseph Townsend in his *Dissertation on the Poor Laws*, published in 1786. Townsend imagined Robinson Crusoe populating his lonely island with goats that multiplied and provided a steady food source for him and his guests. But the goats were also a source of nourishment for pirates who were ruining Spanish trade through waterborne pillage. So Spanish traders dropped off some wild dogs on the island, quickly reducing the number of goats. Townsend took two lessons from his allegory. Firstly, "it was the quantity of food which regulates the number of the human species" and secondly, granting the poor the "right to live" through relief would keep them idle and out of the workforce (Polanyi 1957: 112–113). Townsend's solution was to strip away all relief and threaten the able-bodied unemployed with hunger and starvation. This would spur them to work better than any legislation. Years later, in his *Principle of Population* (1798), the English cleric Thomas Robert Malthus, perhaps with more finesse, essentially plagiarised Townsend's work, arguing that unchecked population growth naturally outstrips the food supply. In Malthus' view, the public did not have a responsibility to feed those who hungered. Parents should simply abstain from having children if they are unable or unwilling to provide for them.

By 1834, this current of thought, among other ruling class ideas, contributed to the Poor Law Amendment Act, which made the search for relief difficult. If in want of clothing, shelter, food or money, the poor would be forced into workhouses. The policy goal was to make conditions in the workhouses so unpalatable that the able-bodied would seek work in the factories and mines. Thus, abolition of the "old poor law" ushered in a labour market for capital, and as Polanyi argued, 1834 can be considered "the true birthday of the modern working class" (1957: 101).

The point of this return to history is twofold. First, due to the circumstances and the monetary power asymmetries between financiers and the Crown in Parliament, a specific fiscal structure was formed based on the belief in limited precious metals as the only "real" money. The public force, or government, was not permitted a free lunch because the Bank of England (and later commercial banks) had control over the issuance of credit. If Parliament wanted to spend more money than it received in taxes, it was structurally forced to go into debt to the private social forces that owned the Bank of England. This is what I call *fiscal lock-in,* and it gives tremendous power to financiers since mounting debt—principally for war at the time—can then be leveraged to influence government policy in favour of bondholders and financiers les the Bank of England turn off the credit tap in an increasingly capitalist society premised on war and industrial development. Secondly, the discussion on pauperisation highlighted the fact that in a capitalist market economy, the able-bodied poor and/or unemployed require money to survive but are to be given as little relief as possible. Modern welfare policies reflect the legacy of these early debates on what to do with the poor. Poverty is viewed as a moral choice, not a structural feature of capitalism. If they are relieved at all, the poor and unemployed are to be given a minimal level of subsistence below or near the national poverty line. As in the past, such treatment is designed to encourage recipients to enter the workforce as soon as is humanly possible. This is despite the widespread liberal belief in a "natural" rate of unemployment. In this view, a degree of unemployment is considered a net positive to the overall economy since the economic suffering of the unemployed is assumed to hold down inflation, as posited by the infamous Philips Curve. Like the government, there *should* be no free lunches for idle hands at the public expense. With this historical background in mind, in the next section, I discuss the virtues of MMT and survey its main criticisms before outlining MMT's oversights on aggregate demand and commercial banking and why this is not only important for our knowledge of the macro-economy but could also theoretically broaden practical policy options, up to and including non-interest bearing and debt-free sovereign money (Crocker 2020; Huber 2017).

MMT, Free Lunches and the Pandemic

As we have discussed, the need to finance fiscal budgets that exceeded tax revenues in the early formation of the English public financial system was largely due to power asymmetries between financiers (who had money) and the state (in need of finance). Originally backed by an unknown quantity of silver, by 1816, England legally adopted a gold standard (Cooper 1982: 3). The development of the British Empire and its financial and industrial power over other colonial and non-colonial powers internationalised the idea that high-powered money consisted of gold. Eventually, foreign powers not under the direct control of the British Empire came to embrace this idea once the United States and Germany—the two other industrial powerhouses—adopted the gold standard from the 1870s. With some exceptions (e.g. China and Persia), "the largest part of the world was on the gold standard" by the end of the century (Eichengreen and Sussman 2000: 20). World War I, the Great Depression and World War II disrupted the international gold standard, but the idea that gold was the only true money remained in the minds of investors, businessmen, economists and politicians. After World War II, this belief was institutionalised in the creation of the International Monetary Fund (IMF). Originally the IMF was designed to facilitate international trade by maintaining relatively fixed exchange rates between currencies and temporarily overcoming balance of payments problems if countries suffered a trade deficit. Under this new regime, the strongest world currency, the U.S. dollar, was pegged to gold at US$35 an ounce. Largely because of the world wars, the United States gained greater industrial might and attracted much of the world's gold because of its investment opportunities and superior technology (Panitch and Gindin 2012: 67–110).

Most of the world struggled with the gold standard until 1971 when the Nixon administration was advised to close the gold window at the Federal Reserve. While the abandonment of the gold standard served American grand strategy in various ways, the move was made because the Nixon administration reasoned that there were too many American dollars outstanding for the stock of gold held by the U.S. Federal Reserve.[5] In other words, countries with surplus dollars could drain away America's gold supply. Relinquishing the gold standard made this option impossible for foreign countries. But it also set the world on a new monetary footing. The world was no longer constrained by the strictures of the gold standard, and currencies now had value, not because they were anchored to a precious metal, but because states enforced their value (Gowan 1999: 19–20). For the first time since the rise of the international gold standard, money was untethered from a precious metal that arbitrarily limited its supply. The move also gave governments more room to deploy deficit spending since outstanding currency could no longer be redeemed in a limited gold supply. However, the intellectual legacy of the gold standard and the need for austerity and fiscal discipline tied to it lingered on in the minds of economists and politicians (Blyth 2015).

This is perhaps the major reason many are sceptical about MMT's claim that currency-issuing governments should not worry about mounting deficits and (national) debt provided they do not contribute to runaway inflation. As in a household, an unbalanced government budget is treated as a vice, not a virtue. Yet, MMT claims the opposite: government deficits can be a virtue if the excess money injected into the economy stimulates real productivity growth, eases the suffering of the unemployed and keeps inflation at bay. If we take Kelton's *The Deficit Myth* as the most recent formulation of MMT, then deficit spending can be used to tackle several social, economic and environmental ills, from needless unemployment to global climate change (Kelton 2020). In other words, the currency issuer has the power of the purse and should spend to increase the nation's well-being and its local communities. Kelton, among others working in the tradition, also calls for a national jobs guarantee that would put willing people to work in their local communities, providing them with worthwhile jobs that add value to their communities (Tcherneva 2018). It should be noted here that no MMT economist argues for wild untargeted deficit spending, particularly where there is little room for productivity growth in the economy and a high probability of inflationary pressure.

MMT could have been brushed aside as a new intellectual fad (or old Keynesian wine in new bottles), but the global pandemic demonstrated how previously inconceivable deficit spending was very useful in propping up economies around the world vastly avoiding the potential for widespread unemployment and bankruptcy. Despite this practical demonstration, however, MMT has its share of critics— with some even labelling it as an "extreme school of thought" (Makin and Tunny 2021: 2). While I will also critique MMT momentarily, I contend here that MMT's critics are tied to the mast of dismal science orthodoxy and have little to no imagination for getting us beyond the legacy of fiscal lock-in. Current fiscal and monetary arrangements, seemingly cast in stone due to decisions made by politicians and financiers in the distant past, need to be re-politicised and rethought for the challenges of the 21st century. But before getting to that, let us briefly survey the main criticisms of MMT and see if they hold any empirical water.

A key criticism of MMT is that it sees the macroeconomic puzzle to solve as only demand related. As such, MMT may under-theorise supply-side constraints and advocate for greater deficit spending, which may help promote inflation by creating too much demand. This is the familiar "inflation is too much money chasing too few goods" maxim of the reigning economic orthodoxy. A second criticism is that we cannot anticipate how much inflation will be caused by what level of deficit spending. This leads to the question: how do we know how much the government can spend on the economy above its revenue before we start seeing dramatic rises in price levels? Furthermore, should inflation rear its ugly head due to deficit spending, the government will have to act fast to tax money out of the economy, lessening the money supply for the circulation of goods and services and potentially angering voters whose discretionary spending may be diminished. The next argument against MMT is the infamous crowding out problem. This problem is premised on the binary assumption: "private sector good"', "public sector bad". According to MMT critics, crowding out can happen in at least three ways. First, borrowing to finance public deficits could lead to mounting interest rates, making it costly for businesses to borrow and grow. Secondly, greater deficit spending could lead citizens to anticipate future tax hikes and therefore save rather than spend their money, creating a greater glut in the economy. Finally, crowding out can occur when foreigners increase their capital investments in the country due to the attraction of higher interest rates. This can lead to currency appreciation and a lack of export competitiveness (Bird et al. 2021: 38–39).

I argue that as long as we remain within the intellectual and structural confines of economic orthodoxy, these critiques appear to have some weight. This is despite the fact that during the pandemic unprecedented deficit spending neither contributed to runaway inflation nor higher interest rates (Anonymous 2020: 14). In fact, in some quarters, there were calls for even more generous deficit spending and the maintenance of low-interest rates to stimulate economic activity even before the pandemic (Putnam 2021: 16). But critics may rightly charge that the pandemic was an exceptional circumstance, leaving considerable room for loose fiscal and monetary policy. However, when things return to "normal", it is presumed that fiscal discipline will be reinstated and that central bankers will raise base interest rates to arrest the flow of cheaper credit. Yet this return to normal only holds if we collectively believe in these strictures in the first place. But if we re-politicise current fiscal-monetary arrangements and imagine how fiscal-monetary relations can be reinvented to better suit public and democratic goals, then we can clearly see that these strictures are not natural laws but the stuff of historical human construction. Let us take the two major critiques—inflation and crowding out—before we move on to our own critique of MMT.

As noted, MMT critics fear that too much deficit spending could lead to increasing prices for goods and services. The assumption here is that deficit spending can be a *primary driver* of inflation. In the economic literature, inflation is said to be ignited by two main forces: cost-push inflation and demand-pull inflation. The first understands rising prices resulting from increasing costs to the business that get pushed on to consumers in the prices they pay for goods and services. A leading example is the oil price shocks of 1973 and 1979, when the price of a barrel of oil increased by 400 per cent. Another tired example of cost-push inflation is increasing wages, primarily attributed to collective bargaining and the power of unions to get their pay indexed to the inflation rate.[6] In this case, since wages are a cost to business, prices have to increase by the logic of cost-plus capitalist accounting (Di Muzio and Robbins 2020). Demand-pull inflation results if demand backed by the ability to pay outstrips the economy's productive capacity. In other words, there is too much demand for fewer goods and services, pushing prices up. These claims are sensible enough, but critics of MMT worry about government deficits driving inflation—a particular claim that, to date, has been asserted without empirical

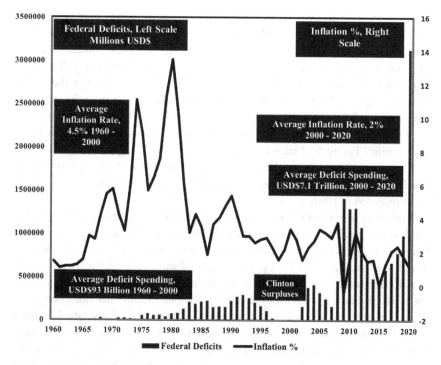

FIGURE 10.1 U.S. federal deficits and inflation rate, 1960–2020

Source: St. Louis Federal Reserve: https://fred.stlouisfed.org/series/FYFSD and https:// fred.stlouisfed.org/series/FPCPITOTLZGUSA.

evidence. Figure 10.1 charts the relationship between federal deficits in the United States of America and inflation in consumer prices. The chart is rather revealing and suggests that federal budget deficits are hardly a primary driver of inflation. In fact, the chart suggests that during the era of higher federal deficit spending (2001– 2020) the inflation rate was two percentage points lower on average than in the period from 1960 to 2000. Thus, the notion that high deficit spending can lead to runaway inflation appears to be a chimaera.[7]

Now that we have debunked the deficit-inflation bug-bear, we can discuss the so-called crowding-out phenomenon.

The crowding out hypothesis claims that deficits will lead to higher interest rates, making it more costly for firms to borrow money to grow their businesses. This view assumes that there is a limited pool of capital that can be lent out. If a government's demand for loans is high, interest rates will be pushed up and crowd out private industry. This is completely incorrect and premised on a false understanding of how new money is created in an economy. In actual fact, loans create deposits, not the other way around. There is no limited pool of capital. When commercial banks purchase government securities, they do not use the savings of their depositors (the assumed but incorrect, limited pool). If banks decide to hold government securities, they merely create the digital money to exchange for the securities and therefore expand their balance sheet. What is more, this is also done through central banking when the central bank purchases government securities. The process is a digital balance sheet operation, pure and simple. This helps explain how suddenly central banks came to the rescue of the banks after the Global Financial Crisis and how they funded stimulus spending throughout the pandemic (Kelton 2020: 34). Where there was a dearth, there is now plenty! But is there any empirical evidence demonstrating that government borrowing will lead to higher interest rates? Figure 10.2 takes a closer look at this claim.

As Figure 10.2 suggests, there is no empirical evidence that federal budget deficits in the United States trigger higher base interest rates and thus crowd out capitalist access to finance.

The next major tenet of the crowding-out hypothesis is that big deficit spending will lead to greater savings because the public anticipates higher taxes in the future. Excess savings can slow demand for goods and services in the economy, thus creating a glut. As Figure 10.3 suggests, savings did increase substantially during the recessionary conditions tied to pandemic lockdowns. But the crowding out claim overlooks the fact that savings are differential. This means that not everyone is saving the same amount, with the better off able to save at a faster rate. According to the Federal Reserve of Kansas, people do not save in anticipation of higher taxes in the future. Saving is normal in recessions because there is less opportunity for consumption, and people tend to save for fear that they will be unemployed or underemployed in future (Smith 2020). Government assistance during the pandemic may have given a boost to household income, but this does not offer strong

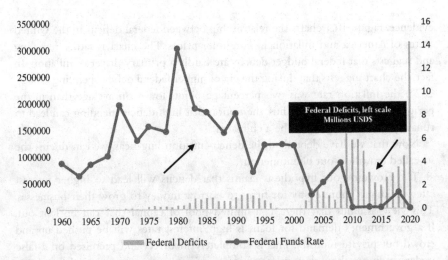

FIGURE 10.2 Federal deficits and federal funds rate 1960–2020

Source: https://fred.stlouisfed.org/series/FYFSD and https://fred.stlouisfed.org/series/FEDFUNDS.

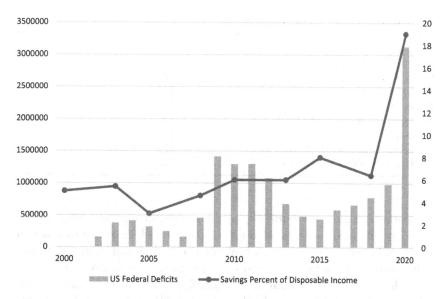

FIGURE 10.3 U.S. Federal deficits and savings per cent of disposable income, 2000–2020

Source: https://fred.stlouisfed.org/series/FYFSD and https://fred.stlouisfed.org/series/PMSAVE.

evidence for the claim that government spending over and above what it takes in in tax, fines, fees and privatisations, contributes to excessive saving by the public, save during a major crisis or the memory of one, such as the GFC.

The final crowding out claim—that higher interest rates will lead to currency appreciation and less export competitiveness can be dismissed as we know that interest rates are at record lows in major capitalist economies (see Figure 10.2 for the USA). Moreover, base interest rates are expected to remain low as economies recover. It is true that analysts continue to debate the possibility of greater inflation, but its primary cause should not be sought in fiscal deficits.[8] In sum, we can largely dispense with the orthodox critiques of MMT. It is now time to offer a new critique of MMT that goes beyond conventional concerns.

The Dearth of Money Revisited and Commercial Banks

As I have already argued, capitalism is born into a world with an artificial shortage of money. This was primarily because power-holders were convinced that gold and silver were the only true money form by history and convention. But there is another major reason why there is a constant shortage of money in modern capitalist economies, and Modern Monetary Theorists seem to be unaware of this: capitalist cost-plus accounting. As originally discovered by C.H. Douglas, the founder of the social credit movement at the start of the twentieth century, it is due to this

TABLE 10.1 Uncle Pepe's super happy fun margarita mix costs

Sugar	$50
Lemon and lime juice	$93
Gas for the stove	$25
Bottles and caps	$44
Labour	$100
Total production cost of one bottle	$3.12
Mark-up	$6.88
Total cost of one bottle with mark-up	$10
Total market value of margarita mix	$1000

accounting that there is a dearth of purchasing power or aggregate demand in the economy. This causes a drastic need for commercial bank credit and increases the power and leverage of commercial banks over individuals and businesses. To provide a simple example here, we can imagine going into business making a margarita mix at home for sale in the local community. All we need is water, sugar, some lime and lemon juice, a stove, some bottles and caps and two labourers paid at minimum wage. Suppose we do one run of 100 bottles at the following costs as shown Table 10.1 below:

While simplified, we can clearly see from this example that there is only US$100 of purchasing power created during the production process of 100 bottles, yet there is a total of US$1,000 worth of margarita mix on the market, for a gap of US$900. But since the labourers cannot purchase all the bottles of the margarita mix, the owner of Uncle Pepe's has to rely on the wider market for sales and the purchasing power created by other capitalists when they pay wages and salaries. But since all capitalist accounting works this way, if we extrapolate across the economy, there is always a shortage of purchasing power for goods and services outstanding. This is shown empirically in Figure 10.4.

Figure 10.4 plots yearly GDP, or the total monetary value of all goods and services produced in the U.S. economy alongside total wage and salary disbursements. The gap between purchasing power and goods outstanding on the market is clear and should not surprise given capitalist cost-plus accounting (Di Muzio and Robbins 2020). Even without the gold standard, *the dearth of money problem is structural* in capitalist economies.[9] If there were no gap, there would be little need for credit, and there would be no talk of an aggregate demand problem and the need for fiscal stimulus. Currently, the only thing that can come remotely close to filling the gap between available purchasing power and the economic goods outstanding on the market is the interest-bearing credit issued by commercial banks as debt to individuals, corporations and governments. This "solution" largely enriches the owners of commercial banks while everyone else sinks deeper into debt. Debt can then be leveraged as a power technology by creditors, especially over governments that want to appear fiscally responsible to their electorates and the international credit rating agencies (Di Muzio and Robbins 1916; Sinclair

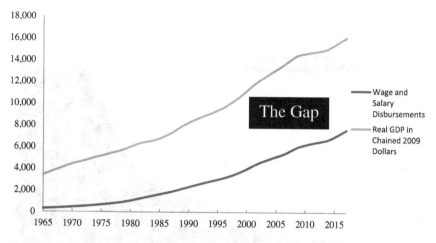

FIGURE 10.4 GDP & wage and salary disbursements in the USA, 1965–2017 (billion US$)

Source: https://fred.stlouisfed.org/series/GDP and https://fred.stlouisfed.org/series/A576RC1.

2005). This structural gap between incomes and outstanding prices for goods and services on the market is why C.H. Douglas argued for all citizens to be issued a social credit by the government. Rather than go into debt to commercial banks to expand purchasing power, Douglas argued that a monetary reward based on a given level of economic productivity be granted to all citizens. This yearly credit does not have to be issued by borrowing from the capital market and going into debt but simply instructing the central bank to credit the treasury. Treasury can then electronically credit the bank accounts of individuals.[10] We can debate the accounting identities for such a transaction and its amount, but that it can be practically done is hardly in doubt. However, there are at least three main obstacles that stand in the way of such a political action (1) the general public and most economists are unaware of the structural gap identified in Figure 10.4; (2) even if knowledge were widespread and the political will was there, the idea of "getting something for nothing" from the government may ignite moral outrage in some quarters—remember the poor are not to be relieved—lest they fall into universal idleness; (3) the owners of commercial banks would be vociferously against such an initiative given that this would radically reduce the need for borrowing at interest. It should be noted here that those against governments issuing a yearly or quarterly social credit to their citizens are implicitly in favour of the current lending regimes of the commercial banks. And this brings me to my final critique of MMT: there is little critical discussion in the literature on how the vast majority of new money enters the economy. It is not by government deficits or borrowing to finance them, albeit important, but by commercial banks issuing loans to willing borrowers.

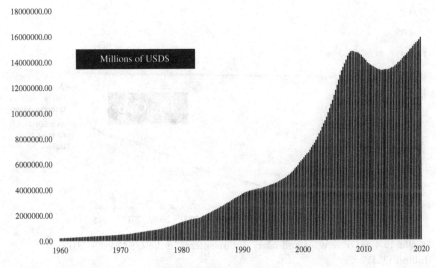

FIGURE 10.5 Mortgage debt outstanding, USA, 1960–2020

Source: www.federalreserve.gov/paymentsystems/coin_data.htm.

To be sure, governments and their agencies create new money as notes and coins and benefit from the difference between the nominal value of the notes and coins and their low cost of production. But notes and coins make up a tiny proportion of the total money supply. For instance, in the United States, notes and coins only make up 8 per cent of the total money supply; the rest of the money supply is digital and created by commercial banks when they issue loans to customers—mostly for home mortgages—see Figure 10.5. This means that *most new money enters the U.S. economy as mortgage debt*, with a total of just under USD$16 tn recorded by the third quarter of 2019.

The following closest categories for commercial bank lending are credit card and other revolving debt, consumer loans, and commercial and industrial loans with a grand total of USD$4.8 tn at the start of 2020—see Figure 10.6.

So while federal deficits can certainly impact the U.S. economy and benefit certain sectors of the economy, commercial bank lending is the primary way new money enters the economy. This means that most new money is allocated by banks, not central governments. And this should be the focus of any so-called "modern monetary theory" because of its perverse implications such as the generation of inequality.[11]

Conclusion

This chapter has argued that the pandemic has opened up intellectual space for rethinking and re-politicising current fiscal and monetary arrangements. To do so, I returned to the transformation of capitalist social relations and to the debates on

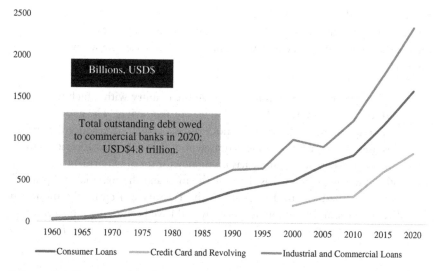

FIGURE 10.6 Commercial Bank Lending, USA, 1960–2020

Source: https://fred.stlouisfed.org/series/CONSUMER, https://fred.stlouisfed.org/ser ies/CCLACBW027SBOG and https://fred.stlouisfed.org/series/BUSLOANS.

the dearth of money and the rise of pauperism. Firstly, to show how the current fiscal-monetary order originated and secondly to demonstrate how economic liberals have always been sceptical about public handouts to the oppressed. The legacy of both events looms like a spectre over current fiscal and welfare policy debates—even though many scholars are unaware of their historical origins. A further point was that the fiscal-monetary regime that advanced capitalist economies are embedded in was a historical creation and gave commercial banks tremendous power over the creation of new money while setting debt traps for governments. I then moved to highlight the virtues of MMT and empirically dismissed some of the major arguments advanced by their critics before proceeding with my critiques, of which there were two. First, MMT has not considered the root cause of a lack of aggregate demand, which we can find in capitalist cost-plus accounting. The dearth of purchasing power is endemic to capitalism because of this accounting logic. Secondly, the gap between purchasing power and outstanding market prices only gets partially solved by individuals, businesses and governments accessing credit at interest from commercial banks. If no one took on debt, capitalism would collapse tomorrow. There is no natural reason why the vast majority of money creation has to be issued by commercial banks and plenty of reasons why it should not— unexplored here due to space constraints.

As in previous crises, the pandemic has revealed that sovereign currency issuers do not have to be chained to a limited pool of capital, balanced budgets, and severe fiscal discipline. However, the question is whether we continue with the current fiscal-monetary arrangement that creates the national debt fright and austerity politics, or whether we push for an alternative way of injecting purchasing power into the economy and change fiscal accounting identities to reflect public investment rather than debt. In the end, we would do well to recall the words of Douglas himself:

> A phrase such as "There is no money in the country with which to do such and so" means simply nothing, unless we are also saying "The goods and services required to do this thing do not exist and cannot be produced, therefore it is useless to create the money equivalent of them." For instance, it is simply childish to say that a country has no money for social betterment, or for any other purpose, when it has the skill, the men and the material and plant to create that betterment. The banks or the Treasury can create the money in five minutes, and are doing it every day, and have been doing it for centuries.
>
> *1923: 9–10*

Notes

1 I wish to thank Matt Dow and Frances Cowell for comments on this chapter.
2 For a breakdown of fiscal spending and initiatives not discussed in this chapter see: www.imf.org/en/Topics/imf-and-covid19/Fiscal-Policies-Database-in-Response-to-COVID-19 (October 9, 2021).
3 www.nationaljusticemuseum.org.uk/museum/news/what-was-the-bloody-code (accessed August 9, 2021).
4 This is likely the earliest formulation of the "crowding out" model cherished by neoclassical economists—though they are unlikely to know from which situation it was derived given the ahistorical nature of their craft.
5 The primary reason for this excess was extravagant U.S. military spending abroad to combat the social forces of communism combined with Johnson's Great Society programs (Gowan 1999: 17).
6 This is also called built-in inflation since collective bargaining agreements can trigger wages to increase relative to inflation so as to maintain living standards.
7 It is beyond the scope of this chapter to discuss the history of U.S. consumer price inflation.
8 For an interesting theory on the source of inflation see, https://strangematters.coop/supply-chain-theory-of-inflation/ (23/05/2022)
9 This helps to explain recurrent Marxist debates on overproduction and underconsumption. The problem is that Marxists have never got to the root of the problem in capitalist accounting and problematically regard the labour theory of value as the primary determinant of prices and profit.
10 Some may note that this is similar to a universal basic income (UBI), but the literature on a UBI is not aware of the structural gap between purchasing power and outstanding market prices for goods and services. The major impetus for a UBI seems to be increasing automation and the threat of mass unemployment—a worthwhile debate but one we cannot address here.
11 www.monetaryalliance.org/the-major-problems-with-bank-money-creation/ (accessed January 10, 2021).

11

CARBON CAPITALISM, THE SOCIAL FORCES OF ANNIHILATION, AND THE FUTURE OF ENERGY

Matt Dow

> Tragic irony indeed if the Anthropocene is cut short by humanity's self-annihilation.
>
> —*William E. Rees (2020: 9)*

Introduction

The latest report from United Nation's Intergovernmental Panel on Climate Change (IPCC 2021) has provided humanity with unequivocal evidence that global climate breakdown and the growing number of extreme weather disasters result from human activities that produce greenhouse-gas emissions, primarily carbon dioxide (CO_2).[1] The primary pathway toward achieving low-carbon patterns of social reproduction has been to reduce, and eventually eliminate, a good portion of humanity's dependency on the carbon energy production and consumption, which accounts for 36.44 bn tonnes (or 99.86 per cent) of all CO_2 emissions (data from Friedlingstein et al. 2020; see also: Blondeel et al. 2021; Kenner and Heede 2021; Newell 2021). There has been rigorous scientific research warning humanity about the connection between CO_2 emissions and global warming since the 1950s, and the coal industry has been aware of this since the 1960s (Mann 2021: 29; see also Franta 2021). In 1982, ExxonMobil's scientists stated, "[t]here is general scientific agreement that...mankind is influencing the global climate...through carbon dioxide release from the burning of fossil fuels" (as cited in Mann 2021: 29; see also Jerving et al. 2015; Supran and Oreskes 2020). With the *burning* awareness and growing acknowledgement of climate change, *this should change everything* (Klein 2019). But will it?

When the Covid-19 pandemic spread exponentially across the globe, some government leaders responded with complete or partial lockdowns in their countries. These lockdowns decelerated almost all aspects of the global economy and

DOI: 10.4324/9781003250432-15

dropped energy demand by 4 per cent in 2020 (IEA 2021a). British Petroleum (2021) reported that oil consumption dropped to 88.48 mn/barrels per day (b/d) in 2020 from 97.60 mn (b/d) in 2019. This 9.1 mn (b/d) decline in oil was mostly in OECD countries at 5.8 mn b/d. Global coal consumption fell by 4 per cent in the first quarter of 2020, but gradually, consumption grew 3.5 per cent higher than in 2019 (IEA 2021b). The reduction in carbon energy consumption led to a decline in global CO_2 emissions by 3 to 7 per cent between January and April 2020 (Le Quéré et al. 2020: 647).

On March 8, 2020, Russia and Saudi Arabia had a short oil price war. Saudi Arabia wanted OPEC+ to cut crude oil production to raise oil prices, Russia refused to comply, and Saudi Arabia responded by flooding the global market with oil (Ward 2020).[2] Therefore, with Covid-19 lockdowns, the oil price war, and the uncertainty about the overall impacts of Covid-19 on the global economy, both the price of oil and global fossil fuels investments plummeted (Hager 2021; Kuzemko et al. 2020; See Table 11.1).

As seen in Table 11.1, the dominant publicly listed oil and gas corporations saw their market capitalisation collapse by roughly half in the first nine months of the pandemic but were already recovering by the end of December 2020 (Passwaters 2020).

Prior to the Covid-19 pandemic and oil price war, there was already speculation that the world order was transitioning towards a new global energy order (Bradshaw et al. 2019; Helm 2017 Kuzemko et al. 2019; Kuzemko et al. 2020; van de Graaf and Bradshaw 2018; Vakulchuk et al. 2020). This new energy order is hypothesised as one where fossil fuels will be abundant, but their demand will have peaked during the adoption of more renewable energy. This hypothesis rests on two assumptions; the first is the recoverability of nonconventional fossil fuels. The second is that global governance takes seriously the growing threats of climate change, and the remaining amounts of fossil fuels will be stranded assets (or wealth). From these perspectives and others, the "coronavirus crisis" may be the decisive event that will peak, and eventually end, most of humanity's dependence on the fossil fuel industries (Carrington et al. 2020; Chapman 2020).

Contrary to the perspectives and assumptions above, this chapter will demonstrate that the current carbon capitalist world order has structured and even intensified the global political economy's reliance on the mass production and consumption of fossil fuels, and the widespread use of fossil fuels is likely to continue. To demonstrate this, I will critique the assumption that the global political economy is transitioning towards a new global energy order. Then, I will provide two additional fundamental social-structural impediments that may prevent this transition towards renewable energy and low-carbon forms of development. The first structure is that neoliberal carbon capitalism reinforces the dependence on fossil fuels for government debt servicing, repayment, and economic growth (measured in gross domestic product). The second structure is how the social reproduction of life and physical infrastructure, especially in the Global North, is reliant on fossil fuels, and there is a growing number of social forces that want to preserve this way

TABLE 11.1 Covid-19 impact on oil and gas corporations by market capitalisation and oil price

Company	Market CAP Dec 30, S2019	Market CAP Mar 30, 2020	Market CAP Jun 30, 2020	Market CAP Sept 30, 2020	Market CAP Dec 30, 2020
Saudi Aramco	1.88T	1.61T	1.92T	2.1T	2.05T
Exxon Mobil	295.45B	160.55B	189.09B	145.16B	174.29B
Chevron	226.82B	135.28B	166.62B	134.45B	162.57B
Royal Dutch Shell	241.03B	144.22B	122.39B	96.28B	136.15B
PetroChina	145.51B	112.94B	102.67B	103.67B	109.36B
Total Energies SE[8]	143.4B	100.44B	101.39B	90.12B	115.19B
Gazpom	97.79B	50.04B	65.33B	51.55B	67.79B
British Petroleum	125.97B	86B	78.70B	58.94B	70.65B
Conoco Phillips	70.55B	33.03B	45.07B	32.84B	42.71B
Equinor	65.77B	41.03B	47.82B	45.56B	54.55B
Oil Prices (Monthly Average) with Percentage of Change	65.03	21.71	41.67	39.00	48.73

Note: CAP = Market Capitalisation, T = Trillions, B = Billions.

Source: https://companiesmarketcap.com/oil-gas/largest-oil-and-gas-companies-by-market-cap/, https://ca.finance.yahoo.com/, https://markets.businessinsider.com/commodities/oil-price on September 30th, 2021.

of existence by any means necessary. Finally, this chapter concludes by suggesting that these social structures must be overcome and that nations need to agree on a Global Carbon Non-Proliferation Agreement. A new global energy order remains doubtful if this alignment cannot happen.

A New Global Energy Order?

This section challenges the hypotheses that fossil fuels are/will be abundant, their demand has peaked and the renewable energy revolution is imminent. This chapter argues that this hypothesis overlooks how the global political economy is completely dependent on fossil fuels and that global financial accumulation is betting on a fossil-fuelled future, not renewable energy.

The assumption that the world order is becoming fossil fuels abundant stems from technology developed in the so-called "shale revolution" in the United States. This development was viewed as a fundamental game changer not only for geopolitics but also for the future of the oil and gas industry (van de Graaf and Bradshaw 2018;Vitalis 2020). The "fracking revolution" in the United States, Canada, and elsewhere has the potential (depending on technology and price) to add 1.9 tn barrels of unconventional oil and gas; this would provide the global political economy with roughly 100+ years of oil-based social reproduction (Bentley 2016: 53, 72ff; IEA 2013: 17–20). From the international relations theoretical approach known as Realism, this is a cause for celebration as the United States will no longer be dependent on foreign oil production and has the potential to become energy independent (Bradshaw et al. 2019). From a liberal geopolitical perspective, the non-conventional fossil fuel revolution now represents the absolute end of high oil prices due to its ever-growing abundance. Oil is no longer on a so-called "commodity supercycle" trend, which means oil has historically traded at a much higher price than it should have been (Helm 2017;Van de Graaf and Bradshaw 2018). This should make investors and publicly listed oil and gas companies extremely nervous as their market value is connected to the price of oil, as are their rates of return (Di Muzio 2012). These perspectives suggest that because oil no longer has geopolitical or market significance this should encourage the world economy to eventually stop the production and consumption of fossil fuels (Blondeel et al. 2021; Kuzemko et al. 2020).

The assumption that fossil fuels will become abundant and their demand has peaked is attached to the confidence that national governments, global governance, and corporations will attempt to meet the United Nations Framework Convention on Climate Change 1.5 °C or 2 °C pathways. As a result, only 20 per cent of current oil reserves can be burned, and the other 80 per cent should be stranded (Carbon Tracker 2017). But there is no current evidence of this happening anytime soon. Studying energy sources is crucial in determining what undergirds financial accumulation, global development, and social reproduction. In 1971, fossil fuels supplied 86.6 per cent of the world's total energy needs, and in 2019, they supplied 80.9 per cent, a decline of only 5.7 per cent (IEA 2021c). When it comes to total final consumption, fossil fuels remain crucial at 70.3 per cent for the OECD and 67 per cent in global terms (IEA 2021d). This suggests that the most advanced economies of the world are nowhere near realising a low-carbon energy future and the middle economies are heading towards the same fossil fuel dominant energy system. While the OECD's demand for energy has relatively peaked, apart from transportation, there will be increases in energy demand from non-OECD countries as they seek more energy-intensive lifestyles and their corporations pursue accumulation both at home and abroad (Di Muzio 2015a; EIA 2021a; Trainer 2007, 2019; IEA 2021d). The International Energy Agency and dominant oil and gas companies' reports have oil and gas potentially not peaking until 2025–2050, but all this is *contingent on the idea that global governance* and *governments will intervene* to wean the global economy and social reproduction off fossil fuels (British Petroleum (2021); EIA 2021a; Exxon Mobil 2019; IEA 2021a).

The United States' shale revolution has only slightly boosted its oil reserves to 47.1 bn proven barrels of oil, ranking it 10th in the world and 5th in proven gas reserves at 494.9 (trillion cubic feet) (EIA 2021b). British Petroleum (2021) reports that there are only "1732 bn barrels" of proven barrels of oil left (at the end of 2020), and at the current rate of world consumption, there are only 47 to 50 years left with OPEC countries owning anywhere from 79.2 to 70.2 per cent of the world's remaining oil reserves (British Petroleum 2021; OPEC 2021). There is ample evidence that we have hit peak conventional oil, which also means the high rates of energy return on energy investment from fossil fuels are coming to an end (Hallock et al. 2014). Historically, conventional oil fields were able to have an energy return on energy invested of 40:1 or higher in some places, which was fundamental for the extraordinary levels of economic growth, especially seen in high-income countries (Hall and Klitgaard 2012; Raworth 2017). Nonconventional oil and gas sources like shale oil, bitumen, tar sands etc., have far lower ratios from 11:1 to 3:1, depending on the source (Hall et al. 2014). This indicates that more fossil fuels will need to be consumed or burned to maintain and reproduce the global political economy and sustain everyday life because the global industrial system needs at least a 10:1 ratio. Finally, the United States may or may not break its energy dependence on foreign oil, but a new problem emerges; the United States is running out of water as each fractured well uses roughly 1.5 mn to 16 mn gallons of water (Heggie 2020: USGS 2021).

Commonplace perspectives see the rise in global investment in renewable energy and the increasing momentum behind the fossil fuel divestment campaigns as reasonable grounds to argue that a renewable energy revolution is underway. The *Go Fossil Free Movement* states there has been approximately US$14.68 tn in fossil fuel divestment, from 2015 to April 2020, an incredible achievement, and hopefully, it continues to grow.[3] However, there are several problems to consider. The database from divesting financial and non-financial organisations appears convincing, yet it is ambiguous how quickly these "commitments" will be enforced (Langey et al. 2021). For example, the qualifications for "low-carbon assets for investment and high-carbon assets for divestment is contingent, contested and compromised" (Langley et al. 2021: 507). Furthermore, the Fossil Free campaign will only be effective if it can fundamentally change the mentality of institutional investors and other financial organisations who have built their financial wealth empires on fossil fuels, labour exploitation, and the tyrannical logic of rate of return that is dependent on further monetising the destruction of the biosphere (Daggert 2019; Di Muzio 2015a; Hamilton 2004; Malm 2016; see also Robbins this volume).

If the carbon energy industry can no longer generate earnings higher than its rivals, nor no longer be the prime mover of global society, then its market capitalisation should be in freefall (Di Muzio 2012). Sandy Hager's (2021) research shows that capitalists (or investors) are still capitalising on an unsustainable future based on non-renewable fossil fuels (see also Banking on Climate Chaos 2021). The capitalisation of the oil and gas industry, listed on the stock exchanges of the world, is about US$5.3 tn consisting of 209 companies.[4] This is a conservative market value estimation as most of the world's oil and gas reserves are government-owned and are either not included or entirely publicly listed. The market value of the global renewable energy industry is only US$186.65 bn, with a total of 28 companies.[5] There are two primary reasons for this tremendous difference and why global investors are gambling on doom (fossil-fuelled future over renewable energy). The first is that in a capitalist system, profitability matters, and the global fossil fuel industries are far more profitable than renewable energy, even with lower oil prices (Hager 2021; Christophers 2021). If the price of oil escalates rapidly, investors in the petroleum industry stand to gain windfall returns as the capitalisation of the industry adjusts their expectations for increasing future profits. The second is that investors attempt to predict or shape the future with their financial power (Nitzan and Bichler 2009). As a result, investors still do not believe that renewable energy can replace fossil fuels as the prime mover for the global society for a variety of technical, political, and social reasons (Di Muzio 2015a; Friedrichs 2013; Sers and Victor 2018; Trainer 2007). With that said, the IEA (2021d) believes that renewable energy is expected "to account for 70% of 2021's total of US$530 bn spent on all new generation capacity" and will account for 90 per cent of new global capacity expansion. The problem with this good news is highlighted by York and Bell (2019), who suggest that energy transitions are misleading because these are simply energy additions to the energy grid. For example, oil replaced coal as the prime mover energy, but coal is still incredibly important in the global energy system (Gellert and Ciccantell 2020). Simply put, renewable energy is adding more energy to the global energy grid in combination with fossil fuels.

In sum, it seems relatively too early to argue that the world order has or is about to enter a new global energy order. To investigate the global energy order, we need to shift our analysis away from state-centric realist geopolitical explanations where states are forever locked-into competition for energy for the so-called "national interest" (Klare 2009). Nor should we trust the liberal assumption that global markets will guide humanity to the most optimistic outcome (Helm 2017). As a result, this chapter now focuses on the global energy order through actual existing structures of the global political economy.

Neoliberal Carbon Capitalism and its Discontents

This section explores the concept of neoliberal carbon capitalism, highlighting how the global political economy has become locked into a debt-growth-inequality restructuring nexus. This nexus, I argue, is tethered to the mass production and consumption of carbon energy. If this underlying logic of neoliberal carbon capitalism remains the dominant mode of development and accumulation, then both governments and corporations may continue to be locked into a carbon-intensive energy-dependent future.

The concept of carbon capitalism highlights the fact that accumulation is bounded by the monetisation of energy across all sectors of the global economy. With the acceleration and relative universalisation of capitalist development, current modes of industrialism and social reproduction would have been impossible without abundant, affordable, and accessible fossil fuels (Di Muzio 2015a). The neoliberal stage of carbon capitalism was conceived during the 1970s global energy crises, intentionally or not, triggering "the unravelling of Keynesian economics" (Mitchell 2013: 199; Smith-Nonini 2016). Mitchell states, "[a]s oil companies prospered in the boom, a handful of families in the United States turned their fortunes from oil into windfall funds for the neoliberal movement" (2013: 197–198). For example, from the 1970s to 2010, US$340 mn was given to neoliberal supporters such as the Heritage Foundation, the American Enterprise Institute, the Hoover Institution, the Manhattan Institute and the Center for Strategic and International Studies (Mitchel 2013: 198). Charles and David Koch, owners of a private oil company in the US, "played a similar role, and Charles Koch co-founded the Cato Institute in 1977" (Mitchell 2013: 198). Since the 1970s, these same think tanks and business elites still attack and disseminate climate change denialism (Franta 2021; Mann 2021; Michaels 2020; Supran and Oreskes 2020). After two decades of on and off again turbulence in the global economy due to high oil prices, the solution was neoliberalism, defined as greater deregulation, market-friendly policies and the quest to lower government deficit with the so-called aim of creating more employment opportunities and economic growth (Brown 2015; Cahill et al. 2018; Eagleton-Pierce 2019; Springer et al. 2016). These policies helped solidify a petro-market civilisation where most of the world's services, commodity production, everyday life and culture are mediated by the capitalist price system and reliant on fossil fuels (Gill 1995; Di Muzio 2011).

Neoliberalism, as a debt-growth-inequality restructuring nexus, highlights how global capitalist development is compelled by the disciplinary power of debt to chase economic growth (Altvater 2002; Di Muzio and Robbins 2016; Gill 1995; Hamilton 2004; Raworth 2017). Debt, as a technology of power, not only propels the need for economic growth but it also transfers considerable income to the banking sector since upwards of 90 per cent of all new money in advanced capitalist economies is created as a digital transaction by commercial banks, which generates an interest stream for the banks (Di Muzio and Robbins 2016. Simply put, the way the current global economy produces new money as debt requires economic

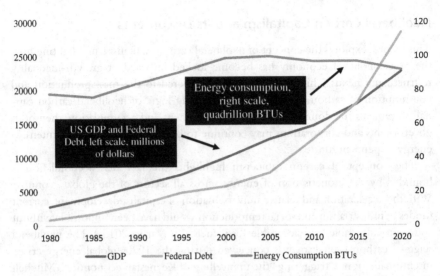

FIGURE 11.1 US federal debt, GDP and energy consumption

Source: https://fred.stlouisfed.org/series/GDP, https://fred.stlouisfed.org/series/GFDE
BTN, www.eia.gov/energyexplained/us-energy-facts/.

growth so that interest on money can be serviced. As the commercial banks do
not create interest when they create new money, there is always more debt in the
economic system than there is the ability to repay (Di Muzio and Noble 2017: 95).
The power of debt and the need for economic growth are two fundamental
social structures that explain why the world order has become path-dependent or
locked-in by what Gill (1995, 2008) calls disciplinary neoliberalism and the new
constitutionalism. The latter are reforms, policies and laws that entrench capitalist
social reproduction and make it more difficult to alter capitalist patterns of energy-
intensive development without real consequences (e.g. capital strikes, suspension of
credit; embargoes, lawsuits, etc.) (see also Roos 2019).

In neoliberal carbon capitalism, the conditions of existence have accelerated the
reciprocal relationship that as debt increases, so must economic growth, which is
contingent on the production and consumption of fossil fuel energy. (Di Muzio
2015a) (see Figure 11.1).

Using the United States as a case study in Figure 11.1, we find both federal
debt and growth steadily rising with energy consumption until 2015, when energy
consumption plateaus. This plateau should not be a cause for celebrating since
the carbon energy needed to sustain the United States' economy is nowhere near
aligned with the 1.5 °C pathway put forward by the IPCC (Kenner and Heede
2021). In the global context, the world's gross domestic product has also been
interconnected to world energy use (see Figure 11.2).

As seen in Figure 11.2, there is a close relationship between energy consumption and economic growth during the transition to neoliberal globalisation. But to

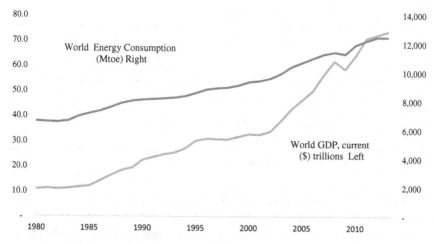

FIGURE 11.2 World GDP in current USA and energy consumption Mtoe, 1980–2017

Source: World Bank 2019 and British Petroleum 2021.

go further back in time, it is interesting to note that the world's GDP increased by 2377 per cent from 1900 to 2020 (World Bank and World of Infinite Data). Global public debt has also increased by 213,223 per cent from 1913 to 2021(Q2) (or roughly 1,776.9 per cent increase each year) (Eichengreen et al. 2019; Ranasinghe 2021). The same exponential growth can be seen in oil consumption. In 1899, 6.4 mn barrels of oil were consumed, in 1980 23 bn, and in 2020, 32.3 bn barrels were consumed for an increase of 504,587 per cent (or 4,170.1 increase each year) (Nye 1998 and British Petroleum 2021). What these trends further illustrate is that during the carbon capitalism era, the global economy has been locked into a single debt-based economy that is dependent on carbon energy and economic growth (Rowbotham 1998: 159).

In conclusion, if carbon capitalist development continues as a debt–growth–inequality nexus, we can make some reasonable prognostications. First, if we assume global public debts increase at a growth rate of 5 per cent, then government debt will stand at US$352.75 tn by 2050. Furthermore, if we assume a 3 per cent growth rate in global GDP, by 2050, GDP will be US$199 tn. In 2050, the global energy needed to supply these possible future scenarios will be 900 quadrillions British Thermal Units (BTU) (up from 620 in 2020) (EIA 2021a). The primary energy provider will still be fossil fuels at 66.7 per cent of the world's total primary energy needs. This is in addition to renewable energy providing 250 quadrillions (BTU) (up from 100 BTU in 2020), at a 3.1 per cent growth rate per year, and nuclear energy remaining stagnant at 48 quadrillions BTU (EIA 2021a). If global governance, institutions, and political leaders continue to allow both global debt and growth to be the driving forces of the world economy, which *will* continue to grow exponentially, it will not be possible without fossil fuels (Raworth 2017). These

TABLE 11.2 Projected carbon budget by IPCC 2018

Temperature	Risks of exceeding (per cent)	Budget of (Gt CO2)	Years remaining at the current emissions rate	Year of Depletion
1.5 °C	33 per cent	340	9	2029
1.5 °C	50 per cent	500	14	2034
2.0 °C	33 per cent	1,090	30	2050
2.0 °C	50 per cent	1,420	39	2059

Source: IPCC 2018 and Carbon Inequality Report 2020.

projections are difficult to grasp, and if they materialised, it would also mean biospheric ruin.

The current rate of CO_2 emissions is already surpassing the carbon budget to meet the 1.5 °C pathway (Kenner and Heede 2021; IPCC 2021; see Table 11.2).

If global governance and political leaders do not stop these trends from intensifying, which seems improbable, then world order will be heading towards a 2 °C or even 3 °C pathway, which will create further climate breakdowns (Plumer and Popovich 2018; Macfarlane 2021).

Carbon Inequality, Petro-Market Civilisation, and the Social Forces of Annihilation

This section investigates carbon inequality and how the social reproduction of life and physical infrastructure relies on the consumption and production of petroleum, especially in the Global North. I also investigate the social forces that seek to protect this civilisational order by any means necessary.

Since 1965, Kenner and Heede (2021) demonstrated that almost the entirety of global CO_2 emissions have been emitted by the Carbon Majors, "64 investor-owned and 35 state-owned companies, of which 73 produce oil and gas, 42 are coal producers, including coal assets owned by oil and gas companies, and four are cement producers" (Kenner and Heede 2021: 2). These Carbon Majors have profited exceptionally from being granted the greatest market subsidy ever, "the privilege to dump its waste products into the atmosphere at no charge" (Mann 2021: 97; McKibben 2012). However, this narrative simplifies the ongoing struggles of transitioning to a new global energy order, emphasising that just Carbon Majors are the primary producer, and, therefore, the *only* obstacle (Gross 2020; Gunderson and Fyock 2021; Paterson 2020). This assumption, intentionally or not, does not address who has largely benefitted besides the Carbon Majors or how the human agency has shaped and reshaped the global political economy and social reproduction to be contingent on fossil fuels. The Carbon Majors have, at times, thwarted other competitive forms of energy, public infrastructure, and information that challenged their profitability and supremacy as *the* global energy suppliers (Di Muzio 2015a; Dow 2019; Supran and Oreskes 2020). But this civilisational order is impossible without the help of governments, other industries (e.g., armament, private transportation, agriculture, shipping, finance, etc.), the global power elite, and a significant amount of humanity who enjoy their carbon energy-intensive livelihoods and lifestyles (Albritton 2009; Di Muzio 2015a; Khalili 2020; McMichael 2009; Bichler and Nitzan 2018).

Global energy consumption, carbon emissions, financial power and inequality are intertwined (Di Muzio 2015b; Kenner 2020). Dario Kenner's (2020) research has demonstrated that the role of the rich in contributing to climate change is disproportionally immense, while those who are resource-poor are impacted disproportionately and have the least capability to deal with the consequences and financial costs of a changing climate (see also Carbon Inequality Report 2020; Otto et al. 2020). Otto (et al. 2019: 83) suggest that "the average lifestyle consumption carbon footprint of someone in the richest 1% could be 175 times that of someone in the poorest 10%" (see also Hardoon et al. 2016 and Popcevski this volume). This should be of no surprise as the luxury lifestyles of the rich and famous and their purchasing power and habits range from private jets, submarines, yachts, islands, and now, space travel which would be best conceived as outrageous carbon emissions (Carson 2021; Di Muzio 2015b; Malm 2021; Kenner 2020).

A fantastic study by Otto (et al. 2020) has attempted to trace the socio-metabolic consumption by global income classes to carbon emissions and their human agency (see Table 11.3). Table 11.3 not only reflects that there is tremendous wealth inequality, but it also illustrates who produces carbon emissions. Obviously, the human agency cannot be just reduced to a person's financial power, as are there other socio-political factors such as discrimination, citizenship, etc. Yet, more energy will be needed to address both the growing global middle class needs and the

TABLE 11.3 Socio-metabolic consumption, carbon emissions, human agency by global income classes

Class Composition	Per cent of Global Population	Per cent of Lifestyle CO2 Emissions	Household Income (in US dollars)	The Level of Human Agency
Underclass	20 per cent	2.5 per cent	<1,000	Extremely Low
Poor Class	30 per cent	7.5 per cent	<10,000	Low
Lower Middle Class	30 per cent	22 per cent	10,000>	Moderate level of collective agency
Middle Class	10 per cent	19 per cent	100,000	Moderate to high
Upper Class	9.5 per cent	35.4 per cent	Net Assets above 1 mn	Very high
Super-Rich	0.54 per cent	13.6 per cent	Net assets above 50 mn	Extremely high

Source: Otto et al. (2020: 20); Credit Suisse (2020).

approximately 1.2 bn people (1 in 6 people) worldwide, who have little or no access to electricity (Kochhar 2021; World Bank 2017). The Covid-19 pandemic has added an additional 100 mn people back into extreme poverty (people living on less than US$1.90 per day), and new research estimates "that climate change will drive 68 million to 132 million into poverty by 2030" (Mahler et al. 2021). In sum, there is a fundamental contradiction between how global development and social reproduction requires evermore energy and how to prevent or limit further climate breakdowns.

If we were to take a global snapshot of how the social reproduction of life is tethered to fossil fuel production and consumption, there is not one sector of the global political economy untouched by carbon energy. But possibly the hardest to liberate from carbon energy is private transportation, shipping, and urbanism because of how neoliberal carbon capitalism has structured the world economy to prioritise urban-centric development, post-Fordist methods of production, and the economies of the Global South, which since European colonialism, have been structured to satisfy the Global North's consumption patterns (Anievas and Nişancioğlu 2015; Gunder-Frank 1967; Harvey 2005; Khalili 2020; Mies 2001; Rodney 1972).

The global shipping and transportation of people, commodities and services have become essential to the global economy and social reproduction. All the Covid-19 pandemic accomplished was a temporary pause on the flow of people, commodities, and services (Murray et al. 2021). In 2018, 53,000 merchant ships sailed transporting roughly 11 bn tonnes of cargo, or 80 per cent of global trade by value, of merchandise internationally (OCED 2019; UNCTAD 2019). In 2019, there were an average of 150,000 flights per day worldwide.[6] This global transportation industry is entirely dependent on oil, accounting for over 90 per cent of its energy needs (British Petroleum 2021). Yet, these industries are expected to expand as global shipping is expected to triple by 2050 and air travel is forecasted to increase by 300 to 700 per cent (OCED 2019; Baker and Grant 2019). While global power contributes the most CO_2 in terms of sectors, global shipping/transportation is secondary (see Table 11.4).

As seen in Table 11.4, in terms of carbon emissions, global power and transportation are some of the primary contributors to the world's CO_2 problem because of their dependence on carbon energy.

Brenner (et al. 2014) notes that the world development trajectory is one of planetary urbanisation as more and more of the world's population (now 54 per cent) and wealth become further concentrated into mega-cities (UN-Habitat 2016). As a result, global cities are collectively responsible for 70 per cent of global CO_2 emissions (UN-Habitat 2016: 1). Since the 1970s, urban and suburban planning has been predominately dependent on the oil and gas and automobile industries for travel which is not dissipating anytime soon despite the temporary lull created during the pandemic (Appel et al. 2015; Brenner et al. 2014; Paterson 2007; Simpson 2020). Since 1971, the transport sector has been the fastest growing sector

TABLE 11.4 CO_2 emissions by sectors and transportation

Industries (Ranked by Emissions)	CO_2 Emissions (in metric tonnes)
Global Electricity and Heat (Power)	14.0 (Gt)
Global Transportation	8.2 (Gt)
Global Industry	6.3 (Gt)
Global Buildings	2.8 (Gt)
Sports Utility Vehicles	544 (M)
Heavy Industry	365 (M
Trucks	311 (M)
Aviation	233 (M)
Sea Shipping	80 (M)
Global CO2 Emissions in Metric Tonnes	36.44 billion metric tonnes

Source: IEA (2019); IEA (2021a).

of CO_2 emissions worldwide, principally from private urban road-based transportation (Mattioli et al. 2020: 2). Road transportation is directly connected to 49 per cent of world oil final consumption (Mattioli et al. 2020: 2). Mattioli (et al. 2020: 2) argue that the Global North and gradually the Global South are becoming a car-dependent transport system defined as "*one in which high levels of car use have become a key satisfier of human needs, largely displacing less carbon-intensive alternatives*." This transport system is one of the fundamental components of the global carbon lock-in, which refers to the "the interlocking technological, institutional and social forces that can create policy inertia towards the mitigation of global climate change" (Unruh 2000: 818). Currently, 44 automakers have a combined market capitalisation of US$2.4 tn, which makes it one of the largest capitalised sectors in the world.[7] This does not include spinoff industries and services such as insurance, parts, and maintenance. In 2017, 88.1 mn automobiles were sold, which is expected to rise from the growing demand of the global middle classes (Parkin et al. 2017). Therefore, what planetary urbanism, shipping, and car dependency suggest is that the transition to a 100 per cent clean and renewable energy future will remain an incredible challenge, particularly because oil and gas remain the prime mover of goods, services, and people (Jacobson et al. 2017). We now turn to the growing climate denialist movement that wants to maintain this current petro-market civilisation despite climate science.

Anthropologist, Karl Polanyi (1957: 3), once stated "*the idea of a self-adjusting market implied a stark utopia. Such an institution could not exist for any length of time without annihilating the human and natural substance of society*" (emphasis added). Polanyi's warning about how unregulated markets would lead to the annihilation of nature and society is very emblematic of the social forces behind climate denialism. The climate denialist movement argues that the global free market should dictate human life, not climate science or the state. Very similar to neoclassical economics and neoliberalism, this quasi–libertarian movement is founded on multiple deceptions (1) hierarchy, social power, and corruption do not exist in the global economy; (2) all social and economic problems are the fault of government intervention and taxation; (3) wealth distribution results from personal effort; and (4) the global free market is an apolitical and non-human global institution (Fix 2021; Nitzan and Bichler 2015; Hunt & Lautzenheiser 2011). What is considerably dangerous about this post-Truth or denialist era is, as Michaels (2020: 14–15) demonstrates, the vast amount of dark money and public relations firms who target, with great specificity, an audience whereby they "manufacture doubt," or "manufacture uncertainty." For example, one-quarter of all tweets denying climate change every day are bots that were paid to be used by someone (Milman 2020). This manufacturing of knowledge and even juridical law has had a long history in liberal capitalist society to protect corporations and their elites (Benson and Kirsch 2010; Oreskes and Conway 2011; Michaels 2020; Pistor 2019). The leaders of this movement are no longer just dominant oil and gas and financial companies providing the "dark money" to promote uncertainty. Russian and Saudi Arabian governments and other petro-nations promote uncertainty (Elliot 2019; Harrison 2019; Mann 2021; Michaels 2020; Sirota and Perez 2020). This movement has now allied with other sympatric reactionary movements—far-right, anti-vaxxers, White Christian supremacy, male and gun rights groups, etc. (Acker 2020; Agius, Rosamond, & Kinnvall 2021; Daggett 2018; Hamilton 2021; Malm 2021; Nelson 2020 Stewart 2020). The commonality of these social forces and their conspiratorial ideologies is that their "civilisation must be defended", to paraphrase Michel Foucault (2003), by any means necessary, even human annihilation (Stewart 2020). As a result, there has been an increase in violence and murders toward minority groups, global land defenders, climate change protestors, scientists, and other people who are struggling for a better world (Tran et al. 2020; Walters and Chang 2021).

The power of the climate denialist movement is not only in creating manufactured mass doubt but also in their ability to prevent or stall the transition towards renewable energy and low carbon patterns of development and social reproduction through the ballot box. In liberal democracies, such as Britain, Australia, the United States and Canada, their constitutions and political institutions are constructed in such a way to prevent the majority from ever truly governing (Pilon 2018; Therborn 1977; Wood 1995). In the last federal elections held in these countries, the population was divided between wanting to mitigate climate change or simply ignoring it (see Table 11.5).

Although, Table 11.5 draws on just the far-right, libertarians, and conservative political parties and members, these groups are not the sole deniers of climate change (Hess and Renner 2019). There is just as much evidence that while centrist parties acknowledge climate change, their policies, instead of mitigating climate change, are doing the opposite (Noakes 2021; Tooze 2021a; Sparrow 2021). The reason for this is that the pursuit of economic growth, the global political economy, employment, and social reproduction are all dependent on fossil fuel consumption

TABLE 11.5 Climate stalling by denialism in the United Kingdom and the Anglo–settler colonies

Countries and Year of Last Election	Population and Percentage of Turnout	Climate Denialist Parties	Popular Vote	Percentage of Voting Population
Australia, 2019	91.89 per cent and 16,419,543	Liberal Liberal National (QLD) Country Liberal (NT) National Kattler's Australia	3,989,404 1,236,401 38,837 642,233 69,736	41.44 per cent
The United Kingdom, 2019	67.3 per cent and 47,568,611	Conservative Party Brexit Party	13,966,454 5,248,533	40.3 per cent
Canada, 2021	62.3 per cent And 10,246,000	Conservative Party People's Party of Canada	5,747,410 840,993	64.3 per cent
The United States, 2020	66.8 per cent and 158,000,000	Republican Party Libertarian Party	74,216,154 1,865,917	48.15 per cent

Source: Australia: https://results.aec.gov.au/24310/Website/HouseDefault-24310.htm. Canada: www.elections.ca/content.aspx?section=ele&dir=enr&document=index&lang=e. United Kingdom: https://commonslibrary.parliament.uk/general-election-2019-the-results-so-far/. United States: www.fec.gov/resources/cms-content/documents/2020presgeresults.pdf.

and production. Moreover, this chapter suggests that there is a dangerous amount of optimism by the majority of humanity that either the global market or a technological fix will solve this burning contradiction between growth, debt and energy (Christopher 2021; Greaves 2013; Langley et al. 2021; Newell 2021; Pearse 2020). No matter what political leadership or global governance attempt to say or agree upon, even during the UN Climate Change Conference (COP26), in terms of mitigating climate change and fossil fuel production and consumption, it *is largely contingent* on their elites voting populations, and political institutions. The outcome of the COP26 conference did not address or even challenge the primary drivers of climate change, which is global carbon capitalism and our petro-market civilisation (Monbiot 2021a). Instead, global leaders placed humanity's faith to solve the climate crisis in the hands of Big Businesses and Finance who are the primary social forces responsible for it (Tooze 2021a). Another aspect of the COP26 plan is to attempt to achieve "net zero" carbon emissions sometime in the mid-21st century. This seems to be another empty promise and places an unbelievable amount of confidence in "carbon dioxide removal" technology that has already been proven cannot prevent climate catastrophe alone (Donald and Dyke 2021). As a result, COP26 is just another failure that highlights how global leadership allows planetary life to be "sacrificed" for capital accumulation that disproportionately benefits the global plutocrat class.

Conclusion

The future is always unknown as it is contested through the dialectics of power and resistance. The recent pandemic illustrates this even further (Berkhout et al. 2021). As seen in the acceleration of consumption as lockdown constraints lifted, the morbid illness embedded in the global political economy must first be cured for a new global energy order to emerge. First, is the power of debt which is not only driving but disciplining global society towards repayment *with interest*. This requires ever-expanding economic growth and predominantly benefits the global plutocratic class (Di Muzio and Robbins 2016, 2017). Second is the need to address the growing power that both global investors and corporations have, as they shape and reshape the global political economy and social reproduction in their favour for profit and power (Nitzan and Bichler 2009). Third is the global political economy, governance, and political and corporate leadership's fetishism of economic growth (Fioramonti 2013; Hamilton 2004). For far too long, global development has been guided by the neoclassical economics fallacies that exponential growth on a finite planet is possible (Hickel and Kallis 2020; Raworth 2017). The fourth is the need to overcome the hurdles of carbon liberal democracies that have attempted to limit more progressive and emancipatory modes of living and governance (Mitchell 2013). The fifth is the need to end the extreme wealth inequality but also acknowledge that the global carrying capacity of the planet is already being overshot by human enterprises by 68 per cent (Rees 2020: 7). The sixth is that fossil fuels have been the fundamental source of energy that has fuelled the prime movers (technology, finance, labour) of history, which has accelerated human development, albeit extremely unevenly, for the last three centuries, this must be stopped, or further climate breakdowns are inevitable (Daggert 2019; Di Muzio 2015a; Malm 2016; Pirani 2018; Smil 1994). The absurdity of this paradox will be if humanity chooses its own annihilation instead of attempting to build a global political economy based on well-being and the logic of livelihood. Finally, it is only through human cooperation, "a power shift", and a binding Global Carbon Non-Proliferation Agreement that we can finally start to head towards a new global energy order and a just transition (Ajl 2021; Newell 2021).

Notes

1 Greenhouse gases include Carbon Dioxide (CO_2), Methane (CH_4), Nitrous Oxide (N_2O), and Fluorinated Gases (F-gases).
2 OPEC+ is just the original OPEC countries with Russia.
3 https://gofossilfree.org/divestment/commitments/ (accessed October 15, 2021).
4 https://companiesmarketcap.com/oil-gas/largest-oil-and-gas-companies-by-market-cap/ (accessed on October 14, 2021).

5 https://companiesmarketcap.com/renewable-energy/largest-companies-by-market-cap/ (accessed on October 14, 2021).
6 www.flightradar24.com/data/statistics (accessed on September 30, 2020).
7 https://companiesmarketcap.com/automakers/largest-automakers-by-market-cap/ (accessed on October 14, 2021).
8 Total SA changed its name to Total Energies SE on May 28, 2021.

12

COVID-19 AND THE FUTURE OF FOOD

Philip McMichael

Introduction

Covid-19 both expressed and precipitated a turning point in the direction of the world food system. This break-down moment revealed transnational food corporations' false claims to "feed the world" via global supply chains often sourced from land appropriated from small farming systems previously supplying local needs. Such claims emerged in the 1990s when the World Trade Organization (WTO) instituted rules liberalising trade and foreign investment. While most countries in the global South were required to reduce protections of their agricultural sectors, the United States and the EU managed to retain protections of their agribusiness by concealing substantial decoupled farm subsidies paid directly to farmers, thereby not distorting "free trade" (Hopewell 2016: 173). This has enabled the northern dumping of artificially cheapened foodstuffs in markets in the global South at the expense of unprotected small farmer cultures unable to compete in their markets. In the second half of the 1990s, a conservative FAO estimate for sixteen southern countries claimed between 20 and 30 mn people lost their land from the impact of liberalisation of agricultural trade (Madeley 2000: 75).

Such directives were reinforced in the new century by foreign investment expansion in agro-exporting. In the name of Public-Private Partnerships (PPPs), public monies subsidised land enclosures and commercial land corridors for producing foods for export. Small-scale farmers were increasingly enclosed in corporate value chains, with commercial agro-inputs encouraging agro-export monocultures geared to supplying corporate processors and global retailers. The Gates Foundation was the exemplar, with its 2006 Alliance for a Green Revolution in Africa (AGRA), supported with public funds to (unsuccessfully) raise the commercial productivity of African land but converting farmers into labourers on their land (Wise 2021).

DOI: 10.4324/9781003250432-16

The deepening of this "*corporate* food regime" through the first two decades of the new century rendered food-dependent populations increasingly vulnerable to disruption of cross-border transport systems, as revealed dramatically by Covid's global impact. Following the spiking of global hunger in 2020, the U.S. Global Leadership Coalition noted that Covid-19's disruption of supply chains drastically raised food prices worldwide:

> exacerbating the severity of food insecurity for 821 mn hungry people in low-income countries … The COVID-19 pandemic exacerbated child hunger and malnutrition as the pandemic forced more than 1.6 bn children out of school in 199 countries, depriving nearly 370 mn children in 150 countries of access to nutritious meals.
>
> *USGLC 2021*

While the pandemic exposed the vulnerabilities of world food marketing, the UN and other international agencies warned against further disruption of global supply chains, given (cultivated) food dependencies. Some governments and public discourses had already begun revaluing shortened supply chains and local provisioning. In this moment of crisis and alternative initiatives, the corporate conclave, the World Economic Forum (WEF), invited the UN to collaborate in a Food Systems Summit in the Fall of 2021.

In effect, this Faustian Bargain enabled corporate capture of the Summit, symbolised in the installation of Dr Agnes Kalibata, the President of AGRA, as convener. This move intensified a substantial Polanyian "countermovement" to protect local farming cultures (and their ecological custodianship), territorial food provisioning, and human rights to food. Such a dramatic "double movement" of market-based solutions to a world food crisis, generating a protective response from a range of frontline food producers and workers, expresses a key contradiction in the global food regime, with ramifications for the future of food.

Food Regime Machinations

International food regimes are transitional, given key tensions in their modes of capital accumulation and associated geopolitical relations (McMichael 2013a). Tensions deepen, triggering crisis and transformation in governance and food provisioning structures. The recent crisis of Covid-19 holds potential for such a transformation—even as the corporate world is attempting to manage the crisis in such a way as to consolidate food regime power. At the same time, resistance intensifies to corporate capture advocating "food sovereignty" solutions via public governance of food systems embodying democratic, ecological practices anchored in territorial markets. The recent farmer (and social) rebellion over Prime Minister Modi's attempts to legislate corporate capture of India's relatively protected territorial farm sector is symbolic of such ongoing and fundamental tension (Ghosh 2020).

This tension is overlaid by questions regarding the sustainability of large-scale chemical and industrial/bio-digital agriculture. While the corporate world's actions are driven by short-term manoeuvres to retain and consolidate power, even as the pandemic reveals its shortcomings, the resistance has its eyes on the long-term viability of the environment, public and planetary health, and the rights of food producers and workers (IPES 2021).

One might say the old is dying, but not without a struggle, as the corporate grip is tightening. Market rule remains the organising principle of a corporate food regime. What form "the new" will take depends on geopolitics, finance capital, grassroots alliances, and the politics of reversal of ecological amnesia.[1]

Market rule involves not only the institution and protection of private property rights by states but also the privileging of a capital logic over a territorial logic (Arrighi 1990). This became the governing principle when states collectively joined the WTO in 1995, adopting its overriding rules of economic liberalisation versus farm protections. WTO Director-General characterised the formation of the WTO as "writing the constitution of a single global economy" (Ruggiero 1996). With the WTO's Agreement on Agriculture, market rule *formally* organised a "corporate food regime", whereby member states privileged agribusiness' claim to "feed the world". Liberalisation enabled the subsequent expansion of agro-exporting from non-western powers such as Brazil, Russia, India, China, Ukraine, Argentina, Thailand and Vietnam competing with the United States and the European Union "global breadbaskets" (Hopewell 2016). Food supply chains proliferated, incorporating local farmland into global networks organised through corporate/state deals.

Formally, this trade arrangement appears multi-polar, but *substantively* the food regime occupies a "multiplex world", where "the nature of economic interdependence today is denser, consisting of trade, finance, and global production networks and supply chains, whereas … multipolarity is mainly trade-based" (Acharya 2017: 11). Such networks are premised on de-territorialisation of landscapes, illuminating the "paradox of sovereignty" (Rosenberg 2001). Here states, as the world market's political scaffolding (enshrined in WTO rules) are subject to competitive interstate relations and compulsions of heightened capital extra-territorial mobility, commodifying land and food on a trans-scale. It was precisely this paradox that the international peasant movement contested during the 1996 World Food Summit in Rome in the name of "food sovereignty". Led by La Vía Campesina, the movement demanded the *sovereign* right of states to organise territorial food systems and protect domestic farmers from cheap food dumping and foreign takeover of land (Desmarais 2007).

In 2000, the leading international peasant organisation, La Vía Campesina, joined 51 other civil society organisations to form the International Planning Committee for Food Sovereignty (IPC), a platform dedicated to strengthening social movement voices within multilateral forums. In 2007–2008, with world food prices spiking, the FAO faced a legitimacy crisis, leading to the reform of its Committee on World Food Security (CFS) in 2010, as food/agrarian movements and supporting NGOs were admitted via a new Civil Society Mechanism (CSM), alongside a Private Sector Mechanism.

Meanwhile, the UN Secretary-General Ban Ki-moon convened a High-Level Conference on World Food Security in June 2008. Its outcome resembled previous food summits in confirming and intensifying market rule in the food regime in terms of productive "efficiency" (Clapp and Moseley 2020). This followed the new agenda of the World Bank's *World Development Report* (2008), where agriculture would be "led by private entrepreneurs in extensive value chains linking producers to consumers", with the expectation that the private sector would drive "the organization of value chains that bring the market to smallholders and commercial farms" (World Bank 2007: 8).[2]

The IPC, in its *Terra Preta* parallel meeting in Rome during the 2008 conference, claimed:

> The serious and urgent food and climate crises are being used by political and economic elites as opportunities to entrench corporate control of world agriculture and the ecological commons. At a time when chronic hunger, dispossession of food providers and workers, commodity and land speculation, and global warming are on the rise, governments, multilateral agencies and financial institutions are offering proposals that will only deepen these crises.[3]

Predictably, the proposed solution was not to support small-scale farming systems worldwide with public subsidies and institutional support, even though they produced two-thirds of the world's food (ETC 2009). While the proximate goal of value-chains is to improve smallholder "productivity", the outcome has been to embed farmers in relations of dependency on agro-inputs and expand food exporting—at the expense of local food provisioning. AGRA exemplified this new approach, investing in an infrastructure of 10,000 agro-dealerships, encompassing farmers in value-chains with agro-inputs (seeds, fertiliser and pesticides) and contracts to deliver products to corporate processors and retailers. It was a model for the increasingly ubiquitous public-private partnerships (PPP), foreshadowing the WEF response during the COVID crisis.[4]

In this way, food regime power deepened beyond simply a license to profit from organised liberalisation of foreign trade and investment. Now states were partnering collectively, through organised alliances, to mobilise public resources and reframe land and agricultural policy in the name of productivity, market supplies, and green practices to be managed by transnational food corporations. Most importantly, *the notion of the "public good" was reframed as best served by private interest.*

Privatisation and the United Nations

Public and private interest blending constitutes a new standard, where the notional "invisible hand" displaces the rights and sovereignty of farmers and civil society at large, as discussed below. This public-private partnership (PPP) model infused food security initiatives during the pandemic in the 2021 UN Food Systems Summit (UNFSS). Here, the WEF represented itself as a global platform for public-private cooperation, having "catalysed stakeholder support for ambitious global political initiatives such as COP21 and the United Nations Sustainable Development Goals... [further] The Forum is officially recognised with a special status to act as the International Organization for Public-Private Cooperation" (WEF 2016: 8, 9).[5] In other words, the WEF has been a key player in promoting PPPs with global consequence—legitimising corporate power in international public reforms. Substantively, this is expressed in WEF claims to have "influenced global thinking by being at the forefront of concepts such as multi-stakeholder engagement, social entrepreneurship, corporate global citizenship and the Fourth Industrial Revolution" (WEF 2016: 8).

In the shadow of Covid-19, the WEF exerted leadership in Summit preparations, proposing reconfiguring "the totality of institutions, policies, norms, procedures and initiatives" through which public-private/"multi-stakeholder" interests "try to bring more predictability and stability to their responses to transnational challenges" (Schwab and Malleret 2020: 47). This claim animated the WEF's override of the CFS as the key UN Organization responsible for global food governance,[6] enabling corporate capture (Chandrasekaran et al. 2021).

Already, the top four global seed and agrochemical firms control "around 70% of the global pesticides market and around 60% of the global seed market" (Clapp 2021: 405), and corporate food chains now account for three-quarters of all global trade (Schwab and Malleret 2020: 72). Further, food corporations "command billions more in infrastructure [beyond] multibillion-dollar markets for their goods" (Philpott 2020: 181–182)—including US$540 bn *annually* in global subsidies, "on track to soar to $1.8 tn (£1.3tn) a year by 2030" (Carrington 2021).

Even so, while in 2018 the global food system was declared "broken" (Carrington 2018), the pandemic compounded the vulnerabilities of such concentrated food provisioning, substantially dependent on global supply chains, including itinerant farmworkers who account for 25 per cent of the world's farm work (Bello 2020). Deforestation, mangrove enclosure and expansion of commercial food frontiers deepen habitat destruction, increasing the likelihood that wild species "come into repeated, intimate contact with the humans spreading into their habitats" (Shah 2020: 6). A recent review claims that 50 per cent of zoonotic diseases are associated with agricultural drivers (Schwab and Malleret 2020: 56). Further, factory farming concentrates and modifies pharmaceutical-laden animals, "providing microbes lush opportunities to turn into deadly pathogens" (Shah 2020: 6).

The question whether Covid-19 originated in Wuhan wet markets in China is not as significant as recognising the role of agro-industrial expansion in China. This pressured small farmers to purvey wild food as enclosures diminished available land, forcing them to "raise or hunt animals closer to or within the forests where the most exotic pathogens might reside" (Whalen 2021: 19). In 2006, "there already were over 19,000 farmers raising wildlife commercially, and their products were processed by about 3,166 companies" (Zhang 2021: 13). Once viruses embed in human intercourse, the food trade and its transport infrastructure act as spreaders. This trade more than tripled in value between 2000 and 2016 to approximately US$1.6 tn (Bello 2020: 5). The wildlife trade is related to such boundary-crossing. Another form of boundary crossing is factory farming, where breeding and antibiotics reduce livestock diversity, exposing confined animals (and workers and consumers) to virus outbreaks (Davis 2020). And this may well affect future food provisioning unless boundaries are respected.

Thus, the multiple global exchanges of food—factory-farmed animal protein and produce transported from field sites elsewhere to a processor, then sold through global retail outlets everywhere—intensifies virus transmissions. With understandable irony, the WTO, the WHO and the FAO issued a joint statement on March 31, 2020:

> Millions of people around the world depend on international trade for their food security and livelihoods… When acting to protect the health and well-being of their citizens, *countries should ensure that any trade-related measures do not disrupt the food supply chain.*[7]

Here, 20 per cent of the calories consumed, such as rice, wheat, soya and grains people eat "cross at least one international border, up by more than 50 per cent since 1980, with one third of the world's food coming from low and middle-income countries" (Shaoul 2020).

This, of course, acknowledges the extent of food-import dependency. Further, Covid-19 spawned extensive reflections on what is recognised to be a global crisis, including public health limitations and failures, government unpreparedness and lack of capacity following decades of privatisation, as well as compromised multilateralism among states, including virulent nativism in the global North. Underscoring this moment, *The Great Reset* declared:

> The worldwide crisis triggered by the coronavirus pandemic has no parallel in modern history… The connectivity between geopolitics and pandemics flows both ways. On the one hand, the chaotic end of multilateralism, a vacuum of global governance and the rise of various forms of nationalism make it more difficult to deal with the outbreak. On the other hand, the pandemic is clearly exacerbating and accelerating [prior] geopolitical trends that were already apparent before the crisis erupted.
>
> *Schwab and Malleret 2020: 8, 44*

The focus on the *crisis of multilateralism* here is critical, since it shaped the WEF-UN partnership in planning the Summit, elevating the concept and practice of "*multi-stakeholderism*" over inter-state obligations and responsibilities in global governance. This proscription, falsely premised on the notion of a "level playing field", consolidates power. Corralling various societal representatives in a multi-stakeholder presence, Summit planning notably ignored small-scale producer constituencies, privileging corporate agribusiness, philanthropic financiers and western science and techno-political hegemony. At the same time, the CFS was sidelined, with further marginalisation of small producers and farmworkers and their representatives in the new Civil Society and Indigenous Peoples' Mechanism (CSM). Known as the most inclusive UN body, the CFS has been divested of its mandate of key responsibility and authority for governing global food security and monitoring the protection of human rights (Canfield et al. 2021).

Such a takeover of the CFS by the WEF was imminent, given the history of the UN-sponsored Public-Private Partnerships (PPP) since 2000.[8] But this was a decisive *private*-public partnership *realignment*, resembling Naomi Klein's "shock doctrine", where the corporate sector seeks to take advantage of market failure "to prevent crises from giving way to organic moments when progressive policies emerge" (Solis 2020).

A cumulative "organic moment" informs *The Great Reset*, which documents a rising tide of social and environmental activism, from food riots to austerity protests, accompanied by alliance-building and initiatives to localise food provisioning when COVID hit. Such challenges "have profoundly altered the environment in which companies operate" (Schwab and Malleret 2020: 73), providing an exceptional moment for intervention to promote corporate capture of the future of food. This required rewriting procedural rules and institutional norms in the governance of the global food system and a WEF takeover of the UN/CFS forum in the 2021 UN Food Systems Summit. The WEF used worldwide distrust of the global system on the order of one in five people to promote a multi-stakeholder approach: "The danger in this development is that scepticism over the value of geostrategic institutions, and even of multilateralism itself, risks eroding the global community's ability to properly manage the primary economic, environmental and technological risks facing the world today" (Brende 2019).

This declaration underscores the evident shortcomings of multilateralism in addressing the global crisis conjuncture but ignores decades of state complicity with "comparative advantage" doctrines undergirding transnational capitalism at the expense of state sovereignty and regulatory efficacy. In other words, overriding multilateral organisations deflects attention from state complicity in elevating market rule. Accordingly, the "shock doctrine" took a giant *global-systemic* leap, with WEF intervention:

> Seeing the failures and fault lines in the cruel light of day cast by the corona crisis may compel us to act faster by replacing failed ideas, institutions, processes and rules with new ones better suited to current and future needs. This is the essence of the Great Reset.
>
> *Schwab and Malleret 2020: 100*

At this juncture, the CSM contested the proposal for multi-stakeholder governance, with platforms to undermine "the clear responsibilities of governments and replace political participation with a model that lacks clear rules of participation, subverts traditional means of political representation and erases mechanisms of accountability" (Canfield et al. 2021: 10). Further, over five hundred civil society organisations warned that the WEF had "emerged as the key space for decision-makers and corporate leaders to roll out initiatives around global public goods—water, food and climate… seeking to shape the future of a wide range of services".[9] And members of the International Panel of Experts on Sustainable Food Systems (IPES-Food) noted: "concerns that the real goal of the Summit was to manufacture a new consensus, to put business-led solutions back in the driving seat, and to shift the locus of food systems governance away from the CFS".[10]

In a system of "multi-stakeholder governance", there are "no recognized standards governing the internal decision-making process of MSGs or ones that clarify the obligations, responsibilities, and liabilities of these new 'governors'" (Gleckman 2016: 102). The default could only be corporate empowerment, given Schwab claims "corporations are the trustees of society" (Schwab 2019). And this form of "governance" is momentous where the Summit's focus was explicitly on food *system* transformation, the emphasis shifting to the role of "science policy" (as distinct from local knowledge): "At the international and multilateral level, there is a growing effort to build collective expertise to formulate state-of-the-art scientific knowledge regarding specific global problems" (Hainzelin et al. 2021: 2). Pertinent to this vector, the Gates Foundation recently formed a new Agricultural Innovations initiative, called "Gates Ag One", with the goal of bringing "climate-smart" scientific breakthroughs to smallholder farmers via "the affordable, high-quality tools, technologies, and resources they need to lift themselves out of poverty". And this is in the context of considering the consolidation of all 15 CGIAR centres into a single-centre, co-chaired by the Senior Program Officer of the Gates Foundation, which would blur the "lines between the private and public sectors" and fulfil the Gates Foundation website's claim: "a key trigger of agricultural transformation is a conducive policy environment" (Navdanya 2020: 67, 70).

In short, whereas CFS inclusiveness embodies debate and recognition of eco-knowledge of decentralised food-producing cultures, the WEF Reset beyond the CFS privileges elite science policy governance along techno-political lines. In this way, the PPP nexus is reformulated in such a way as to legitimise centralised institutional power for corporate food. This was expressed by a Scientific Group led by academic scientists, and certainly not frontline small-scale farmer practitioners. While acknowledging that "food is a contentious topic" (e.g. agro-ecology vs biotechnology), they conclude that the Scientific Group aims "to offer a scientific basis to this diversity of perspectives" (von Braun et al. 2021: 30). The implicit message is that smallholder farming and landscape knowledge are of minimal value, even as they remain a powerful and democratic solution to reproducing biodiversity and reducing emissions (Rosset and Altieri 2017).

Turning Point in the Food Regime?

The UNFSS expressed a culminating shock doctrine operation, with the UN surrender of multilateral governance as the Great Reset's ultimate goal. The attempt to marginalise the CFS undermines its inclusive reform acknowledging frontline producers, workers, and Indigenous peoples who in the corporate scheme are redundant. The ultimate object of agribusiness is seeking to colonise these spaces along with its current and future enablers, namely financial and bio-digital and data platform corporations (Mooney 2018).

The global food system oligopoly peaked in 2015, centralising market power in each segment of the industrial food chain. However: "the *bête noirs* of the food chain used to be Monsanto at one end and Walmart at the other" (Mooney 2018: 5). Now the Fourth Industrial Revolution is restructuring food systems, with agribusiness mergers via asset managers such as BlackRock and the Carlyle Group and half a dozen top asset management companies owning 10–30 per cent of the shares of top agribusinesses (Clapp 2019: 614). Their access to information via algorithms on their Big Data platforms provides strategic knowledge of market and merger conditions. Amazon and China's JD.com e-commerce platforms are among the top ten global retailers: "with agribusinesses increasingly reliant on the cloud, AI, and data processing services, big tech firms like Amazon, Alibaba, Microsoft, Google, and Baidu are moving into food production" (Jacobs 2021). Such data-driven technologies, offering "climate-smart" and "precision farming" as silver bullets to policymakers grappling with pandemic legacies, environmental deterioration and climate emergencies, inform UNFSS revisioning via the exclusive Science Policy Interface (von Braun et al. 2021).

Combinations of digitalisation and financialisation may substantially transform global foodscapes and their governance, in line with WEF ambitions. At the commercial level, insider knowledge about weather and markets traditionally held by commodity traders, such as ADM and Cargill, is now rendered almost public property by Big Data. In recent years, "the share of trade in soybeans and wheat ... conducted via blockchains and through Dark Pools has risen from 39% to almost 50%" and will continue to grow (Mooney 2018: 13). Blockchains, as digital ledgers revealing complete transaction processes, and Dark Pools, as opaque Internet trading platforms using blockchains, collectivise strategic information on supply chains or financial deals, enabling new frontiers of market power.

Digital blockchains can reduce transaction costs by removing intermediaries and encouraging start-up fresh/organic foods in competition with corporate food processors like Nestlê, Coca-Cola, Tyson and Unilever. However, given financial market instabilities, with continual buyouts, such new sustainability initiatives may be unrealised as large processors like Unilever, Pepsi, General Mills and ConAgra buy out niche market start-ups, claiming green nutritional standards (Mooney 2017). The Amazon-Whole Foods merger (backed by BlackRock) in 2017 signalled "a race to the bottom", displacing smaller suppliers of Whole Foods with industrial-scale organics or relaxing their standards as Amazon implements downward price pressures (Mooney 2017: 19, 61).

The recent controversy regarding the substantial climatic impact of animal protein production has generated alternative protein in the form of "Food-as-Software".

This is symbolised by Soylent, an invented drink offering a complete (protein-enriched) meal in a bottle (Mann 2021: 69). And profitable green-washing has encouraged Tyson, a major global meat processor, to invest in Beyond Meat, a plant-based fake meat start-up. Meanwhile, the leading food-tech startup, Impossible Foods, leverages climate change challenges, including water shortages and land degradation, as well as population growth, to promote new functional/ultra-processed foods (Mann 2021: 89). Nevertheless, the non-corporate scientific community claims that the animal protein alternative, the bean patty, or veggie-burger, has a footprint one-fifth of that of plant-based meat substitutes (Creswell 2021; Mann 2021: 80).

Digital technologies may intensify displacement of humans from food landscapes, in a trade-off between reductions in energy and chemical use and human touch. Aerial drones can spot and target-spray weeds – and they monitor one-third of Japanese rice fields, aging farmers, and Malaysian and Indonesian oil palm plantations to overs deforestation, infestation and workers (Mooney 2018: 15). Such "precision farming" perpetuates monocultural industrial logic, fetishising information technology and converting "agriculture without farmers" to "agriculture without humans", as the analogue to "Food-as-Software".

Such intensified displacement is implicit in the Earth Bank of Codes (EBC), proposed at the 2018 World Economic Forum. As an extension of the Norwegian Svalbard Seed Bank, which assumes the loss of thousands of seed varieties used by peasants across the world, the EBC could upload genomic information onto a blockchain to ensure, in EBC's words, that "nature's biological and biomimetric assets [are] accessible to innovators around the world". And if energy costs of block-chaining decline, "fintech will inevitably reduce the transaction costs of major corporations, though without improving transparency and to the disadvantage of (already) marginalized peoples" (Mooney 2018: 26–27). The overall consequence would be an intensified commodified enclosure of global biodiversity: the ultimate corporate food regime frontier.

The threat to small-scale farming systems and indigenous rights is built into this vision of agricultural methods privileging monoculture, reliance on proprietary inputs and specialised knowledge (ETC Group 2018: 29). This technology appears to be a next-generation investment vehicle for agribusiness, alongside CRISPR overtaking GM, with gene editing to customise a living organism's genetic sequence, altering its DNA.

Of immediate relevance is the possibility that the pandemic helps "to position agri-food tech innovation as altruistic and uncontroversial" (Reisman 2021: 7). This includes a vision of sterile environments, with Vertical Farming for expanding cities, replacing vulnerable laboring bodies with automation to sustain commodity flows, flexible and reliable data monitoring of food supplies, and even the promise of decentralisation. This latter promise indicates the shortcoming of such narratives, where the cost of the new infrastructure may well be borne by small farms and local food businesses under contract to industry giants such as Walmart and Cargill

(Reisman 2021: 18). With respect to digitalisation, an executive of Nutrien (the world's largest fertiliser company) suggested:

> It's an opportunity to recognize how important a resilient supply chain is to ensure farmers have what they need to continue producing food and a supply chain that can operate under any and all conditions ... Digital tools will play a role ... [to] ensure the critical paths to food security will be able to support societal confidence and create new value.
>
> *Quoted in Reisman 2021: 16*

Looking forward, digital power portends revolutionary change in the structure and operations of the economic, genomic and informational dimensions of the food regime. For a start, the long-standing divisions between (1) agrochemical and seed firms, (2) grain traders and plant breeders, and (3) retailers and farm machinery firms are no longer the case. Here: "the new Big Data platform invites—almost requires—cross-sectoral convergence, and those who control the platform can literally regroup the industrial landscape" (Mooney 2018: 5). Furthermore, these developments outpace regulatory conventions in the general corporate interest, especially as multilateralism falters.

How this will play out in national politics is unclear. However, more substantive public intervention is increasingly mooted and expected as Washington Consensus legitimacy unravels:

> Whereas the Washington Consensus minimized the state's role in the economy and pushed an aggressive free-market agenda of deregulation, privatization, and trade liberalization, the Cornwall Consensus (reflecting commitments voiced at the G7 summit in Cornwall last June) would invert these imperatives ... [in the interest of] a new international social contract.
>
> *Mazzucato 2021*

In this moment, the Chinese model of state-directed capitalism may set the tone, if not the agenda.

China in the Food Regime

Complicating the future of food is China's growing weight in the food regime. China is now the largest trading partner of the United States and has "surpassed the United States as the world's top choice of foreign direct investment" (Pieterese 2018:11). It is now the largest farm produce importer at 10 per cent of global farm produce trade, including bulk agricultural products such as grains, edible oils, sugar, meat, and milk (FAO 2019: 34; Xinhua 2018). It is also the third largest exporter of agricultural commodities globally, by value (Zhan 2019: 51), its food exports concentrating on fish, fruits, vegetables, and processed foods.

Since China has only 9 per cent of the world's arable land to feed 20 per cent of the world's population, access to resources requires stable bilateral relations to replace the instability of finance-driven, globally mobile private capital. China's new Belt and Road Initiative (BRI), connecting with Europe and Africa, includes infrastructural investments in "modernizing" Southeast Asian, and Central and West Asian agricultures and cultivating Africa as an agricultural incubator (McMichael 2020). As the FAO notes: "Chinese science and agriculture have much to offer developing countries, since intensive small-scale agriculture has been practised in China for centuries" (quoted in Buckley 2013: 43).

Compared with the initial food regime, in which British settlers occupied and cultivated New World frontiers, sourcing wage-foods for European industrial labour forces, China captures offshore food supplies from *extant* food systems and farmers in Southeast Asia and Central Asia, Australia and New Zealand, South America, and Africa for wage-foods, feedstuffs, *and* its rising consumer class—expected to double from 480 to 780 mn by 2025. In 2014 the PRI's No. 1 Central Document stated: "China must be more active in utilizing international food market and agricultural resources to effectively coordinate and supplement domestic supply" (Cited in Zhang 2019, 46). And here, the BRI has the potential to realign the global wheat trade in Asia, by establishing a grain futures market with Kazakhstan, Russia and other post-Soviet states, with China's substantial state-owned enterprise, COFCO, as a significant buyer (Kanao and Bisenov 2017).

China's BRI includes a form of agro-security neo-mercantilism, as key states in the Middle East and East Asia lease or enclose land for offshore investment in food production to address ecological limits and ensure food supplies for their domestic citizens (McMichael 2013b). Compared with Northern states and agribusinesses and their global corporate supply chains, Southern states substitute sovereign wealth funds and government firms and banks to acquire land. Bypassing grain trader monopoly with new hybrid state-capital combinations not only deepens agro-exporting, but also underscores the strategic role of state-owned enterprises to bypass WTO trade rules, and thereby Northern dominance. As a U.S. Trade Representative observed: "The WTO's rules were not written with an economy like China's in mind, and critics say the organisation has failed to adequately police Beijing for using a mix of private enterprise and state support to dominate global industries" (Swanson 2019; cf, Hopewell 2020).

Thus, while China complements food regime patterning, its forms of engagement nevertheless represent newly emergent relations, inverting western PPPs to recenter public initiative, in a *centralised* state-capitalist development model, alongside a substantially protected peasant sector (van der Ploeg and Ye 2016). The state has a strong hand in regulating and standardising a "top down" form of organic agriculture and recently pursued policies promoting green and sustainable agriculture. Alongside this sector, informal grass-roots networks of self-managing organic farmers work with participatory monitoring of organic practices. While China adopts western-style agro-technologies to feed its urban middle class, retention of the peasant sector offers an alternative path to de-territorialisation of food systems and large-scale high-tech agriculture.

Via the BRI, the Chinese state-capitalist model of "development cooper-ation" among southern states (Scoones et al. 2016) may well universalise, given the combined and intensifying crises of social inequality and global ecology. But public intervention remains the default,[11] even while corporate globalism resists irrele-vance, showing its teeth—most recently in the UNFSS and echoed in PM Modi's India. Further, COP26 was notable for not including a substantive theme session on agro-industrialisation and the climate emergency.[12]

Emancipatory Possibilities

The corporate path to global food governance is not preordained, despite its claims to have the resources and know-how to manage effective food system transform-ation in environmental stabilisation and world-scale food security. At present, capital may have the upper hand in remaking agriculture with "precision" technologies, generally designed to greenwash and cover tracks (e.g. GM failures, superweeds, toxic chemicals), and securing corporate impunity vested in algorithms to engin-eering ecosystems.

However, such techno-politics is not working on a clean slate and must reckon with the mass exodus of over a billion rural peoples and undermining of their diversified farming systems that manage half the world's land and three-quarters of its fresh water and provide the majority of the world's food (Cribb 2017). It is here that socio-ecological relations over-determine the "future of food", given massive biodiversity decline, soil and water degradation, global heating, and public health deterioration. The UN projects that at current soil loss rates, the world has about 60 years of food harvests left (Monbiot 2015). Given this scenario, future food provisioning founders on contention between green agro-industrial food systems (e.g. climate-smart agriculture, sustainable intensification) and agro-ecological systems geared to reproducing natural processes and cycles. While these systems represent distinctive practices, they overlap in practice across time and space, where economic and environmental pressures are forcing adaptations in both forms of agriculture (IPES-food 2020; Philpott 2020).

Agroecology is gaining ground and/or legitimacy in international organisations, such as the FAO (HLPE 2019), and among producers—either by political-ecological motivation or necessity, where farmers of varying scales are unable to afford the inflated costs of monopolised agro-inputs (lacking the public subsidies that target agribusiness), counter with seed sharing and rural/urban solidarity alliances (Da Viá 2012). It is a practice widespread in Europe (Levidow 2015; Ploeg 2018; Williamson 2019), Latin America, Africa and parts of South Asia, such as local state support for intensifying Zero Budget Natural Farming in southern India, where millions of farmers are rejecting credit and chemicals (Khadse and Rosset 2019), and the System of Rice Intensification

(SRI) producing above-average yields without external inputs now spread across Southeast Asia and into Africa (Vidal 2014). It is also emergent in North America, where farm debt, soil decline and water shortages threaten family farm viability (e.g. Hylton 2012; Greenaway 2017; PAN 2019; Philpott 2020), and ecosystem repair is capturing the attention of some food companies to modify supply chains and appropriate organic initiatives, in context of a Regenerative Organic Certification movement to restore "organic" to its original meaning[13] (Reguzzoni 2018; see also Blesh and Galt 2017), and meanwhile, an active U.S. National Family Farm Coalition (NFFC) encourages agroecological farming. Not unique to "peasant" agriculture, widespread farmer movement adoption of restorative agriculture by reducing agro-inputs avoids debt relations and the ecocide of industrial agriculture.[14] It signals a palpable tension *internal* to the food regime that allows/anticipates the possibility/likelihood of widespread territorial-based restorative agroecological farming systems (cf, Rosset and Altieri 2017). Here, governments, ultimately responsible and vulnerable to food riots, may well "recognise land and landscapes as a special sphere of exchange that is exempt from … global competition" (Hornborg 2011: 154).

Conclusion

A principal tension in the corporate food regime is an expanding "agriculture without farmers"—La Vía Campesina's arresting catchphrase invoking the now deepening precarity of food security and the abstraction of food and land via commodity fetishism. Ultimately, commodification entails simplification, economic compulsion and destruction of the knowledge systems and life worlds of humans and other species we depend on. As the World Bank sponsored International Assessment of Agricultural Science and Technology for Development recommended: "business as usual is no longer an option" as markets cannot register social and environmental harm (IAASTD 2008). And lab food is no answer to extreme global inequalities.

In *The Long Food Movement*, IPES-food and the ETC Group, in observing that civil society and trans-local food movements today are now more networked, knowledgeable and critical of "agriculture without farmers", and aware "that the role of governments is essential", forecast that:

> By 2045 or sooner, civil society is capable of reducing the industrial food chain's horrendous health and environmental damages *and* shifting unproductive or counter-productive funding flows towards territorial markets and agroecology … [with] an estimated 75% reduction in the GHG emissions of the industrial food chain.
>
> *IPES-food & ETC Group 2021: 16–17*

This, of course, will require cumulative international solidarities. The pandemic has focused citizens on the vulnerabilities of global supply chains and the threat of information technologies, and governments unprepared to address food and public health crises. The UNFSS attack on the CFS and the possibility of silencing the CSM voice has sparked an unprecedented movement of global solidarity against corporate capture and its changing faces.

Meanwhile, the Indian farmer rebellion against corporate capture has spawned a broad citizen alliance of lawyers, chefs, drivers, healthcare workers, recognising the significance of a national food culture. A quarter of a century ago, the peasant demand for "food sovereignty" pinpointed fundamental limits to the claim to "feed the world" via a corporate food regime premised on *dispossession* by accumulation of small-scale food systems. With multiple meanings, "sovereignty" requires restoration of territorial self-determination in food and nutrition policy coupled with protection and support of *self-organising* rural and urban food provisioning across various political-ecological systems including Indigenous territories (Mayes 2018; Schiavoni 2017). The future of (real) food depends on this compelling vision.

Notes

1 "Politics" includes contention between green capitalism and genuine ecological renewal (cf Ajl 2021).
2 This was the Bank's first annual report on agriculture, following almost three decades of a global agrarian crisis (McMichael 2009).
3 https://viacampesina.org/en/civil-society-declaration-of-the-terra-preta-forum/ (accessed on December 11, 2021).
4 For example, multi-state corporate agro-industrial ventures such as the G-7 sponsored New Alliance for Food Security and Nutrition in Africa (NAFSN), and the Global Alliance for Climate Smart Agriculture (GACSA) with 14 governments partnered with corporations such as Dupont, Dow, Kelloggs, McDonalds, Monsanto, Walmart, Tyson Foods, Syngenta, Unilever and Yara (McKeon 2013; Taylor 2018).
5 www3.weforum.org/docs/WEF_Institutional_Brochure_2016.pdf (accessed on December 11, 2021).
6 Ignoring the recent HLPE 2020 report extending the concept of "food security" in socio-ecological terms (McKeon 2021).
7 www.dailysabah.com/world/world-to-face-food-crisis-if-coronavirus-pandemic-not-managed-properly-un-wto/news (emphasis added, accessed on December 11, 2021).
8 With the UN Social Compact, encouraging corporate social and environmental responsibility in return for its brand.
9 www.iatp.org/blog/202003/world-economic-forum-and-corporate-takeover-global-governance-our-food-systems (accessed on December 11, 2021).
10 www.newsbreak.com/news/0OTrWLJe/op-ed-the-2021-food-systems-summit-has-started-on-the-wrong-foot-but-it-could-still-be-transformational (accessed on 12/11/2021).
11 Notably, the Mexican government is phasing out glyphosate use and GM corn for human consumption by 2024: www.agrinews-pubs.com/business/2021/01/18/mexico-bans-gmo-corn-2024-deadline-includes-elimination-of-glyphosate-herbicide/ (accessed on December 11, 2021).

12 See https://thetricontinental.org/newsletterissue/agricultural-technology/ (accessed on December 11, 2021).

13 https://regenorganic.org

14 van der Ploeg characterises this as a movement towards "re-peasantisation"—essentially withdrawing from commercial inputs and rebuilding ecological wealth on the farm (2018).

CONCLUSION THE ONGOING COVID-19 DYSTOPIA

A Crossroads for Critical IPE and Humanity

Tim Di Muzio and Matt Dow

The system isn't broken it was built this way

Protest Statement

Corona is the virus, capitalism is the pandemic.

Graffiti on a Wall in Toronto, Canada

Introduction

This edited collection was composed throughout 2021 as the pandemic continued to afflict multiple communities and economies differently. In addition, new variants of the virus like Delta and Omicron were uncovered as public health care systems struggled to cope with rising infections, hospitalisations and death rates. In the rich countries, thanks largely to publicly funded research and development and mass vaccinations, life appeared to be returning to semi-normal as more of the population was double vaccinated, and in some countries, boosters were offered. But the global poor have not been so fortunate; they have suffered disproportionately throughout the pandemic with little access to reliable health care. Due to the inequality generated by capitalist accumulation, the legacy of colonialism, slavery, and the power of pharmaceutical firms to sabotage vaccine availability by patent and price, the world's poorest countries, mostly on the African continent, remain unvaccinated (see Andersen this volume). As of December 6, 2021, 4.33 bn people have received at least one dose of the vaccine, mostly in wealthy countries.[1] This represents only 56.5 per cent of the global population since the virus was first detected in Wuhan, China, on December 21, 2019. By March 11th, the World Health Organization (WHO) declared the Covid-19 outbreak a pandemic and serious threat to the global population's health. As is well known, albeit, with

DOI: 10.4324/9781003250432-17

different speeds and capacities, public health officials and their governments soon moved to put in place public health protocols such as social distancing, local and state-level lockdowns and the wearing of personal protective equipment such as masks and face shields. Almost instantly, there was a feel-good sense that "we are all in this together". This was because the virus did not respect the human construct of national borders and required an international effort of epic proportions to combat it. At first, there appeared to be a "commitment to shared responsibility and collective endeavour" (Alexiou 2021: 286; Sobande 2020: 1034). But, as scholars have been at pains to point out, we were not really "all in this together". Although billionaires escaped on their superyachts and white-collar workers hunkered down at home to work remotely, it was the most vulnerable in every nation and community who suffered the worst of the novel coronavirus (see Popcevski this volume). The level of suffering often fell along the intersections of age, class, racial and gender lines and, on top of this, access to quality care and money—the latter typically determined by where one stood in the hierarchy of global capitalism before the pandemic (see Bousfield, Smith-Nonini, Davy and Dickinson). Even in the wealthiest nation on earth, the United States, the most vulnerable barely stood a chance whereas protected workers stayed home, and billionaires witnessed their wealth soar (Warf 2021; see Robbins this volume).

As the pandemic progressed, the world, it seemed, had been turned upside down. But to critical scholars, the casualties were largely predictable after four decades of neoliberal rule and healthcare systems transformations (Navarro 2020; see Benatar and Wamsley this volume). This chapter's goal is to tease out some of what we have learned from the Covid-19 crisis from the point of view of the contributions in this volume. Our argument is not only that the crisis has starkly revealed many of the contradictions of global capitalism but also that the pandemic opens up opportunities for thinking about the world anew. Indeed, humanity seems at a crossroads of crises, and we contend here that we need to shift away from the 19th- and 20th-century political theory and economy and use new tools of analysis to struggle for a more just, sustainable, and equitable global order. This chapter is organised in the following way; first, we highlight some of the key findings of this study. We recognise that we are in no way the final word on what our fellow political economists have learned from the pandemic, but we do hope our readership and future generations can gain some important knowledge on how global society responded to the crisis and what opportunities for progressive and humane social change may have been missed. Second, we examine what we call the "crossroads of crisis" and briefly consider the prospects of neoliberal capitalism continuing as the world's chief governance framework in what will hopefully be a post-pandemic world. Here we should recall that during the global financial crisis (GFC), many heralded the "death of neoliberalism" as a mode of governance (Cooper 2011). This has been true of the pandemic as well. It seems that neoliberalism is always about to die as more of its contradictions are compounded and exposed in periods of crisis. Yet somehow, neoliberalism is like the walking dead. In the aftermath of the GFC, one scholar labelled this the "zombie" phase of neoliberalism. The following quote is also apropos for our current conjuncture:

> Exploiting crisis conditions, we must remember, has been a hallmark of neo-liberal governance, even if the recent pattern of events seems less and less like a "normal crisis". But again, the jaded and discredited project threatens to lurch haphazardly onward (if not forward)—that is, unless concerted political opposition blocks its path, and until an alternative socio-political program begins to fill the attendant vacuum. "Dead but dominant", neoliberalism may indeed have entered its zombie phase. The brain has apparently long since ceased functioning, but the limbs are still moving, and many of the defensive reflexes seem to be working too. The living dead of the free-market revolution continue to walk the earth, though with each resurrection their decidedly uncoordinated gait becomes even more erratic.
>
> Peck 2010: 109

Like Peck, we will argue that there is little evidence to suggest the emergence of an alternative governance framework roughly two years after the virus first appeared and proliferated from Wuhan. In fact, some have suggested that the deficits built up during the crisis will eventually give way to greater neoliberal austerity as governments cut back on their budgets to "balance the books" (Kentikelenis and Stubbs 2021). In the third section, we consider some of the key reasons for why the multiple crises we face, exacerbated by the pandemic, are not being addressed sufficiently by world leaders. The chapter offers a brief conclusion.

Main Achievements

Our study is not exhaustive, and there will be still much to learn in the years to come. This volume has tried to bring critical scholars together in IPE around three major themes we deemed important to explore to understand better the global political economy and where we might be headed. These themes were (1) Global Power, Inequality, and Climate Change; (2) Global Health, Social Care, and Reproduction during the Covid-19 Pandemic; (3) The Future of Production, Money, Energy, and Food Regimes. Each chapter is revealing in its own right, but we offer a general summary here.

As evidenced by the chapters in this volume, one of the fundamental achievements of this edited collection is that we offer a critical, diversified reflection on how the Covid-19 pandemic has impacted the global political economy through a variety of conceptual lenses and approaches. At the heart of our theorisation, we demonstrate that Covid-19 has and will continue to impact and intensify the dialectical nature embedded in the global political economy between power and resistance. Moreover, this volume critiques hegemonic social myths created by neoclassical economics, neoliberal politicians, think tanks and scholarship on a variety of topics such as wealth distribution, monetary and fiscal policy, care, social reproduction and the future of work, as well as the climate, food and energy. This political project attempts to create new critical common sense in international political economy and potentially other fields of study. We aimed to challenge the inherent biases in government policies riddled with orthodox economic assumptions. Collectively, these chapters reveal that humanity is at a crossroads of crises or a fundamental tipping point where humanity should not *return to normalcy* even when Covid-19 finally dissipates as perhaps the seasonal flu. This is because normalcy, under neoliberal or even Keynesian capitalism, helped create the very social, economic, and environmental conditions for the Covid-19 pandemic to occur and spread. The Covid-19 pandemic has exposed and worsened the already existing systematic social and environmental problems that are plaguing humanity: ignorance, racism, white supremacy and sexism, unpaid gendered labour and the devaluation of biological, social reproduction, global inequality and precarisation, austerity, privatisation and climate denialism. The primary lesson learned from the novel coronavirus outbreak has been that both global political economy and liberal governance are largely more concerned with corporate profitability. At the same time, more worthwhile endeavours that target overall social well-being are viewed as largely expendable when confronted with the need for economic growth. In this sense, the normalisation of neoliberal capitalism is not a viable option *if humanity* wants to live on a habitable planet. A secondary takeaway from this volume is how we interpret and govern risk in capitalist democracies. Although this book has not specifically used the lens of risk to evaluate the pandemic, it is clear that the risk of virus transmission and death was shared unequally and that many health systems were stretched to the brink during the crisis. Part of the explanation for this unevenness is not just systemic inequality but the increasing privatisation of risk under neoliberalism. Individualising risk opens the door to exacerbating pre-existing vulnerabilities where people may not have the financial means to insure their lives or livelihoods in the private market. Thus, one key challenge for critical political economists might be to challenge the privatisation of risk, particularly when the law of large numbers suggests that collective risks should be pooled and insured by society as a whole (Di Muzio 2014). The law of large numbers suggests that the cost of risks diminishes as the population of people insured increases. The public health response to the pandemic and the mass vaccination campaigns in the Global North is but one prominent example of how public institutions can help insure the entire population, albeit with outliers who refuse vaccination. In this sense, the critical left should argue for more nation-based insurance schemes when it comes to protecting society from various harms and crises—the math is on their side to argue for the greater socialisation of risk. However, the chief difficulty other than political opposition from some ideological quarters is that the politicians of indebted states will argue that "there is no money" for such social programs. Claiming a dearth of money is a nonsense so long as the human and natural resources are available within the community and the government is monetarily sovereign over its currency issuance (see Di Muzio this volume).

Thus, taken as a whole, what this volume reveals is that humanity is at a crossroads of multiple crises, with the most vulnerable suffering the greatest risk to their livelihoods and life chances despite the level of wealth produced since the Industrial Revolution. We explain this concept in the following section and discuss the prospects of neoliberal capitalism continuing as the world's chief governance framework.

The Crossroads of Multiple Crises

As critical scholars have suggested long before the recent pandemic, as a socio-economic system, capitalism is prone to repeated crisis (Harvey 2015). Viewed in this light, the pandemic can be considered among a long list of capitalist crises, but has been qualitatively unique in the current conjuncture. Yet, as we have stressed in this volume, the pandemic was not born in a vacuum but in specific historical circumstances accompanied by several ongoing crises in food and agriculture, care and social reproduction, income and wealth inequality and energy and the sustainability of the biosphere. We call this the "crossroads of multiple crises" and conceptualise these crises as interrelated, interconnected and intertwined. Much like the feminist concept of "intersectionality" that draws our attention to the fact that oppression and domination can have multiple root causes, we too find numerous root causes for the crises faced by humanity. However, many of these current crises can be traced back to the differential accumulation of capital and the rise and spread of neoliberal forms of rule (Nitzan and Bichler 2009; Cahill and Konings 2017). This suggests that the pandemic is just one of many morbid symptoms that need to be taken seriously and addressed globally if we want to avoid the demolition of society and our biosphere (Polanyi 1957). In other words, we must tackle all crises at once, but how to do so is up for debate in a world of so-called "fiscal constraints" and unequal access to resources.

If we imagine a crossroad as a metaphor for our current predicament, we always have options at particular moments of crisis. At present, it seems as though there are two dominant *capitalist* routes we can take. The first is to continue with the neoliberal policies of fiscal discipline, privatisation and re-regulation that prioritise capital, creditors and markets over debtors, the poor and everyday working people. The hope here is that capitalists will innovate us out of our current predicament of multiple crises with the right policy framework and incentive structures. In this view, individual and corporate entrepreneurialism and innovation will grow the economic pie while addressing existential issues such as climate change and the future of food, water and energy. Never mind that for everyone to live like a North American, we would need multiple planets (Di Muzio 2017: 150; see Dow this volume). The current incarnation of this vision is the Great Reset proposed by the elite World Economic Forum (WEF) and its founder Klaus Schwab. Highly abstract, the discourse of the Great Reset consists of three components that make for a post-pandemic plan of international governmental and business action. The first is to create a "stakeholder economy" alongside a shareholder economy where governments act to steer market forces towards more equitable outcomes. The second is that public investments should advance shared goals such as sustainability and greater equity. The third component of the "Great Reset" is to marshal the so-called forces of the fourth industrial revolution to forces to solve social and health challenges.[2] Although the far-right fears that a "Great Reset" is a hidden path to global socialism lead by a capitalist elite—a strange new take on political theory—its agenda largely entails continuing to pursue greater economic growth with new technology and perhaps alleviating some of the worst excesses of capitalist accumulation (Slobodian 2020). In essence, if it were ever to be enacted, it would be neoliberalism 2.0—capitalism with a kinder face and not too radically different from Keynesianism.

The second capitalist option seems to be some renewed form of Keynesianism where the state takes on a larger role in investing in the economy, as we saw during the pandemic and in other capitalist crises. Even the editorial board of the *Financial Times* resounded that:

> Radical reforms—reversing the prevailing policy direction of the last four decades—will need to be put on the table. Governments will have to accept a more active role in the economy. They must see public services as investments rather than liabilities, and look for ways to make labour markets less insecure. Redistribution will again be on the agenda; the privileges of the elderly and wealthy in question. Policies until recently considered eccentric, such as basic income and wealth taxes, will have to be in the mix.
>
> *cited in Matthewman and Huppatz 2020: 678*

There is little doubt that the pandemic demonstrated the importance of fiscal policy—particularly in the OECD—where monetary policy, even before the pandemic, appeared to be running out of steam to stimulate economic activity. Moreover, since the Global Financial Crisis (2007–2009), most of the new money created as public debt by digital balance sheet operations between governments and central banks appear to have contributed to urban real estate and stock market inflation in the Global North. This trend is worrisome for two main reasons. The first is that rising prices for homes and inequality in access to mortgages have caused an urban housing affordability crisis, effectively locking people of many countries out of their domestic housing market and engendering greater insecurity of life chances (Soederberg 2021; Wetzstein 2017). Or course, we must recognise here that a significant portion of humanity inhabits informal settlements, which can also generate considerable insecurity. The second reason for concern has to do with the fear that stock markets have become a house of cards that will collapse without further stimulus money and cause another—and perhaps greater—financial crisis. But even if governments could direct stimulus spending to where it is needed, like public infrastructure, health and education, a universal basic income and a jobs guarantee, a rebooted Keynesianism following Modern Monetary Theory would not challenge capitalism as the root of our multiple crises in any serious way. The imperatives of economic growth and the differential accumulation of capital would remain, as would, presumably, the current fiscal-monetary debt-based order. This historical order allows commercial banks to produce the majority of new money as personal and corporate debt and sees the government forced into debt if it spends more than its revenue. The prevalence of debt can have severe impacts on all levels of society, and in many countries since the 1980s, it has been used to plug the gap between stagnant wages, consumer spending and increasingly, for necessities like access to healthcare (Soederberg 2014; Di Muzio and Robbins 2016). For individuals, it can lead to bankruptcy, greater housing inflation, stress and anxiety and acquiescence to the power of creditors. For corporations, debt service can lead to downsizing, the greater capacity to degrade the environment through extraction, production and consumption and even the potential for insolvency. For states, mounting deficits and debt can cut public service provisioning and investment as politicians seek to "balance the books" in the post-pandemic world. In this sense, scaremongering over mounting national debts could supercharge neoliberal policies such as the privatisation of public assets as governments seek to reintroduce fiscal discipline and, therefore, the approval of their credit rating agencies (Di Muzio and Robbins 2016). What all this amounts to is that there is a real danger of the "new normal" being much of the same in post-pandemic world order and that the "emergency Keynesianism" experienced throughout the pandemic was an aberration only deemed necessary at the time due to the nature and scale of the crisis (Šumonja 2020: 216). In other words, we find no clear, hopeful signs that neoliberalism will be replaced by some other form of governance focused on prioritising and overcoming the multiple crises we face. In the following section, we examine why this might be so.

Neoliberalism, the Pandemic and Post-Capitalism?

One of the major lessons of the pandemic is that the state can help protect the health of their populations and economies through concerted and coordinated action. Yet, despite this demonstration, governments worldwide are doing precious little to combat the multiple crises we face. This is not to suggest that governments are doing nothing but that their measures are piecemeal and largely inadequate related to the scope and scale of the crises we and future generations face. In this section, we want to take a closer look at why this may be the case and pose three interrelated hypotheses for consideration. The first we call the "democracy and class society hypothesis", the second the "Carr–Diamond hypothesis" and the third, the "accounting and capitalism hypothesis". Theoretically and practically, we understand them as interrelated.

In most quarters, liberal democracy is lauded as an ideal form of governance even with its large range of institutional, racial, gendered, and classist embedded "deficits" (discriminations) that limit the actual democratic process (Pilon 2018). Although imperfect, liberal representative democratic institutions are supposed to, at the very least, allow individuals of a certain age to participate in their governance, be it as a government representative or by voting for an individual or political party. This participatory approach—even at a distance—is said to be far superior to other forms of government like fascism, communism, or totalitarianism (Dahl 1998). But there is a dark side to liberal democracy that very few are willing to discuss besides that most are founded on colonialism, slavery, genocides, and war (Mann 2004). Although the demand for "more democracy" is a default position of the political and critical left, with many viewing capitalism and democracy as fundamentally opposed to one another, there is a different view. (Carey 1997; Losurdo 2011; Macpherson 1962; Wood 1995). As Graeber and Wengrow (2021) masterfully show, both democratic and egalitarian principles are not liberal, capitalist, or even European inventions but have existed consistently throughout human history, especially in the Indigenous communities of North America. With this said, "borrowed ideas" from non-European populations and Indigenous tribes, European wars, capitalism, and liberalism were central features that gave birth to European democracy unevenly and differentially (Davidson 2012; Graeber and Wengrow 2021). But there is one similarity within European-based liberal constitutional democracies: they were structured and built by a minority of property owners who have created political institutions and laws to ensure the protection of their property and the accumulation of wealth based on their ownership (Di Muzio 2008).

The primary contradiction in contemporary democracies is that the majority interest is supposed to have power over individual or minority interests. Yet, liberalism's ontological starting point for explaining how the social universe is supposed to be governed begins with abstract individualism (Rand 1957) or better conceptualised by what C. B. Macpherson (1962) called "possessive individualism." In other words, the very fabric of governance, societal aims, human development, and even imaginations under liberalism is becoming ever more tethered to a market supremacist civilisation that rewards individuals and corporations that pursue wealth, power, and materialism at the expense of the majority of humanity and biosphere *writ large*. (Gill 1995; Di Muzio 2015b) Therefore, the aim of liberal-capitalist hegemonies is to mask how social power still dictates everyday life. For example, liberal elite intellectuals and their followers continually justify the persistence of inequalities in human societies as inherently connected to human nature, natural competition, individual behaviour patterns, or some other preordained factor or natural structure (Lévi-Strauss 1974). This attempts to rewrite history by eliding the fact that the capitalist class has historically structured inequality within society and political institutions along racialist, sexist, and classist lines. As a result, one fundamental task for both critical scholars and the left, in general, is to bring the social forces of power back into the spotlight. Yet, tremendous hurdles need to be addressed to rely on democracy and governmental accountability to keep power in check. As Gill (2008) has pointed out, global development has for the last three decades been rooted in "locking in" the rights of capital accumulation and "locking out" democracy. Simply put, nation-states have become extremely subordinate to social forces of market civilisation over most of the needs of their populations. For this to change, both state and government officials/workers and the majority of the population will need to prepare for the threat of the capitalist class and market forces striking back (Roos 2019). Thus, one central future research question becomes how do we reorient society towards more egalitarian and inclusive principles and away from extreme individualism which is interconnected to the daily oppressions of liberal governmentality and capitalism that the Covid-19 pandemic has exposed.

The limits of democracy are further highlighted by Bell and Henry (2001), who suggest that far from being completely opposed to one another, capitalism and democracy develop alongside one another with money and the inequality of property ownership. To make their argument, Bell and Henry juxtapose an egalitarian non-property-based community that follows the ethic of hospitality and a propertied based community where owners follow their individual self-interest, often to the determinant of communal well-being. As they suggest:

> In an egalitarian society where the interests of the individual are those of the collective, coercive behavior leading to non-egalitarian consequences is incomprehensible. Such behavior connotes a rupture in the egalitarian principle of equal rights and responsibilities, and this would be reflected in a breach in the principle of hospitality—a violation of the main social relationship fortifying the underlying collective production process, thus placing the entire population in economic jeopardy.
>
> *2001: 212*

But as we know, the current world order is radically unequal by income, wealth and life chances (Credit Suisse 2020). In other words, all modern societies are hierarchical and according to the Pew Research Center, about half of these have democratic arrangements of one kind or another.[3] Bell and Henry explain that these disparities are not aberrations from a perfect form but should be expected of democratic and propertied societies:

> Democratic arrangements, in whatever form, would be foreign to [a non-propertied] population. Democracy connotes division, fractiousness, inequality. Agreement cannot be reached as interests are not the same. Hence, democracy appears with the development of class society (or civilization), where the egalitarian relationships have been destroyed (though they may appear to continue in certain formal arrangements). Democracy or any other political structure is symptomatic of propertied economies.
>
> *2001: 213*

Although Bell and Henry may go too far in suggesting agreements can never be reached in democracies, they do make the important point about the fractiousness of democracy and how the battle between different and unequal interests is rooted in property ownership. For instance, the Koch brothers in the United States who derive their billions from fossil fuels, mining and manufacturing, do not have the same interests as the Manning brothers who made their fortunes playing American football. The takeaway here is that we should not be so quick to treat liberal democratic forms of governance as a panacea for our problems, as some voices and interests can be prioritised above others (Gilens and Page 2014). This is not to suggest that we should be against democratic political arrangements, but it does indicate that we need to be aware that current forms of democracy and modern capitalism may not be as opposed to one another as we often think. In this sense, global capitalism does not necessarily undermine democracy *per se* but promotes a particular version of it where property and the self-interest in the accumulation of money are largely protected within the law (Commons 1959; Gill and Cutler 2014). Recognising the class divided nature of our democracies may go a far way in helping us to explain why known problems persist. To elaborate on this point, we now discuss the Carr–Diamond hypothesis first introduced by Tim Di Muzio in *Carbon Capitalism* (2015a: 170).

In writing about the problem of civilisation's reliance on fossil fuels and the climate emergency, Di Muzio proposed a merger of Carr and Diamond's thinking to help explain why more was not being done about a needed energy transition. E.H. Carr was an international relations theorist whereas Jared Diamond is a geographer and historian. In their own way, both suggested that known international problems endure because, for a minority, these harms are beneficial to them. For example, it is very advantageous to the owners of fossil fuel companies and the state governments that oversee the ownership of their national oil and gas to go on producing and selling petroleum. With climate disasters on the rise and future threats looming, it can hardly be argued with any credibility that these practices and the subsidies that underwrite them are beneficial to the vast majority of humanity even in the short run (see Lucas this volume).[4] In fact, as NASA's former climate scientist, James Hanson, said just before the most recent pandemic:

> All we've done is agree there's a problem. We agreed that in 1992 [at the Earth summit in Rio] and re-agreed it again in Paris [at the 2015 climate accord]. We haven't acknowledged what is required to solve it. Promises like Paris don't mean much, it's wishful thinking. It's a hoax that governments have played on us since the 1990s.
>
> *cited in Milman 2018 np*[5]

Thus, the climate emergency persists, and as Hansen suggests, governments worldwide are doing precious little to solve the problem (see Dow and Lucas this volume). *The Guardian* asked a Harvard historian of science what she made of Hansen's decades-long plight to get the U.S. government to do something about climate change based on scientific observations. Professor Naomi Oreskes offered the following:

> Poor Jim Hansen. He's a tragic hero. The Cassandra aspect of his life is that he's cursed to understand and diagnose what's going on but unable to persuade

people to do something about it. We are all raised to believe knowledge is power but Hansen proves the untruth of that slogan. Power is power.

cited in Milman 2018 np

Power is indeed power and although it concedes nothing without a demand, it can also ignore these demands or choose which demands it wants to respond to, as has been demonstrated in multiple cases of crisis. So here, we would do well to recall that problems persist because they are beneficial to a particular group of people.

Both the "democracy and class society" and "Carr–Diamond" hypotheses link up with a third suggestion for why we experience multiple crises that could potentially be solved—the "capitalism and accounting" hypothesis. There is a little doubt that we are a society governed in large measure by symbolic numbers (Fioramonti 2014). These quantifications of qualitative things—the price of food, our heart rates, population levels, morbidity etc.—all matter for how we understand our world and behave in it. Our civilisational order is governed by one overarching number that virtually all politicians adhere to, gross domestic product or GDP. A calculation first worked out in the 1930s by a team of American economists to help the Allies war effort, the computation of national wealth has become ubiquitous through the United Nations' System of National Accounts. Since GDP is largely an adding up exercise that calculates the monetary value of all goods and services produced in an economy, it is viewed as a poor indicator of overall societal well-being (Fioramonti 2013). For instance, the construction of more nuclear weapons, the cost of cleaning up oil spills and automotive accidents among other harmful things, all contribute to GDP. Yet, despite GDP masking societal well-being, it remains the key indicator for most economists and politicians worldwide. If GDP is increasing, we are succeeding in managing the economy correctly. If GDP is faltering, society is failing and something must be done to reignite growth lest business fails, unemployment increases and depressed conditions lead to social misery and political instability. For decades scholars have pointed out the deficiency of this indicator for guiding and improving society, but it appears hard-wired into the brains of the present *zeitgeist* (Daly 1996; Hamilton 2004; Fioramonti 2013; Jackson 2009; Kempf 2008). As Jackson (2009: 103) asserted in his important study on sustainability and growth commissioned by the U.K. government: "Questioning growth is deemed the act of lunatics, idealists and revolutionaries". Thus, although many proposals exist from pursuing de-growth economics to finding other indicators that better measure social well-being, none (save perhaps in Bhutan, where they have introduced a "gross national happiness" indicator), are currently adopted by national governments. It is as if we are locked into a Cold War mentality where material economic growth on a finite planet remains the key goal for all our endeavours. Warning students at the University of Kansas that they may not like what he was about to say, Robert F. Kennedy noted as far back as 1968 that:

Our Gross National Product, now, is over $800 billion dollars a year, but that Gross National Product—if we judge the United States of America by

that—that Gross National Product counts air pollution and cigarette advertising, and ambulances to clear our highways of carnage. It counts special
locks for our doors and the jails for the people who break them. It counts
the destruction of the redwood and the loss of our natural wonder in chaotic
sprawl. It counts napalm and counts nuclear warheads and armored cars for
the police to fight the riots in our cities. It counts Whitman's rifle and Speck's
knife, and the television programs which glorify violence in order to sell toys
to our children. Yet the gross national product does not allow for the health of
our children, the quality of their education or the joy of their play. It does not
include the beauty of our poetry or the strength of our marriages, the intelligence of our public debate or the integrity of our public officials. It measures
neither our wit nor our courage, neither our wisdom nor our learning, neither our compassion nor our devotion to our country, it measures everything
in short, except that which makes life worthwhile. And it can tell us everything about America except why we are proud that we are Americans. If this
is true here at home, so it is true elsewhere in world.[6]

If GDP is such a poor indicator of our social well-being as Kennedy suggests, why
does it persist as our leading indicator for economic achievement? Why are our
political leaders obsessed with growing the economy in a world of non-renewable
resources? Is there a structural reason for the continued reliance on GDP found in
the very dynamics and math of capitalism? We think there is, and until we learn to
account for things anew—that is to say, find new accounting identities and prioritise what we find valuable—our problems will persist, and crises will compound.
Our goal here is not to offer a list of brand new accounting identities for the
national accounts or to tell the reader what should or should not be counted and
measured/valued but to raise the idea that IPE needs to make a more profound
contribution to this area of knowledge if we are to address the multiple crises we
face. This has become all the more clear since the pandemic. A good start, we argue,
is to understand the math of capitalism, commercial bank lending and their relationship with the pursuit of GDP (Di Muzio and Robbins 2021).[7]

The first thing to notice is that all for-profit businesses use a form of cost-plus
accounting. Rather than being price-takers as in traditional economic theory, the
largest firms are *price makers* (Nitzan and Bichler 2009: 240ff). This means they cal-
culate the cost of producing their products for sale and add a percentage mark-up
aligned with a specific profit target.[8] For example, Table C.1 shows the mark-up
for the twenty-five leading companies on the *Forbes* Global 2000.[9] Pressured by
owners/investors to accumulate, businesses do their best to reduce costs, kill or
absorb their competition and use their power and influence to shape the terrain of
accumulation through political lobbying and donations. But they also borrow from
commercial banks for a variety of reasons. For instance, as of Q3 2021, the amount
of non-financial corporate debt is just over US$11 tn, on which interest has to be
paid.[10] This suggests that the drive to grow and accumulate is rooted not just in the
desire to please owner/investors with differential returns but also to service loans

TABLE C.1 Mark-up for the twenty-five leading companies

Company	Country	Sales (Billions)	Profits (Billions)	Assets (Billions)	Market Value (Billions)	Costs (billions)	Mark-up (%)
Saudi Arabian Oil Company (Saudi Aramco)	Saudi Arabia	$329.80	$88.20	$398.30	$1,684.80	$241.60	36.51
Microsoft	United States	$138.60	$46.30	$285.40	$1,359	$92.30	50.16
Apple	United States	$267.70	$57.20	$320.40	$1,285.50	$210.50	27.17
Amazon	United States	$296.30	$10.60	$221.20	$1,233.40	$285.70	3.71
Alphabet	United States	$166.30	$34.50	$273.40	$919.30	$131.80	26.18
Facebook	United States	$73.40	$21	$138.40	$583.70	$52.40	40.08
Alibaba	China	$70.60	$24.70	$189.40	$545.40	$45.90	53.81
Tencent Holdings	China	$54.60	$13.50	$137	$509.70	$41.10	32.85
Berkshire Hathaway	United States	$254.60	$81.40	$817.70	$455.40	$173.20	47.00
Johnson & Johnson	United States	$82.80	$17.20	$155	$395.30	$65.60	26.22
Walmart	United States	$524	$14.90	$236.50	$344.40	$509.10	2.93
Nestlé	Switzerland	$93.10	$12.70	$132.10	$304.10	$80.40	15.80
Roche Holding	Switzerland	$61.90	$13.60	$85.80	$297.40	$48.30	28.16
Procter & Gamble	United States	$70.30	$5	$118.60	$291.80	$65.30	7.66
JPMorgan Chase	United States	$142.90	$30	$3,139.40	$291.70	$112.90	26.57
Samsung Electronics	South Korea	$197.60	$18.40	$304.90	$278.70	$179.20	10.27
UnitedHealth Group	United States	$246.30	$13.80	$189.10	$277.10	$232.50	5.94
Intel	United States	$75.70	$22.70	$147.70	$254	$53.00	42.83
ICBC	China	$177.20	$45.30	$4,322.50	$242.30	$131.90	34.34
Verizon Communications	United States	$131.40	$18.40	$294.50	$237.70	$113.00	16.28
AT&T	United States	$179.20	$14.40	$545.40	$218.60	$164.80	8.74
Pfizer	United States	$50.70	$15.80	$167.50	$212.80	$34.90	45.27
Bank of America	United States	$112.10	$24.10	$2,620	$208.60	$88.00	27.39
China Construction Bank	China	$162.10	$38.90	$3,822	$203.80	$123.20	31.57

Source: Forbes (2021) *Global 2000.* Available at: www.forbes.com/lists/global2000/#78d3c7465ac0 (Accessed on January 1, 2022).

by commercial banks and other financial institutions. Put simply, businesses need to expand not simply to grow their profit share but because they *are compelled to by the debt burdens they must service.*

The second thing to notice is that commercial banks are special entities within capitalism. Although ordinary firms cannot produce new money, commercial banks do so by extending loans to willing borrowers (Werner 2014a and 2014b). The problem is that when commercial banks make loans, they *do not* create the interest that is to be repaid on the loan (Di Muzio and Robbins 2016; Di Muzio and Noble 2017; Di Muzio and Robbins 2017). This means that there is always more debt owed within capitalist economies than the ability to repay the outstanding loans. In other words, if commercial banks called in all their loans tomorrow, there would not be enough money to discharge all accumulated liabilities. This fundamental fact spurs the need for greater economic growth, or what is the same, the expansion of the economy.

In short, capitalism is a debt-based system of political economy founded on commercial bank money creation and supported by fossil fuel energy (Rowbotham 1998; Di Muzio and Robbins 2016; Di Muzio 2017). This suggests that GDP is not simply a measure of the goods and services produced within an economy over a year but a weathervane for how well individuals, businesses and governments can service their debts to commercial banks and other lenders. Under the current order of things, if economic growth slows or collapses, debts become more difficult to service, and commercial banks fear creating more money as loans, freezing credit, and further exacerbating the problems of a debt-based monetary system. Thus, it makes little sense to call for a form of post-capitalism or the abolition of the growth economy until we abolish a system of money creation largely founded on commercial bank debt and interest, which compels growth and the further destruction of the biosphere. The good news is that many scholars, concerned citizens and practitioners are working on transforming the fiscal-monetary system (for a summary of monetary reformers, see, Scott 2018). Whether they succeed and in what measure remains an open question, but it will bear incredible importance for how we overcome a growth-driven system on a finite planet.

Conclusion

This chapter began with a brief review of some of the key achievements of this study. We then discussed what we have called the "crossroads of multiple crises." We have suggested that these interrelated crises persist for three main reasons and that our current governance structures are either unwilling or inadequate to meet them before these crises become exponentially worse. Although the pandemic exacerbated and exposed many morbid symptoms of our capitalist societies, it also revealed many horizons for hope as people across the world continue to struggle and fight for a better, fairer, and more environmentally sustainable world order. In conclusion, we agree with Roy's statement that the Covid-19 pandemic is a part of a larger "*doomsday machine we have built ourselves. Nothing could be worse than a return to normality"* (Roy 2020, emphasis added). As a result, the Covid-19 pandemic has provided humanity with two options for the future:

> *We can choose to walk through it, dragging the carcasses of our prejudice and hatred, our avarice... Or we can walk through lightly, with little luggage, ready to imagine another world.*
>
> Roy 2020, emphasis added

Notes

1 www.nytimes.com/interactive/2021/world/covid-vaccinations-tracker.html (accessed July 12, 2021).
2 www.weforum.org/agenda/2020/06/now-is-the-time-for-a-great-reset/ (August 12, 2021).
3 www.pewresearch.org/fact-tank/2019/05/14/more-than-half-of-countries-are-democratic/ (accessed December 14, 2021).
4 www.imf.org/en/Topics/climate-change/energy-subsidies (accessed October 1, 2022).
5 Hansen first testified to Congress about global warming in 1988.
6 www.jfklibrary.org/learn/about-jfk/the-kennedy-family/robert-f-kennedy/robert-f-kennedy-speeches/remarks-at-the-university-of-kansas-march-18-1968 (accessed March 1, 2022).
7 We must recall that although there are different forms of accounting, at base, like the price system, the accounting system is a system of information. What we count and why therefore matters a great deal.
8 For most industries, mark-up is a conventional percentage. However, firms with greater market power may have a higher mark-up than smaller or weaker firms.
9 The metric used to rank the companies consider: assets, market value, sales and profits.
10 https://fred.stlouisfed.org/series/BCNSDODNS (accessed May 1, 2021).

BIBLIOGRAPHY

Abramsky, K. (Ed.). (2010). *Sparking a worldwide energy revolution: Social struggles in the transition to a post-petrol world*. Oakland: AK Press.

ABS (2019), Housing occupancy and costs, 2017–2018, Cat. No. 4130.0. Available at: www.abs.gov.au/statistics/people/housing/housing-occupancy-and-costs/2017-18, (Accessed: 01/01/22).

ABS. (2018). Population projections, Australia. Available at: www.abs.gov.au/statistics/people/population/population-projections-australia/2017-base-2066 (Accessed: 01/01/22).

ABS. (1996). Trade union members Australia, Cat. No. 6325.0. Available at: www.abs.gov.au/ausstats/abs@.nsf/mf/6325.0 (Accessed: 01/01/22).

ABS. (2008). Industrial disputes Australia, Cat. No. 6321.0.55.001. Available at: www.abs.gov.au/AUSSTATS/abs@.nsf/DetailsPage/6321.0.55.001Jun%202008?OpenDocument (Accessed: 01/01/22).

ABS. (2013). Employee earnings, benefits and trade union membership Australia, Cat. No. 6310.0. Available at: www.abs.gov.au/ausstats/abs@.nsf/mf/6310.0 (Accessed: 01/01/22).

ABS. (2020b). Trade union membership, August 2020, Cat. No. 6335.0. Available at: www.abs.gov.au/statistics/labour/earnings-and-work-hours/trade-union-membership/latest-release (Accessed: 01/01/22).

ABS. (2020c). Industrial disputes Australia, Cat. No. 6321.0.55.001. Available at: www.abs.gov.au/statistics/labour/earnings-and-work-hours/industrial-disputes-australia/sep-2020 (Accessed: 01/01/22).

Acharya, A. (2017). After liberal hegemony: The advent of a multiplex world order. *Ethics & International Affairs, 31*(3), 271–285.

Acker, A. (2020). What could *carbofascism* look like? A historical perspective on reactionary politics in the COVID-19 pandemic. *Journal for the History of Environment and Society, 5*, 135–148.

Adkisson, J. (2021). Warren-Nadler consumer bankruptcy reform act portends biggest changes to bankruptcy code since 2005. *Forbes*. Available at: www.forbes.com/sites/jayadkisson/2021/01/27/warren-nadler-consumer-bankruptcy-reform-act-portends-biggest-changes-to-bankruptcy-code-since-2005/ (Accessed: 01/01/22).

Adorno, T. W., & Crook, S. (2007). *The stars down to earth and other essays on the irrational in culture*. London: Routledge.

Agius, C., Rosamond, A. B., & Kinnvall, C. (2020). Populism, ontological insecurity and gendered nationalism: Masculinity, climate denial and Covid-19. *Politics, Religion & Ideology*, *21*(4), 432–450.

Agius, C., Rosamond, A. B., & Kinnvall, C. (2020). Populism, ontological insecurity 16 and gendered nationalism: Masculinity, climate denial and Covid-19. *Politics, 17 Religion & Ideology*, *21*(4), 432–450.

AIHW (Australian Institute of Health and Welfare). (2020). People with disability in Australia 2020: In brief. Available at: www.aihw.gov.au/reports/disability/people-with-disability-in-australia-2020-in-brief/contents/about-people-with-disability-in-australia-2020-in-brief (Accessed: 01/01/22).

AIHW (Australian Institute of Health and Welfare). (2021). Aged care snapshot. Available at: www.aihw.gov.au/reports/australias-welfare/aged-care (Accessed: 01/01/22).

Ajl, M. (2021). *A people's green new deal*. London: Pluto Press.

Alberti, G., Bessa, I., Hardy, K., Trappmann, V., & Umney, C. (2018). In, against and beyond precarity: Work in insecure times. *Work, Employment and Society*, *32*(3), 447–457.

Albertson, B. L. (2015). Dog-whistle politics: Multivocal communication and religious appeals. *Political Behavior*, *37*(1), 3–26.

Albo, G., Gindin, S., & Panitch, L. (2010). *In and out of crisis: The global financial meltdown and left alternatives*. Oakland: PM Press.

Albritton, R. (2009). *Let them eat junk: How capitalism creates hunger and obesity*. Winnipeg: Arbeiter Ring Publishing.

Aldo, Musacchio and Sergio Lazzarini. (2014). *Reinventing State Capitalism*. Harvard University Press.

Alerigi, Alberto and Thais Freitas. (2017). 'Operation Weak Flesh' takes bite out of Brazil's meat exports. *Reuters*. March 24. Available at: www.reuters.com/article/us-brazil-corruption-food-exports/operation-weak-flesh-takes-bite-out-of-brazils-meat-exports-idUSKBN16V281 (Accessed: 05/13/22).

Alexiou, C. (2021). Covid-19, capitalism and political elites: The real threat to humanity. *Human Geography*, Vol. *14*(2): pp. 284–287.

Alfani, G. (2020). Pandemics and inequality: A historical overview. Available at: https://voxeu.org/article/pandemics-and-inequality-historical-overview (Accessed: 01/01/22).

Alfani, G. (2021). Economic inequality in preindustrial times: Europe and beyond. *Journal of Economic Literature*, *59*(1), 3–44.

Alimahomed-Wilson, J., & Reese, E. (Eds.). (2020). *The cost of free shipping: Amazon in the global economy*. London: Pluto Press.

Alperovitz, G., & Daly, L. (2008). *Unjust deserts: How the rich are taking our common inheritance*. New Press: W. W. Norton & Co.

Alston, P. (2018). Report of the special rapporteur on extreme poverty and human rights on his mission to the United States of America. Available at: https://digitallibrary.un.org/record/1629536?ln=en (Accessed: 01/01/22).

Alston, P. (2020). The parlous state of poverty eradication. Report of the Special rapporteur on extreme poverty and human rights. Human Rights Council. Available at: www.ohchr.org/EN/Issues/Poverty/Pages/parlous.aspx (Accessed: 01/01/22).

Altvater, E. (2002). The Growth Obsession. In Leo Panitch and Colin Leys (eds.), *The Socialist Register 2002: A World of Contradictions* (pp. 73–92). London: Merlin Press.

Amir-Aslani, A., & Chanel, M. A. (2016). Innovation through M&A in the biopharmaceutical sector. *Strategic Direction*, *32*(6), 27–29.

Amnesty International. (2020). Brazil: Cattle illegally grazed in the Amazon found in supply chain of leading meat-packer JBS. July 15. Available at: www.amnesty.org/en/latest/news/2020/07/brazil-cattle-illegally-grazed-in-the-amazon-found-in-supply-chain-of-leading-meat-packer-jbs/ (Accessed: 05/13/22).

Amnesty International. (2020, July 15). Brazil: Cattle illegally grazed in the Amazon found in supply chain of leading meat-packer JBS. Available at: www.amnesty.org/en/latest/news/2020/07/brazil-cattle-illegally-grazed-in-the-amazon-found-in-supply-chain-of-leading-meat-packer-jbs/ (Accessed: 01/01/22).

Anderson, E. (2021). *Epistemic bubbles and authoritarian politics in (Eds.) Edenberg, E., & Hannon, M. Political epistemology*. Oxford: Oxford University Press.

Anderson, K. L., Mander, S. L., Bows, A., et al. (2008). The Tyndall decarbonisation scenarios—Part II: Scenarios for a 60% CO2 reduction in the UK. *Energy Policy, 36*(10), 3764–3773.

Anievas, A. (2015). *How the west came to rule: The geopolitical origins of capitalism*. London: Pluto Press.

Anievas, A. and K. Nişancioğlu. (2015). *How the West Came to Rule: The Geopolitical Origins of Capitalism*. London: Pluto Press.

Anievas, A., & Saull, R. (2020). Reassessing the Cold War and the far-right: Fascist legacies and the making of the liberal international order after 1945. *International Studies Review, 22*(3), 370–395.

Anievas, A., Manchanda, N., & Shilliam, R. (Eds.). (2015). *Race and racism in international relations: Confronting the global colour line*. London: Routledge.

Anonymous (2019). McKinsey & Company: Capital's willing executioners. *Current Affairs*. Available at: www.currentaffairs.org/2019/02/mckinsey-company-capitals-willing-executioners (Accessed: 01/01/22).

Anonymous. (2020, July 25). Starting over again. *The Economist*, 13–16.

Appel, H., Mason, A., Watts, M., & Huber, M. T. (Eds.). (2015). *Subterranean estates: Life worlds of oil and gas*. Ithaca: Cornell University Press.

Arbutus Biopharma. (2010). Tekmira awarded up to $140 Million U.S. Government contract to develop RNAi therapeutic against Ebola virus. Available at: https://investor.arbutusbio.com/news-releases/news-release-details/tekmira-awarded-140-million-us-governm ent-contract-develop-rnai (Accessed: 01/01/22).

Arbutus Biopharma. (2020). Investor FAQ. Available at: https://investor.arbutusbio.com/investor-faq (Accessed: 01/01/22).

Ardia, D. S. (2010). Free speech savior or shield for scoundrels: an empirical study of intermediary immunity under section 230 of the communications decency act. *Loyola of Los Angeles Law Review, 43*(2), 373–506.

Arendt, H. (1973). *The origins of totalitarianism*. London: Harcourt Brace.

Ariyarathna, L. and Kariyawasam, K. (2020) 'Pharmaceutical patents and access to generic medicines in developing countries', *European Intellectual Property Review, 42*(2), pp. 108–118.

Arlidge, J. (2009). I'm doing "God's Work". Meet Mr Goldman Sachs. *New York Times*. Available at: https://dealbook.nytimes.com/2009/11/09/goldman-chief-says-he-is-just-doing-gods-work/ (Accessed: 01/01/22).

Arnn, L. P., Swain, C. M., & Spalding, M. (Eds.). (2021). *The 1776 report*. New York: Encounter Books.

Arrighi, G. (1990). The three hegemonies of historical capitalism. *Review* (Fernand Braudel Center), *13*(3), 365–408.

Arrighi, G. (2008). *Adam Smith in Beijing: Lineages of the twenty-first century*. London: Verso.

Assa, J. and Calderon, C. (2020). *Privatization and Pandemic: A cross-country analysis of COVID-19 rates and health-care financing structures*. UNDP.

Astor, M. (2019). Should billionaires exist? Sanders, Warren and Steyer debate it. *New York Times*. Available at: www.nytimes.com/2019/10/15/us/politics/us-billionaires.html?smtyp=cur&smid=fb-nytimes (01/01/2022).

Australian Department of Health. (2021). Coronavirus (COVID-19) case numbers and statistics. Available at: www.health.gov.au/news/health-alerts/novel-coronavirus-2019-ncov-health-alert/coronavirus-covid-19-case-numbers-and-statistics (Accessed: 01/01/22).

Australian Government Labour Market Information Portal. (2018). The labour market for personal care workers in aged and disability care: Australia 2017. Available at: https://lmip.gov.au/default.aspx?LMIP/GainInsights/SpecialTopicReports (Accessed: 01/01/22).

Australian Government Labour Market Information Portal. (2021b). Education and training: Employment characteristics data. Available at: https://lmip.gov.au/default.aspx?LMIP/GainInsights/IndustryInformation/EducationandTraining (Accessed: 01/01/22).

Australian Government Labour Market Information Portal. (2021c). Construction: Employment characteristics data. Available at: https://lmip.gov.au/default.aspx?LMIP/GainInsights/IndustryInformation/Construction (Accessed: 01/01/22).

Babic, M. (2020). Let's talk about the interregnum: Gramsci and the crisis of the liberal world order. *International Affairs*, *96*(3), 767–786.

Baer, B. (2020). Why we need antitrust enforcement during the COVID-19 pandemic. *Brookings*. Available at: www.brookings.edu/blog/techtank/2020/04/22/why-we-need-antitrust-enforcement-during-the-covid-19-pandemic/ (Accessed: 01/01/22).

Bailey, A. (2007) Strategic Ignorance in (Eds.) Sullivan, S., & Tuana, N. *Race and epistemologies of ignorance*. New York: SUNY Press.

Baker, D., J. B. De Long, and P. R. Krugman. (2005). Asset returns and economic growth. *Brookings Papers on Economic Activity*, *1*, 289–330.

Baker, K. and Grant, J. (2019). How will we travel the world in 2050? *Salon*. Available at: www.salon.com/2019/08/16/how-will-we-travel-the-world-in-2050_partner/ (Accessed: 01/01/22).

Bakker, I. (2007). Social reproduction and the constitution of a gendered political economy. *New Political Economy*, *12*(4), 541–556.

Bakker, I., & Gill, S. (2003). *Power, production, and social reproduction: Human in/security in the global political economy*. London: Palgrave Macmillan.

Bakker, I., & Gill, S. (2019). Rethinking power, production, and social reproduction: Toward variegated social reproduction. *Capital & Class*, *43*(4), 503–523.

Bambra, C., Riordan, R., Ford, J., & Matthews, F. (2020). The COVID-19 pandemic and health inequalities. *Journal of Epidemiology and Community Health*, 74(11), jech-2020-214401.

Banking on Climate Chaos (2021). Fossil fuel finance report card 2021. *Rainforest Action Network*. Available at: www.ran.org/wp-content/uploads/2021/03/Banking-on-Climate-Chaos-2021.pdf (Accessed: 01/01/22).

Barbara, V. (2021). The unveiling of Bolsonaro's supervillain plot is weirdly gripping. May 27. *The New York Times*. Available at: www.nytimes.com/2021/05/27/opinion/brazil-covid-inquiry-bolsonaro.html (Accessed: 01/01/22).

Barbara, Vanessa. (2021). The Unveiling of Bolsonaro's Supervillain Plot Is Weirdly Gripping. May 27. *The New York Times*. Opinion. Available at: www.nytimes.com/2021/05/27/opinion/brazil-covid-inquiry-bolsonaro.html. (Accessed: 05/13/22).

Barkawi, T., & Laffey, M. (1999). The imperial peace: Democracy, force and globalization. *European Journal of International Relations*, *5*(4), 403–434.

Barnes, T. (2021). Pathways to precarity: Work, financial insecurity and wage dependency among Australia's retrenched auto workers. *Journal of Sociology*, *57*(2), 443–463.

Barnes, T., & Weller, S. A. (2020). Becoming precarious? Precarious work and life trajectories after retrenchment. *Critical Sociology, 46*(4–5), 527–541.

Barnosky, A. D., Hadly, E. A., Bascompte, J., et al. (2012). Approaching a state shift in Earth's biosphere. *Nature, 486*(7401), 52–58.

Barnum, M. (2020). Asked whether she is using crisis to support private school choice, DeVos says 'Yes, Absolutely.' *Chalkbeat.* Available at: www.chalkbeat.org/2020/5/20/21265527/devos-using-coronavirus-to-boost-private-schools-says-yes-absolutely, accessed November 25, 2021 (Accessed: 01/01/22).

Barro, R. J., & Sala-i-Martin, X. (2004). *Economic growth.* Cambridge: MIT Press.

Barro, R., J. Ursúa, & J. Weng. (2020). The Coronavirus and the great influenza pandemic: Lessons from the "Spanish Flu" for the Coronavirus's potential effects on mortality and economic activity. w26866. Cambridge, MA: National Bureau of Economic Research. Available at: www.nber.org/papers/w26866.pdf, accessed July 13, 2021 (Accessed: 01/01/22).

Basu, K. (2017). The global economy in 2061. *Project Syndicate.* Available at: www.project-syndicate.org/commentary/long-term-global-economic-prospects-by-kaushik-basu-2017-06 (Accessed: 01/01/22).

Baumgartner, F. R., & Jones, B. D. (2009). *Agendas and instability in American politics.* Illinois: The University of Chicago Press.

BBC News (2021) *'Greed' and 'capitalism' helped UK's vaccines success, says PM, BBC News.* Available at: www.bbc.com/news/uk-politics-56504546 (Accessed: 15 October 2021).

Beck, U. (2010). Climate for change, or how to create a green modernity? *Theory, Culture & Society, 27*(2–3), 254–266.

Beder, S. (2000). *Global spin: The corporate assault on environmentalism.* Melbourne: Scribe.

Bell, S. & Henry, J. (2001). Hospitality versus exchange: The limits of monetary economies. *Review of Social Economy. 59*(2), 203–226.

Bell, V. (2015) The state giveth and the state taketh away: Patent rights under the Bayh-Dole act. *Southern California Interdisciplinary Law Journal, 24*, 491–527.

Bello, W. (2020, April 22). The corporate food system is making the corona virus crisis worse. *Foreign Policy in Focus.* Available at: https://fpif.org/the-corporate-food-system-is-making-the-coronavirus-crisis-worse/ (Accessed: 01/01/22).

Belot, H. (2017, February 2). Clean energy subsidies could be used to build new coal power plants, Scott Morrison says. *ABC News.* Available at: www.abc.net.au/news/2017-02-02/clean-energy-money-could-fund-coal-power-stations-morrison-says/8234118 (Accessed: 01/01/22).

Benanav, A. (2019). Automation and the future of work—2. *New Left Review, 12*, 117–146

Benanav, A. (2020). *Automation and the future of work.* London: Verso.

Benatar S. R., Upshur, R., & Gill, S. (2021). Understanding the relationship between ethics, neoliberalism and power as a step towards improving the health of people and our planet. In S. Benatar & G. Brock (Ed.), *Global health: Ethical challenges* (230–241). Cambridge: Cambridge University Press.

Benatar, S. (2016). Politics, power, poverty and global health: Systems and frames. *International Journal of Health Policy and Management, 5*(10), 599–604.

Benatar, S. R. (2002). The HIV/AIDS pandemic: A sign of instability in a complex global system. *The Journal of Medicine and Philosophy, 27*(2), 163–177.

Benatar, S. R., Daar, A. S., & Singer, P. A. (2003). Global health ethics: The rationale for mutual caring. *International Affairs, 79*(1), 107–138.

Benatar, S. R., Sanders, D., & Gill, S. (2018). The global politics of healthcare reform in (Eds.) McInnes, C., Lee, K., & Youde, J. *The Oxford handbook of global health politics* (445–468). Oxford: Oxford University Press.

Beneria, L. (1979). Reproduction, production and the sexual division of labour. *Cambridge Journal of Economics*, Vol. *3*(3), 203–225.

Beneria, L. (1999). Globalization, gender and The Davos Man. *Feminist Economics*, *5*(3), 61–83.

Benson, P., & Kirsch, S. (2010). Capitalism and the politics of resignation. *Current Anthropology*, *51*(4), 459–486.

Bentley, R. W. (2016). *Introduction to peak oil* (1st ed. 2016). New York: Springer.

Berberoglu, B. (Ed.). (2020). *The global rise of authoritarianism in the 21st Century: Crisis of neo-liberal globalization and the nationalist response*. New York: Routledge.

Berkhout, E., Galasso, N., Lawson, M., et al. (2021, January 25). The Inequality Virus. *Oxfam*: London. Available at: https://oxfamilibrary.openrepository.com/bitstream/handle/10546/621149/bp-the-inequality-virus-250121-en.pdf (Accessed: 01/01/22).

Bernstein, A. and R. N. Salas. (2020). Coronavirus and Climate Change. *Harvard T. H. Chan School of Public Health*. Available at: www.hsph.harvard.edu/c-change/subtopics/coronavirus-and-climate-change/ (Accessed: 01/01/22).

Betts, R. A., Collins, M., Hemming, D., et al. (2011). When could global warming reach 4°C? *Philosophical Transactions of the Royal Society A: Mathematical, Physical and Engineering Sciences*, *369*(1934), 67–84.

Betts, R. A., et al. (2011). When could global warming reach 4°C? *Philosophical Transactions of the Royal Society*, *369*, 67–84.

Bhambra, G. K., Medien, K., & Tilley, L. (2020). Theory for a global age: From nativism to neoliberalism and beyond. *Current Sociology*, *68*(2), 137–148.

Bhattacharya, T., & Vogel, L. (Eds.). (2017). *Social reproduction theory: Remapping class, recentering oppression*. London: Pluto Press.

Bhattacharya, T., & Vogel, L. (Eds.). (2017). *Social reproduction theory: Remapping 8 class, recentering oppression*. London: Pluto Press.

Bichler, S., & Nitzan, J. (2007). The Rockefeller Boys. *Science & Society*, *71*(2), 243–250.

Bichler, S., & Nitzan, J. (2018). Arms and oil in the Middle East: A biography of research. *Rethinking Marxism*, *30*(3), 418–440.

Bienkov, A. and T. Colson. (2021, May 26). Boris Johnson wanted to be infected with COVID-19 on live TV to show it's nothing to be scared of, Dominic Cummings says. *Business Insider*. Available at: www.businessinsider.com/boris-johnson-dominic-cummings-covid-infected-on-tv-kung-flu-2021-5 (Accessed: 01/01/22).

Bigby, C., and Beadle-Brown, J. (2018). Improving quality of life outcomes in supported accommodation for people with intellectual disability: What makes a difference? *Journal of Applied Research in Intellectual Disabilities*, *31*(2), e182–e200.

Birch, K. (2015). *We have never been neoliberal: A manifesto for a doomed youth*. London: Zero Books.

Birch, K. (2017). Rethinking *value* in the bio-economy: Finance, assetization, and the management of value. *Science, Technology, & Human Values*, *42*(3), 460–490.

Birch, K. (Ed.). (2020). *Assetization: Turning things into assets in technoscientific capitalism*. Cambridge: The MIT Press.

Birch, K. and Muniesa, F. (eds) (2020) *Assetization: Turning Things into Assets in Technoscientific Capitalism*. United States: Massachusetts Institute of Technology Press.

Birch, K., & Tyfield, D. (2013). Theorizing the bioeconomy: Biovalue, biocapital, bioeconomics or . . . what? *Science, Technology, & Human Values*, *38*(3), 299–327.

Bird, G., E. Pentecost, & T. Willett. (January–March 2021). Modern monetary theory and the policy response to COVID-19. *World Economics*, *22*(1), 31–53.

Blondeel, M., Bradshaw, M. J., Bridge, G., & Kuzemko, C. (2021). The geopolitics of energy system transformation: A review. *Geography Compass*, *15*(7), e12580.

BLS. (2017). *The Economics Daily*, Labor share of output has declined since 1947. Available at: www.bls.gov/opub/ted/2017/labor-share-of-output-has-declined-since-1947.htm (Accessed: 01/01/22).

BLS. (2019). Characteristics of minimum wage workers, 2018. Available at: www.bls.gov/opub/reports/minimum-wage/2018/pdf/home.pdf (Accessed: 01/01/22).

BLS. (2020). Current employment statistics, US Bureau of Labour Statistics. Available at: www.bls.gov/ces/publications/highlights/2020/current-employment-statistics-highlights-09-2020.pdf (Accessed: 01/01/22).

BLS. (2020a). Employment by major industry sector, US Bureau of Labour Statistics. Available at: www.bls.gov/emp/tables/employment-by-major-industry-sector.htm (Accessed: 01/01/22).

BLS. (2021). Labor force statistics from the current population survey, LNS14000000. Available at: https://data.bls.gov/cgi-bin/surveymost?ln (Accessed: 01/01/22).

BLS. (2021a). Labor force statistics from the current population survey, LNS12032194, LNS12000000. Available at: https://data.bls.gov/cgi-bin/surveymost?ln (Accessed: 01/01/22).

BLS. (2021b). Employment cost index (NAICS), CIU1010000000000A. Available at: https://data.bls.gov/cgi-bin/surveymost?ci (Accessed: 01/01/22).

BLS. (2021c). Chained CPI for all urban consumers, U.S. city average (C-CPI-U), SUUR0000SA0. Available at: https://data.bls.gov/cgi-bin/surveymost?su (Accessed: 01/01/22).

Blyth, M, and Sommers, J. (April 2020). COVID-19 and the return of a dangerous idea, austerity. *Brave New Europe*. Available at: https://braveneweurope.com/mark-blyth-jeffrey-sommers-covid-19-and-the-return-of-a-dangerous-idea-austerity (Accessed: 01/01/22).

Blyth, M. (2013). *Austerity: The history of a dangerous idea*. Oxford: Oxford University Press.

Bodley, J. H. (2015). *Victims of progress*. London: Rowman & Littlefield.

Boland, Michael James. (2021). Why Big Pharma had a responsibility to profit from the pandemic. *The Conversation*. Available at: http://theconversation.com/why-big-pharma-had-a-responsibility-to-profit-from-the-pandemic-160826 (Accessed: 01/01/22).

Bonam, D, & A. Smădu. (2021). The long-run effects of pandemics on inflation: Will this time be different? *Economics Letters*, 208, 110065.

Bond, S. (2021). Just 12 People Are Behind Most Vaccine Hoaxes On Social Media, Research Shows. *NPR*. May 14, 2021. Available at: www.npr.org/2021/05/13/996570855/disinformation-dozen-test-facebooks-twitters-ability-to-curb-vaccine-hoaxes (Accessed: 01/01/22).

Bose, K. S., & Sarma, R. H. (1975). Delineation of the intimate details of the backbone conformation of pyridine nucleotide coenzymes in aqueous solution. *Biochemical and Biophysical Research Communications*, 66(4), 1173–1179.

Botsman, R. (2017). *Who can you trust? How technology brought us together and why it might drive us apart*. New York: Public Affairs.

Bottan, N., B. Hoffmann, and D. Vera-Cossio (2020). The unequal impact of the coronavirus pandemic: Evidence from seventeen developing countries. *PLoS ONE 15*(10): e0239797. https://doi.org/10.1371/journal.pone.0239797

Bottan, N., Hoffmann, B., & Vera-Cossio, D. (2020). The unequal impact of the coronavirus pandemic: Evidence from seventeen developing countries. *PLOS ONE, 15*(10), e0239797.

Bourzac, K. (2010, October 4). Tapping the powers of persuasion. MIT Technology Review. Available at: www.technologyreview.com/2010/10/04/200160/tapping-the-powers-of-persuasion/ (Accessed: 01/01/22).

Boxall, H., Morgan, A., Brown, R., & Australian Institute of Criminology. (2020). *The prevalence of domestic violence among women during the COVID-19 pandemic.* Australian Institute of Criminology.

Boxall, M. (2021, March 19). Does the deficit myth apply in a post-Covid world? *Financial Times.*

Bradbury, S. (2020a, May 7). Two JBS Greeley employees say they were fired after staying home sick during coronavirus pandemic. *The Denver Post.* Available at: www.denverpost. com/2020/05/07/coronavirus-jbs-greeley-plant-fired-sick/ (Accessed: 01/01/22).

Bradbury, S. (2020b, July 12). How coronavirus spread through JBS's Greeley beef plant. *The Denver Post.* Available at: www.denverpost.com/2020/07/12/jbs-greeley-coronavirus-investigation/ (Accessed: 01/01/22).

Bradbury, Shelly. (2020a). Two JBS Greeley employees say they were fired after staying home sick during coronavirus pandemic. *The Denver Post.* May 7. Available at: www.den verpost.com/2020/05/07/coronavirus-jbs-greeley-plant-fired-sick/ (Accessed: 05/13/22).

Bradbury, Shelly. (2020b). How coronavirus spread through JBS's Greeley beef plant. *The Denver Post.* July 12. Available at: www.denverpost.com/2020/07/12/jbs-greeley-coro navirus-investigation/. (Accessed: 05/13/22).

Bradley, C. & P. Stumpner. (2021). The impact of COVID-19 on capital markets | McKinsey. Available at: www.mckinsey.com/business-functions/strategy-and-corporate-finance/ our-insights/the-impact-of-covid-19-on-capital-markets-one-year-in (Accessed: 01/01/ 22).

Bradshaw, M., Van de Graaf, T., & Connolly, R. (2019). Preparing for the new oil order? Saudi Arabia and Russia. *Energy Strategy Reviews, 26,* 100374.

Brandt, L. (2020). US renters paid around $4.5 trillion in rent over the past decade—and New York city renters have been leading the list for 15 years in a row. *Business Insider.* Available at: www.businessinsider.com/total-money-spent-on-rent-usa-past-decade-2020-1 (Accessed: 01/01/22).

Brannen, S. & K. Hicks. (2020). We Predicted a Coronavirus Pandemic. Here's What Policymakers Could Have Seen Coming. *Politico.* September 7, 2020. Avaiable at: www. politico.com/news/magazine/2020/03/07/coronavirus-epidemic-prediction-policy-advice-121172 (Accessed: 01/01/22).

Braudel, F. (1981). *The Structures of Everyday Life: The Limits of the Possible. Civilization and Capitalism 15th to 18th Century.* Trans. by Sian Reynolds. London: William Collins Sons & Co Ltd.

Braudel, F. (1982). *Civilization and capitalism, 15th–18th century, vol. II: The wheels of commerce.* London: Collins.

Braudel, F. (1982). *On history.* Illinois: University of Chicago Press.

Brenner, N. (ed.). (2014a) *Implosions-Explosions: Towards A Study of Planetary Urbanization.* Berlin: Deutsche Nationalbibliothek.

Brenner, N., Peck, J., & Theodore, N. (2010). Variegated neoliberalization: Geographies, modalities, pathways. *Global Networks, 10*(2), 182–222.

Brenner, R. (2020). Escalating plunder. *New Left Review,* (123), 5–22.

Brenner, R. (July-August 1977). The origins of capitalist development: A critique of neo-Smithian Marxism. *New Left Review, I*(104), 25–92.

Brewer, J. (1989). *The sinews of power: War, money and the English state, 1688–1783.* London: Unwin Hyman.

British Petroleum. (2020). Energy outlook. Available at: www.bp.com/en/global/corporate/ energy-economics/energy-outlook.html (Accessed: 01/01/22).

British Petroleum. (2021a). Oil. Available at: www.bp.com/en/global/corporate/energy-economics/statistical-review-of-world-energy/oil.html (Accessed: 01/01/22).

Brown, S. (2021). Canada's COVID-19 vaccine fix. *Canadian Foreign Policy Journal, 28*(1), 98–106.

Brown, W. (2015). *Undoing the demos: Neoliberalism's stealth revolution.* Brooklyn: Zone Books.

Brown, Wendy. (2015). *Undoing the Demos: Neoliberalism's Stealth Revolution.* Zone Books.

Brownie, S., Horstmanshof, L., and Garbutt, R. (2014). Factors that impact residents' transition and psychological adjustment to long-term aged care: A systematic literature review. *International Journal of Nursing Studies, 51*(12), 1654–1666.

Buckley, L. (2013). Chinese agriculture development cooperation in Africa: narratives and politics. *IDS Bulletin, 44*(4), 42–52.

Burleigh, N. (2021). How the Covid-19 vaccine injected billions into Big Pharma—and made its executives very rich. *Forbes.* Available at: www.forbes.com/sites/forbesdigitalcov ers/2021/05/14/virus-book-excerpt-nina-burleigh-how-the-covid-19-vaccine-injec ted-billions-into-big-pharma-albert-bourla-moncef-slaoui/ (Accessed: 01/01/22).

Busse, R., Blümel, M., Knieps, F., & Bärnighausen, T. (2017). Statutory health insurance in Germany: A health system shaped by 135 years of solidarity, self-governance, and competition. *The Lancet, 390*(10097), 882–897.

Byanyima, W. (2021, January 29). A global vaccine apartheid is unfolding. People's lives must come before profit. *The Guardian.* www.theguardian.com/global-development/2021/ jan/29/a-global-vaccine-apartheid-is-unfolding-peoples-lives-must-come-before-profit (Accessed: 01/01/22).

Byrnes, A. (2020). 'Human rights unbound: An unrepentant call for a more complete application of human rights in relation to older persons—And beyond', *Australasian Journal on Ageing 39* (2), 91–9

Byrnes, A. (2020). Human rights unbound: An unrepentant call for a more complete application of human rights in relation to older persons—and beyond. *Australasian Journal on Ageing, 39*(2), 91–98.

Cahill, D., & Konings, M. (2017). *Neoliberalism.* London: Polity Press.

Cahill, D., M. Cooper, M. Konnings, D. Primrose. (2018). *The SAGE Handbook of Neoliberalism.* SAGE Publishing: California.

Campanale, M., J. Leggett, & J. Leaton (2011). *Unburnable carbon: Are the world's financial markets carrying a carbon bubble?* London: *Carbon Tracker Initiative.*

Campbell, I., & Price, R. (2016). Precarious work and precarious workers: Towards an improved conceptualisation. *The Economic and Labour Relations Review, 27*(3), 314–332.

Camus, A. (1947). *The Plague.* Knopf: New York.

Canfield, M., Anderson, M. D., & McMichael, P. (2021). UN food systems summit 2021: Dismantling democracy and resetting corporate control of food systems. *Frontiers in Sustainable Food Systems, 5,* 661552.

Capurro, G., Greenberg, J., Dubé, E., et al. (2018). Measles, moral regulation and the social construction of risk: Media narratives of "Anti-Vaxxers" and the 2015 Disneyland outbreak. *Canadian Journal of Sociology, 43*(1), 25–48.

Carbon Inequality Report 2020. (2020). The carbon inequality era: An assessment of the global distribution of consumption emissions among individuals from 1990 to 2015 and beyond. *Oxfam and Stockholm Environment Institute.* Available at: https://policy-practice. oxfam.org/resources/the-carbon-inequality-era-an-assessment-of-the-global-distribut ion-of-consumpti-621049/ (Accessed: 01/01/22).

Carbon Tracker. (2017, August 23). Stranded assets. Available at: www.carbontracker.org/ terms/stranded-assets/ (Accessed: 01/01/22).

Carey, A. (1997). *Taking the risk out of democracy: Corporate propaganda versus freedom and liberty*. Chicago: University of Illinois Press.

Carrington, D. (2021, September 14). 90% of global farm subsidies damage people and planet, says UN. *The Guardian*. Available at: www.theguardian.com/environment/2021/sep/14/global-farm-subsidies-damage-people-planet-un-climate-crisis-nature-inequality (Accessed: 01/01/22).

Carrington, D., Ambrose, J. & Taylor, M. (2020, April 1). Will the coronavirus kill the oil industry and help save the climate? *The Guardian*. Available at: www.theguardian.com/environment/2020/apr/01/the-fossil-fuel-industry-is-broken-will-a-cleaner-climate-be-the-result (Accessed: 01/01/22).

Carroll, W. K. (2010). *The making of a transnational capitalist class: Corporate power in the twenty-first century*. London: Zed Books.

Carson, R. (2021). Billionaires In Space: Privilege Or Progress? *Forbes*. August 17, 2021. Available at: www.forbes.com/sites/rcarson/2021/08/17/billionaires-in-space-privilege-or-progress/?sh=1f6219fa3e36 (Accessed on 01/01/2022).

Casale, M. (2020). COVID-19: Can this crisis be transformative for global health? *Global Public Health*, 15(11), 1740–1752.

Cassidy, J. (2021, September 30). How (not) to tax billionaires. *The New Yorker*. Available at: www.newyorker.com/news/our-columnists/how-not-to-tax-billionaires (Accessed: 01/01/22).

CDC. (2019). Outbreak of *Salmonella* Infections Linked to Ground Beef. Centers for Disease Control and Prevention. *Food Safety Alert*. March 22. Available at: www.cdc.gov/salmonella/newport-10-18/index.html (Accessed: 05/13/22).

CDC. (2019, March 22). Outbreak of Salmonella infections linked to ground beef. Centers for Disease Control and Prevention. Food Safety Alert. Available at: www.cdc.gov/salmonella/newport-10-18/index.html (Accessed: 01/01/22).

CDC. (2021). Centers for Disease Control and Prevention. Available at: www.cdc.gov/coronavirus/2019-ncov/need-extra-precautions/older-adults.html (Accessed: 01/01/22).

Center for Responsive Politics. (2021). Open Secrets: Money to Congress. Agribusiness: Meat processing and products. Available at: www.opensecrets.org/industries/summary.php?cycle=2020&ind=G2300 (Accessed: 05/23/22).

Centers for Disease Control and Prevention. (2020a). CDC SARS response timeline. Available at: www.cdc.gov/about/history/sars/timeline.htm (Accessed: 01/01/22

Centers for Disease Control and Prevention. (2020b). Seasonal flu death estimate increases worldwide. Available at: www.cdc.gov/media/releases/2017/p1213-flu-death-estimate.html (Accessed: 01/01/22).

Centers for Disease Control and Prevention. (2021a). About variants of the virus that causes COVID-19. Available at: www.cdc.gov/coronavirus/2019-ncov/transmission/variant.html (Accessed: 01/01/22).

Chain Reaction. (2017). JBS: Financial Restructuring Could Be Delayed Due to Serious Allegations. *Chain Reaction Research*. Washington, DC. June 28.

Chakrabarty, D. (2017). The politics of climate change is more than the politics of capitalism. *Theory, Culture & Society, 34*(2–3), 25–37.

Chapman, B. (2020, April 21). Could the coronavirus crisis be the beginning of the end for the oil industry. *The Independent*. Available at: www.independent.co.uk/climate-change/news/coronavirus-oil-gas-industry-climate-change-renewable-energy-a9453756.html (Accessed: 01/01/22).

Chotiner, I. (2020, December 18). The influence of the anti-vaccine movement. *The New Yorker*. Available at: www.newyorker.com/news/q-and-a/the-influence-of-the-anti-vaccine-movement (Accessed: 01/01/22).

Christakis, N. A. (2020). *Apollo's arrow: The profound and enduring impact of coronavirus on the way we live*. New York: Little Brown Spark.

Christoff, P. (2013). Climate discourse complexes, national climate regimes and Australian climate policy. *Australian Journal of Politics & History, 59*(3), 349–367.

Christoff, P. (2016, 15 April), Ideas for Australia: A six-point plan for getting climate policy back on track, *The Conversation*.

Christophers, B. (2021). Fossilised capital: Price and profit in the energy transition. *New Political Economy, 27*(1), 1–14.

Christopherson, G. T., & Nesti, L. J. (2011). Stem cell applications in military medicine. *Stem Cell Research & Therapy, 2*(5), 40.

Chung, H., Birkett, H., Forbes, S., & Seo, H. (2021). Covid-19, flexible working, and implications for gender equality in the United Kingdom. *Gender & Society, 35*(2), 218–232.

CIPD. (2021). Coronavirus (Covid-19): Furlough guide. Available at: www.cipd.co.uk/knowledge/fundamentals/emp-law/employees/post-furlough#gref (Accessed: 01/01/22)

Clancy, M. (2020) The case for remote work. Economics Working Paper 2007, Department of Economics, Iowa State University.

Clapp, J. (2021). The problem with growing corporate concentration and power in the global food system. *Nature Food, 2*(6), 404–408.

Clapp, J., & Moseley, W. G. (2020). This food crisis is different: COVID-19 and the fragility of the neoliberal food security order. *The Journal of Peasant Studies, 47*(7), 1393–1417.

Clark, G. (2010). *A farewell to alms: A brief economic history of the world*. New Jersey: Princeton University Press.

Clark, J. (2019). U.S. renters paid $4.5 trillion in rent in the 2010s Zillow research. Available at: www.zillow.com/research/total-rent-paid-2010-2019-26112/ (Accessed: 01/01/22).

Climate Action Tracker. (2021). Temperatures: Addressing global warming. Available at: https://climateactiontracker.org/global/temperatures/ (Accessed: 01/01/22).

Climate Action Tracker. (2021a). Countries: Find your country. Available at: https://climateactiontracker.org/countries/ (Accessed: 01/01/22).

Coburn, D. (2000). Income inequality, social cohesion and the health status of populations: The role of neo-liberalism. *Social Science & Medicine, 51*(1), 135–146.

Collins et al. 2020, *Billionaire Bonanza 2020: Wealth Windfalls, Tumbling Taxes, and Pandemic Profiteers*, Available at: https://ips-dc.org/billionaire-bonanza-2020/ Accessed: 01/01/2022

Collins, C., (2020). *US Billionaire wealth surges past $1 trillion since beginning of pandemic*, Inequality.org. Available at: https://inequality.org/great-divide/u-s-billionaire-wealth-surges-past-1-trillion-since-beginning-of-pandemic/ (Accessed: 01/01/22).

Collins, C., Landivar, L. C., Ruppanner, L., & Scarborough, W. J. (2021). COVID-19 and the gender gap in work hours. *Gender, Work & Organization, 28*(S1), 101–112.

Collins, N. (2018). Stocks more rewarding than lending to governments. *Financial Times*. Available at: www.ft.com/content/afa024b8-3e55-11e8-bcc8-cebcb81f1f90 (Accessed: 01/01/22).

Commons, John R. (1959) *Legal Foundations of Capitalism*. (Madison: University of Wisconsin Press).

Connell, R. (2020). COVID-19/Sociology. *Journal of Sociology, 56*(4), 745–751.

Cooper, P. (2021, October 6). Moderna wants Fed. Cir. help to avoid Covid vaccine patent suits. *Bloomberg Law*. Available at: https://news.bloomberglaw.com/ip-law/moderna-wants-fed-cir-help-to-avoid-covid-vaccine-patent-suits (Accessed: 01/01/22).

Cooper, R. N. (1982). The gold standard: Historical facts and future prospects. *Brookings Papers on Economic Activity*, No. 1, 1–56.

Coriat, B & Weinstein, O. (2012). Patent regimes, firms and the commodification of knowledge. *Socio-Economic Review, 10*(2), 267–292.

Corkery, M. and Yaffe-Bellany, D. (2020). As meat plants stayed open to feed Americans, exports to China surged. *The New York Times*. June 16. Available at: www.nytimes.com/2020/06/16/business/meat-industry-china-pork.html (Accessed: 06/17/20).

Correa, C. M. (2004). Supplying pharmaceuticals to countries without manufacturing capacity: Examining the solution agreed upon by the WTO on 30th August, 2003. *Journal of Generic Medicines: The Business Journal for the Generic Medicines Sector, 1*(2), 105–119.

Cortis, N., and van Toorn, G. (2020). *The disability workforce and COVID-19: initial experiences of the outbreak*. Social Policy Research Centre, UNSW Sydney: http://doi.org/10.26190/5eb0e680cbb04.

Cousins, S. (2020). Experts criticise Australia's aged care failings over COVID-19. *The Lancet, 396*(10259), 1322–1323, doi: 10.1016/S0140-6736(20)32206-6

Cox, R. W. (1987). *Production, power, and world order: Social forces in the making of history*. Columbia: Columbia University Press.

Crane, L. D., R. A. Decker, et al. (2021). Business exit during the COVID-19 pandemic: Non-traditional measures in historical context. *Finance and Economics Discussion Series, 2021*(025), 1–59.

Credit Suisse, (2021), *Global Wealth Report 2021*, Available at: www.credit-suisse.com/about-us/en/reports-research/global-wealth-report.html Accessed: 01/01/2022

Credit Suisse, Research Institute. (2020). *Global Wealth Report 2020*. Zurich: Credit Suisse. Available at: www.credit-suisse.com/media/assets/corporate/docs/about-us/research/publications/global-wealth-report-2020-en.pdf (Accessed on 01/01/2022).

Credit Suisse, Research Institute. (2020). *Global Wealth Report 2020*. Zurich: Credit Suisse. Available at: www.credit-suisse.com/media/assets/corporate/docs/about-us/research/publications/global-wealth-report-2020-en.pdf (Accessed on 01/01/2022).

Credit Suisse, Research Institute. (2020). Global Wealth Report 2020. Zurich: Credit Suisse. Available at: www.credit-suisse.com/media/assets/corporate/docs/about-us/research/publications/global-wealth-report-2020-en.pdf (Accessed on 01/01/2022).

Creswell, J. (2021, October 18). Plant-based food companies face critics: Environmental advocates. *New York Times*. Available at: www.nytimes.com/2021/10/15/business/beyond-meat-impossible-emissions.html?referringSource=articleShare (Accessed: 01/01/22).

Cribb, J. (2011). *The coming famine: The global food crisis and what we can do to avoid it*. Berkely: University of California Press.

Crocker, G. (2020). *Basic income and sovereign money: The alternative to economic crisis and austerity policy*. London: Palgrave Macmillan.

Crossa, Mateo & James M. Cypher. (2020). Essential—and Expendable—Mexican Labor. *Dollars and Sense*. July–August. Available at: www.dollarsandsense.org/archives/2020/0720crossa-cypher.html (Accessed: 05/13/22).

Cullen, D. (2019). Medium- and long-term pressures on the system: the changing demographics and dynamics of aged care. Royal Commission on Aged Care Quality and Safety, Office of the Royal Commission. Available at: https://apo.org.au/node/232991 (Accessed: 01/01/22).

Curnow, S., March, S., & Selvaratnam, N. (2020). Epping Gardens Aged Care coronavirus outbreak led to desperation behind the scenes, records reveal. *ABC News*. Available at: www.abc.net.au/news/2020-08-18/epping-gardens-aged-care-coronavirus-outbreak-in-melbourne/12551524 (Accessed: 01/01/22).

Da Vià, E. (2012). Seed diversity, farmers' rights, and the politics of re-peasantization. *The International Journal of Sociology of Agriculture and Food, 19*, 229–242.

Daggett, C. (2018). Petro-masculinity: Fossil fuels and authoritarian desire. *Millennium: Journal of International Studies*, 47(1), 25–44.

Daggett, C. N. (2019). *The birth of energy: Fossil fuels, thermodynamics, and the politics of work*. Durham: Duke University Press.

Dahl, R. A. (1998). *On Democracy*. New Haven: Yale University Press.

Daley, F. et al. (2021). *The fossil fuelled 5: Comparing rhetoric with reality on fossil fuels and climate change*. Fossil Fuel Non-Proliferation Treaty. Available at: https://fossilfueltreaty.org/fossil-fuel-5 (Accessed: 01/01/22).

Daly, H. E. (1996). *Beyond Growth: The Economics of Sustainable Development*. Boston: Beacon Press.

Davidson, N. *How Revolution were the Bourgeois Revolutions?* Chicago: Haymarket Books.

Davies, G. (2002). *A history of money: From ancient times to the present day*. Cardiff: University of Wales Press.

Davis, M. (2020). *The monster enters: COVID-19, Avian flu and the plagues of capitalism*. New York: OR Books.

Davy, L. (2019). Between an ethic of care and an ethic of autonomy. *Angelaki*, 24(3), 101–114.

Dawson, A. (2016). *Extinction: A radical history*. New York: OR Books.

De Loecker, J., Eeckhout, J., & Unger, G. (2020). The rise of market power and the macroeconomic implications. *The Quarterly Journal of Economics*, 135(2), 561–644.

Dean, J. (2012). Still Dancing: drive as a category of political economy. *International Journal of Žižek Studies*, 6(1), 1–19.

Deangelis, C. D. (2016). Big Pharma profits and the public loses: Big Pharma profits and the public loses. *The Milbank Quarterly*, 94(1), 30–33.

Debtwire. (2018). Batista Family fights to stay atop as scandals deepen. *JBS Shareholder Profile*. March 28. Available at: www.debtwire.com/info/shareholder-profile-batista-family-fights-stay-atop-jbs-scandals-deepen (Accessed: 05/13/22).

Delfanti, A. (2021). Machinic dispossession and augmented despotism: Digital work in an Amazon warehouse. *New Media & Society*, 23(1), 39–55.

Delina, L. L. (2016). *Strategies for Rapid Climate Mitigation: Wartime mobilisation as a model for action*, London: Routledge.

Dell, R., Costa Dias, M., Joyce, R., & Xu, X. (2020). COVID-19 and inequalities⋆. *Fiscal Studies*, 41(2), 291–319.

Deloitte Access Economics. (2020). The value of informal care in 2020. Available at: https://apo.org.au/node/307225 (Accessed: 01/01/22).

Dembicki, Geoff. (2020). Trump Is Bailing Out Big Meat—and Further Screwing the Planet. *The New Republic*. June 1. Available at: https://newrepublic.com/article/157913/trump-bailing-big-meatand-screwing-planet (Accessed: 05/23/22).

Democracy NC. (1995). Hog Money Pollutes NC General Assembly. Democracy North Carolina. July 13. Available at: https://democracync.org/research/july-1995-hog-money-pollutes-nc-general-assembly/ (Accessed: 05/13/22).

Deonandan, K., & Bell, C. (2019). Discipline and punish: Gendered dimensions of violence in extractive development. *Canadian Journal of Women and the Law*, 31(1), 24–57.

Desan, C. (2014). *Making money: Coin, currency, and the coming of capitalism*. Oxford: Oxford University Press.

Di Muzio, T. & L. Noble. (2017). The coming revolution in political economy: money creation, Mankiw and macroeconomics. *Real-world Economics Review*, 80, 85–108.

Di Muzio, T. (2008). *Towards a Genealogy of Militant Liberalism*. Doctoral Thesis. Toronto: York University.

Di Muzio, T. (2011). The crisis of petro-market civilization: The past as prologue? In Stephen Gill (ed.), *Global crises and the crisis of global leadership* (73–88). Cambridge: Cambridge University Press.

Di Muzio, T. (2012). Capitalizing a future unsustainable: Finance, energy and the fate of market civilization. *Review of International Political Economy*, *19*(3), 363–388.

Di Muzio, T. (2014). Toward a genealogy of the new constitutionalism: the empire of liberty and domination. In Claire A. Cutler and Stephen Gill (eds.), *New Constitutionalism and World Order* (pp. 81–94). London UK: Cambridge University Press.

Di Muzio, T. (2015a). *Carbon capitalism: Energy, social reproduction and world order*. London: Rowman & Littlefield.

Di Muzio, T. (2015b). *The 1% and the rest of us: A political economy of dominant ownership*. London: Zed Books.

Di Muzio, T. (2017). *The Tragedy of Human Development: A Genealogy of Capital as Power*. London: Rowman and Littlefield International.

Di Muzio, T., & Dow, M. (2017). Uneven and combined confusion: On the geopolitical origins of capitalism and the rise of the west. *Cambridge Review of International Affairs*, *30*(1), 3–22.

Di Muzio, T., & Robbins, R. (2020). Capitalized money, austerity and the math of capitalism. *Current Sociology*, *68*(2), 149–168.

Di Muzio, T., & Robbins, R. H. (2016). *Debt as power*. Manchester: Manchester University Press.

Di Muzio, T., & Robbins, R. H. (2017). *An anthropology of money: A critical 19 introduction*. London: Routledge.

Di Muzio, T., & Robbins, R. H. (2017). *An anthropology of money: A critical 19 introduction*. London: Routledge.

Di Muzio, T., & Robbins, R. H. (n.d.). *An anthropology of money: A critical introduction*. London: Routledge.

Diamond, D. (2021, January 17) The crash landing of "Operation Warp Speed." *POLITICO*. Available at: www.politico.com/news/2021/01/17/crash-landing-of-operation-warp-speed-459892 (Accessed: 01/01/22).

Dias, F. A., Chance, J., & Buchanan, A. (2020). The motherhood penalty and the fatherhood premium in employment during COVID-19: Evidence from the United States. *Research in Social Stratification and Mobility*, *69*, 100542.

Dickinson H; Smith C, 2021, 'Leadership in integrated care', in *How to Deliver Integrated Care A Guidebook for Managers*, Emerald Group Publishing, pp. 39–58

Dickinson, H., Carey, G., & Kavanagh, A. (2020). Personalisation and pandemic: An unforeseen collision course? *Disability and Society*, *35*(6), 1012–1017.

Dickinson, H., Llewellyn, G. & Kavanagh, A. (2022). In F. Felder, L. Davy & R. Kayess *Disability law and human rights: Theory and policy*. Palgrave Macmillan, pp. 239–262

Dickinson, H., Smith, C., Carey, N. et al. (2021). Exploring governance tensions of disruptive technologies: The case of care robots in Australia and New Zealand. *Policy and Society*, *40*(2), 232–249.

Dickson, P. G. M. (1993). *The financial revolution in England: A study in the development of public credit, 1688–1756*. London: Gregg Revivals.

DiMasi, J. A., & Grabowski, H. G. (2007). The cost of biopharmaceutical R&D: Is biotech different? *Managerial and Decision Economics*, *28*(4–5), 469–479.

DiMuzio, T., & Robbins, R. (2020). Capitalized money, austerity and the math of capitalism. *Current Sociology*, *68*(2), 149–168. https://doi.org/10.1177/0011392119886876

Disterhoft, J. (2021). The net-zero banking alliance's $40B Exxon problem. Available at: www.ran.org/the-understory/the-net-zero-banking-alliances-40-billion-exxon-problem/ (Accessed: 01/01/22).

Do Rosario, J. & P. Gillespie. (2019, December 6). MF critic close to Stiglitz made Argentine economy minister. Bloomberg. Available at: www.bloomberg.com/news/articles/2019-12-06/argentina-s-fernandez-names-martin-guzman-as-economy-minister (Accessed: 01/01/22).

Documenting Covid-19. (2020). Brown Institute for Media Innovation. Columbia University. Available at: https://documentingCovid-19.io/ (Accessed: 08/15/20).

DOD. (2020, July 7). HHS, DOD collaborate with Regeneron on large-scale manufacturing demonstration project of COVID-19 investigational therapeutic treatment. United States Department of Defense. Available at: www.defense.gov/News/Releases/Release/Article/2310882/hhs-dod-collaborate-with-regeneron-on-large-scale-manufacturing-demonstration-p/ (Accessed: 01/01/22).

Donald and Dyke 2021

Dorling, D. (2015). *Injustice: Why social inequality still persists.* London: Policy Press.

Douglas, C. H. (1922) *The control and distribution of production.* London: Cecil Palmer.

Douglas, Leah and Marema, Tim. (2020). When Covid-19 hits a rural meatpacking plant, county infection rates soar to five times the average. Food and Environmental Reporting Network. 28 May. Available at: https://thefern.org/2020/05/when-Covid-19-hits-a-rural-meatpacking-plant-county-infection-rates-soar-to-five-times-the-average/ (Accessed: 07/16/20).

Douglas, Leah. (2020a). Mapping Covid-19 outbreaks in the food system April 22. Food and Environmental Reporting Network. Available at: https://thefern.org/2020/04/mapping-Covid-19-in-meat-and-food-processing-plants/ (Accessed: 02/02/21).

Douglas, Leah. (2020b). Few states release data about Covid-19 in the food system. Food and Environmental Reporting Network. August 17. Available at: https://thefern.org/ag_insider/few-states-release-data-about-Covid-19-in-the-food-system/ (Accessed: 08/25/20).

Douglas, Leah. (2020c). Charting the spread of Covid-19 in the food system. Food and Environmental Reporting Network, May 19. Available at: https://thefern.org/2020/05/charting-the-spread-of-Covid-19-in-the-food-system/ (Accessed: 07/02/20).

Douglas, Leah. (2020d). Covid-19 shows no sign of slowing among food-system workers. Food and Environmental Reporting Network. June 22. Available at: https://thefern.org/2020/06/Covid-19-shows-no-sign-of-slowing-among-food-system-workers/ (Accessed: 07/05/20).

Dow, M. (2019). *Canada's Carbon Capitalism in the Age of Climate Change.* PhD Thesis. Toronto: York University. Available at: http://130.63.180.190/xmlui/handle/10315/38141 (Accessed on 01/01/2022).

DSS (Department of Social Services). (2021). DSS Demographics—March 2021. Available at: https://data.gov.au/data/dataset/dss-payment-demographic-data/resource/e9de2352-c21b-4c5f-bb5b-02020227f1eb (Accessed: 01/01/22).

Du Bois, W. E. B. (1910). The souls of white folk. The Independent.

Du Bois, W. E. B. (1998). *Black reconstruction in America: 1860–1880.* New York: The Free Press.

Dubé, E., & MacDonald, N. (2017). *Vaccine hesitancy.* Oxford: Oxford University Press.

Dubé, E., Laberge, C., Guay, M., Bramadat, P., Roy, R., & Bettinger, J. A. (2013). Vaccine hesitancy: an overview. *Human vaccines & immunotherapeutics, 9*(8), 1763–1773.

Dunlap, R., M. C. J. Stoddart & D. Tindall (eds) (2022), *Handbook of anti-environmentalism.* Cheltenham: Edward Elgar Publishing.

Dwoskin, E. (2020). American might never come back to the office, and Twitter is leading the charge. *Washington Post.* Available at: www.washingtonpost.com/technology/2020/10/01/twitter-work-from-home/ (Accessed: 01/01/22).

Dyke, J. & R. Watson. (2021). Climate scientists: concept of net zero is a dangerous trap. *The Conversation.* Available at: https://theconversation.com/climate-scientists-concept-of-net-zero-is-a-dangerous-trap-157368 (Accessed on 01/01/2022).

Eagleton-Pierce, M. (2019). Neoliberalism. In T. M. Shaw, L. C. Mahrenbach, R. Modi, et al. (eds.), *The Palgrave handbook of contemporary international political economy* (119–134). London: Palgrave Macmillan.

Eccles, B. (2019). Concentration in the asset management industry: Implications For corporate engagement. *Forbes*. Available at: www.forbes.com/sites/bobeccles/2019/04/17/concentration-in-the-asset-management-industry-implications-for-corporate-engagement/ (Accessed: 01/01/22).

Economic Policy Institute. N.D. Nominal Wage Tracker. Economic Policy Institute. Available at: www.epi.org/nominal-wage-tracker/ (Accessed: 01/01/22)

Edenberg, E., & Hannon, M. (2021). *Political epistemology*. Oxford: Oxford University Press.

Eede, C. (2020). Elon Musk throws 9000-person rave at Berlin Tesla Factory. *DJMag*. Available at: https://djmag.com/news/elon-musk-throws-9000-person-rave-berlin-tesla-factory (Accessed: 01/01/22).

Eichengreen, B. & N. Sussman. (2000). The international monetary system in the (very) long run. *IMF Working Paper, 43*, 1–56.

Eichengreen, B. et al. (2019). Public Debt Through the Ages. *IMF*. Working Paper *19*(6), 1–59. Available at: www.imf.org/en/Publications/WP/Issues/2019/01/15/Public-Debt-Through-the-Ages-46503 (Accessed on 01/01/2022).

Eisinger, J., Ernsthausen, J., & Kiel P. (2021, June 8). The Secret IRS files: Trove of never-before-seen records reveal how the wealthiest avoid income tax. *ProPublica*. Available at: www.propublica.org/article/the-secret-irs-files-trove-of-never-before-seen-records-reveal-how-the-wealthiest-avoid-income-tax (Accessed: 01/01/22).

Elias, J., & Rai, S. M. (2019). Feminist everyday political economy: Space, time, and violence. *Review of International Studies, 45*(2), 201–220.

Elliot, J. K. (2019, September 18). When does an 'I love Canadian oil & gas' shirt become political? *Global News*. Available at: https://globalnews.ca/news/5913362/i-love-canadian-oil-and-gas-shirt-political/ (Accessed: 01/01/22).

Ellwanger, J. H., Kulmann-Leal, B., Kaminski, V. L., et al. (2020). Beyond diversity loss and climate change: Impacts of Amazon deforestation on infectious diseases and public health. *Anais Da Academia Brasileira de Ciências, 92*(1), e20191375.

Ellwanger, Joel H., Bruna Kulmann-Leal & Valéria Kaminski, et. al. (2020). Beyond diversity loss and climate change: Impacts of Amazon deforestation on infectious diseases and public health. *Annals of the Brazilian Academy of Sciences. 92*(1): 1–33.

Engelmann, Fabiano. (2020). The 'Fight Against Corruption.' In: Brazil from the 2000s: A Political Crusade Through Judicial Activism. *Journal Of Law and Society*. Volume 47, Issue S1, October. ISSN: 0263-323X, S74–S89.

Ensign R L., & Rubin, R. (2021, July 13). Buy, borrow, die: How rich Americans live off their paper wealth. *Wall Street Journal*. Available at: www.wsj.com/articles/buy-borrow-die-how-rich-americans-live-off-their-paper-wealth-11625909583 (Accessed: 01/01/22).

Epstein, G. (2020). The MMT free lunch mirage can lead to a perverse outcome. *Challenge, 63*(1), 2–13.

Estrada, Rodrigo. (2017). Greenpeace Brazil Suspends Negotiations with Cattle Giant JBS. Greenpeace. March 23. Available at: www.greenpeace.org/usa/news/greenpeace-brazil-suspends-negotiations-cattle-giant-jbs/ (Accessed: 05/13/22).

Exxon Mobil. (2019). Outlook for energy. Available at: https://corporate.exxonmobil.com/-/media/Global/Files/outlook-for-energy/2019-Outlook-for-Energy_v4.pdf (Accessed: 01/01/22).

FAO. (2019). *World food and agriculture statistical pocketbook*. Rome: FAO.

Federal Reserve Bank of St. Louis (2022) Velocity of M2 money stock [M2V], retrieved from FRED, Federal Reserve Bank of St. Louis; https://fred.stlouisfed.org/series/M2V (Accessed: 02/22/2022).

Federici, S. (2004). *Caliban and the witch*. Brooklyn: Autonomedia Press.

Ferguson, N. (2001). *The cash nexus: Money and power in the modern world, 1700–2000*. Basic Books.

Ferguson, T., P. Jorgensen, and J. Chen. (2017). Fifty shades of green: high finance, political money, and the U.S. Congress. Roosevelt Institute. Available at: https://rooseveltinstitute. org/wp-content/uploads/2017/05/FiftyShadesofGreen_0517.pdf (Accessed: 01/01/22).

Ficke, J. R., Obremskey, W. T., Gaines, R. J., et al. (2012). Reprioritization of research for combat casualty care. *Journal of the American Academy of Orthopaedic Surgeons*, 20, S99–S102.

Fine, B. (2013). *Labour market theory: A constructive reassessment*. London: Routledge.

Fioramonti, L. (2013). *Gross domestic problem: The politics behind the world's most powerful number*. London: Zed Books.

Fioramonti, L. (2014). *How Numbers Rule the World: The Use and Abuse of Statistics in Global Politics*. London: Zed Books.

Fioramonti, L. (2017, October 10). Why capitalism wins and how a simple accounting move can defeat it. *The Conversation*. Available at: https://theconversation.com/why-capitalism -wins-and-how-a-simple-accounting-move-can-defeat-it-83821 (Accessed: 01/01/22).

Firozi, P. (2020, February 17). Tom Cotton keeps repeating a coronavirus conspiracy theory that was already debunked. *Washington Post*. Available at: https://web.archive.org/web/ 20210528031737if_/https://www.washingtonpost.com/politics/2020/02/16/tom-cot ton-coronavirus-conspiracy/ (Accessed: 01/01/22).

Fisher, P., and V. Byrne. (2012). Identity, emotion and the internal goods of practice: A study of learning disability professionals. *Sociology of Health & Illness*, 34(1), 79–94.

Fisher, P., and V. Byrne. 2012. "Identity, Emotion and the Internal Goods of Practice: A Study of Learning Disability Professionals." Sociology of Health & Illness *34* (1): 79–94. doi:10.1111/j.1467-9566.2011.01365.x

Fix, B. (2021). How the rich are different: Hierarchical power as the basis of income size and class. *Journal of Computational Social Science*, 4(2), 403–454.

Flaherty, C. (2021, January 21). A push for patriotic education. *Inside Higher Ed*. Available at: www.insidehighered.com/news/2021/01/20/historians-trump-administrations-rep ort-us-history-belongs-trash (Accessed: 01/01/22).

Flannery, M. E. (2020). With pandemic, privatization advocates smell a big opportunity | *NEA*. Available at: www.nea.org/advocating-for-change/new-from-nea/pandemic- privatization-advocates-smell-big-opportunity (Accessed: 01/01/22).

Food Safety News. (2020a). DeLauro challenges USDA officials about JBS corruption in meat industry. February 13. Available at: www.foodsafetynews.com/2020/02/delauro- challenges-usda-officials-about-jbs-corruption-in-meat-industry/. (Accessed: 05/13/22).

Food Safety News. (2020b). JBS, S.A. shareholders agree to sue Joesley and Wesley Batista. November 9. Available at: www.foodsafetynews.com/2020/11/jbs-s-a-shareholders- agree-to-sue-joesley-and-wesley-batista/ (Accessed: 05/23/22).

Forbes, 2021a (April 6), Forbes' 35th Annual World's Billionaires List: Facts And Figures 2021, available at: www.forbes.com/sites/kerryadolan/2021/04/06/forbes-35th-annual-wor lds-billionaires-list-facts-and-figures-2021/?sh=4dcd6d15e587 Accessed: 01/01/22

Forbes. (2018). *Forbes' 32nd Annual World's Billionaires Issue*. Available at: www.forbes.com/ sites/forbespr/2018/03/06/forbes-32nd-annual-worlds-billionaires-issue/?sh=7fac3 44910e0 (Accessed: 01/01/22).

Forbes. (2021). *Forbes worlds billionaire list the richest in 2021*. Available at: www.forbes.com/ billionaires/ (Accessed: 01/01/22).

Forster, T., Kentikelenis, A. E., Stubbs, T. H., & King, L. P. (2020). Globalization and health equity: The impact of structural adjustment programs on developing countries. *Social Science & Medicine, 267*, 112496.

Forster, T., Kentikelenis, A. E., Stubbs, T. H., & King, L. P. (2020). Globalization 10 and health equity: The impact of structural adjustment programs on 11 developing countries. *Social Science & Medicine, 267*, 112496.

Foucault, M. (1995). *Discipline and punish: The birth of the prison*. New York: Vintage Books.

Foucault, M. (2003). *Society Must be Defended*. Lectures at the College de France, 1975–1976. Edited by Mauro Bertani and Alessandro Fontana. Translated by David Macey. New York: Picador.

Foucault, M. (2008). *The Birth of Biopolitics: Lectures at the Collège de France, 1978-1979*. Edited by Michel Senellart. Translated by Graham Burchell. New York: Palgrave MacMillan.

Frank, A. G. (2009). *Capitalism and underdevelopment in Latin America: Historical studies of Chile and Brazil*. New York: Monthly Review Press.

Franta, B. (2021). Weaponizing economics: Big oil, economic consultants, and climate policy delay. *Environmental Politics*, 1–21.

FRBNY-Federal Reserve Bank of New York. (2021). Total household debt climbs in Q2 2021, new extensions of credit hit series highs. Available at: www.newyorkfed.org/new sevents/news/research/2021/20210803 (Accessed: 01/01/22).

Freitas, Jr., Gerson, Tatiana Freitas and Jeff Wilson. (2017). The Dirty family secret behind JBS' $20 billion buying spree. *The Grand Island Independent*. Bloomberg - Washington Post News Service, June 3. Available at: https://theindependent.com/news/dirty-family-sec ret-behind-jbs-20-billion-buying-spree/article_367033a2-48a7-11e7-b6bf-93bbde853 c2d.html (Accessed: 05/13/22).

Fremstad, S., Rho, H.J., Brown, H. (2020). Meatpacking workers are a diverse group who need better protections. Center for Economic and Policy Research. April 29. Available at: https://cepr.net/meatpacking-workers-are-a-diverse-group-who-need-better-prot ections/#:~:text=almost%20one%2dhalf%20(44.4%20percent,and%2022.5%20perc ent%20are%20black) (Accessed: 05/13/22).

Friedlingstein, P., O'Sullivan, M., Jones, M.W., et al. (2020). Global carbon budget 2020. *Earth System Science Data, 12*(4), 3269–3340.

Friedman, Z. (2021, June 27). 46% of stimulus checks were invested in the stock market? *Forbes*. Available at: www.forbes.com/sites/zackfriedman/2021/06/27/46-of-people-invested-their-stimulus-checks-in-the-stock-market/?sh=450a6bd72f01 (accessed 9/11/2021).

Friedrichs, J. (2013). *The future is not what it used to be: Climate change and energy scarcity*. Cambridge: MIT Press.

Frumhoff, P. C., Heede, R., & Oreskes, N. (2015). The climate responsibilities of industrial carbon producers. *Climatic Change, 132*(2), 157–171.

Fthenakis, V. M., Kim, H. C., & Alsema, E. (2008). Emissions from photovoltaic life cycles. *Environmental Science & Technology, 42*(6), 2168–2174.

Gabriel, J. M. (2020). *Medical monopoly: Intellectual property rights and the origins of the modern pharmaceutical industry*. Chicago: The University of Chicago

Gabriel, J.M. (2014) *Medical Monopoly: Intellectual Property Rights and the Origins of the Modern Pharmaceutical Industry*. Chicago: University of Chicago Press.

Garner, S. (2007). *Whiteness: An introduction*. London: Routledge.

Garrett, L. (2020). *The coming plague: Newly emerging diseases in a world out of balance*. New York: Penguin Books.

Garrett, T. A. (2005). 100 years of bankruptcy: Why more Americans than ever are filing. *Federal Reserve Bank of St. Louis*. Available at: www.stlouisfed.org/publications/brid ges/spring-2006/100-years-of-bankruptcy-why-more-americans-than-ever-are-filing (Accessed: 01/01/22).

Garthwaite, J. (2021). Stanford-led research shows carbon emissions have rebounded to near pre-pandemic levels. *Stanford News*. Available at: https://news.stanford.edu/2021/11/03/carbon-emissions-rebound-near-pre-pandemic-levels/ (Accessed: 01/01/22).

Gates, B. & M. F. Gates. (2020, September). COVID-19 a global perspective. 2020 goalkeepers report, *Bill & Melinda Gates Foundation*. Available at: www.gatesfoundation.org/goalkeepers/report/2020-report/#GlobalPerspective (Accessed: 01/01/22).

Gaviria, M., & Kilic, B. (2021). A network analysis of COVID-19 mRNA vaccine patents. *Nature Biotechnology*, *39*(5), 546–548.

Gebrekidan, S. (2020). For Autocrats, and Others, Coronavirus Is a Chance to Grab Even More Power. *The New York Times*. April 14, 2020. Available at: www.nytimes.com/2020/03/30/world/europe/coronavirus-governments-power.html (Accessed: 01/01/22).

Gellert, P. K., & Ciccantell, P. S. (2020). Coal's persistence in the capitalist world-economy. *Sociology of Development*, *6*(2), 194–221.

George, Eric (2019) *Digitalization of society and socio-political issues 1: Digital, communication and culture*. New York: Hoboken: Wiley.

George, S. (1990). *A fate worse than debt*. New York: Grove Press.

George, S. (2010). *Whose crisis, whose future? Towards a greener, fairer, richer world*. London: Polity Press.

Gerber, P. J., Steinfeld, H., Henderson, B., et al. (2013). *Tackling climate change through livestock—A global assessment of emissions and mitigation opportunities*. Rome: FAO.

Gerber, P. J., Steinfeld, H., Henderson, B., et. al. (2013). *Tackling Climate Change through Livestock —A Global Assessment of Emissions and Mitigation Opportunities*. Food and Agriculture Organization. Rome. Available at: www.fao.org/3/i3437e/i3437e.pdf (Accessed: 05/23/22).

Gereffi, G. (2014). Global value chains in a post-Washington consensus world. *Review of International Political Economy*, *21*(1), 9–37.

Gezici, A. (2020). Monopoly everywhere. *Dollars and Sense*. Available at: www.dollarsandsense.org/archives/2020/0120gezici.html (Accessed: 01/01/22).

Gezici, Armağan. (2020). Monopoly Everywhere. *Dollars and Sense*. January/February. Available at: www.dollarsandsense.org/archives/2020/0120gezici.html (Accessed: 05/13/22).

Gilens, M., & Page, B. I. (2014). Testing theories of American politics: Elites, interest groups, and average citizens. *Perspectives on Politics*, *12*(3), 564–581.

Gill, S. (1995). Globalisation, market civilisation, and disciplinary neoliberalism. *Millennium: Journal of International Studies*, *24*(3), 399–423.

Gill, S. (1999). The geopolitics of the Asian crisis. *Monthly Review*, *50*(10), 1.

Gill, S. (2008). *Power and resistance in the new world order*. London: Palgrave Macmillan.

Gill, S. (2014). Market Civilization, New Constitutionalism and World Order. In Claire A. Cutler and Stephen Gill (eds.), *New Constitutionalism and World Order* (pp. 29–42). London UK: Cambridge University Press.

Gill, S. (2019). Global governance "as it was, is and ought to be": A critical reflection. *Global Governance: A Review of Multilateralism and International Organizations*, *25*(3), 371–392.

Gill, S. (Ed.). (2012). *Global crises and the crisis of global leadership*. Cambridge: Cambridge University Press.

Gill, S. R., & Benatar, S. R. (2020). Reflections on the political economy of planetary health. *Review of International Political Economy*, *27*(1), 167–190.

Gill, S. R., & Law, D. (1989). Global hegemony and the structural power of capital. *International Studies Quarterly*, *33*(4), 475–495.

Gill, S., & Benatar, S. (2016a). Global health governance and global power: A critical commentary on the Lancet-University of Oslo Commission Report. *International Journal of Health Services, 46*(2), 346–365.

Gill, S., & Benatar, S. R. (2016b). History, structure and agency in global health governance comment on "Global Health Governance Challenges 2016—Are We Ready?" *International Journal of Health Policy and Management, 6*(4), 237–241.

Gill, S., & Cutler, A.C. (Eds.). (2014). *New constitutionalism and world order*. Cambridge: Cambridge University Press.

Gill, S., Bakker, I., & Wamsley, D. (2021). Morbid symptoms, organic crisis and enclosures of the commons: Global health since the 2008 world economic crisis. In S. Benatar & G. Brock (Ed.), *Global health: Ethical challenges* (242–256). Cambridge: Cambridge University Press.

Gindin, S., & Panitch, L. (2012). *The making of global capitalism: The political economy of American empire*. London: Verso.

Giroux, H. A. (2004). *The terror of neoliberalism*. Aurora: Garamond Press.

Giroux, H. A. (2008). *Against the terror of neoliberalism: politics beyond the age of greed*. Boulder: Paradigm.

Gleckman, H. (2016). Multi-stakeholder governance: A corporate push for a new form of global governance. *State of Power*. Transnational Institute (TNI). Available at: www.tni.org/en/publication/multi-stakeholderism-a-corporate-push-for-a-new-form-of-global-governance (Accessed: 01/01/22).

Global Alliance for Tax Justice. (2020). *$427 billion lost to tax havens every year*. Available at: www.globaltaxjustice.org/en/latest/427-billion-lost-tax-havens-every-year (Accessed: 01/01/22).

Godfray, C., P. Aveyard, & T. Garnett et al. (2018). Meat consumption, health, and the environment. *Science, 361*(6399), 1–8.

Godfray, Charles, Paul Aveyard, and Tara Garnett et. al. (2018). Meat consumption, health, and the environment. *Science*. Vol. *361*, Issue 6399, 1–8. Available at: https://science.sciencemag.org/content/361/6399/eaam5324. (Accessed: 05/13/22).

Goldenberg, M. J. (2021). *Vaccine hesitancy: Public trust, expertise, and the war on science*. Pittsburgh: University of Pittsburgh Press.

Goldin, I., (2021 May 20) COVID-19: how rising inequalities unfolded and why we cannot afford to ignore it, *The Conversation*, https://theconversation.com/covid-19-how-rising-inequalities-unfolded-and-why-we-cannot-afford-to-ignore-it-161132 Accessed: 01/01/22

Gore, E., & LeBaron, G. (2019). Using social reproduction theory to understand unfree labour. *Capital & Class, 43*(4), 561–580.

Gotzsche, P. C. (2012). Big Pharma often commits corporate crime, and this must be stopped. *BMJ, 345*(December 14, 3), e8462–e8462.

Gould, E. (2019). *Wages 2018*. Washington, DC: Economic Policy Institute.

Gowan, P. (1999). *The global gamble: Washington's Faustian bid for world dominance*. London: Verso.

Graeber D. & D. Wengrow. (2021). *Dawn of Everything: A New History of Humanity*. Bristol: Allen Lane.

Graeber, D. (2019). *Bullshit jobs*. New York: Simon & Schuster.

Greaves, W. (2013). Risking rupture: integral accidents and in/security in Canada's bitumen sands. *Journal of Canadian Studies, 47*(3), 169–199.

Green, C., Dickinson, H., Carey, G., and Joyce, A. (2020). Barriers to policy action on social determinants of health for people with disability in Australia. *Disability & Society*, https://doi.org/10.1080/09687599.2020.1815523.

Green, J. A. (2006). *La Vie Campesina: Globalization and the power of peasants*. Halifax: Fernwood Publishing.

Greenaway, T. (2017, November 26). Where corn is king, the stirrings of a renaissance in small grains. *YaleEnvironment360*. Available at: http://e360.yale.edu/features/where-corn-is-king-the-stirrings-of-a-small-grain-renaissance (Accessed: 01/01/22). Available at: www.greenpeace.org/static/planet4-international-stateless/2021/03/77f3941a-0988_gp_pan_mincemeat_v9.95_mixedres.pdf (Accessed: 01/01/22).

Greenpeace. (2021). Making mincemeat of the Pantanal: The markets for beef. *Greenpeace International*.

Greenpeace. (2021). Making Mincemeat of the Pantanal: The Markets for Beef. March 3. Greenpeace International. Amsterdam. Available at: www.greenpeace.org/static/planet4-international-stateless/2021/03/77f3941a-0988_gp_pan_mincemeat_v9.95_mixedres.pdf (Accessed: 05/13/22).

Greenwood, R., and D. Scharfstein. (2013). The growth of finance. *Journal of Economic Perspectives, 27*(2), 3–28.

Grey, M. (1999). Immigrants, migration and worker turnover at the hog pride pork processing plant. *Human Organization, 58*, 16–27.

Grey, Mark. (1999). "Immigrants, migration and worker turnover at the hog pride pork processing plant" *Human Organization* Vol. 58: 16–27.

Gross, M., McGoey, L., (Eds.). (2018). *Routledge international handbook of ignorance studies*. London: Routledge.

Gross, S. (2020). Why are fossil fuels so hard to quit? *Brookings*. Available at: www.brookings.edu/essay/why-are-fossil-fuels-so-hard-to-quit/#:~:text=We%20understand%20to day%20that%20humanity's,climate%20of%20our%20entire%20planet (Accessed: 01/01/22).

Guan, W. (2016). IPRs, public health, and international trade: An international law perspective on the Trips Amendment. *Leiden Journal of International Law, 29*(2), 411–440.

Guida. V. (2020). Small businesses sue wells, JPMorgan, other banks over PPP loans. *Politico*. Available at: www.politico.com/news/2020/04/20/small-business-sue-wells-jpmorgan-197456 (Accessed: 01/01/22).

Gunder-Frank, A. (1967). *Capitalism and Underdevelopment in Latin America: Historical Studies of Chile and Brazil*. New York: Monthly Review Press.

Gunderson, R., & Fyock, C. (2021). The political economy of climate change litigation: Is there a point to suing fossil fuel companies? *New Political Economy*, 1–14.

Hagar, S. (2014). The vast majority of U.S. federal debt is now held by the richest households and largest companies, raising concerns about inequality and power. Available at: http://eprints.lse.ac.uk/58495/1/__lse.ac.uk_storage_LIBRARY_Secondary_libfile_shared_repository_Content_American%20Politics%20and%20Policy_2014_January_blogs.lse.ac.uk-The_vast_majority_of_US_federal_debt_is_now_held_by_the_richest_households_and_largest_companies_rais.pdf (Accessed: 01/01/22).

Hager, S. B. (2021). A requiem for carbon capitalism? Available at: https://sbhager.com/a-requiem-for-carbon-capitalism/?utm_source=rss&utm_medium=rss&utm_campaign=a-requiem-for-carbon-capitalism (Accessed: 01/01/22).

Hall, C. A. S., & Klitgaard, K. A. (2012). *Energy and the wealth of nations*. New York: Springer.

Hall, C. A. S., Lambert, J. G., & Balogh, S. B. (2014). EROI of different fuels and the implications for society. *Energy Policy, 64*, 141–152.

Hallock, J. L., Wu, W., Hall, C. A. S., & Jefferson, M. (2014). Forecasting the limits to the availability and diversity of global conventional oil supply: Validation. *Energy, 64*, 130–153.

Halpern, Rick 2005. Packinghouse unions. *The Electronic Encyclopedia of Chicago*. Chicago Historical Society. Available at: www.encyclopedia.chicagohistory.org/pages/943.html (Accessed: 01/01/22).

Halpern, Rick. (2005). Packinghouse unions. *The Electronic Encyclopedia of Chicago*. Chicago Historical Society. Available at: www.encyclopedia.chicagohistory.org/pages/943.html (Accessed: 09/12/20).

Hamilton, C. (2004). *Growth fetish*. London: Pluto Press.

Hamilton, C. (2007). *Scorcher: The dirty politics of climate change.* Victoria: Black Inc. Agenda.

Hamilton, C. (2021, September 12). What would it take for antivaxxers and climate science deniers to 'wake up'? *The Guardian*. Available at: www.theguardian.com/australia-news/commentisfree/2021/sep/13/what-would-it-take-for-antivaxxers-and-climate-science-deniers-to-wake-up (Accessed: 01/01/22).

Hamilton, J. D. (1983). Oil and the macroeconomy since World War II. *Journal of Political Economy, 91*(2), 228–248.

Hamilton, S. (2020). From survival to revival: How to help small businesses through the Covid-19 crisis: 31. *The Hamilton Project*. Available at: www.brookings.edu/wp-content/uploads/2020/09/PP_Hamilton_Final.pdf (Accessed: 01/01/22).

Hamlin, J. (2021). BlackRock, the world's biggest asset manager, is also the world's strongest asset management brand. *Institutional Investor*. Available at: www.institutionalinvestor.com/article/b1r5jzgktf21t6/BlackRock-the-World-s-Biggest-Asset-Manager-Is-Also-the-World-s-Strongest-Asset-Management-Brand (Accessed: 01/01/22).

Hammond, M. L. (2020). *Epidemics and the modern world.* Toronto: University of Toronto Press.

Handley, E. (2020, August 1). Why are there are more COVID-19 cases in private aged care than the public sector? *ABC News*. Available at: www.abc.net.au/news/2020-08-01/why-more-covid-19-cases-in-private-aged-care-than-public-sector/12503212 (Accessed: 01/01/22).

Haney-López, I. (2015). *Dog whistle politics: How coded racial appeals have reinvented racism and wrecked the middle class*. Oxford: Oxford University Press.

Hanrieder, T. (2020). Priorities, partners, politics: The WHO's mandate beyond the crisis. *Global Governance: A Review of Multilateralism and International Organizations, 26*(4), 534–543.

Hanson, M. (2021). U.S. public education spending statistics: Per pupil + total education data initiative. Available at: https://educationdata.org/public-education-spending-statistics (Accessed: 01/01/22).

Hardoon, D., R. Fuentes-Nieva, S. Ayele. (2016). "An Economy For the 1%: How privilege and power in the economy drive extreme inequality and how this can be stopped", *Oxfam International*: pp. 1–44. Retrieved from: https://oxfamilibrary.openrepository.com/handle/10546/592643.

Harrington, B. (2016). *Capital without borders: Wealth managers and the one percent*. Cambridge: Harvard University Press.

Harrison, T. (2019). Morbid symptoms: Alberta's Yellow Vest Movement. *Canadian Dimension*. Available at: https://canadiandimension.com/articles/view/morbid-symptoms-albertas-yellow-vest-movement (Accessed: 01/01/22).

Harvey, D. (2005). *A brief history of neoliberalism*. Oxford: Oxford University Press.

Harvey, D. (2007). Neoliberalism as creative destruction. *The ANNALS of the American Academy of Political and Social Science, 610*(1), 21–44.

Harvey, D. (2011). *The enigma of capital: And the crises of capitalism*. Oxford: Oxford University Press.

Harvey, D. (2015). *Seventeen Contradictions and the End of Capitalism*. Oxford: Oxford University Press.

Harvey, David. (2005). *A Brief History of Neoliberalism*. Oxford: Oxford University Press.

Harvey, F. (2016). World on track for 3C of warming under current global climate pledges, warns UN. *The Guardian*. Available at: www.theguardian.com/environment/2016/nov/03/world-on-track-for-3c-of-warming-under-current-global-climate-pledges-warns-un (Accessed: 01/01/22).

Harvey, F. (2020). Rebound in carbon emissions expected in 2021 after fall caused by Covid. *The Guardian*. Available at: www.theguardian.com/environment/2020/dec/11/rebound-in-carbon-emissions-expected-in-2021-after-fall-caused-by-covid (Accessed: 01/01/22).

Haunss, S. (2013). *Conflicts in the knowledge society: The contentious politics of intellectual property*. Cambridge: Cambridge University Press.

Heede, R. (2014). Tracing anthropogenic carbon dioxide and methane emissions to fossil fuel and cement producers, 1854–2010. *Climatic Change*, 122, 229–241.

Heggie, J. (2020). Why is America running out of water? *National Geographic*. Available at: www.nationalgeographic.com/science/article/partner-content-americas-looming-water-crisis (Accessed: 01/01/22).

Heilweil, R. (2020, May 12). Why Elon Musk disobeyed government orders and reopened a tesla factory. *Vox*. Available at: www.vox.com/recode/2020/5/12/21255812/elon-musk-tesla-factory-coronavirus-reopening (Accessed: 01/01/22).

Heinberg, R. (2011). *The end of growth: Adapting to our new economic reality*. Gabriola: New Society Publishers.

Helm, D. (2017). *Burn out: The endgame for fossil fuels*. New Haven: Yale University Press.

Helmreich, S. (2008). Species of biocapital. *Science as Culture*, 17(4), 463–478.

Henig, R. M. (2020, April 8). Experts warned of a pandemic decades ago. Why weren't we ready? *National Geographic*. Available at: www.nationalgeographic.com/science/article/experts-warned-pandemic-decades-ago-why-not-ready-for-coronavirus (Accessed: 01/01/22).

Henry, J. (2012). The price of offshore revisited. Tax Justice Network. Available at: www.taxjustice.net/cms/upload/pdf/Price_of_Offshore_Revisited_120722.pdf (Accessed: 01/01/22).

Henry, J. S. (2016). Taxing tax havens: How to respond to the Panama Papers. *Foreign Affairs*, Available at: www.foreignaffairs.com/articles/panama/2016-04-12/taxing-tax-havens (Accessed: 01/01/22).

Hertel-Fernandez, A. (2019), *State capture: How conservative activists, big businesses, and wealthy donors reshaped the American states—and the nation*. New York: Oxford University Press.

Hertwich, E. G. et al. (2015), Integrated life-cycle assessment of electricity-supply scenarios confirms global environmental benefit of low-carbon technologies, *Proceedings of the National Academy of Sciences*, 112(20), 6277–6282.

Hess, D. J., & Renner, M. (2019). Conservative political parties and energy transitions in Europe: Opposition to climate mitigation policies. *Renewable and Sustainable Energy Reviews*, 104, 419–428.

HHS. (2020, May 15). Trump administration announces framework and leadership for "Operation Warp Speed." United States Department of Health and Human Services. Available at: https://public3.pagefreezer.com/browse/HHS.gov/31-12-2020T08:51/https://www.hhs.gov/about/news/2020/05/15/trump-administration-announces-framework-and-leadership-for-operation-warp-speed.html (Accessed: 01/01/22).

Hickel, J., & Kallis, G. (2020). Is green growth possible? *New Political Economy*, 25(4), 469–486.

High Level Panel of Experts on Food Security and Nutrition (HLPE). (2020). *Food security and nutrition. Building a global narrative towards 2030*. Available at: www.fao.org/cfs/cfs-hlpe/en/ (Accessed: 01/01/22).

High Level Panel of Experts on Food Security and Nutrition (HLPE). (2019). *Agroecology and Other Innovative Approaches*. UN Committee on World Food Security.

Hirsch, L. (2021, August 3). After mandate, 91% of Tyson workers are vaccinated. *New York Times*. Available at: www.nytimes.com/2021/09/30/business/tyson-foods-vaccination-mandate-rate.html (Accessed: 01/01/22).

Hirsch, Lauren. (2021). After mandate, 91% of Tyson workers are vaccinated. *New York Times*. September 30. Available at: www.nytimes.com/2021/09/30/business/tyson-foods-vacc ination-mandate-rate.html (Accessed: 05/23/22).

Hodder, A. (2020). New technology, work and employment in the era of COVID-19: Reflecting on legacies of research. *New Technology, Work and Employment*, *35*(3), 262–275.

Holst, J. (2020). Global health—emergence, hegemonic trends and biomedical reductionism. *Globalization and Health*, *16*(1), 42.

Hooijer, G., & King, D. (2021). The racialized pandemic: Wave one of COVID-19 and the reproduction of global north inequalities. *Perspectives on Politics*, 1–21.

Hopewell, K. (2016). *Breaking the WTO: How emerging powers disrupted the neoliberal project*. Stanford: Stanford University Press.

Hopewell, K. (2020). *Clash of Powers: US-China rivalry in global trade governance*. Cambridge: Cambridge University Press.

Hornborg, A. (2012). *Global ecology and unequal exchange: Fetishism in a zero-sum world*. London: Routledge.

Horne, G. (2018). *The apocalypse of settler colonialism: The roots of slavery, white supremacy, and capitalism in seventeenth-century North America and the Caribbean*. New York: Monthly Review Press.

Horne, G. (2020). *The dawning of the apocalypse: The roots of slavery, white supremacy, settler colonialism, and capitalism in the long sixteenth century*. New York: Monthly Review Press.

Horsefield, K. J. (1960) *British monetary experiments, 1650–1710*. (Cambridge: Harvard University Press).

Hswen, Y., Xu, X., Hing, A., Hawkins, et al. (2021). Association of "#covid19" Versus "#chinesevirus" with anti-Asian sentiments on Twitter: March 9–23, 2020. *American Journal of Public Health*, *111*(5), 956–964.

Huber, J. (2017). *Sovereign money: Beyond reserve banking*. London: Palgrave Macmillan.

Hughes, B., McKie, L., Hopkins, D., et al. (2005). Love's labours lost? Feminism, the disabled people's movement and an ethic of care. *Sociology*, *39*(2), 259–275.

Hunt, E. K., & Lautzenheiser, M. (2011). *History of economic thought: A critical perspective*. New York: M.E. Sharpe.

Hunter, B. M., & Murray, S. F. (2019). Deconstructing the financialization of healthcare. *Development and Change*, *50*(5), 1263–1287.

Hylton, W. S. (2012). Broken heartland. The looming collapse of agriculture on the great plains. *Harper's Magazine*. Available at: https://harpers.org/blog/2012/06/from-broken-heartland-the-looming-collapse-of-agriculture-on-the-great-plains/ (Accessed: 01/01/22).

Iacobucci, G. (2021). Covid-19: How will a waiver on vaccine patents affect global supply? *BMJ*, n1182.

IBM. (2020). Retail technology for the evolving consumer landscape, US Retail Index Report. Available at: www.ibm.com/industries/retail (Accessed: 01/01/22)

Ido, V.H.P. (2021) 'The Role of Courts in Implementing TRIPS Flexibilities: Brazilian Supreme Court Rules Automatic Patent Term Extensions Unconstitutional', *The South Centre Policy Brief*, (94), pp. 1–8.

IEA (2021b). Global coal demand surpassed pre-Covid levels in late 2020, underlining the world's emissions challenge. IEA: Paris. Available at: www.iea.org/commentaries/global-coal-demand-surpassed-pre-covid-levels-in-late-2020-underlining-the-world-s-emissions-challenge (Accessed: 01/01/22).

IEA. (2013). *Tracking clean energy progress 2013*. France: Paris.

IEA. (2019). Growing preference for SUVs challenges emissions reductions in passenger car market. Available at: www.iea.org/commentaries/growing-preference-for-suvs-challenges-emissions-reductions-in-passenger-car-market (Accessed: 01/01/22).

IEA. (2021a). Global energy review: CO2 emissions in 2020. IEA: Paris. Available at: www.iea.org/articles/global-energy-review-co2-emissions-in-2020 (accessed on (Accessed: 01/01/22).

IEA. (2021c) Total primary energy supply by fuel, 1971 and 2019. IEA: Paris. Available at: www.iea.org/data-and-statistics/charts/total-primary-energy-supply-by-fuel-1971-and-2019 (Accessed: 01/01/22).

IEA. (2021d). World energy balances: Overview. IEA: Paris. Available at: www.iea.org/reports/world-energy-balances-overview (Accessed: 01/01/22).

Ikenberry, J. G. (2018). The end of liberal international order? *International Affairs*. Vol 94(1): 7–23.

ILO. (2020). The impact of the COVID-19 pandemic on jobs and incomes in G20 economies. International Labour Organisation: Geneva.

IMF Blog. (2019). Corporate tax rates: How low can you go. IMF Blog. Available at: https://blogs.imf.org/2019/07/15/corporate-tax-rates-how-low-can-you-go/ (Accessed: 01/01/22).

IMF. (2018). World economic outlook update, January 2018: Brighter prospects, optimistic markets, challenges ahead. Available at: www.imf.org/en/Publications/WEO/Issues/2018/01/11/world-economic-outlook-update-january-201 (Accessed: 01/01/22).

IMF. (2020). World economic outlook update, June 2020: A crisis like no other, An uncertain recovery. Available at: www.imf.org/en/Publications/WEO/Issues/2020/06/24/WEOUpdateJune2020 (Accessed: 01/01/22).

Institute of International Finance. (2021). Global debt monitor: COVID drives debt surge—stabilization ahead? Available at: www.iif.com/Research/Capital-Flows-and-Debt/Global-Debt-Monitor (Accessed: 01/01/22).

International Assessment of Agricultural Science and Technology for Development (IAASTD). (2008). Executive summary of the synthesis report. Available at: www.agassessment.org/docs/ SR_Exec_Sum_280508_English.pdf (Accessed: 01/01/22).

International Panel of Experts on Sustainable Food Systems (IPES-Food). (2020). Available at: The added value(s) of agroecology. Unlocking the potential for transition in West Africa. www.ipes-food.orgn (Accessed: 01/01/22).

International Panel of Experts on Sustainable Food Systems (IPES-Food), & ETC Group. (2021). The long food movement. Transforming food systems by 2045. Available at: www.ipes-food.org (Accessed: 01/01/22).

IPCC. (2007). *IPCC fourth assessment report: Climate change 2007—synthesis report*. Cambridge: Cambridge University Press.

IPCC. (2018). Summary for Policymakers. In: Climate Change 2014: Mitigation of Climate Change. Contribution of Working Group III to the Eighth Assessment Report of the Intergovernmental Panel on Climate Change: pp. 1–32. Cambridge UK: Cambridge University Press.

IPCC. (2021) *Climate change 2021: The physical science basis. Contribution of working group I to the sixth assessment report of the Intergovernmental Panel on Climate Change*. Cambridge: Cambridge University Press.

Jackson, T. (2009). *Prosperity without Growth: Economics for a Finite Planet*. London: Earthscan.

Jacobs, N. (2021, April 7). Six months to prevent a hostile takeover of food systems, and 25 years to transform them. *Common Dreams*. Available at: www.commondreams.org/views/2021/04/07/six-months-prevent-hostile-takeover-food-systems-and-25-years-transform-them (Accessed: 01/01/22).

Jacobson, M. Z., Delucchi, M. A., Bauer, Z. A. F., et al. (2017). 100% clean and renewable wind, water, and sunlight all-sector energy roadmaps for 139 countries of the world. *Joule*, *1*(1), 108–121.

Jacques, P. J., R. E. Dunlap & M. Freeman. (2008). The organisation of denial: Conservative think tanks and environmental scepticism. *Environmental Politics*, *17*(3), 349–385.

Jagoda, N. (2021). Republicans focus tax hike opposition on capital gains change. Text. *The Hill*. Available at: https://thehill.com/policy/finance/564639-republicans-focus-tax-hike-opposition-on-capital-gains-change (Accessed: 01/01/22).

Jahn, B. (2013). *Liberal internationalism: Theory, history, practice*. Basingstoke: Palgrave MacMillan.

James, C. D., Hanson, K., McPake, B., et al. (2006). To retain or remove user fees?: Reflections on the current debate in low- and middle-income countries. *Applied Health Economics and Health Policy*, *5*(3), 137–153.

Jay, J., Bor, J., Nsoesie, E.O. *et al.* Neighbourhood income and physical distancing during the COVID-19 pandemic in the United States. *Nature Human Behaviour*, Vol. 4: pp. 1294–1302.

Jerving, S., K. Jennings, M. M. Hirsch & S. Rust. (2015, October 9). What Exxon knew about earth's melting Arctic. *LA Times*. Available at: http://graphics.latimes.com/exxon-arctic/ (Accessed: 01/01/22).

Jetten, J., Mols, F., & Selvanathan, H. P. (2020). How economic inequality fuels the rise and persistence of the Yellow Vest Movement. *International Review of Social Psychology*, *33*(1), 2.

Jin, Y., Iles, I. A., Austin, L., Liu, B., & Hancock, G. R. (2020). The Infectious Disease Threat (IDT) appraisal model: How perceptions of IDT predictability and controllability predict individuals' responses to risks. *International Journal of Strategic Communication*, *14*(4), 246–271.

Johns Hopkins University of Medicine. COVID-19 Dashboard by the Center for Systems Science and Engineering (CSSE) at Johns Hopkins University (JHU). Available at: https://coronavirus.jhu.edu/map.html (Accessed: 01/01/22).

Johnstone, P., A. Stirling & B. Sovacool. (2017). Policy mixes for incumbency: Exploring the destructive recreation of renewable energy, shale gas "fracking" and nuclear power in the United Kingdom. *Energy Research and Social Science*, *33*, 147–162.

Jones, C. et al. (2017). An approach to prospective consequential life cycle assessment and net energy analysis of distributed electricity generation. *Energy Policy*, *100*, 350–358.

Jones, M. (2021, February 17). COVID response drives $24 trillion surge in global debt: IIF. *Reuters*. Available at: www.reuters.com/article/us-global-debt-iif-idUSKBN2AH285 (Accessed: 01/01/22).

Jordà, Ò., K. Knoll, D. Kuvshinov, M., et al. (2019). The rate of return on everything, 1870–2015. *Quarterly Journal of Economics 134*, 1225–1298.

Jordà, Ò., S. R. Singh, and A. M. Taylor. (2020). Longer-run economic consequences of pandemics. Working Paper, 26934. Working Paper Series. National Bureau of Economic Research. Available at: www.nber.org/papers/w26934 (Accessed: 01/01/22).

Kalb, Don. (2018). Challenges to the European State: The deep play of finance, demos and ethnos in the new old Europe. In B. Kapferer (Ed.), *State, Resistance, Transformation: Anthropological Perspectives on the Dynamics of Power in Contemporary Global Realities*. Herefordshire, UK: Sean Kingston Publishing, 23–65.

Kalleberg, A. L. (2018). *Precarious lives: Job insecurity and well-being in rich democracies*. London: Polity Press.

Kanao, H., & N. Bisenov. (2017, November 30). China's Belt and Road sparks battle of the breadbaskets. *Nikkei Asian Review*. Available at: https://asia.nikkei.com/Spotlight/Asia-Insight/China-s-Belt-and- Road-sparks-a-battle-of-the-breadbaskets (Accessed: 01/01/22).

Kang, H.Y. (2020) 'Patents as Assets: Intellectual Property Rights as Market Subjects and Objects', in Birch, K. and Muniesa, F. (eds) *Assetization: Turning Things into Assets in Technoscientific Capitalism*. Massachusetts Institute of Technology Press, pp. 45–74.

Kang, H.Y. (2021) *Patent Capital in the Covid-19 Pandemic: Critical Intellectual Property Law, Critical Legal Thinking*. Available at: https://criticallegalthinking.com/2021/02/09/patent-capital-in-the-covid-...1 (Accessed: 10/11/2021).

Kang,C & McCabe D (2020) Oct 6, House Lawmakers Condemn Big Tech's 'Monopoly Power' and Urge Their Breakups, *The New York Times*, available at: www.nytimes.com/2020/10/06/technology/congress-big-tech-monopoly-power.html (Accessed 01/01/2022)

Kapferer, B. (2004). Old permutations, new formations? war, state, and global transgression. *Social Analysis*, 48(1), 64–72.

Kapferer, Bruce. (2004). Old Permutations, New Formations? War, State, and Global Transgression. *Social Analysis, 48*(1): 64–72.

Kapferer, Bruce. (2018). Introduction: Crises of the power and the state in global realities. In B. Kapferer (Ed.), *State, Resistance, Transformation: Anthropological Perspectives on the Dynamics of Power in Contemporary Global Realities*. Herefordshire, UK: Sean Kingston Publishing, 1–12.

Kapur, R. (2020). *Gender, alterity and human rights: Freedom in a fishbowl*. Cheltenham: Edward Elgar Publishing.

Kavanagh, A., Dickinson, H., Carey, G., Llewellyn, G., Emerson, E., Disney, G., & Hatton, C. (2021). Improving health care for disabled people in COVID-19 and beyond: Lessons from Australia and England. *Disability and Health Journal, 14*(2), 101050.

Kavanagh, A., Dimov, S., Shields, M., McAllister, A., Dickinson, H., Kavenagh, M. (2020). Disability support workers: the forgotten workforce during COVID-19. University of Melbourne. Available at https://apo.org.au/node/307257

Kellogg, K. C.,Valentine, M. A., & Christin, A. (2020). Algorithms at work: The new contested terrain of control. *Academy of Management Annals, 14*(1), 366–410.

Kelton, S. (2020). *The deficit myth: Modern monetary theory and the birth of the people's economy*. New York Public Affairs.

Kempf, H. (2008). *How the rich are destroying the Earth*. New York: Green Books.

Kempf, H., & Kempf, H. (2008). *How the rich are destroying the Earth*. New York: Green Books.

Kenner, D. (2020). *Carbon inequality: The role of the richest in climate change*. London: Routledge.

Kenner, D., & Heede, R. (2021). White knights, or horsemen of the apocalypse? Prospects for Big Oil to align emissions with a 1.5 °C pathway. *Energy Research & Social Science, 79*, 102049.

Kentikelenis, A., Karanikolos, M., Reeves, A., McKee, M., & Stuckler, D. (2014). Greece's health crisis: From austerity to denialism. *The Lancet, 383*(9918), 748–753.

Khadse, A., & Rosset, P. M. (2019). Zero budget natural farming in India—from inception to institutionalization. *Agroecology and Sustainable Food Systems, 43*(7–8), 848–871.

Khalili, L. (2020). *Sinews of war and trade: Shipping and capitalism in the Arabian Peninsula*. London: Verso.

Kiersz, A. (2021, May 6). A judge ordered Tesla to turn over documents related to Elon Musk's $55 Billion compensation plan. Here's how the elaborate pay agreement works. *Business Insider.* Available at: www.businessinsider.com/elon-musk-tesla-compensation-package-tranches-explainer (Accessed: 01/01/22).

Kim, J. H., P. Hotez, C. Batista, et al. (2021). Operation Warp Speed: Implications for Global Vaccine Security. *The Lancet Global Health 9*(7). Elsevier: e1017–e1021.

Kindy, K. (2019, November 7). This foreign meat company got U.S. tax money. Now it wants to conquer America. *Washington Post.* Available at: www.washingtonpost.com/politics/this-foreign-meat-company-got-us-tax-money-now-it-wants-to-conquer-america/2019/11/04/854836ae-eae5-11e9-9306-47cb0324fd44_story.html (Accessed: 01/01/22).

Kindy, Kimberly. (2019). This foreign meat company got U.S. tax money. Now it wants to conquer America. *Washington Post.* November 7. Available at: www.washingtonpost.com/politics/this-foreign-meat-company-got-us-tax-money-now-it-wants-to-conquer-america/2019/11/04/854836ae-eae5-11e9-9306-47cb0324fd44_story.html. (Accessed: 05/13/22).

Kipfer, S. (2019). What colour is your vest? Reflections on the Yellow Vest Movement in France. *Studies in Political Economy, 100*(3), 209–231.

Kirigia, J. M., Nganda, B. M., Mwikisa, C. N., & Cardoso, B. (2011). Effects of global financial crisis on funding for health development in nineteen ountries of the WHO African Region. *BMC International Health and Human Rights, 11*(1), 4.

Kirkham, C. (2021, February 18). Exclusive: Most U.S. firms hit with COVID-19 safety fines aren't paying up. Available at: www.reuters.com/article/us-health-coronavirus-workplace-fines-ex/exclusive-most-u-s-firms-hit-with-covid-19-safety-fines-arent-paying-up-idUSKBN2AI1JT (Accessed: 01/01/22).

Kirkham, Chris. (2021). Exclusive: Most U.S. firms hit with COVID-19 safety fines aren't paying up February 18. *Reuters.* Available at: www.reuters.com/article/us-health-coronavirus-workplace-fines-ex/exclusive-most-u-s-firms-hit-with-covid-19-safety-fines-arent-paying-up-idUSKBN2AI1JT (Accessed: 05/13/22).

Klare, M. T. (2009). *Rising powers, shrinking planet: The new geopolitics of energy.* New York: Holt.

Klein, N. (2017, July 6). How power profits from disaster. *The Guardian.* Available at: www.theguardian.com/us-news/2017/jul/06/naomi-klein-how-power-profits-from-disaster (Accessed: 01/01/22).

Klein, N. (2019). *On fire: The (burning) case for a green new deal.* New York: Simon & Schuster.

Kochhar, R. (2021). The pandemic stalls growth in the global middle class, pushes poverty up sharply. *Pew Research Center.* Available at: www.pewresearch.org/global/2021/03/18/the-pandemic-stalls-growth-in-the-global-middle-class-pushes-poverty-up-sharply/ (Accessed: 01/01/22).

Kolbert, E. (2015). *The Sixth Extinction: An Unnatural History.* New York: Picador Books.

Koons, C., Chen, C. and Langreth, R. (2014) *Ebola Drug by Tekmira May Be Used on Infected Patients, Bloomberg.* Available at: www.bloomberg.com/news/articles/2014-08-07/ebola-drug-by-tekmira-may-be-used-on-infected-patients-fda-says (Accessed: 9/12/20).

Koons, C., Chen, C. and Langreth, R. (2014) *Ebola Drug by Tekmira May Be Used on Infected Patients, Bloomberg.* Available at: www.bloomberg.com/news/articles/2014-08-07/ebola-drug-by-tekmira-may-be-used-on-infected-patients-fda-says (Accessed: 9/12/20).

Kose, M. Ayhan, Peter Nagle, Franziska Ohnsorge, et al. (2020). *Global waves of debt: Causes and consequences.* Washington, DC: World Bank.

Kraus, M. W., Brown, X., & Swoboda, H. (2019). Dog whistle mascots: Native American mascots as normative expressions of prejudice. *Journal of Experimental Social Psychology, 84*, 103810.

Krier, D. (2009). Speculative profit fetishism in the age of finance capital. *Critical Sociology*, *35*(5), 657–675.

Krugman, P. (2021, April 16). Opinion | Krugman wonks out: The case for supercore inflation. *The New York Times*. Available at: www.nytimes.com/2021/04/16/opinion/econ omy-inflation-retail-sales.html (Accessed: 01/01/22).

Kuter, B. J., Offit, P. A., & Poland, G. A. (2021). The development of COVID-19 vaccines in the United States: Why and how so fast? *Vaccine*, *39*(18), 2491–2495.

Kuzemko, C., Bradshaw, M., Bridge, G., Goldthau, A., Jewell, J., Overland, I., Scholten, D., Van de Graaf, T., & Westphal, K. (2020). Covid-19 and the politics of sustainable energy transitions. *Energy Research & Social Science*, *68*, 101685.

Kuzemko, C., Lawrence, A., & Watson, M. (2019). New directions in the international political economy of energy. *Review of International Political Economy*, *26*(1), 1–24.

Kwarteng, K. (2014). *War and gold: A 500-year history of empires, adventures, and debt.* New York: PublicAffairs.

Labonté, R., Johri, M., Plamondon, K., & Murthy, S. (2021). Canada, global vaccine supply, and the TRIPS waiver: Le Canada, l'offre mondiale de vaccins et l'exemption ADPIC. *Canadian Journal of Public Health*, *112*(4), 543–547.

Labour market insights (2021a; 2021b; 2021c); Labour Market Information Portal (2018).

Labour market insights. 2021a. Retail Trade: Overview. Available at: https://labourmarketi nsights.gov.au/industries/industry-details?industryCode=G (Accessed 22/5/22)

Labour market insights. 2021b. Education and Training: Overview. Available at: https://labou rmarketinsights.gov.au/industries/industry-details?industryCode=P (Accessed 22/5/22)

Labour market insights. 2021c. Construction: Overview. Available at: https://labourmarketi nsights.gov.au/industries/industry-details?industryCode=E (Accessed 22/5/22)

Lakoff, A. (2017). *Unprepared: Global health in a time of emergency.* Berkely: University of California Press.

Lancet Commission Task Force Members. (2021). Operation Warp Speed: implications for global vaccine security. *The Lancet Global Health*, 9(7), e1017–e2021.

Langley, P., Bridge, G., Bulkeley, H., & van Veelen, B. (2021). Decarbonizing capital: Investment, divestment and the qualification of carbon assets. *Economy and Society*, *50*(3), 494–516.

Langlois, S. (2020). The coronavirus has given investors a 'Once-in-a-Lifetime Opportunity,' says hedge-fund billionaire, *MarketWatch*. Available at: www.marketwatch.com/story/the-coronavirus-has-given-investors-a-once-in-a-lifetime-opportunity-says-hedge-fund-bill ionaire-2020-07-08 (Accessed: 01/01/22).

Le Fanu, J. (2014). *The rise & fall of modern medicine.* Toronto: Abacus.

Le Quéré, C., Jackson, R. B., Jones, M. W. *et al.* (2020). Temporary reduction in daily global CO_2 emissions during the COVID-19 forced confinement. *Natural Climate Change*, *10*, 647–653.

Lee, E. K., & Parolin, Z. (2021). The care burden during COVID-19: A national database of child care closures in the United States. *Socius: Sociological Research for a Dynamic World*, 7, 237802312110320.

Lenton, T. M. (2011). Beyond 2°C: Redefining dangerous climate change for physical systems. *Wiley Interdisciplinary Reviews: Climate Change*, *2*(3), 451–461.

Levidow, L. (2015). European transitions towards a corporate-environmental food regime: Agroecological incorporation or contestation? *Journal of Rural Studies*, *40*, 76–89.

Levitsky, S. & D. Ziblatt. (2018). *How democracies die: What history reveals about our future.* New York: Viking.

Lewchuk, W., Clarke, M., & de Wolff, A. (2008). Working without commitments: Precarious employment and health. *Work, Employment and Society*, *22*(3), 387–406.

Lindsey, B. & S. M. Teles. (2017). *The captured economy: How the powerful become richer, slow down growth, and increase inequality.* New York: Oxford University Press.

Lonas, L. (2021, October 6). Moderna founders crack Forbes list for wealthiest people in US. *The Hill.* Available at: https://thehill.com/policy/healthcare/575582-moderna-founders-crack-forbes-list-for-wealthiest-people-in-us (Accessed: 01/01/22).

Londoño, E. (2021, December 26). Brazil is famous for its meat. But vegetarianism is soaring. *New York Times.* Available at: www.nytimes.com/2020/12/26/world/americas/brazil-vegetarian.html (Accessed: 01/01/22).

Londoño, Ernesto. (2021). Brazil Is Famous for Its Meat. But Vegetarianism Is Soaring. *The New York Times.* December 26. Available at: www.nytimes.com/2020/12/26/world/americas/brazil-vegetarian.html (Accessed: 05/13/22).

Long, H., A. Van Dam, A. Fowers, and L. Shapiro. (Sept. 30, 2020). The covid-19 recession is the most unequal in modern U.S. history. *Washington Post.* Available at: www.washingtonpost.com/graphics/2020/business/coronavirus-recession-equality/ (Accessed: 01/01/22).

Losurdo, D. (2011). *Liberalism: A Counter-History.* London: Verso.

Losurdo, D., & Elliott, G. (2014). *Liberalism: A counter-history.* London: Verso.

Lucas, A. (2020). Risking the Earth Part 1: Reassessing dangerous anthropogenic interference and climate risk in IPCC processes. *Climate Risk Management,* 31, 100257.

Lucas, A. (2020a). Risking the Earth Part 2: Power politics and structural reform of the IPCC and UNFCCC. *Climate Risk Management,* 31, 100260.

Lucas, A. (2021). Investigating networks of corporate influence on government decision-making: The case of Australia's climate change and energy policies. *Energy Research and Social Science,* 81, xx.

Lucas, A. (2022). Fossil networks and dirty power: The politics of decarbonisation in Australia. In R. Dunlap, M. C. J. Stoddart and D. Tindall (Eds), *Handbook of anti-environmentalism* (xx–xx). Cheltenham: Edward Elgar Publishing.

Luscome, R. (2020, March 28). Billionaire David Geffen criticized for tone-deaf self-isolation post. *The Guardian.* Available at: www.theguardian.com/us-news/2020/mar/28/billionaire-david-geffen-isolation-coronavirus (Accessed: 01/01/22).

Luxton, M., & Bezanson, K. (Eds.). (2006). *Social reproduction: Feminist political economy challenges neo-liberalism.* Montreal: McGill-Queen's University Press.

Macfarlane, L. (2021, January 7). Why 2021 is humanity's make-or-break moment on climate breakdown. *Open Democracy.* Available at: www.opendemocracy.net/en/oureconomy/why-2021-is-humanitys-make-or-break-moment-on-climate-breakdown/ (Accessed: 01/01/22).

MacLean, N. (2017). *Democracy in chains: The deep history of the radical right's stealth plan for America.* New York: Viking.

Macpherson, C.B. (1962). *The Political Theory of Possessive Individualism: Hobbes to Locke.* Oxford: Oxford University Press.

Madeley, J. (2000). *Hungry for trade: How the poor pay for free trade.* London: Zed Books.

Mahler, D. G. et al. (2021). Updated estimates of the impact of COVID-19 on global poverty. *World Bank.* Available at: https://blogs.worldbank.org/opendata/updated-estimates-impact-covid-19-global-poverty-turning-corner-pandemic-2021#:~:text=We%20find%20that%20the%20pandemic,the%20course%20of%20the%20pandemic) (Accessed on 01/01/2022).

Makin, T. & G. Tunny. (2021). The MMT hoax. The center for independent studies. *Policy Paper,* 41, 1–10.

Malbon, E., Carey, G., & Meltzer, A. (2019). Personalisation schemes in social care: Are they growing social and health inequalities? *BMC Public Health,* 19(1), 805.

Mallapaty S. How sewage could reveal true scale of coronavirus outbreak. *Nature.* Apr 2020;*580*(7802):176–177. doi: 10.1038/d41586-020-00973-x PMID: 32246117.

Malm, A. (2016). *Fossil capital:The rise of steam-power and the roots of global warming.* London:Verso.

Malm, A. (2021). *White skin, black fuel: On the danger of fossil fascism.* London:Verso.

Malthus, T. (1798)[1998]. An Essay on the Principle of Population. London: J. Johnson, in St. Paul's Church-Yard.

Malthus, T. (1798)[1998]. An Essay on the Principle of Population. London: J. Johnson, in St. Paul's Church-Yard.

Malthus, T. R. (1992). *An essay on the principle of population.* Cambridge: Cambridge University Press.

Mann, M. (1993)[2012]. *The Sources of Social Paper. The rise of classes and nation-states, 1760–1914.* Volume 2. Cambridge UK: Cambridge University Press.

Mann, M. (2004). *The Dark side of Democracy:Explaining Ethnic Cleansing.* Cambridge:Cambridge University Press.

Mann, M. E. (2021). *The new climate war:The fight to take back our planet.* New York: Public Affairs.

Mano, A. (2020a, August 14). Update: 1-Brazil's JBS resumes U.S. share listing plan after COVID-19 fallout, CEO says. *Reuters.* Available at: www.reuters.com/article/jbs-outl ook/update-1-brazils-jbs-resumes-u-s-share-listing-plan-after-covid-19-fallout-ceo-says-idUSL1N2FG0L2 (Accessed: 01/01/22).

Mano, A. (2020b, September 8). Special report: How Covid-19 swept the Brazilian slaughterhouses of JBS, world's top meatpacker. *Reuters.* Available at: www.reuters. com/article/us-health-coronavirus-jbs-specialreport/special-report-how-covid-19-swept-the-brazilian-slaughterhouses-of-jbs-worlds-top-meatpacker-iduskbn25z1hz (Accessed: 01/01/22).

Mano, A. (2021, March 19). JBS ordered to pay $3.6 million after Brazil beef plant's COVID outbreak. *Reuters.* Available at: www.reuters.com/article/us-jbs-covid-payment/jbs-orde red-to-pay-3-6-million-after-brazil-beef-plants-covid-outbreak-idUSKBN2BB1XB (Accessed: 01/01/22).

Mano, Ana. (2020a). Update: 1-Brazil's JBS resumes U.S. share listing plan after COVID-19 fallout, CEO says. *Reuters.* August 14. Available at: www.reuters.com/article/jbs-outlook/ update-1-brazils-jbs-resumes-u-s-share-listing-plan-after-covid-19-fallout-ceo-says-idUSL1N2FG0L2 (Accessed: 05/13/22).

Mano, Ana. (2020b). Special Report: How Covid-19 Swept the Brazilian Slaughterhouses of JBS, World's Top Meatpacker. *Reuters.* September 8. Available at: www.reuters.com/arti cle/us-health-coronavirus-jbs-specialreport/special-report-how-covid-19-swept-the-brazilian-slaughterhouses-of-jbs-worlds-top-meatpacker-iduskbn25z1hz (Accessed: 08/ 17/21)

Mano, Ana. (2021). JBS ordered to pay $3.6 million after Brazil beef plant's COVID out-break. *Reuters.* March 19. Available at: www.reuters.com/article/us-jbs-covid-payment/ jbs-ordered-to-pay-3-6-million-after-brazil-beef-plants-covid-outbreak-idUSKBN2BB 1XB (Accessed: 05/13/22).

Marema, T. (2020, June 15). The rural counties with highest rate of new infections. *Daily Yonder.* Available at: https://dailyyonder.com/new-infections-hit-counties-with-meatpacking-plants-prisons-and-non-white-populations/2020/06/15/ (Accessed: 01/ 01/22).

Marema, Tim. (2020). The rural counties with highest rate of new infections. *Daily Yonder.* June 15. Available at: https://dailyyonder.com/new-infections-hit-counties-with-meat packing-plants-prisons-and-non-white-populations/2020/06/15/ (Accessed 07/15/20).

Marmot, M. (2020). Health equity in England: The Marmot review 10 years on. *BMJ*, 368, m683.

Marquis, R., & Jackson, R. (2000). Quality of life and quality of service relationships: Experiences of people with disabilities. *Disability & Society*, *15*(3), 411–425.

Marx, K., Fowkes, B., & Fernbach, D. (1981). *Capital: A critique of political economy*. London: Penguin Books.

Matthewman, S. & Huppatz, K. (2020). A sociology of Covid-19. *Journal of Sociology*, *56*(4), 675–683.

Mattioli, G., Roberts, C., Steinberger, J. K., & Brown, A. (2020). The political economy of car dependence: A systems of provision approach. *Energy Research & Social Science*, *66*, 101486.

Mauritsen, T. & R. Pincus. (2017). Committed warming inferred from observations. *Nature Climate Change*, 31 July, 652–656.

Mayer, J. (2017). *Dark money: The hidden history of the billionaires behind the rise of the radical right*. New York: Anchor Books.

Mayes, C. (2018). *Unsettling food politics: Agriculture, dispossession and sovereignty in Australia*. London: Rowman & Littlefield.

Mazzucato, M. (2014). *The entrepreneurial state: Debunking public vs. private sector myths*. New York: Anthem Press.

Mazzucato, M. (2018a) *The Entrepreneurial State: Debunking Public vs Private Sector Myths*. Revised Edition. Great Britain: Penguin Books.

Mazzucato, M. (2018b) *The Value of Everything: Making and Taking in the Global Economy*. New York: Public Affairs.

Mazzucato, M. (2020). *The value of everything: Making and taking in the global economy*. New York: Public Affairs.

Mazzucato, M. (2021, October 13). A new global economic consensus. *Project Syndicate*.

McCausland, P. (2021, October 2) The price of meat is going up. Ranchers and corporations are split on why. *NBC News*. Available at: www.nbcnews.com/politics/politics-news/farmers-biden-admin-push-change-meatpackers-status-quo-rcna2511 (Accessed: 01/01/22).

McCausland, Phil. (2021). The Price of Meat is going up. Ranchers and Corporations are split on why. *NBC News*, October 2. Available at: www.nbcnews.com/politics/politics-news/farmers-biden-admin-push-change-meatpackers-status-quo-rcna2511 (Accessed 05/23/22).

McCormick, C., L. Torres, C. Benhamou, M. and D. Pogkas. (2021, January 29). The Covid-19 pandemic has added $19.5 trillion to global debt. *Bloomberg*. Available at: www.bloomberg.com/graphics/2021-coronavirus-global-debt/ (Accessed: 01/01/22).

McDonald, M. (2015). Climate security and economic security: The limits to climate change action in Australia? *International Politics*, *52*(4), 484–501.

McGrael, C. (2020). A disgraced scientist and a viral video: how a Covid conspiracy theory started. *The Guardian*. May 14, 2020. Available at: www.theguardian.com/world/2020/may/14/coronavirus-viral-video-plandemic-judy-mikovits-conspiracy-theories (Accessed: 01/01/22).

McGrath, M. (2021). COP26: Fossil fuel industry has largest delegation at climate summit. *BBC News*. Available at: www.bbc.co.uk/news/science-environment-59199484 (Accessed: 01/01/22).

McKeon, N. (2014). *The new alliance for food security and nutrition: A coup for corporate capital?* Amsterdam: Transnational Institute.

McKeon, N. (2015). *Food security governance: Empowering communities, regulating corporations*. London: Routledge.

McKibben, B. (2012). Fossil-fuel subsidies: Helping the richest get richer. *LA Times*. April 5 2012. Available at: www.latimes.com/opinion/la-xpm-2012-apr-05-la-oe-mckibben-stop-oil-subsidies-20120404-story.html (Accessed on 01/01/2022).

McLeay, M. and A. Radia and R. Thomas. (2014). Money creation in the modern economy. *Quarterly Bulletin Q1* Bank of England.

McMahon, A. (2021). Global equitable access to vaccines, medicines and diagnostics for COVID-19: The role of patents as private governance. *Journal of Medical Ethics, 47*(3), 142–148.

McMichael, P. (2009a). A food regime genealogy. *The Journal of Peasant Studies, 36*(1), 139–169.

McMichael, P. (2009b). Banking on agriculture: A review of the *World Development Report 2008*. *Journal of Agrarian Change, 9*(2), 235–246.

McMichael, P. (2013a). *Food regimes and agrarian questions*. New York: Practical Action Publishing.

McMichael, P. (2013b). Land grabbing as security mercantilism in international relations. *Globalizations, 10*(1), 47–64.

McMichael, P. (2020). Does China's 'going out' strategy prefigure a new food regime? *The Journal of Peasant Studies, 47*(1), 116–154.

McNally, D. (1988). *Political Economy and the Rise of Capitalism: A Reinterpretation*. Berkeley: California University Press.

McNally, D. (2011). *Global Slump: The Economics and Politics of Crisis and Resistance*. Oakland: PM Press.

McNeill, W. H. (1989). *Plagues and peoples*. New York: Anchor Books.

Mellish, Luzmore, & Shahbaz. (2020). Why were the UK and USA unprepared for the COVID-19 pandemic? The systemic weaknesses of neoliberalism: A comparison between the UK, USA, Germany, and South Korea. *Journal of Global Faultlines, 7*(1), 9.

Meyer, S. B., Violette, R., Aggarwal, R., et al. (2019). Vaccine hesitancy and Web 2.0: Exploring how attitudes and beliefs about influenza vaccination are exchanged in online threaded user comments. *Vaccine, 37*(13), 1769–1774.

Michaels, D. (2020). *The triumph of doubt: Dark money and the science of deception*. Oxford: Oxford University Press.

Mies, M. (2001). *Patriarchy and accumulation on a world scale: Women in the international division of labour*. London: Zed Books.

Mihaly, C., & Heavenrich, S. (2019). *Diet for a changing climate: Food for thought*. New York: Twenty-First Century Books.

Milanović, B. (2018). *Global inequality: A new approach for the age of globalization*. Harvard: Harvard University Press.

Millar, K. M. (2017). Toward a critical politics of precarity. *Sociology Compass, 11*(6), e12483.

Mills, C. W. (1999). The Racial Contract. Cornell University Press.

Mills, C. W. (2009). Critical race theory: A reply to Mike Cole. Ethnicities, 9(2), 270–281.

Mills, C. W. (2011). *The racial contract*. Durham: Cornell University Press.

Mills, C. W. (2017). *Black rights/white wrongs: The critique of racial liberalism*. Oxford: Oxford University Press.

Milman, O. (2018). Ex-Nasa scientist: 30 years on, world is failing 'miserably' to address climate change. *The Guardian*. Available at: www.theguardian.com/environment/2018/jun/19/james-hansen-nasa-scientist-climate-change-warning#:~:text=%E2%80%9CAll%20we've%20done%20is,mean%20much%2C%20it's%20wishful%20thinking. (Accessed on 01/01/2022).

Milman, O. (2018). Ex-Nasa scientist: 30 years on, world is failing 'miserably' to address climate change. *The Guardian*. Available at: www.theguardian.com/environment/2018/jun/19/james-hansen-nasa-scientist-climate-change-warning#:~:text=%E2%80%9CAll%20we've%20done%20is,mean%20much%2C%20it's%20wishful%20thinking. (Accessed on 01/01/2022).

Milman, O. (2020, February 23). Revealed: Quarter of all tweets about climate crisis produced by bots. *The Guardian*. Retrieved from: www.theguardian.com/technology/2020/feb/21/climate-tweets-twitter-bots-analysis (Accessed: 01/01/22).

Mirowski, P., & Plehwe, D. (Eds.). (2009). *The road from Mont Pèlerin: The making of the neoliberal thought collective*. Cambridge: Harvard University Press.

Mitchell, B. (2020). A cause for celebration: A paradigm shift in macroeconomics is underway. *AQ: Australian Quarterly*. *91*(4), 18–29.

Mitchell, C. (2019, October 3). In Nebraska, cattle ranchers rally against big agribusiness. *The Counter*. Available at: https://thecounter.org/nebraska-cattle-ranchers-rally-ocm-usda/ (Accessed: 01/01/22).

Mitchell, Charlie. (2019). In Nebraska, cattle ranchers rally against big agribusiness. *The Counter*. October 3. Available at: https://thecounter.org/nebraska-cattle-ranchers-rally-ocm-usda/ (Accessed: 05/13/22).

Mitchell, T. (2009). Carbon democracy. *Economy and Society*, *38*(3), 399–432.

Mitchell, T. (2013). *Carbon democracy: Political power in the age of oil*. London: Verso.

Mittra, J., & Zoukas, G. (2020). Unpacking the concept of bioeconomy: Problems of definition, measurement, and value. *Science & Technology Studies*, *33*(1), 2–21.

Monbiot, G. (2021). Capitalism is killing the planet – it's time to stop buying into our own destruction. *The Guardian*. October 30, 2021. Available at: www.theguardian.com/environment/2021/oct/30/capitalism-is-killing-the-planet-its-time-to-stop-buying-into-our-own-destruction (Accessed on 01/01/2022).

Moody, K. (2018). High tech, low growth: Robots and the future of work. *Historical Materialism*, *26*(4), 3–34.

Moore, J. W. (2015). *Capitalism in the web of life: Ecology and the accumulation of capital*. London: Verso.

Moore, P.V., & Woodcock, J. (Eds.). (2021). *Augmented exploitation: Artificial intelligence, automation and work*. London: Pluto Press.

Moravcsik, A. (2004). Is there a 'democratic deficit' in world politics? A Framework for analysis. *Government and Opposition*, *39*(2), 336–363.

Morgan, M. L. (Ed.). (2011). *Classics of moral and political theory*. New York: Hackett.

Morrison, C., & Lähteenmäki, R. (2016). Public biotech in 2015—the numbers. *Nature Biotechnology*, *34*(7), 709–715.

Morrison, O. (2021, February 12). JBS doubles down on deforestation as Greenpeace denounces 'five more years of inaction' Food Navigator. Available at: www.foodnavigator.com/Article/2021/02/12/JBS-doubles-down-on-deforestation-as-Greenpeace-denounces-five-more-years-of-inaction (Accessed: 01/01/22).

Morrison, Oliver. (2021). JBS doubles down on deforestation as Greenpeace denounces 'five more years of inaction' *Food Navigator*. February 12. Available at: www.foodnavigator.com/Article/2021/02/12/JBS-doubles-down-on-deforestation-as-Greenpeace-denounces-five-more-years-of-inaction (Accessed: 05/13/22).

Morton, A. & B. Pridham. (2021). Australia considering more than 100 fossil fuel projects that could produce 5% of global industrial emissions. *The Guardian*. Available at: www.theguardian.com/environment/2021/nov/03/australia-considering-more-than-100-fossil-fuel-projects-that-could-produce-5-of-global-industrial-emissions (Accessed: 01/01/22).

Morton, A. & G. Readfearn. (2021). "Not too late": Australian scientists call for urgent action to avoid worst of climate crisis. *The Guardian*. Available at: www.theguardian.com/austra lia-news/2021/aug/09/not-too-late-australian-scientists-call-for-urgent-action-to-avoid-the-worst-of-climate-crisis (Accessed: 01/01/22).

Murphy, R. H. (2019). The rationality of literal tide pod consumption. *Journal of Bioeconomics* 21(2), 111–122.

Murray, B., Curran, E., Chipman, K. (2021, May 17). The world economy is suddenly running low on everything. *Bloomberg*. Available at: www.bloomberg.com/news/articles/2021-05-17/inflation-rate-2021-and-shortages-companies-panic-buying-as-supplies-run-short (Accessed: 01/01/22).

Nanda, P. (2002). Gender dimensions of user fees: Implications for women's utilization of health care. *Reproductive Health Matters*, 10(20), 127–134.

Nasralla, S. & K. Abnett. (2021). "Beyond Oil" alliance adds members, but shunned by UK climate summit host. *Reuters*. Available at: www.reuters.com/business/cop/beyond-oil-allia nce-lands-members-shunned-by-uk-climate-summit-host-2021-11-11/ (Accessed: 01/01/22).

National Disability Insurance Agency. (2021). NDIS Annual Report 2020-21. Accessed at www.ndis.gov.au/media/3593/download?attachment

Navarro V. The consequences of neoliberalism in the current pandemic. *Int J Health Serv* 2020; *50*: 271–75.

NC Watchdog Reporting Network. (2020). How NC chose cooperation over transparency on meatpacking plants with virus outbreaks. *Raleigh News and Observer*. August 11. Available at: www.newsobserver.com/news/coronavirus/article244672767.html?fbclid= IwAR3Hu6elRWHY6EQKgfO4N_G_jeKafCxbXOuWhpTYhc00pWGFNYjD-exg rpM (Accessed: 08/18/20).

NC Watchdog Reporting Network. (2020, August 11). How NC chose cooperation over transparency on meatpacking plants with virus outbreaks. Raleigh News and Observer. Available at: www.newsobserver.com/news/coronavirus/article244672767.html?fbclid= IwAR3Hu6elRWHY6EQKgfO4N_G_jeKafCxbXOuWhpTYhc00pWGFNYjD-exg rpM (Accessed: 01/01/22).

Ndikumana, L., & Boyce, J. K. (2011). *Africa's odious debts: How foreign loans and capital flight bled a continent*. London: Zed Books.

Nederveen Pieterse, J. (2018). *Multipolar globalization: Emerging economies and development*. London: Routledge.

Neghaiwi, B. H., Jessop, S. (2021, March 25). In 2020 the ultra-rich got richer. Now they're bracing for the backlash, *Reuters*, www.reuters.com/article/us-wealth-billionaires-outl ook-insight-idUSKBN2BH0J7

Nelson, B. M., & Schultz, P. L. (2019). The Tide Pod Challenge: Responding to The Threat of Viral Internet Phenomena. Journal of Case Studies, 37(2), 43–55.

Nelson, J. (2020). Petro-masculinity and climate change denial among white, politically conservative American males. *International Journal of Applied Psychoanalytic Studies*, 17(4), 282–295.

Nestle, M. (2007). *Food politics: How the food industry influences nutrition and health*. Berkley: University of California Press.

Nestle, Marion. (2007). *Food Politics: How the Food Industry Influences Nutrition and Health*. University of California Press.

Newell, P. (2021). *Power shift: The global political economy of energy transitions*. Cambridge: Cambridge University Press.

Nguyen, C. T. (2020). Echo chambers and epistemic bubbles. *Episteme*, *17*(2), 141–161.

Nitzan, J. & Bichler, S. (2015). *The scientists and the Church*. World Economic Association.

Nitzan, J. (2001). Regimes of differential accumulation: Mergers, stagflation and the logic of globalization. *Review of International Political Economy*, 8(2), 226–274.

Nitzan, J., & Bichler, S. (2009). *Capital as power: A study of order and reorder*. London: Routledge.

Noakes, T. C. (2021, May 24). The myth of a green Canada. *Foreign Policy*. Available at: https://foreignpolicy.com/2021/05/24/green-canada-trudeau-oil-gas-keystone-xl-energy-sector/ (Accessed: 01/01/22).

Noble, S. U. (2018). *Algorithms of oppression: How search engines reinforce racism*. New York: New York University Press.

Noman, A. H. M., Griffiths, M. D., Pervin, S., & Ismail, M. N. (2021). The detrimental effects of the COVID-19 pandemic on domestic violence against women. *Journal of Psychiatric Research*, *134*, 111–112.

Nonini, Donald. n.d. Our Food, The Alliance, and the Corporate State. In Donald Nonini and Dorothy Holland, *Food Activism in the Current Crises*. (In prep) New York City: New York University Press.

Nordhaus, W. D. (2013). *The climate casino: Risk, uncertainty, and economics for a warming world*. New Haven: Yale University Press.

Notzon, F. C. (1998). Causes of declining life expectancy in Russia. *JAMA*, *279*(10), 793.

Nye, D. E. (1998). *Consuming power: A social history of American energies*. Cambridge: MIT Press.

Nye, J. S. (2001). Globalization's democratic deficit: How to make international institutions more accountable. *Foreign Affairs*, *80*(4), 2.

Obama White House. (2012). *National bioeconomy blueprint*, Executive Office of the President of the United States. Available at: https://obamawhitehouse.archives.gov/administration/eop/ostp/library/bioeconomy (Accessed: 01/01/22).

Oberst, C. (2015). JBS turns to Europe for processed foods expansion. Available at: www.delimarketnews.com/jbs-turns-europe-processed-foods-expansion/christofer-oberst/mon-09212015-1218/2131 (Accessed: 01/01/22).

Oberst, Christofer. (2015). JBS turns to Europe for Processed Foods Expansion. Available at: www.delimarketnews.com/jbs-turns-europe-processed-foods-expansion/christofer-oberst/mon-09212015-1218/2131. (Accessed: 05/13/22).

OECD (2020a, May 20) *Supporting livelihoods during the COVID-19 crisis: Closing the gaps in safety nets*. Available at: www.oecd.org/coronavirus/policy-responses/supporting-livelihoods-during-the-COVID-19-crisis-closing-the-gaps-in-safety-nets-17cbb92d/ (Accessed: 01/01/22).

OECD (2020b, October 12) *Job retention schemes during the COVID-19 lockdown and beyond*. Available at: www.oecd.org/coronavirus/policy-responses/job-retention-schemes-during-the-covid-19-lockdown-and-beyond-0853ba1d/ (Accessed: 01/01/22).

OECD (2020c, November 19) *Government financial management and reporting in times of crisis*. Available at: www.oecd-ilibrary.org/social-issues-migration-health/government-financial-management-and-reporting-in-times-of-crisis_3f87c7d8-en (Accessed: 01/01/22).

OECD (2020d June 10) **Global economy faces a tightrope walk to recovery** Available at: www.oecd.org/newsroom/global-economy-faces-a-tightrope-walk-to-recovery.htm accessed Nov 4th 2021

OECD. (2019). Ocean shipping and shipbuilding. Available at: www.oecd.org/ocean/topics/ocean-shipping/ (Accessed: 01/01/22).

ONS. (2001). Family Resources Survey 2000–2001. Available at: https://webarchive.nationalarchives.gov.uk/20121003132950/http://statistics.dwp.gov.uk/asd/frs/2000_01/index.php?page=intro (Accessed: 01/01/22).

ONS. (2002). Family Resources Survey 2001–2002. Available at: https://webarchive.nationalarchives.gov.uk/20121003133002/http://statistics.dwp.gov.uk/asd/frs/2001_02/index.php?page=intro (Accessed: 01/01/22).

ONS. (2005). Family Resources Survey 2004–2005. Available at: https://webarchive.natio nalarchives.gov.uk/20121003153003/http://statistics.dwp.gov.uk/asd/frs/2004_05/ pdfonly/frs_2004_05_report.pdf (Accessed: 01/01/22).

ONS. (2006). Family Resources Survey 2005–2006. Available at: https://webarchive.natio nalarchives.gov.uk/20121003132920/http://statistics.dwp.gov.uk/asd/frs/2005_06/ index.php?page=intro (Accessed: 01/01/22).

ONS. (2007). Family Resources Survey 2006–2007. Available at: https://webarchive.natio nalarchives.gov.uk/20121003132831/http://statistics.dwp.gov.uk/asd/frs/2006_07/ index.php?page=intro (Accessed: 01/01/22).

OPEC. (2021). *OPEC Share of World Crude Oil Reserves, 2018*. Retrieved from: www.opec. org/opec_web/en/data_graphs/330.htm.

OpenSecrets. (n.d) Donor demographics. Available at: www.opensecrets.org/elections-overv iew/donor-demographics (Accessed: 01/01/22).

Oppenheim, V. H. (1976–1977). The past: We pushed them. *Foreign Policy*, 25, 24–57.

Oreskes, N., & Conway, E. M. (2011). *Merchants of doubt: How a handful of scientists obscured the truth on issues from tobacco smoke to global warming*. New York: Bloomsbury Press.

Ortega, F., & Orsini, M. (2020). Governing COVID-19 without government in Brazil: Ignorance, neoliberal authoritarianism, and the collapse of public health leader-ship. *Global Public Health*, *15*(9), 1257–1277.

Ortiz-Ospina, E., & Roser, M. (2016, August 22). *Global Health*. Our World in Data. Available at: https://ourworldindata.org/health-meta (Accessed: 01/01/22).

Ostry, J. D., Loungani, P., & Furceri, D. (2016). *Neoliberalism: Oversold?* IMF. Available at: www. imf.org/external/pubs/ft/fandd/2016/06/ostry.htm (Accessed: 01/01/22).

Otto, I. M., Kim, K. M., Dubrovsky, N., et al. (2019). Shift the focus from the super-poor to the super-rich. *Nature Climate Change*, *9*(2), 82–84.

Otto, I. M., Wiedermann, M., Cremades, R., et al. (2020). Human agency in the Anthropocene. *Ecological Economics*, *167*, 106463.

Ouellet, M. (2019). Capital as power: Facebook and the symbolic monopoly rent. *Digitalization of Society and Socio-political Issues 1: Digital, Communication and Culture*, 81–94.

Our World in Data. (2021a). World GDP over the last two millennia. Available at: https://our worldindata.org/grapher/world-gdp-over-the-last-two-millennia (Accessed: 01/01/22).

Oxfam International. (2021). Mega-rich recoup COVID-losses in record-time yet billions will live in poverty for at least a decade. Available at: www.oxfam.org/en/press-relea ses/mega-rich-recoup-covid-losses-record-time-yet-billions-will-live-poverty-least (Accessed: 01/01/22).

Oxfam, 2020, *Pandemic Profits Exposed*, Available at: www.oxfamamerica.org/explore/resea rch-publications/pandemic-profits-exposed/ Accessed: 01/01/2022

Pachana, N. A., Beattie, E., Byrne, G. J., et al. (2020). COVID-19 and psychogeriatrics: The view from Australia. *International Psychogeriatrics*, *32*(10), 1135–1141.

Page, B. I., & Gilens, M. (2017). *Democracy in America? What has gone wrong and what we can do about it*. Illinois: The University of Chicago Press.

Pahnke, A. (2017). The Brazilian crisis: Corruption, neoliberalism and the primary sector. *Monthly Review* 68(9), 43–54.

Pahnke, Anthony. (2017). The Brazilian Crisis: Corruption, Neoliberalism and the Primary Sector. *Monthly Review Press.* Vol. *68*(9): 43–54.

Pan, K. Y. (2015, March 15). Boom time for Brazil's JBS as real slides. *Financial Times*.

Pan, Kwan Yuk. (2015). Boom time for Brazil's JBS as real slides. *Financial Times*. March 30.

PAN. 2019. *Agroecology. Sustainable & successful agricultural practices in the United States.* Available at: www.panna.org/sites/default/files/AgroecologyInUSbriefENG201909_FINAL.pdf (Accessed: 01/01/22).

Parkin, R., R. Wilk, E, Hirsh, et al. (PWC 2017). 2017 automotive trends. Strategy and PWC. Available at: www.strategyand.pwc.com/trend/2017-automotive-industry-trends. (Accessed: 01/01/22).

Parkinson, G. (2018). Unsubsidised wind and solar now cheapest form of bulk energy, *Renew Economy*. Available at: https://reneweconomy.com.au/unsubsidised-wind-and-solar-now-cheapest-form-of-bulk-energy-96453/ (Accessed: 01/01/22).

Parks, M. (2021). Few Facts, Millions Of Clicks: Fearmongering Vaccine Stories Go Viral Online. *NPR*. March 25, 2021. Available at: www.npr.org/2021/03/25/980035707/lying-through-truth-misleading-facts-fuel-vaccine-misinformation (Accessed: 01/01/22).

Passwaters, M. (2020). Difficult 2020 leaves oil and gas producers' market caps devastated. *S&P Global Market Intelligence*. Available at: www.spglobal.com/marketintelligence/en/news-insights/latest-news-headlines/difficult-2020-leaves-oil-and-gas-producers-market-caps-devastated-60650553 (Accessed: 01/01/22).

Paterson, M. (2007). *Automobile politics: Ecology and cultural political economy*. Cambridge: Cambridge University Press.

Paterson, M. (2020). 'The end of the fossil fuel age'? Discourse politics and climate change political economy. *New Political Economy*, 1–14.

Pearse, G. (2007). *High and dry: John Howard, climate change and the selling of Australia's future*. Camberwell: Viking.

Pearse, G. (2009). Quarry Vision: Coal, climate change and the end of the resources boom. *Quarterly Essay*, *33*, 1–122.

Pearse, R. (2020). Theorising the political economy of energy transformations: Agency, structure, space, process. *New Political Economy*, *26*(6), 951–963.

Pechlaner, G. (2010). The sociology of agriculture in transition: The political economy of agriculture after biotechnology. *Canadian Journal of Sociology*, *35*(2), 243–270.

Peck J. (2010). Zombie neoliberalism and the ambidextrous state. *Theoretical Criminology*, *14*(1), 104–110.

Peetz, D. (2019). *The realities and futures of work*, Canberra: ANU Press.

Pehl, M. et al. (2017). Understanding future emissions from low-carbon power systems by integration of life-cycle assessment and integrated energy modelling. *Nature Energy*, *2*, 939–945.

Peisah, C., Byrnes, A., Doron, I., et al. (2020). Advocacy for the human rights of older people in the COVID pandemic and beyond: A call to mental health professionals. *International Psychogeriatrics*, *32*(10), 1199–1204.

Persaud, R. B. (2016). Neo-Gramscian theory and third world violence: A time for broadening. *Globalizations*, *13*(5), 547–562.

Petras, J. (2008). Global ruling class: Billionaires and how they "make it." *Journal of Contemporary Asia*, *38*(2), 319–329.

Philippon, T. (2019). *The great reversal: How America gave up on free markets*. Cambridge: Harvard University Press.

Phillips D. (2019, July 2). The swashbuckling meat tycoons who nearly brought down a government. *The Guardian*. Available at: www.theguardian.com/environment/2019/jul/02/swashbuckling-meat-tycoons-nearly-brought-down-a-government-brazil (Accessed: 01/01/22).

Phillips D. (2020, July 15). There's a direct relationship': Brazil meat plants linked to spread of Covid-19. *The Guardian*. Available at: www.theguardian.com/environment/2020/jul/15/brazil-meat-plants-linked-to-spread-of-covid-19 (Accessed: 01/01/22).

Phillips, A. (1958). The relationship between unemployment and the rate of change of money wage rates in the United Kingdom, 1861–1957. *Economica*, *25*(100), 283–299.

Phillips, Dom. (2019). The swashbuckling meat tycoons who nearly brought down a government. *The Guardian.* July 2. Available at: www.theguardian.com/environment/2019/jul/02/swashbuckling-meat-tycoons-nearly-brought-down-a-government-brazil (Accessed: 05/13/22).

Phillips, Dom. (2020). 'There's a direct relationship': Brazil meat plants linked to spread of Covid-19. *The Guardian.* July 15. Available at: www.theguardian.com/environment/2020/jul/15/brazil-meat-plants-linked-to-spread-of-covid-19 (Accessed: 05/13/22).

Philpott, T. (2020). *Perilous bounty: The looming collapse of American farming and how we can prevent it.* New York: Bloomsbury Publishing.

PhRMA. (2021, May 5). PhRMA statement on WTO TRIPS Intellectual Property Waiver, PhRMA. Available at: www.phrma.org/coronavirus/phrma-statement-on-wto-trips-intellectual-property-waiver (Accessed: 01/01/22).

Pidcock, R. (2016). Analysis: What global emissions in 2016 mean for climate change goals, *Carbon Brief.* Available at: www.carbonbrief.org/what-global-co2-emissions-2016-mean-climate-change (Accessed: 01/01/22).

Pijl, K. van der. (1998). *Transnational classes and international relations.* London: Routledge.

Pijl, K. van der. (2012). *The making of an Atlantic ruling class.* London: Verso.

Piketty, T. (2017). *Capital in the twenty-first century.* Cambridge: Harvard University Press.

Piketty, T., & Goldhammer, A. (2020). *Capital and ideology.* Cambridge: Harvard University Press.

Pilon, D. (2018). The struggle over actually existing democracy. In Leo Panitch and Greg Albo (eds.), *Socialist register 2018: Rethinking democracy* (24–49). London: Merlin Press.

Pimentel, D. and Pimentel, M. (2003). Sustainability of meat-based and plant-based diets and the environment. *American Jour. Clinical Nutrition,* 78: 660S–663S. Available at: https://doi.org/10.1093/ajcn/78.3.660S (Accessed: 05/13/22).

Pimentel, D., & Pimentel, M. (2003). Sustainability of meat-based and plant-based diets and the environment. *The American Journal of Clinical Nutrition,* 78(3), 660S-663S.

Pinker, S. (2018). *Enlightenment now: The case for reason, science, humanism, and progress.* New York: Penguin Books.

Piquero, A. R., Jennings, W. G., Jemison, E., Kaukinen, C., & Knaul, F. M. (2021). Domestic violence during the COVID-19 pandemic—Evidence from a systematic review and meta-analysis. *Journal of Criminal Justice,* 74, 101806.

Pirani, S. (2018). *Burning up: A global history of fossil fuel consumption.* London: Pluto press.

Pistor, K. (2019). *The code of capital: How the law creates wealth and inequality.* New Jersey: Princeton University Press.

Pittock, B. (2006). Are scientists underestimating climate change? *Eos,* 87(34), 340–341.

Plehwe, D., Slobodian, Q., & Mirowski, P. (Eds.). (2020). *Nine lives of neoliberalism.* London: Verso.

Ploeg, J. D. van der, & Ye, J. (Eds.). (2016). *China's peasant agriculture and rural society: Changing paradigms of farming.* London: Routledge.

Ploeg, J. D. van der. (2018). *The new peasantries: Rural development in times of globalization.* London: Routledge.

Plumber, B., & Popovich, N. (2018, October 7). Why half a degree of global warming is a big deal. *New York Times.* Available at: www.nytimes.com/interactive/2018/10/07/climate/ipcc-report-half-degree.html?mtrref=www.google.com&assetType=REGIWALL (Accessed: 01/01/22).

Polanyi, K. (1957). *The Great Transformation: The Political and Economic Origins of Our Times* Boston, MA: Beacon Press.

Polanyi, K. (1985). *The great transformation.* New York: Beacon Press.

Ponciano (2021) Oct 27, new billionaire wealth tax targeting assets of 700 richest Americans unveiled, *Forbes*, available at: www.forbes.com/sites/jonathanponciano/2021/10/27/new-billionaire-wealth-tax-targeting-assets-of-700-richest-americans-unveiled-heres-how-the-democratic-plan-would-work/?sh=1dc574633f5c Accessed: 01/01/22

Ponsar, F., Tayler-Smith, K., Philips, M., Gerard, S., Van Herp, M., Reid, T., & Zachariah, R. (2011). No cash, no care: How user fees endanger health—lessons learnt regarding financial barriers to healthcare services in Burundi, Sierra Leone, Democratic Republic of Congo, Chad, Haiti and Mali. *International Health*, 3(2), 91–100.

Porter, T. (2001). The democratic deficit in the institutional arrangements for regulating global finance. *Global Governance: A Review of Multilateralism and International Organizations* 7(4), 427–439.

Puri, N., Coomes, E. A., Haghbayan, H., & Gunaratne, K. (2020). Social media and vaccine hesitancy: New updates for the era of COVID-19 and globalized infectious diseases. *Human Vaccines & Immunotherapeutics*, 16(11), 2586–2593.

Putnam, B. H. (2021). From phase transitions to Modern Monetary Theory: A framework for analyzing the pandemic of 2020. *Review of Financial Economics*, 39(1), 3–19.

Qin, V. M., Hone, T., Millett, C., et al. (2019). The impact of user charges on health outcomes in low-income and middle-income countries: A systematic review. *BMJ Global Health*, 3(Suppl 3), e001087.

Ranasinghe, D. (2021). Global debt is fast approaching record $300 trillion – IIF. *Reuters*. September 19, 2021). Available at: www.reuters.com/business/global-debt-is-fast-appr oaching-record-300-trillion-iif-2021-09-14/ (Accessed on 01/01/2022).

Rand, A. (1957). *Atlas Shrugged*. New York: Random House.

Rapley, J. (2021). Empires, pandemics and the economic future of the West. *Aeon*. Available at: https://aeon.co/essays/empires-pandemics-and-the-economic-future-of-the-west (Accessed: 01/01/22).

Raworth, K. (2017). *Doughnut economics: Seven ways to think like a 21st century economist*. New York: Green Publishing.

Reed, A. (2013). Marx, race, and neoliberalism. *New Labor Forum*, 22(1), 49–57.

Rees, W. E. (2020). Ecological economics for humanity's plague phase. *Ecological Economics*, 169, 106519.

Reinhart, C. M. & K. S. Rogoff. (2009). *This time is different: Eight centuries of financial folly*. New Jersey: Princeton University Press.

Reisman, E. (2021). Sanitizing agri-food tech: COVID-19 and the politics of expectation. *The Journal of Peasant Studies*, 48(5), 910–933.

Reppy, J. (2008). A biomedical military – industrial complex? *Technovation*, 28(12), 802–811.

Reuters (2015) *Tekmira shares soar on deal with OnCore Biopharma, Reuters*. Available at: www.reuters.com/article/us-tekmira-deal/tekmira-shares-soar-on-deal-with-oncore-biopha rma-idUSKBN0KL1SO20150112 (Accessed: 9/12/20). *Review*, I. 103, 3–41.

Richards, D. (2020, April 27). Industry: Georgia chicken plant production unabated by Covid-19. *11 Alive News*. Available at: www.11alive.com/article/news/health/coro navirus/poultry-industry-Covid-19/85-76a95ff2-4668-419e-ae48-e069de380f80 (Accessed: 01/01/22).

Richards, Doug. (2020). Industry: Georgia chicken plant production unabated by Covid-19. *11Alive News*. April 27. Available at: www.11alive.com/article/news/health/coronavirus/poultry-industry-Covid-19/85-76a95ff2-4668-419e-ae48-e069de380f80 (Accessed: 08/18/20).

Rincon, P. (2021, July 20). Jeff Bezos launches to space aboard New Shepard rocket ship. *BBC*. Available at: www.bbc.com/news/science-environment-57849364 (Accessed: 01/01/22).

Ripple, W. J., C. Wolf, T. M. Newsome, et al., and 15,364 scientist signatories from 184 countries. (2017). 'World Scientists' Warning to Humanity: A Second Notice. *BioScience*, Vol. 67(12), 1026–1028.

Robbins, R. H. & R. D. Beech (2018) *Global problems and the culture of capitalism*, 7th edition. London: Pearson Publishing.

Robbins, R. H. (2022). Financialization. In *The handbook of economic anthropology*, (3rd edition), edited by James Carrier. Oxford: Berg Publishers.

Robinson W., & Harris, J., (2000). Towards a global ruling class? Globalization and the transnational capitalist class. *Science & Society*, 64(1), 11–54.

Robinson, C. J. (2021). *Black Marxism: The making of the Black radical tradition*. Chapel Hill: The University of North Carolina.

Robinson, S., Graham, A., Fisher, K. R., Neale, K., Davy, L., Johnson, K., & Hall, E. (2021). Understanding paid support relationships: Possibilities for mutual recognition between young people with disability and their support workers. *Disability & Society*, 36(9), 1423–1448.

Robinson, W. I. (2017). Debate on the new global capitalism: Transnational capitalist class, transnational state apparatuses, and global crisis. *International Critical Thought*, 7(2), 171–189.

Rockström, J., H. J. Schellnhuber, B. Hoskins, et. al. (2016). The world's biggest gamble. *Earth's Future*, Vol. 4(10), 465–470.

Rodney, W. (1972). *How Europe underdeveloped Africa*. Bogle-L'Ouverture Publications.

Romanelli, E., & Tushman, M. L. (1994). Organizational transformation as punctuated equilibrium: An empirical test. *Academy of Management Journal*, 37(5), 1141–1166.

Roos, J. (2019). *Why not default? The political economy of sovereign debt*. New Jersey: Princeton University Press.

Rosenberg, J. (1994). *The empire of civil society: A critique of the realist theory of international relations*. London: Verso.

Ross, M. & N. Bateman. (2020). Low unemployment isn't worth much if the jobs barely pay. *Brookings*. Available at: www.brookings.edu/blog/the-avenue/2020/01/08/low-unemployment-isnt-worth-much-if-the-jobs-barely-pay (Accessed: 01/01/22).

Rosset, P., & Altieri, M.A. (2017). *Agroecology: Science and politics*. Halifax: Fernwood Publishing.

Rowbotham, M. (1998). *The grip of death: A study of modern money, debt slavery, and destructive economics*. New York: Jon Carpenter.

Rowden, R. (2009). *The deadly ideas of neoliberalism: How the IMF has undermined public health and the fight against AIDS*. London: Zed Books.

Rowlatt, J. & T. Gerken. (2021). COP26: Document leak reveals nations lobbying to change key climate report. *BBC News*. Available at: www.bbc.com/news/science-environment-58982445.amp (Accessed: 01/01/22).

Rowley, R. (2022). American insurrection. *PBS Frontline*. Available at: www.pbs.org/wgbh/frontline/film/american-insurrection/ (Accessed: 01/01/22).

Roy, A. (2020, April 3). The pandemic is a portal. *Financial Times*. Available at: www.ft.com/content/10d8f5e8-74eb-11ea-95fe-fcd274e920ca (Accessed: 01/01/22).

Roy, V. (2020) 'A Crisis for Cures: Tracing Assetization and Value in Biomedical Innovation', in Birch, K. and Muniesa, F. (eds) *Assetization: Turning Things into Assets in Technoscientific Capitalism*. United States: The MIT Press.

Royal Commission into Aged Care Quality and Safety. Final Report: Care, Dignity and Respect. Volume 1: Summary and recommendations. Available at: https://agedcare.royalcommission.gov.au/publications/final-report (Accessed: 01/01/22).

Royal Commission into Violence, Abuse, Neglect and Exploitation of People with Disability. (2020). Interim report. Available at: https://disability.royalcommission.gov.au/publications/interim-report (Accessed: 01/01/22).

Royal Commission into Violence, Abuse, Neglect and Exploitation of People with Disability. (2021). Public hearing 12: The experiences of people with disability, in the context of the Australian Government's approach to the COVID 19 vaccine rollout. Draft Commissioner's Report. Available at: https://disability.royalcommission.gov.au/publicati ons/report-public-hearing-12-experiences-people-disability-context-australian-gove rnments-approach-covid-19-vaccine-rollout-commissioners-draft-report (Accessed: 01/ 01/22).

Rudin, J., & Sanders, D. (2021). Debt, structural adjustment and health. In S. Benatar & G. Brock (Eds.), *Global health: Ethical challenges* (170–181). Cambridge: Cambridge University Press.

Runciman, D. (2018). *How democracy ends*. New York: Profile Books.

Saad-Filho, A. (2020). From COVID-19 to the end of neoliberalism. *Critical Sociology, 46*(4–5), 477–485.

Sachs, J. (Mar. 12, 2012). What I did in Russia. Available at: https://static1.squarespace.com/ static/5d59c0bdfff8290001f869d1/t/5ed7d8e248deea6dbee5d577/1591204091062/ Sachs+%282012%29_What+I+did+in+Russia.pdf (Accessed: 01/01/22).

Saez, E. and G. Zucman. (2019a). Progressive wealth taxation. Brookings Papers on Economic Activity. BPEA Conference Drafts, September 5–6. Available at: www. brookings.edu/wp-content/uploads/2019/09/Saez-Zucman_conference-draft.pdf (Accessed: 01/01/22).

Saez, E.& G. Zucman. (2019b). *The triumph of injustice: How the rich dodge taxes and how to make them pay*. New York: W.W. Norton.

SafeWork NSW. (2020, November 24). New taskforce to investigate gig economy deaths. Available at: www.safework.nsw.gov.au/news/safework-media-releases/new-taskforce-to-investigate-gig-economy-deaths (Accessed: 01/01/22).

Sanders, D., Nandi, S., Labonté, R., Vance, C., & Van Damme, W. (2019). From primary health care to universal health coverage—One step forward and two steps back. *The Lancet, 394*(10199), 619–621.

Sanofi. (2021a, April 9). Sanofi acquires Tidal Therapeutics, adding innovative mRNA-based research platform with applications in oncology, immunology, and other disease areas. *Sanofi*, Available at: www.sanofi.com/en/media-room/press-releases/2021/2021-04-09-19-45-00-2207664 (Accessed: 01/01/22).

Sanofi. (2021b, August 3). Sanofi to acquire Translate Bio; advances deployment of mRNA technology across vaccines and therapeutics development. *Sanofi*, Available at: www.sanofi.com/en/media-room/press-releases/2021/2021-08-03-07-00-00-2273 307 (Accessed: 01/01/22).

Sartre, J. P. (October 1957). *Les temps modernes*. Éditions Gallimard: Paris.

Saunders, J. (2020, April 7). Poultry processor sends 415 South Georgia employees home with pay. *Atlanta Business Journal*. Available at: www.bizjournals.com/atlanta/news/2020/ 04/07/poultry-processor-sends-415-south-georgia.html (Accessed: 01/01/22).

Saunders, Jessica. (2020). Poultry processor sends 415 South Georgia employees home with pay. *Atlanta Business Journal*. April 7. Available at: www.bizjournals.com/atlanta/news/ 2020/04/07/poultry-processor-sends-415-south-georgia.html . (Accessed: 05/13/22).

Schaoul, J. (2020, March 30). UN warns that COVID-19 pandemic could trigger global food shortage. Available at: www.wsws.org/en/ articles/2020/03/30/unit- m30.html (Accessed: 01/01/22).

Schiavoni, C. M. (2017). The contested terrain of food sovereignty construction: Toward a historical, relational and interactive approach. *The Journal of Peasant Studies, 44*(1), 1–32.

Schneider, S. (2009). The worst-case scenario. Nature, *458*, 1104–1105.

Schnirring, L. (2015) *Experimental Ebola drug shelved; study explores virus clearance, Center for Infectious Disease and Research Policy.* Available at: www.cidrap.umn.edu/news-pers pective/2015/07/experimental-ebola-drug-shelved-study-explores-virus-clearance (Accessed: 9/12/20).

Schnirring, L. (2015) *Experimental Ebola drug shelved; study explores virus clearance, Center for Infectious Disease and Research Policy.* Available at: www.cidrap.umn.edu/news-pers pective/2015/07/experimental-ebola-drug-shelved-study-explores-virus-clearance (Accessed: 9/12/20).

Schoch-Spana, M., M. Shearer, E. Brunson, et al. (2017). The SPARS pandemic 2025–2028. *John Hopkins Bloomberg School of Public Health.* Available at: www.centerforhea lthsecurity.org/our-work/pubs_archive/pubs-pdfs/2017/spars-pandemic-scenario.pdf (Accessed: 01/01/22).

Schwab, K. (2019). Why we need the 'Davos Manifesto' for a better kind of capitalism. Available at: www.weforum.org/agenda/2019/12/why-we-need-the-davos-manifesto-for-better-kind-of-capitalism/ (Accessed: 01/01/22).

Schwab, K. and Malleret, T. (2020). *COVID-19: The great reset.* Little Island: Forum Publishing.

Scoones, I., Amanor, K., Favareto, A., & Qi, G. (2016). A new politics of development cooper-ation? Chinese and Brazilian engagements in African agriculture. *World Development, 81,* 1–12.

Scott, Brett (2018) 'These 5 Rebel Movements Want To Change How Money Works' *Huffington Post,* September 17. www.huffpost.com/entry/five-monetary-rebellions-cha nge-money-system_n_5b9a819ae4b0b64a336ca248 (25/05/2022).

Seabrook, V. (2021). Climate change: UK's $1bn support for Mozambique gas project assessed pollution against 2°C warming—not 1.5°C. Available at: https://news.sky.com/story/ climate-change-uks-1bn-support-for-mozambique-gas-project-assessed-pollution-agai nst-20c-warming-not-1-50c-12440917 (Accessed: 01/01/22).

Sers, M. R., & Victor, P. A. (2018). The energy-emissions trap. *Ecological Economics, 151,* 10–21.

Seth, S. (2020). *Beyond reason: Postcolonial theory and the social sciences.* Oxford: Oxford University Press.

Seth, S. G., C. Doxsee, & N. Harrington. (2020). The escalating terrorism problem in the United States. *Center for Strategic & International Studies.* Available at: https://csis-webs ite-prod.s3.amazonaws.com/s3fs-public/publication/200612_Jones_DomesticTerrorism _v6.pdf (Accessed: 01/01/22).

Shah, S. (2020, March 16). The other pandemic: habitat destruction. *The Nation.*

Sharma, R. (2021, May 14). The billionaire boom: How the super-rich soaked up COVID cash. *Financial Times.*

Sharma, S. (2018). Mighty giants: Leaders of the Global Meat Complex Inst. for Agriculture and Trade Policy. Available at: www.iatp.org/blog/leaders-global-meat-complex (Accessed: 01/01/22).

Sharma, Shefali. (2018). Mighty Giants: Leaders of the Global Meat Complex. Inst. for Agriculture and Trade Policy. April 10. Available at: www.iatp.org/blog/leaders-global-meat-complex. (Accessed: 05/13/22).

Shaxson, N. (2011). *Treasure islands: Uncovering the damage of offshore banking and tax havens.* London: Palgrave Macmillan.

Shead, S. (2020, December 3). COVID has accelerated the adoption of online food delivery by 2 to 3 years, Deliveroo CEO says. *CNBC.* Available at: www.cnbc.com/2020/12/ 03/deliveroo-ceo-says-covid-has-accelerated-adoption-of-takeaway-apps.html(Acces sed: 01/01/22).

Shilliam, R. (2018). *Race and the undeserving poor: From abolition to Brexit*. London: Agenda Publishing.

Silverstein, J. (2019, 20 December). We respond to the historians who critiqued the 1619 project. *The New York Times Magazine*. Available at: www.nytimes.com/2019/12/20/magaz ine/we-respond-to-the-historians-who-critiqued-the-1619-project.html (Accessed: 01/ 01/22).

Simpson, M. (2020). Fossil urbanism: Fossil fuel flows, settler colonial circulations, and the production of carbon cities. *Urban Geography*, 1–22.

Sims, B. & E. Shaffer. (2020, March 27). JBS sets earnings record in 2019. JBS SA. Available at: www.meatpoultry.com/articles/22838-jbs-sets-earnings-record-in-2019#:~:text= JBS%20USA%20Beef%2C%20which%20includes,compared%20to%208%25%20 in%202018 (Accessed: 01/01/22).

Sims, Bob and Erica Shaffer. (2020). JBS sets earnings record in 2019. JBS SA. March 27. Available at: www.meatpoultry.com/articles/22838-jbs-sets-earnings-record-in-2019#:~:text=JBS%20USA%20Beef%2C%20which%20includes,compared%20to%20 8%25%20in%202018. (Accessed: 05/13/22).

Sinclair, T. J. (2008). *The new masters of capital: American bond rating agencies and the politics of creditworthiness*. Ithaca: Cornell University Press.

Sirota, D. and Perez, A. (2020, October). The fossil fuel industry's dark money is getting even darker. *Jacobin*. Available at: https://jacobinmag.com/2020/10/fossil-fuel-extraction-oil-gas-citizens-united (Accessed: 01/01/22).

Skidelsky, R. (2011). The relevance of Keynes. *Cambridge Journal of Economics*, *35*(1), 1–13.

Sklair, L. (2001). *The transnational capitalist class*. New York: Blackwell.

Sklair, L. (2002). Democracy and the transnational capitalist class. *The ANNALS of the American Academy of Political and Social Science*, *581*(1), 144–157.

Slaoui, M., & Hepburn, M. (2020). Developing safe and effective Covid vaccines—Operation Warp Speed's strategy and approach. *New England Journal of Medicine*, *383*(18), 1701–1703.

Slobodian, Q. (2018). *Globalists: The end of empire and the birth of neoliberalism*. Cambridge: Harvard University Press.

Slobodian, Q. (2020). How the 'great reset' of capitalism became an anti-lockdown conspiracy. *The Guardian*. Available at: www.theguardian.com/commentisfree/2020/dec/ 04/great-reset-capitalism-became-an-anti-lockdown-conspiracy (Accessed on 01/01/ 2022).

Sloterdijk, P. (1987). *Critique of cynical reason*. Minneapolis: University of Minnesota Press.

Smessaert, J., Missemer, A., & Levrel, H. (2020). The commodification of nature, a review in social sciences. *Ecological Economics*, *172*, 106624.

Smil, V. (1994). *Energy in world history*. Colorado: Westview Press.

Smith C; Dickinson H; Carey N; Carey G, 2021, 'The Challenges and Benefits of Stewarding Disruptive Technology', in *The Palgrave Handbook of the Public Servant*, Springer International Publishing, pp. 1021–1036, http://dx.doi.org/10.1007/978-3-030-29980-4_56

Smith, M. (2021, April 20). JBS buys European plant-based food producer Vivera. ProFood World. Available at: www.profoodworld.com/industry-news/news/21391581/jbs-acqu isition-raises-its-global-position-in-the-plant-protein-market (Accessed: 01/01/22).

Smith, M. J., & Upshur, R. E. G. (2015). Ebola and learning lessons from moral failures: Who cares about ethics?: Table 1. *Public Health Ethics*, phv028.

Smith, Morgan. (2021). JBS Buys European Plant-based Food Producer Vivera. *ProFood World*. April 20. Available at: www.profoodworld.com/industry-news/news/21391581/ jbs-acquisition-raises-its-global-position-in-the-plant-protein-market. (Accessed: 05/ 13/22).

Smith-Nonini, S. & O. Paschal (2020, September 8). As COVID-19 hit Georgia meatpacking counties, officials and industry shifted blame Facing South. Institute for Southern Studies. Available at: www.facingsouth.org/2020/09/covid-19-hit-georgia-meatpacking-count ies-officials-and-industry-shifted-blameTop(Accessed: 01/01/22).

Smith-Nonini, S. & T. Marema. (2020, July 29). We tracked the rural epicenters of corona-virus spread in North Carolina. The data point to meat-processing plants. *INDY Week*, 9–11. Available at: https://indyweek.com/news/northcarolina/coronavirus-meatpack ing-plants-data/ (Accessed: 01/01/22).

Smith-Nonini, S. (2016). The role of corporate oil and energy debt in creating the neoliberal era: Role of energy debt in creating the neoliberal era. *Economic Anthropology*, *3*(1), 57–67.

Smith-Nonini, S. (2020, July 1). Covid confidential. The coronavirus is surging in rural counties with meatpacking plants. North Carolina officials are hiding data on clusters from the public. *INDY Week*, 12–13. Available at: https://indyweek.com/news/northc arolina/covid-19-meatpacking-plants/ (Accessed: 01/01/22).

Smith-Nonini, Sandy and Olivia Paschal. (2020). As COVID-19 hit Georgia meatpacking counties, officials and industry shifted blame. *Facing South*. Institute for Southern Studies. Sept. 8. Available at: www.facingsouth.org/2020/09/covid-19-hit-georgia-meatpacking-counties-officials-and-industry-shifted-blameTop. (Accessed: 05/13/22).

Smith-Nonini, Sandy and Tim Marema. (2020). We Tracked the rural epicenters of corona-virus spread in North Carolina. The data point to meat-processing plants. *INDY Week*, 9–11, July 29. Available at: https://indyweek.com/news/northcarolina/coronavirus-meat packing-plants-data/. (Accessed: 05/13/22).

Smith-Nonini, Sandy. (2020). Covid Confidential. The coronavirus is surging in rural counties with meatpacking plants. North Carolina officials are hiding data on clusters from the public. *INDY Week*, 12–13, July 1. Available at: https://indyweek.com/news/ northcarolina/covid-19-meatpacking-plants/.(Accessed: 05/13/22).

Smith-Nonini, Sandy. (2021). "When Workers' Health is Public Health:" Meat-Processing, COVID-19 Spread and the Structural Complicity of Local and State Health Departments. In M. Singer, P. Erickson, & C. Abadia (Eds.), *A Companion to Medical Anthropology*. 2nd edition. Hoboken, NJ: Wiley-Blackwell.

Snowden, F. M. (2020). *Epidemics and society: From the Black Death to the present*. New Haven: Yale University Press.

Sobande, F. (2020). 'We're all in this together': Commodified notions of connection, care and community in brand responses to COVID-19. *European Journal of Cultural Studies*. Vol. *23*(6): pp. 1033–1037.

Soederberg, S. (2014). *Debtfare states and the poverty industry: Money, discipline and the surplus population*. London: Routledge.

Soederberg, S. (2021). *Urban Displacements Governing Surplus and Survival in Global Capitalism*. London: Routledge.

Sokol, M., & Pataccini, L. (2020). Winners and losers in coronavirus times: Financialisation, financial chains and emerging economic geographies of the Covid-19 pandemic. *Tijdschrift Voor Economische En Sociale Geografie*, *111*(3), 401–415.

Solty, I. (2020). When the state steps in to save profit. *Jacobin*. Available at: www.jacobinmag. com/2020/03/coronavirus-recession-global-economy-stimulus-state (Accessed: 01/01/ 22).

Sonnemaker, T. (2021). IBM's CEO predicts a hybrid remote-work model for 80% of employees post-pandemic. *Business Insider*. Available at: www.businessinsider.com. au/ibm-ceo-hybrid-remote-work-for-most-employees-post-pandemic-2021-3?r= US&IR=T (Accessed: 01/01/22).

Sparrow, J. (2021). Neoliberalism wrecked our chance to fix the climate crisis – and leftwing statements of faith have changed nothing. *The Guardian*. Available at: www.theguardian.com/commentisfree/2021/nov/17/neoliberalism-wrecked-our-chance-to-fix-the-climate-crisis-and-leftwing-statements-of-faith-have-changed-nothing (Accessed on 01/01/2022).

Speights, K. (2021, August 10). Here's who's making a $1 Billion bet on Moderna. *NASDAQ*, Available at: www.nasdaq.com/articles/heres-whos-making-a-%241-billion-bet-on-moderna-2021-08-10 (Accessed: 01/01/22).

Spina, A. G. (2016). The sound of silence: international treaties and data exclusivity as a limit to compulsory licensing. *European Intellectual Property Review, 38*(12), 746–756.

Spiro, D. E. (1999). *The hidden hand of American hegemony: Petrodollar recycling and international markets*. Ithaca: Cornell University Press.

Springer, S., K. Birch, and J. MacLeavy. (2016). *The Handbook of Neoliberalism*. London and New York: Routledge.

Stahl, R. M. (2019). Ruling the interregnum: Politics and ideology in nonhegemonic times. *Politics & Society, 47*(3), 333–360.

Standing, G. (2014). *The precariat: The new dangerous class*. New York: Bloomsbury.

Standing, G. (2014a). *The precariat: The new dangerous class*. New York: Bloomsbury.

Starblanket, T. (2018). 'Kill the Indian in the child': Genocide in international law in (Ed.) Watson, I. Indigenous Peoples as Subjects of International Law. New York: Routledge.

StatsCan. (2020). COVID-19 in Canada: A six-month update on social and economic impacts. Available at: www150.statcan.gc.ca/n1/pub/11-631-x/11-631-x2020003-eng.htm (Accessed: 01/01/22).

Steele, L., Swaffer, K., Phillipson, L., & Fleming, R. (2019). Questioning segregation of people living with dementia in Australia: An international human rights approach to care homes. *Laws, 8*(3), 18.

Steffen, W. & M. Rice. (2015). Unburnable carbon: why we need to leave fossil fuels in the ground. *The Conversation*. Available at: http://theconversation.com/unburnable-carbon-why-we-need-to-leave-fossil-fuels-in-the-ground-40467 (Accessed: 01/01/22).

Stern, N. (2006). *Stern review on the economics of climate change*. London: HM Treasury.

Stewart, B. (2020). The rise of far-right civilizationism. *Critical Sociology, 46*(7–8), 1207–1220.

Stiglitz, J. E. (2003). *Globalization and its discontents*. New York: W.W. Norton.

Stiglitz, J. E. (2012). *The price of inequality: How today's divided society endangers our future*. New York: W.W. Norton & Co.

Stiglitz, J. E. (2016). *The great divide: Unequal societies and what we can do about them*. New York: W.W. Norton & Company.

Stiglitz, J. E. (2019). *People, power, and profits: Progressive capitalism for an age of discontent*. New York: W.W. Norton & Company.

Stroud, S. (2020). Poverty and Covid-19. *Social Metrics Commission*. Available at: https://socialmetricscommission.org.uk/poverty-and-covid/ (Accessed: 01/01/22).

Stubbs, T., Kring, W., Laskaridis, C., Kentikelenis, A., & Gallagher, K. (2021). Whatever it takes? The global financial safety net, Covid-19, and developing countries. *World Development, 137*, 105171.

Stuckler, D., & Basu, S. (2013). *The body economic: Why austerity kills: recessions, budget battles, and the politics of life and death*. New York: Basic Books.

Stuckler, D., King, L., & McKee, M. (2009). Mass privatisation and the post-communist mortality crisis: A cross-national analysis. *The Lancet, 373*(9661), 399–407.

Stuckler, D., Reeves, A., Loopstra, R., Karanikolos, M., & McKee, M. (2017). Austerity and health: The impact in the UK and Europe. *European Journal of Public Health, 27*(suppl_4), 18–21.

Subotić, J. (2015). Narrative, ontological security, and foreign policy change. *Foreign Policy Analysis*, n/a-n/a.

Sugawara, M. A. Kose, F. Ohnsorge, & Naotaka (2021). Navigating the debt legacy of the pandemic. *Brookings*. Available at: www.brookings.edu/blog/future-development/2021/10/20/navigating-the-debt-legacy-of-the-pandemic/(Accessed: 01/01/22).

Sultana, F. (2021, May 16). Climate and Covid-19 crises both need feminism—Here's why opinion. *The Hill*. Available at: https://thehill.com/opinion/energy-envi ronment/553707-climate-and-covid-19-crises-both-need-feminism-heres-why (Accessed: 01/01/22).

Sultana, Farhana. (2021). Climate and Covid-19 Crises Both Need Feminism – Here's Why. Opinion. *The Hill*. May 16. Available at: https://thehill.com/opinion/energy-environment/553707-climate-and-covid-19-crises-both-need-feminism-heres-why. (Accessed: 05/13/22).

Sumagaysay, L. (2020, November 7) The pandemic has more than doubled food-delivery apps' business: Now what? *Market Watch*. Available at: www.marketwatch.com/story/the-pandemic-has-more-than-doubled-americans-use-of-food-delivery-apps-but-that-doe snt-mean-the-companies-are-making-money-11606340169 (Accessed: 01/01/22).

Šumonja, M. (2020). Neoliberalism is not dead – On political implications of Covid-19. *Capital and Class*. Vol. *45*(2): pp. 215–227.

Sun, H., Y. Xiao, J. Liu, D. et al. (2020). Prevalent Eurasian avian-like H1N1 swine influenza virus with 2009 pandemic viral genes facilitating human infection. *Proceedings of the National Academy of Sciences of the United States of America*, *116*(29), 17204–17210.

Supran, G. & N. Oreskes. (2017, August 22). What Exxon Mobil didn't say about climate change. *The New York Times*. Available at: www.nytimes.com/2017/08/22/opinion/exxon-climate-change-.html (Accessed: 01/01/22).

Supran, G., & Oreskes, N. (2020). Addendum to 'Assessing ExxonMobil's climate change communications (1977–2014)' Supran and Oreskes (2017 *Environ. Res. Lett.* 12 084019). *Environmental Research Letters*, *15*(11), 119401.

Takagi, Y., & Shikita, M. (1975). The active form of cytochrome P-450 from bovine adrenocortical mitochondria. *The Journal of Biological Chemistry*, *250*(21), 8445–8448.

Tanzi, A. (2018, April 9). Global debt jumped to record $237 Trillion last year. *Bloomberg*. Available at: www.bloomberg.com/news/articles/2018-04-10/global-debt-jumped-to-record-237-trillion-last-year (Accessed: 01/01/22).

Taylor, C., Boulos, C., & Almond, D. 2020. Livestock plants and COVID-19 transmission. *Proceedings of the National Academy of Sciences of the United States of America*, 117, 31706–31715. Available at: www.pnas.org/content/117/50/31706/tab-article-info (Accessed: 01/01/22).

Taylor, C., Boulos, C., and Almond, D. (2020). Livestock plants and COVID-19 transmission. *Proceedings of the National Academy of Sciences* 117: 31706–31715. Available at: www.pnas.org/content/117/50/31706/tab-article-info (Accessed: 01/31/21).

Taylor, M. (2018). Climate-smart agriculture: What is it good for? *The Journal of Peasant Studies*, *45*(1), 89–107.

TBIR (2019, February 7). Revealed: How the global beef trade is destroying the Amazon. The Bureau of Investigative Reporting. Available at: www.thebureauinvestigates.com/stories/2019-07-02/global-beef-trade-amazon-deforestation (Accessed: 01/01/22).

TBIR. (2019). Revealed: How the Global Beef Trade is Destroying the Amazon. The Bureau of Investigative Reporting. February 7. Available at: www.thebureauinvestigates.com/stor ies/2019-07-02/global-beef-trade-amazon-deforestation. (Accessed: 05/13/22).

Tcherneva, P. R. (2018). The job guarantee: Design, jobs, and implementation. *SSRN Electronic Journal*.

Temin, P., & Voth, H.-J. (2013). *Prometheus shackled: Goldsmith banks and England's financial revolution after 1700*. Oxford: Oxford University Press.

Terry, J. (2017). *Attachments to war: Biomedical logics and violence in twenty-first-century America*. Durham: Duke University Press.

Thambisetty, S., McMahon, A., McDonagh, L., Kang, H.Y., & Dutfield, G. (2021). The TRIPS intellectual property waiver proposal: Creating the right incentives in patent law and politics to end the COVID-19 pandemic. *SSRN Electronic Journal*.

The information from this government website was migrated to a new website after we submitted this chapter. The original website for 2021a no longer displays the relevant information. Please update all references as follows below. The data in this table has also been updated in line with the updated data presented on the new website.

(ILO). (2021). ILO monitor: COVID-19 and the world of work. Available at: www.ilo.org/wcmsp5/groups/public/---dgreports/---dcomm/documents/briefingnote/wcms_767028.pdf https://www.ilo.org/global/about-the-ilo/newsroom/news/WCMS_766949/lang--en/index.htm (Accessed: 01/01/22).

Therborn, G. (May-June 1977). The Rule of Capital and the Rise of Democracy: Capital and Suffrage. *New Left Review*, I (103): pp. 3–41.

Tiftik, E., K. Mahmood, & S. Gibbs. (Nov. 18, 2020). Global debt monitor: Attack of the debt tsunami. *Institute of International Finance*. Available at: www.iif.com/Research/Capital-Flows-and-Debt/Global-Debt-Monitor (Accessed: 01/01/22).

Tooze, A. (2020). Is the coronavirus crash worse than the 2008 financial crisis? *Foreign Policy*. Available at: https://foreignpolicy-com.ezproxy.library.yorku.ca/2020/03/18/coronavirus-economic-crash-2008-financial-crisis-worse/?_ga=2.138643891.1821605023.1617036955-583163173.1617036955 (Accessed: 01/01/22).

Tooze, A. (2020, August 2). By pushing for more oil production, the US is killing its climate pledges. *The Guardian*. Available at: www.theguardian.com/commentisfree/2021/aug/12/pushing-oil-production-us-joe-biden-killing-climate-pledges (Accessed: 01/01/22).

Tooze, A. (2021, September 2). Has COVID ended the Neoliberal Era? *The Guardian*. Available at: www.theguardian.com/news/2021/sep/02/covid-and-the-crisis-of-neoliberalism (Accessed: 01/01/22).

Tooze, Adam. (2021). Has Covid ended the Neoliberal Era? *The Guardian*, September 2. Available at: www.theguardian.com/news/2021/sep/02/covid-and-the-crisis-of-neoliberalism. (Accessed: 05/13/22).

Tooze, J.A. (2018). *Crashed: How a decade of financial crises changed the world*. New York: Viking.

Trainer, T. (2007). *Renewable energy cannot sustain a consumer society*. New York: Springer.

Trainer, T. (2019). Entering the era of limits and scarcity: The radical implications for social theory. *Journal of Political Ecology*, *26*(1).

Trainor, Sean. (2015) The long, twisted history of your credit score. *Time*. Available at: https://time.com/3961676/history-credit-scores/ (Accessed: 01/01/22).

Tran, D., Navas, G., Martinez-Alier, J., et al. (2020). Gendered geographies of violence: A multiple case study analysis of murdered women environmental defenders. *Journal of Political Ecology*, *27*(1).

Turnbull, N. (2021, November 17). PM ignores our modelling experts and hires a controversial global consultant. *Pearls and Irritations*. Available at: https://johnmenadue.com/pm-ignores-our-experts-on-modelling-and-hires-a-controversial-global-consultant/ (Accessed: 01/01/22).

Turshen, M. (1999). *Privatizing health services in Africa*. New Jersey: Rutgers University Press.

Tyfield, D. (2008). Enabling TRIPs: The pharma—biotech—university patent coalition. *Review of International Political Economy*, *15*(4), 535–566.

U.S. Bureau of Economic Analysis. (2022b). Federal government current tax receipts [W006RC1Q027SBEA], retrieved from FRED, Federal Reserve Bank of St. Louis; https://fred.stlouisfed.org/series/W006RC1Q027SBEA

U.S. Bureau of Economic Analysis. (2022c) Federal government current tax receipts [W006RC1Q027SBEA], retrieved from FRED, Federal Reserve Bank of St. Louis; https://fred.stlouisfed.org/series/W006RC1Q027SBEA

U.S. Bureau of Economic Analysis. 2022a. Gross domestic product [GDP]. retrieved from FRED, Federal Reserve Bank of St. Louis; https://fred.stlouisfed.org/series/GDP

U.S. Congressional Research Service, 2021, *Operation Warp Speed contracts for COVID-19 vaccines and ancillary vaccination materials.*

U.S. House of Representatives, 2021, *Drug pricing investigation: Industry spending on buybacks, dividends, and executive compensation,* 1–12, Committee on Oversight and Reform U.S. House of Representatives.

UCL IIPP (2018) *The people's prescription: Re-imagining health innovation to deliver public value.* UCL Institute for Innovation and Public Purpose, pp. 1–60.

UN Women (2020) Whose time to care? Unpaid care and domestic work during COVID-19. Available at: https://data.unwomen.org/sites/default/files/inline-files/Whose-time-to-care-brief_0.pdf (Accessed: 01/01/22).

UNCTAD. (2019). Trade and development report 2019. Available at: https://unctad.org/webflyer/trade-and-development-report-2019 (Accessed: 01/01/22).

UNEP (United Nations Environment Program). (2020). *Emissions gap report 2020.* Nairobi: Kenya.

United Nations Human Settlements Programme (UN-Habitat). (2016). *Urbanization and development: Emerging futures: World cities report 2016.* Nairobi: Kenya. Available at: http://wcr.unhabitat.org/main-report/ (Accessed: 01/01/22).

United Nations International Strategy for Disaster Reduction (UNISDR). (2016). The human cost of weather related disasters, 1995–2015. Available at: www.unisdr.org/2015/docs/climatechange/COP21_WeatherDisastersReport_2015_FINAL.pdf (Accessed: 01/01/22).

United Nations. (2020). World social report 2020: Inequality in a rapidly changing world. *Department of Economic and Social Affairs.* (New York: United Nations). Available at: www.un.org/development/desa/dspd/wp-content/uploads/sites/22/2020/02/World-Social-Report2020-FullReport.pdf (Accessed: 01/01/22).

United States Energy Information Administration (EIA). 2021a. Annual energy outlook 2021. Available at: Retrieved from: www.eia.gov/outlooks/aeo/ (Accessed: 01/01/22).

United States Energy Information Administration (EIA). 2021b. U.S. crude oil and natural gas proved reserves, year-end 2019. Available at: www.eia.gov/naturalgas/crudeoilreserves/ (Accessed: 01/01/22).

Unruh, G. C. (2000). Understanding carbon lock-in. *Energy Policy, 28,* 817–930.

US Census Bureau. (2021). Housing inventory estimate: Total housing units in the United States [ETOTALUSQ176N]. Available at: FRED, Federal Reserve Bank of St. Louis; https://fred.stlouisfed.org/series/ETOTALUSQ176N (Accessed: 01/01/22).

US Census Bureau. (2021a). Housing inventory estimate: Renter occupied housing units in the United States [ERNTOCCUSQ176N]. Available at: FRED, Federal Reserve Bank of St. Louis; https://fred.stlouisfed.org/series/ERNTOCCUSQ176N (Accessed: 01/01/22).

US Treasury. (2021). COVID-19 economic relief, US Department of the Treasury, Washington DC. Available at: https://home.treasury.gov/policy-issues/coronavirus(Accessed: 01/01/22).

USGS. (2021). How much water does the typical hydraulically fractured well require? Available at: www.usgs.gov/faqs/how-much-water-does-typical-hydraulically-fractured-well-require?qt-news_science_products=0#qt-news_science_products (Accessed: 01/01/22).

Vakulchuk, R., Overland, I., & Scholten, D. (2020). Renewable energy and geopolitics: A review. *Renewable and Sustainable Energy Reviews, 122,* 109547.

Van de Graaf, T. (2017). Is OPEC dead? Oil exporters, the Paris agreement and the transition to a post-carbon world. *Energy Research & Social Science, 23,* 182–188.

Van de Graaf, T., & Bradshaw, M. (2018). Stranded wealth: Rethinking the politics of oil in an age of abundance. *SSRN Electronic Journal, 94*(6), 1309–1328.

Veblen, T, 1904, *The theory of business enterprise (Reprints of Economics Classics),* A. M. Kelley.

Vilar, P. (1984). *A history of gold and money, 1450 to 1920.* London: Verso.

Vitalis, R. (2017). *White world order, black power politics: The birth of American international relations.* Ithaca: Cornell University Press.

Vitalis, R. (2020). *Oilcraft: The haunting of U.S. grand strategy in the Gulf.* Stanford: Stanford University Press.

Wade, N. (2021, May 5). The origin of COVID: Did people or nature open Pandora's box at Wuhan? *Bulletin of the Atomic Scientists.* Available at: https://thebulletin.org/2021/05/the-origin-of-covid-did-people-or-nature-open-pandoras-boxat-wuhan/ (Accessed: 01/01/22).

Wagstyl, St. (2019, December 13). Billionaires feel the sting of a populist backlash. *Financial Times.*

Wajcman, J. (2017). Automation: Is it really different this time?: Review essay: Automation. *The British Journal of Sociology, 68*(1), 119–127.

Wallace, R. (2020). *Dead epidemiologists: On the origins of Covid-19.* New York: Monthly Review Press.

Wallace, Rob. (2020). *Dead Epidemiologists: On the Origins of Covid-19.* Monthly Review Press.

Wallerstein, I. (1974). *The modern world system I: Capitalist agriculture and the origins of the European world-economy in the sixteenth century.* New York: Academic Press.

Walters, J. & Chang, A. (2021, September 8). Far-right terror poses bigger threat to US than Islamist extremism post-9/11. *The Guardian.* Available at: www.theguardian.com/us-news/2021/sep/08/post-911-domestic-terror (Accessed: 01/01/22).

Ward, A. (2020, March 9). The Saudi Arabia-Russia oil war, explained. *Vox.* Available at: www.vox.com/2020/3/9/21171406/coronavirus-saudi-arabia-russia-oil-war-explained (Accessed: 01/01/22).

Warf, B. (2021). The Coronavirus Pandemic and American Neoliberalism. *Geographical Review.* Vol. *111*(4): pp. 496–509.

Watson, I. (Ed.). (2018). *Indigenous peoples as subjects of international law.* London: Routledge.

Weatherford, J. M. (1997). *The history of money: From sandstone to cyberspace.* New York: Three Rivers Press.

Weber, I. (2021). *How China escaped shock therapy: The market reform debate.* London: Routledge.

Webster, C. (2002). *The national health service: A political history.* Oxford: Oxford University Press.

Weisser, D. (2007). A guide to life-cycle greenhouse gas (GHG) emissions from electric supply technologies. *Energy, 32*(9), 17.

Wendling, M. (2020, January 6). QAnon: What is it and where did it come from? *British Broadcasting Company.* Available at: www.bbc.com/news/53498434 (Accessed: 01/01/22).

Wennerlind, C. (2011). *Casualties of credit: The English financial revolution, 1620–1720.* Cambridge: Harvard University Press.

Werner, R. A. (2014a). Can Banks Individually Create Money out of Nothing? –The Theories and the Empirical Evidence' *International Review of Financial Analysis,* Vol. *36*: pp. 1–19.

Werner, R. A. (2014b). How do Banks Create Money, and Why Can Other Firms Not Do the Same? An Explanation for the Coexistence of Lending and Deposit-Taking. *International Review of Financial Analysis,* Vol *36:* pp. 71–77.

Wetzstein, S. (2017). The global urban housing affordability crisis. *Urban Studies,* Vol. *54*(14): pp. 3159–3177.

White, S. and Burger, L. (2021) *Sanofi ditches mRNA COVID-19 vaccine after rivals' success, Reuters.* Available at: www.reuters.com/business/healthcare-pharmaceuticals/frances-san ofi-announces-positive-update-mrna-based-covid-19-vaccine-candidate-2021-09-28/ (Accessed: 10/15/21).

WHO and UNICEF. (2018). *A vision for primary healthcare in the twenty first century: toward universal health coverage and the sustainable development goals.* Available at: www.who.int/docs/default-source/primary-health/vision.pdf (Accessed: 01/01/22).

WHO. (1991). Maternal mortality ratios and rates, A tabulation of available information, Third ed. WHO. Available at: https://apps.who.int/iris/handle/10665/272290 (Accessed: 01/01/22).

WHO. (1998). *The world health report 1998: Life in the 21st century, A vision for all.* Available at: www.who.int/whr/1998/en/whr98_en.pdf (Accessed: 01/01/22).

WHO. (2010). Trends in maternal mortality: 1980 to 2008. WHO. Available at: https://apps.who.int/iris/bitstream/handle/10665/44423/9789241500265_eng.pdf (Accessed: 01/01/22).

WHO. (2020). Global spending on health 2020: Weathering the storm. Available at: https://apps.who.int/iris/handle/10665/337859 (Accessed: 01/01/22).

Wigglesworth, R. (2020). Long live Jay Powell, the new monarch of the bond market. *Financial Times.*

Wilkinson, R. G., & Pickett, K. (2011). *The spirit level: Why greater equality makes societies stronger.* New York: Bloomsbury Press.

Williamson, J. (1990). What Washington means by policy reform. In John Williamson (ed.), *Latin American adjustment: How much has happened?* (pp. 5–20). Washington: Institute for International Economics.

Williamson, S. (2019). *Agroecology. First steps by British farmers Towards agroecological systems.* Brighton, UK: The Brighthelm Centre.

WMO (World Meteorological Organization). (2020). *State of the global climate 2020: Unpacking the indicators.* Available at: https://public.wmo.int/en/our-mandate/climate/wmo-statem ent-state-of-global-climate (Accessed: 01/01/22).

Wolff, E. N. (2012). *The asset price meltdown and the wealth of the middle class.* Cambridge, MA: *National Bureau of Economic Research.*

Wolff, E. N. (2013). The asset price meltdown and the wealth of the middle class. *Journal of Economic Issues, 47,* 333–342.

Wolff, E. N. (2017) Household wealth trends in the United States, 1962 to 2016: Has middle class wealth recovered? Working Paper, 24085. *National Bureau of Economic Research.* Available at: www.nber.org/papers/w2408 (Accessed: 01/01/22).

Wolin, S. S. (2010), *Democracy incorporated: Managed democracy and the specter of inverted totalitarianism.* New Jersey: Princeton University Press.

Wood, A. J. (2020). *Despotism on demand: How power operates in the flexible workplace.* Ithaca: Cornell University Press.

Wood, E. M. (1995). *Democracy against capitalism: Renewing historical materialism.* Cambridge: Cambridge University Press.

Wood, E. M. (2002). *The origin of capitalism: A longer view.* London: Verso.

Woolhandler, S., Himmelstein, D. U., Ahmed, S., et al. (2021). Public policy and health in the Trump era. *The Lancet, 397*(10275), 705–753.

World Bank (2018) Nearly half the world lives on less than $5.50 a day. Available at: www. worldbank.org/en/news/press-release/2018/10/17/nearly-half-the-world-lives-on-less-than-550-a-day. (Accessed: 01/01/22).

World Bank (2022) Inflation, consumer prices for the United States [FPCPITOTLZGUSA], retrieved from FRED, Federal Reserve Bank of St. Louis; https://fred.stlouisfed.org/ser ies/FPCPITOTLZGUSA

World Bank 2020. 5-Bank asset concentration for United States. FRED, Federal Reserve Bank of St. Louis. FRED, Federal Reserve Bank of St. Louis. Available at: https://fred.stl ouisfed.org/series/DDOI06USA156NWDB (Accessed: 01/01/22).

World Bank. (2017). *Access to electricity (% of population).* Available at: https://data.worldbank. org/indicator/EG.ELC.ACCS.ZS. (Accessed: 01/01/22).

World Bank. (2019). World gross domestic product. Available at: https://data.worldbank.org/ indicator/NY.GDP.MKTP.CD (Accessed: 01/01/22).

World Bank. (2020). *Gross domestic product 2020.* Available at: https://databank.worldbank. org/data/download/GDP.pdf (Accessed: 01/01/22).

World Bank. (2021). GDP (current US$). Available at: https://data.worldbank.org/indica tor/NY.GDP.MKTP.CD (Accessed: 01/01/22).

World Health Organization. (2021). Coronavirus. Available at: www.who.int/health-topics/ coronavirus#tab=tab_1 (Accessed: 01/01/22).

World Intellectual Property Organization. (2020). WIPO search international and national patent collections: FP: (tekmira pharmaceuticals). World Intellectual Property Organization (WIPO). Available at: https://patentscope.wipo.int/search/en/result.jsf?_vid=P12-KEZ 7LJ-24178 (Accessed: 01/01/22).

Wright, E. O. (2000). Working-class power, capitalist-class interests, and class compromise. *American Journal of Sociology, 105*(4), 957–1002.

Wright, E. O. (2021). *How to be an anticapitalist in the twenty-first century.* London: Verso.

Yates, S., & Dickinson, H. (2021). Navigating complexity in a global pandemic: The effects of COVID-19 on children and young people with disability and their families in Australia. *Public Administration Review, 81*(6), 1192–1196.

Yerardi, J. and Fernández Campbell, A. (2020). Fewer inspectors, more deaths: The Trump administration rolls back workplace safety inspections. *Vox News.* August 18. Available at: www.vox.com/2020/8/18/21366388/osha-worker-safety-trump (Accessed:08/29/ 20).

Yinliang, L. (2014). An American intangible empire of intellectual property rights and its dilemmas. *Peking University Law Journal, 2*(1), 227–256.

York, R., & Bell, S. E. (2019). Energy transitions or additions? *Energy Research & Social Science, 51*, 40–43.

Zahn, M. with A. Serwer (2020). Coronavirus a "once-in-a-lifetime opportunity" for debt investors: Billionaire Marc Lasry. *Yahoo Finance.* Available at: https://finance.yahoo.com/ news/coronavirus-a-onceinalifetime-opportunity-for-debt-investors-billionaire-marc-lasry-122736571.html (Accessed: 01/01/22).

Zhan, S. (2020). *Land question in China: Agrarian capitalism, industrious revolution, and east Asian development.* London: Routledge.

Zhang, L. (2021). *The origins of COVID-19: China and global capitalism.* Stanford: Stanford University Press.

Zuboff, S. (2019). *The age of surveillance capitalism: The fight for a human future at the new frontier of power.* New York: PublicAffairs.

INDEX

Note: Figures are indicated by *italics* and tables by **bold type**. Endnotes are indicated by the page number followed by "n" and the endnote number e.g., 186n9 refers to endnote 9 on page 186.

Printed in the United States
by Baker & Taylor Publisher Services